Articles on Women Writers

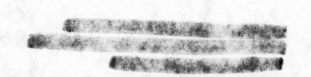

Articles on Women Writers
A Bibliography

Narda Lacey Schwartz

ABC-Clio, Inc.

Santa Barbara, California
Oxford, England

Library of Congress Cataloging in Publication Data
Schwartz, Narda Lacey, 1948–
    Articles on women writers.

    Includes index.
    1. English literature—Women authors—History
and criticism—Bibliography. 2. American literature—Women authors—History and criticism—
Bibliography. I. Title.
Z2013.5.W6S37 [PR111] 016.82'09'9287 77-9071

ISBN 0-87436-252-0

Second printing, February 1979

American Bibliographical Center—Clio Press
Riviera Campus, 2040 A.P.S., Box 4397
Santa Barbara, California 93103

Clio Press, Ltd.
Woodside House, Hinksey Hill
Oxford OX1 5BE, England

Manufactured in the United States of America

To the women of all time who had the courage to express their ideas.

To my mother, father, and brother, who recognized my desire to write.

Contents

Contents

Contents   x

Contents

Contents

Contents   *xviii*

Contents

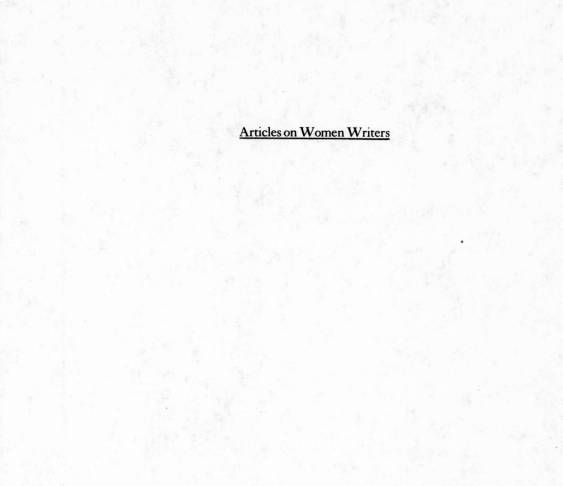

Articles on Women Writers

Preface

This bibliography originated in fall 1973 in the course of compiling an index to a collection of women's movement newsletters being prepared for microfilming. The changing attitude of the women themselves evident in that collection suggested a need to evaluate the possibility of a change in the role of women in literature. Why, for example, do the works of Aphra Behn, Eliza Haywood, and Mary Davys so rarely appear in anthologies along with those of Daniel Defoe, Jonathan Swift, and Alexander Pope? Searching the literature of women writers led to my discovery of a reprint of Arundell Esdaile's *List of English Tales and Prose Romances Printed Before 1740* (written in 1910 and since superseded by other works). Esdaile's work revealed the names of authors I had not encountered in my study of English literature—Jane Barker, Aphra Behn, Margaret Cavendish, Mary Davys, and Eliza Haywood (to mention just a few) were rarely noticed, and remain unmentioned, in most college courses and in most critical literature.¶   An examination of an anthology of English literature then in use at the University of Nevada showed reference to only two women writers. Anne Finch, Countess of Winchilsea, was briefly cited as the author of three poems under the heading "A Miscellany of Poems." Lady Mary Wortley Montagu was included as the author of a single poem. However, much of the prose fiction published in English during the eighteenth century—not to mention poetry and plays—was written by women authors. I asked a professor and he replied that the writing of eighteenth-century women is "bad," mostly unintelligible to twentieth-century readers, and that most women writers of that period were merely scandalmongers.¶   Up to the present time, this has been the widely held literary critic's opinion of women writers. Filling the need for a reference to the criticism of women writers, this bibliography provides the basis for researching such past opinion. It is also intended to encourage the study of neglected authors and to suggest a reevaluation of the status of women in the literary world.

Introduction

This bibliography is a handlist of articles published in English about over 600 women writers. It cites works published between 1960 and 1975 in popular as well as scholarly periodicals. It includes writers from the United States, Great Britain, Ireland, Australia, Canada, New Zealand, and writers in English from countries in Africa. It cites articles published in the following bibliographies:

Abstracts of English Studies
American Literature
American Quarterly
Australian Literary Studies
Biography Index
Canadian Literature
English Language Notes
English Literature in Transition
Explicator
Humanities Index
Keats-Shelley Journal
Modern Language Association Bibliography
Modern Drama
Philological Quarterly
Review of English Studies
Studies in Philology
Studies in Short Fiction
Twentieth Century Literature
Victorian Poetry
Victorian Studies
Western American Literature

In addition, *Dissertation Abstracts International* is frequently mentioned because it cites research about uncharted topics and neglected authors.¶ The bibliography lists women writers alphabetically by last name—maiden name, married name, title, or pseudonym, depending on which is most commonly known. When available, birth and death dates are given, as well as the country where most of the writing was done. Each author entry is divided into subcategories: Bibliography, General Works, and Individual Works.¶ The *Bibliography* section cites collections of critical studies about the author and her work. Under *General Works,* biographical and thematic articles and articles comparing one author to another are entered according to critic. *Individual Works* lists the primary literature alphabetically by title, followed by secondary literature about each work.¶ Cross-references are not used. Articles which mention two or more authors, or two or more individual works, are cited in full under each category. Thus, an entry may be repeated several times. ¶ The criteria used to select women writers for inclusion was intended to be extensive. Those writers who had at least one article written about them between 1960 and 1975 are included. Letters, diaries, and memoirs, previously valued by the literary establishment only as resource material to explain novels and poems, or as contributions to bibliographies, are cited as primary literature in this bibliography. It encompasses letter writers, diarists, essayists, novelists, poets, short-story writers, and dramatists from the Middle Ages to the present day. Generally, book reviews are excluded unless they contribute new information about the author or her work.¶ The contemporary time frame 1960–1975 was chosen because with the growing consciousness about women, by women, the published scholarship exploring women's role in literature has increased.¶ This bibliography will enable scholars to record the changes in attitudes about women writers from the early 1960s to the 1970s. It is a guide to the independent study of women, their works, and literary contributions. It is a beginning, an acknowledgment of women writers who have been long neglected, and a promise that the literary contribution of women will be fully explored in the future.¶ I would like to acknowledge Dr. Janet Bolton, who helped me appreciate the beauty of oral literature; Dr. Norma Engberg, whose practice of the scholarly life expanded my horizons; Dr. Donald Davie, who helped me appreciate poetry; Dr. W. Ross Winterowd, whose example as a scholar led me to compile this bibliography; and Stephen Becker, who cared while I did the research. Finally I wish to express my appreciation to my publisher, especially Myrt Leimer, Vice President, whom I met at the California Library Association Convention in San Diego, and who encouraged me to submit the manuscript.¶ I am nonetheless responsible for the content and accuracy of this bibliography. Comments and recommendations for changes that should be made in future editions will be considered and appreciated.

NARDA LACEY SCHWARTZ

A

HANNAH ADAMS (1755–1831) U.S.
General Works
Gleason, G. "Mere Woman." *American Heritage* 24 (December 1972): 81–84

Renata Adler (1938?–) U.S.
General Works
"Does She, or Doesn't She?" *Newsweek* (April 15, 1968): 94.

"Interesting Women." *McCall's* (March 1969): 99.

"Liberated, all Liberated." *Vogue* (June 1970): 115.

"Peculiar Experience." *Newsweek* (February 2, 1970): 80.

"Rigors of Criticism." *Time* (December 1, 1967): 38.

"Third Journalist." *Time* (February 16, 1970): 92.

CHRISTINA AMA ATA AIDOO (1942–) Ghana
General Works
Bamikunle, A. "The Two Plays of Aidoo: A Commentary." *Work in Progress* 1 (1973): 169–83.

Burness, Donald Bayer. "Womanhood in the Short Stories of Ama Ata Aidoo." *Studies in Black Literature* 4 (Summer 1973): 21–23.

Conde, M. "Three Female Writers in Modern Africa: Flora Nwapa, Ama Ata Aidoo and Grace Ogot." *Présence Africaine* 82 (1973): 132–43.
Individual Works
Dilemma of a Ghost (1965)

Jones, Eldred. "A Note on the Lagos Production of Christina Aidoo's *Dilemma of a Ghost.*" *Bulletin of the Association* of African Literature in English 2 (1968): 37–38.

LOUISA MAY ALCOTT (1832–1888) U.S.
Bibliography
Payne, Alma J. "Louisa May Alcott, (1832–1888)."

American Literary Realism 6 (1973): 27–44.
General Works
Brophy, Brigid. "A Masterpiece, and Dreadful." *New York Times Book Review* (January 17, 1965): 1.

Carpenter, Nan Cooke. "Louisa May Alcott and 'Thoreau's Flute': Two Letters." *Huntington Library Quarterly* 24 (November 1960): 71–74.

Gay, Carol. "The Philosopher and His Daughter: Amos Bronson Alcott and Louisa." *Essays in Literature* 2 (Fall 1975): 181–91.

Hamblen, Abigail Ann. "Louisa May Alcott and the Racial Question." *University Review* (Kansas) 37 (1971): 307–13.

Hamblen, Abigail Ann. "Louisa May Alcott and the 'Revolution' in Education." *Journal of General Education* 22 (July 1970): 81–92.

Haverstick, I. "To See Louisa Plain." *Saturday Review* (October 19, 1968): 35.

Janeway, Elizabeth. "Meg, Jo, Beth, Amy and Louisa." *New York Times Book Review* (September 29, 1968): 42.

O'Faolain, S. "This Is Your Life, Louisa May Alcott." *Holiday* (November 1968): 18.

Payne, Alma J. "Duty's Child: Louisa May Alcott." *American Literary Realism* 6 (1973): 260–61.

Peattie, Donald, and Louisa Peattie. "Louisa May Alcott: Greatest of 'Little Women.'" *Reader's Digest* (June 1960): 256–64.
Individual Works
Behind a Mask (1975)

Bannon, B.A. "Story behind the Book: *Behind a Mask:* The Unknown Thrillers of Louisa May Alcott." *Publishers Weekly* (June 30, 1975): 40.

Bedell, M. "Forward: Why Miss Alcott Turned Her Pen to the Lurid Style." *Redbook* (December

1975): 149–50.

Little Women (1868–1869)

Crompton, Margaret. *"Little Women:* The Making of a Classic." *Contemporary Review* 218 (1971): 99–104.

Morley, Olive J. *"Little Women:* Dramatization of a Novel by L.M. Alcott." *Plays* 35 (December 1975): 85–95.

Steegmuller, Francis. "House of *Little Women." Holiday* (March 1960): 191–92.

BESS STREETER ALDRICH (1881–1954) U.S.
General Works

Meier, A. Mabel. "Bess Streeter Aldrich: A Literary Portrait." *Nebraska History* 50 (1969): 67–100.

ELIZABETH AKERS ALLEN, née Chase [pseud. Florence Percy] (1832–1911) U.S.
General Works

Cary, Richard. "The Misted Prism: Paul Akers and Elizabeth Akers Allen." *Colby Library Quarterly* 7 (March 1966): 193–227.

MARGERY ALLINGHAM (1904–1966) Great Britain
General Works

Peters, Margot, and Agate N. Krouse. "Women and Crime: Sexism in Allingham, Sayers, and Christie." *Southwest Review* 59 (Spring 1974): 144–52.

SUSAN MARY PATTEN ALSOP, née Jay (1919?–) U.S.
General Works

Lyon, L. "To Marietta from Paris." *New York Times Book Review* (September 14, 1975): 37.

HELEN B. ANDELIN (1919?–) U.S.
General Works

"Total Fascination." *Time* (March 10, 1975): 77.

MARGARET ANDERSON (1891?–1973) U.S.
General Works

Edelstein, J.M. "Exuberance and Ecstasy." *New Republic* (June 13, 1970): 19–22.

MAYA ANGELOU (1928–) U.S.
General Works

Benson, C. "Out of the Cage and Still Singing: Interview." *Writer's Digest* 55 (January 1975): 18–20.

Gross, R.A. "Growing Up Black," *Newsweek*

(March 2, 1970): 90.

Julianelli, J. "Maya Angelou: Interview." *Harper's Bazaar* (November 1972): 124.

JOAN WALSH ANGLUND (1926–) U.S.
General Works

"Joan Walsh Anglund and Her Books." *Publishers Weekly* (July 8, 1963): 104–6.

HANNAH ARENDT (1906–1975) U.S.
General Works

Glazer, N. "Hannah Arendt's America." *Commentary* 60 (September 1975): 61–67.

"Notes and Comment." *New Yorker* (December 22, 1975): 27.

CHARLOTTE ARMSTRONG (1905–1969) U.S.
General Works

Waldron, Ann. "Charlotte Armstrong." *Journal of Popular Culture* 5 (Fall 1971): 435–45.

HARRIETTE ARNOW, [pseud. Louisa Simpson] (1908–) U.S.
General Works

Oates, Joyce Carol. "An American Tragedy." *New York Times Book Review* (January 24, 1971): 12.

HELEN ASHTON (1891–1958) Great Britain
General Works

Wordan, J. D. "Doctors as Men of Letters." *Bulletin of the New York Public Library* 68 (November 1964): 599.

EMILIA ASHURST, née Hawkes (fl. 1850s) Great Britain
General Works

Daniels, Elizabeth A. "Collaboration of Mazzini on an Article in the *Westminster Review." Bulletin of the New York Public Library* 65 (November 1961): 577–82.

LADY CYNTHIA MARY EVELYN ASQUITH, née Charteris (1887–1960) Great Britain
General Works

"Modern Beauty." *Newsweek* (March 17, 1969): 124.

MARY ASTELL (1666–1731) Great Britain
General Works

Norton, J. E. "Some Uncollected Authors 27: Mary

Astell, 1666–1731." *Book Collector* 10 (Spring 1961): 58–65.

THEA ASTLEY (1925–) Australia
General Works
Couper, Thea. "The Novels of Thea Astley." *Meanjin Quarterly* 26 (1967): 332–37.
Matthews, Brian. "Life in the Eye of the Hurricane: The Novels of Thea Astley." *Southern Review* (Australia) 6 (1973): 148–73.
Individual Works
The Slow Natives (1966)
Burns, Robert. "The Underdog-Outsider: The Achievement of Mather's Trap." *Meanjin Quarterly* 29 (1970): 95–105.

GERTRUDE ATHERTON (1857–1948) U.S.
General Works
Forman, Henry James. "A Brilliant California Novelist: Gertrude Atherton." *California Historical Society Quarterly* 40 (March 1961): 1–10.
Forrey, Carolyn D. "Gertrude Atherton and the New Woman." *Dissertation Abstracts International* 32 (1971): 2684A–85A (Yale).
Richey, Elinor. "The Flappers Were Her Daughters: The Liberated Literary World of Gertrude Atherton." *American West* 11 (July 1974): 4.
Van Domelen, John E. "Gertrude Atherton Inscriptions." *American Notes and Queries* 10 (September 1971): 7.
Weir, Sybil. "Gertrude Atherton: The Limits of Feminism in the 1890's." *San Jose Studies* 1 (February 1975): 24–31.

FLORENCE ATKINSON (fl. 1880s) U.S.
General Works
Sharkey, Eugene G. "The Diary of Florence Atkinson, 1883–1886." *Journal of the Rutgers University Library* 34 (December 1970): 23–27.

MARGARET ATWOOD (1939–) Canada
General Works
Glicksohn, Susan W. "The Martian Point of View." *Extrapolation* 15 (1974): 161–73.
Harcourt, Joan. "Atwood Country." *Queen's Quarterly* 80 (1973): 278–81.
MacCallum, Hugh. "Poetry." *University of Toronto Quarterly* 36 (July 1967): 354–79.
Onley, Gloria. "Power Politics in Bluebeard's Cas-

tle." *Canadian Literature*, no. 60 (Spring 1974): 21–42.
Rogers, Linda. "Margaret the Magician." *Canadian Literature*, no. 60 (Spring 1974): 83–85.
Individual Works
The Circle Game (1966)
Ross, Gary. "*The Circle Game*." *Canadian Literature*, no. 60 (Spring 1974): 51–63.
Surfacing (1972)
Schaeffer, S.F. "'It Is Time That Separates Us': Margaret Atwood's *Surfacing*." *Centennial Review* 18 (1974): 319–37.
Survival (1972)
Macri, F.M. "Survival Kit: Margaret Atwood and the Canadian Scene." *Modern Poetry Studies* 5 (Autumn 1974): 187–95.
Morley, Patricia. "Survival, Affirmation, and Joy." *Lakehead University Review* 4 (1971): 21–30.

JANE AUSTEN (1775–1817) Great Britain
Bibliography
Gilson, D.J. "Jane Austen Bibliography." *Times Literary Supplement* (April 17, 1973): 4151.
Page, Norman. "A Short Guide to Jane Austen Studies." *Critical Survey* 3 (1968): 230–34.
Southam, B.C. "General Tilney's Hot-House: Some Recent Jane Austen Studies and Texts." *Ariel* 2 (1971): 52–62.
General Works
Acabal, Perla G. "Jane Austen's Moral Vision: Form and Function." *Dissertation Abstracts International* 33 (1973): 6297A–98A (Indiana).
Adams, J. Donald. "Speaking of Books." *New York Times Book Review* (March 20, 1960): 2.
Anderson, Walter E. "Jane Austen's Novels as Represented Actions." *Dissertation Abstracts International* 29 (1969): 4448A (California, Berkeley).
Arthurs, Alberta. "Arrangements with the Earth: Jane Austen's Landscapes." *Dissertation Abstracts* 34 (1974): 4185A–86A (Bryn Mawr).
Auerbach, Nina J. "Reality as Vision in the Novels of Jane Austen and George Eliot." *Dissertation Abstracts International* 31 (1971): 4701A–2A (Columbia).
Beach, Luann. "A Rhetorical Analysis of Jane Austen's Novels." *Dissertation Abstracts International* 32 (1972): 5730A (Stanford).
Binkley, William O. "Comic Self-Discovery in Jane Austen's Novels." *Dissertation Abstracts* 22 (1961): 1992–93 (Wisconsin).

Bogh, Kirsten, et al., eds. "Jane Austen: Criticism and Ideological Debate." *Language and Literature* 1 (1973): 17–23.

Bradbrook, Frank W. "Dr. Johnson and Jane Austen." *Notes and Queries* 7 (April 1960): 108–12.

Bramer, George R. "The Quality of Love in Jane Austen's Novels." *Dissertation Abstracts* 27 (1966): 1779A (Notre Dame).

Brophy, Brigid. "Miss J. Austen." *New Statesman* (December 4, 1964): 879–80.

Brown, Julia Prewitt. "The Bonds of Irony: A Study of Jane Austen's Novels." *Dissertation Abstracts International* 35 (1975): 1517A–18A (Columbia).

Brown, Lloyd W. "The Comic Conclusion in Jane Austen's Novels." *Publications of the Modern Language Association* 84 (1969): 1582–87.

Brown, Lloyd W. "Jane Austen and the Feminist Tradition." *Nineteenth Century Fiction* 28 (December 1973): 321–38.

Cady, Joseph, and Ian Watt. "Jane Austen's Critics." *Critical Quarterly* 5 (Spring 1963): 49–63.

Chabot, Charles B. "The Vicissitudes of Desire: Jane Austen and the Concept of Style." *Dissertation Abstracts International* 33 (1973): 4403A (S.U.N.Y., Buffalo).

Chandler, Alice. " 'A Pair of Fine Eyes': Jane Austen's Treatment of Sex." *Studies in the Novel* 7 (Spring 1975): 88–103.

Citino, David J. "From Pemberly to Eccles Street: Families and Heroes in the Fiction of Jane Austen, Charles Dickens, and James Joyce." *Dissertation Abstracts International* 35 (1974): 1090A–91A (Ohio State).

Constantine, Annette V. "Wit in Jane Austen's Novels: An Expression of the Conflict between Duty and Desire." *Dissertation Abstracts International* 34 (1973): 721A–22A (Illinois).

Cope, Zachary. "Who Was Sophia Sentiment?" *Book Collector* 15 (Summer 1966): 143–51.

Corwin, Laura J. "Character and Morality in the Novels of Jane Austen." *Revue des Langues Vivantes* 38 (1972): 363–79.

Corwin, Laura J. "The Concept of the Self in the Novels of Jane Austen." *Dissertation Abstracts International* 31 (1971): 5356A–57A (Penn.).

Crewe, J.V. "Correspondence: Jane Austen." *Theoria* 36 (1971): 67–68.

Crowder, Tudja. "The Rational Treatment of Emotion: An Essay on Jane Austen's Style." *Spectrum* 5 (Summer 1961): 91–96.

Crowley, J. Donald. "Jane Austen Studies: A Portrait of the Lady and Her Critics." *Studies in the Novel* 7 (Spring 1975): 137–60.

Davis, Earle. "Jane Austen and the Comic Flaw." *Kansas Quarterly* 5 (Summer 1973): 23–24.

Delaney, Janice F. "Chapter Design in Jane Austen's Novels." *Dissertation Abstracts International* 31 (1971): 5394A–95A (Temple).

DeRose, Peter Louis. "Jane Austen and Samuel Johnson." *Dissertation Abstracts International* 35 (1975): 6662A (Indiana).

Derry, Warren. "Jane Austen." *Times Literary Supplement* (December 29, 1961): 929.

Dodds, M. Hope. "Daughters of the Clergy." *Brontë Society Transactions* 14 (1965): 20–24.

Dornberg, Curtis L. "Three Prospects of the Comic Landscape." *Mankato State College Studies* 1 (May 1966): 69–86.

Draffan, Robert A. "Jane Austen and Her Time." *History Today* 20 (March 1970): 190–97.

Duckworth, A.M. "Jane Austen Criticism on the Eve of the Bicentenary." *Sewanee Review* 83 (Summer 1975): 493–502.

Dylla, Sandra Marie. "Jane Austen and George Eliot: The Influence of Their Social Worlds on Their Women Characters." *Dissertation Abstracts International* 35 (1975): 899A (Wisconsin, Milwaukee).

Eisner, Seth A. "Jane Austen's Characters: Manners of Being." *Dissertation Abstracts International* 34 (1974): 7747A (Penn.).

Elsbree, Langdon. "The Breaking Chain: A Study of the Dance in the Novels of Jane Austen, George Eliot, Thomas Hardy, and D.H. Lawrence." *Dissertation Abstracts* 24 (1963): 2476 (Claremont).

Elsbree, Langdon. "Jane Austen and the Dance of Fidelity and Complaisance." *Nineteenth Century Fiction* 15 (September 1960): 113–36.

Emmett, Victor J., Jr. "Jane Austen's Plots." *Midwest Quarterly* 11 (Summer 1970): 393–409.

Fergus, Jan Stockton. "Jane Austen's Early Novels: The Educating of Judgment and Sympathy." *Dissertation Abstracts International* 35 (1975): 2218A (C.U.N.Y.).

Fowler, Marian E. "Patterns of Prudence: Courtship Conventions—Jane Austen's Novels." *Dissertation Abstracts International* 32 (1971): 917A–18A (Toronto).

Fryxell, Donald Raymond. "The Patterns of Jane Austen's Novels." *Dissertation Abstracts* 20 (1960): 4110 (Kentucky).

Gilson, D.J. "The Early American Editions of Jane

Austen." *Book Collector* 18 (Autumn 1969): 340–52; 20 (Autumn 1971): 388–89.

Gilson, D.J. "The First American Editions of Jane Austen." *Book Collector* 16 (Winter 1967): 512.

Gilson, D.J. "Jane Austen's Books." *Book Collector* 23 (Spring 1974): 27–39.

Gilson, D.J. "Letters of Jane Austen." *Times Literary Supplement* (November 9, 1973): 1372–73.

Glucksman, Stuart. "The Happy Ending in Jane Austen." *Dissertation Abstracts International* 34 (1973): 2559A–60A (S.U.N.Y., Stony Brook).

Gornall, F.G. "Marriage, Property, and Romance in Jane Austen's Novels." *Hibbert Journal* 65 (1967): 151–56.

Greenstein, Susan Mitchell. "The Negative Principle and the Virtuous Character Undercutting in the Work of Richardson, Austen and James." *Dissertation Abstracts International* 35 (1975): 4521A (Indiana).

Griffin, Cynthia. "The Development of Realism in Jane Austen's Early Novels." *English Literary History* 30 (March 1963): 36–52.

Gross, John. "Your Comical Cousin." *New Statesman* (February 14, 1964): 256–57.

Hamilton, Jack. "A Conversation with Jane Austen." *Intellectual Digest* 3 (May 1973): 16–18.

Harding, D.W. "Two Aspects of Jane Austen's Development." *Theoria* 35 (1970): 1–16.

Hardy, Barbara. "The Change of Heart in Dickens' Novels." *Victorian Studies* 5 (September 1961): 49–67.

Harris, Stephen Le Roy. "The Mask of Morality: A Study of the Unconscious Hypocrite in Representative Novels of Jane Austen, Charles Dickens, and George Eliot." *Dissertation Abstracts* 25 (1965): 4699 (Cornell).

Hartley, L.P. "Jane Austen and the Abyss." *Essays by Divers Hands* 35 (1969): 85–100.

Hartzler, Sara K.K. "Marriage as Theme and Structure in Jane Austen's Novels." *Dissertation Abstracts International* 32 (1971): 389A (Indiana).

Hennedy, Hugh L. "Acts of Perception in Jane Austen's Novels." *Studies in the Novel* 5 (Spring 1973): 22–38.

Herold, J. Christopher. "Our Great Favourite, Miss Austen." *Horizon* (New York) 6 (Spring 1964): 41–48.

Higbie, Robert G. "Characterization in the English Novel: Richardson, Jane Austen, and Dickens." *Dissertation Abstracts International* 34 (1974): 4263A–64A (Indiana).

Hill, Patricia A.N. "The Function of Setting in Jane Austen's Novels." *Dissertation Abstracts International* 32 (1971): 3252A (Auburn).

Hodge, Jane Aiken. "Jane Austen and the Publishers." *Cornhill Magazine*, no. 1071 (Spring 1972): 188–94.

Hogan, Charles Beecher. "Jane Austen." *Times Literary Supplement* (January 11, 1963): 25.

Hough, Graham. "Narrative and Dialogue in Jane Austen." *Critical Quarterly* 12 (Autumn 1970): 201–29.

Irvine, Ian M. "Figurative Representation in the Novels of Jane Austen: A Study of Style." *Dissertation Abstracts International* 33 (1973): 6913A (Penn.).

Jackel, David A. "Jane Austen and the Concept of the Novelist's Art 1775–1820." *Dissertation Abstracts International* 32 (1971): 3308A (Toronto).

Jackel, David A. "Jane Austen and 'through Novel Slang.'" *Notes and Queries* 20 (February 1973): 46–47.

Jason, Philip K. "Off-stage Characters in Jane Austen's Novels." *Southern Humanities Review* 8 (Winter 1974): 55–66.

Joukovsky, Nicholas A. "Another Unnoted Contemporary Review of Jane Austen." *Nineteenth Century Fiction* 29 (December 1974): 336–38.

Kauvar, Elaine M. "Jane Austen and *The Female Quixote*." *Studies in the Novel* 2 (Summer 1970): 211–21.

Kestner, Joseph A., III. "The 'I' Persona in the Novels of Jane Austen." *Studies in the Novel* 4 (Spring 1972): 6–16.

Kestner, Joseph A., III. "Intimacy in the Novels of Jane Austen." *Iowa English Bulletin: Yearbook* 21 (1971): 52–59.

Kestner, Joseph A., III. "Jane Austen: Seven Themes in Variation." *Dissertation Abstracts International* 33 (1972): 6379A–80A (Columbia).

Kestner, Joseph A., III. "Silence and Shyness in the Novels of Jane Austen: 'The Quietness of It Does Me Good.'" *Descant* 16 (1971): 40–47.

Kiley, Anne W. "The Art of Living: Jane Austen's Social Aesthetic." *Dissertation Abstracts* 29 (1968): 873A (Wisconsin).

Kissane, Joseph M. "Richardson and Jane Austen." *Dissertation Abstracts* 29 (1968): 1899A (Columbia).

Koppel, Gene Stuart. "The Moral Basis of Jane Austen's Novels." *Dissertation Abstracts* 26 (1966): 4663–64 (Washington).

Kormali, Sema G. "The Treatment of Marriage in Representative Novels of Jane Austen and Henry James." *Dissertation Abstracts International* 35 (1974): 2228A–29A (Texas Tech).

Kumar, Anita S. "Jane Austen—The Feminist Sensibility." *Indian Journal of English Studies* 3 (1962): 135–59.

Kunkel, Francis L. "Jane Austen." *Critic* 21 (December 1962–January 1963): 38–41.

Lachman, Michele Schurgin. "Jane Austen: Studies in Language and Values." *Dissertation Abstracts International* 35 (1975): 2848A (Brandeis).

Lauber, John. "Heroes and Anti-Heroes in Jane Austen's Novels." *Dalhousie Review* 51 (Winter 1971–1972): 489–503.

Lauber, John. "Jane Austen's Fools." *Studies in English Literature, 1500–1900* 14 (Autumn 1974): 511–24.

Lerner, Laurence. " 'This Old Maid.' " *Listener* (February 23, 1963): 340–41.

Levin, Harry. "Janes and Emilies, or the Novelist as Heroine." *Southern Review* (U.S.) 1 (1965): 735–53.

Linder, C.A. "The Ideal Marriage as Depicted in the Novels of Jane Austen and Charlotte Brontë." *Standpunte,* 24 (1971): 20–30.

Litz, Walton. "*The Loiterer:* A Reflection of Jane Austen's Early Environment." *Review of English Studies* 12 (August 1961): 251–61.

Lochhead, Marion. "Jane Austen and the Seven Deadly Sins." *Quarterly Review* 305 (October 1967): 429–36.

Lock, F.P. "Jane Austen: Some Non-Literary Manuscripts in the Fitzwilliam Museum and the University Library, Cambridge." *Transactions of the Cambridge Bibliographic Society* 5 (1970): 145–48.

Lock, F.P. "A Jane Austen Quotation Identified." *Notes and Queries* 20 (August 1973): 289.

Lynch, Catherine M. "The Reader as Guest: Jane Austen's Audience." *Dissertation Abstracts International* 35 (1974): 1627A–28A (Pittsburgh).

Magee, William H. "The Happy Marriage: The Influence of Charlotte Smith on Jane Austen." *Studies in the Novel* 7 (Spring 1975): 120–32.

Maniar, U.M. "The Immortal Mr. Collins." *Literary Half-Yearly* 6 (July 1965): 46–48.

Maxwell, J.C. "Jane Austen and *Belinda*." *Notes and Queries* 21 (May 1974): 175–176.

McIlroy, Ellen. "Jane Austen's Families." *Thoth* 3 (1962): 24–31.

McIlroy, Ellen. "Realism and Anti-Realism in the Novels of Jane Austen." *Dissertation Abstracts* 24 (1963): 1617–18 (Syracuse).

McMaster, Juliet. "The Continuity of Jane Austen's Novels." *Studies in English Literature, 1500–1900* 10 (Autumn 1970): 723–39.

McMaster, Juliet. "Surface and Subsurface in Jane Austen's Novels." *Ariel* 5 (1974): 5–24.

Measham, D.C. "Sentiment and Sentimental Psychology in Jane Austen." *Renaissance and Modern Studies* 16 (1972): 61–85.

Moraham, Richard E. "I. Samuel Johnson and William Lauder's Milton Forgeries. II. Poetry in Space: Disjunction in Language and Stage Action in Jonson's *Sejanus*. III. Jane Austen's Endings." *Dissertation Abstracts International* 32 (1971): 3318A–19A (Rutgers).

Munday, M. "Jane Austen, Women Writers, and *Blackwood's Magazine*." *Notes and Queries* 20 (August 1973): 290.

Murrah, Charles C. "Jane Austen In America: Some Observations." *Polemic* 7 (1962): 12–18.

Myers, Sylvia H. "Womanhood in Jane Austen's Novels." *Novel* 3 (Spring 1970): 225–32.

Newman, Donald Bruce. "Life Style in the Novels of Jane Austen." *Dissertation Abstracts International* 35 (1975): 7262A–63A (Michigan).

Noel-Bentley, E.R. "Jane Austen and Regina Maria Roche." *Notes and Queries* 22 (September 1975): 390–91.

North, Douglas M. "Inheritance in the Novels of Jane Austen, Charles Dickens, and George Eliot." *Dissertation Abstracts International* 31 (1971): 5419A (Virginia).

Odumu, Ocheibi. "Women Talk about Women: The Image of Women in the Novels of Jane Austen and Emily Brontë." *Horizon* (Ibadan) 9 (1973): 47–54.

Orum, Tania. "History/Herstory: Pictures from Jane Austen's Novels." *Language and Literature* 1 (1973): 24–29.

Page, Norman. " 'The Best Chosen Language': Stylistic Modes in Jane Austen." *Ariel* 2 (1971): 45–51.

Page, Norman. "Jane Austen and the 'Best Chosen Language.' " *Wascana Review* 4 (1969): 67–76.

Page, Norman. "Standard of Excellence: Jane Austen's Language." *Review of English Literature* 7 (July 1966): 91–98.

Pati, Prafulla Kumar. "Jane Austen: Her Relationships to the Romantic and Realistic Traditions of English Fiction." *Dissertation Abstracts* 24 (1964): 4681 (Minnesota).

Pevsner, Nikolaus. "The Architectural Setting of Jane Austen's Novels." *Journal of the Warburg and Courtauld Institutes* 31 (1968): 404–22.

Phillipps, K.C. "Jane Austen's English." *Neuphilologische Mitteilungen* 70 (1969): 319–38.

Pickering, Jean E. "Comic Structure in the Novels of Jane Austen." *Dissertation Abstracts International* 33 (1973): 6681A (Stanford).

Podis, Jo Anne Med. " 'The Way They Should Go': Family Relationships in the Novels of Jane Austen." *Dissertation Abstracts International* 35 (1975): 6153A–54A (Case Western Reserve).

Post, Alfred P., III. "Jane Austen and *The Loiterer:* A Study of Jane Austen's Literary Heritage." *Dissertation Abstracts International* 34 (1973): 333A (North Carolina).

Raz, Robert W. "Syntactic Variation in Jane Austen's Dialogue." *Dissertation Abstracts International* 31 (1971): 6584A–85A (Michigan).

Rosenfeld, Sybil. "Jane Austen and Private Theatricals." *Essays and Studies* 15 (1962): 40–51.

Ross, Mary Beth. "The 'Bisexual' World of Jane Austen." *Aphra* 6 (Winter 1974–1975): 2–15.

Rubinstein, E. "Jane Austen's Novels: The Metaphor of Rank." *Literary Monographs* 2 (1969): 101–93.

Rudolf, Jo-Ellen S. "The Novels That Taught the Ladies: A Study of Popular Fiction Written by Women, 1702–1834." *Dissertation Abstracts International* 33 (1972): 1695A (California, San Diego).

Ryle, Gilbert. "Jane Austen and the Moralists." *Oxford Review* 1 (1966): 5–18.

Scholes, R. "Dr. Johnson and Jane Austen." *Philological Quarterly* 54 (Winter 1975): 380–90.

Simon, Irene. "Jane Austen and the Art of the Novel." *English Studies* 43 (1962): 225–39.

Slattery, Sister Margaret P. "The Technique of Balance in the Construction of Character in the Novels of Jane Austen." *Dissertation Abstracts* 27 (1967): 3063A–64A (Catholic U.).

Sobiston, Elizabeth J. "The Provincial Heroine in Prose Fiction: A Study in Isolation and Creativity." *Dissertation Abstracts* 30 (1969): 1150A (Cornell).

Southam, B.C. "Jane Austen: A Broken Romance?" *Notes and Queries* 8 (December 1961): 464–65.

Southam, B.C. "Letter to Editor." *Ariel* 3 (1972): 79.

Southam, B.C. "Mrs. Leavis and Miss Austen: The 'Critical Theory' Reconsidered." *Nineteenth Century Fiction* 17 (June 1962): 21–32.

Stoller, Annette Linda. "Jane Austen's Rhetorical Art: A Revaluation." *Dissertation Abstracts International* 35 (1975): 7271A (Brown).

Strauch, Gerard. "Jane Austen's Response to Fanny Burney." *Bulletin de la Faculté des Lettres de Strasbourg* 47 (1969): 217–32.

Taylor, Roselle. "The Narrative Technique of Jane Austen: A Study in the Use of Point of View." *Dissertation Abstracts International* 35 (1975): 912A (Texas).

Ten Harmsel, Henrietta. "Jane Austen's Use of Literary Conventions." *Dissertation Abstracts* 23 (1963): 3902–3 (Michigan).

Wade, Rosalind. "The Anatomy of Jane Austen (1775–1817)." *Contemporary Review* 218 (1971): 132–36.

Waidner, Maralee L. "From Reason to Romance: A Progression from an Emphasis on Neoclassic Rationality to Romantic Intuition in Three English Woman Novelists." *Dissertation Abstracts International* 34 (1973): 1259A–60A (Tulsa).

Walls, A.F. "Miss Austen on Sunday." *Trivium* 6 (May 1971): 92–102.

Walls, A.F. "Miss Austen's Theological Reading." *Anglican Theological Review* 47 (1965): 49–58.

Ward, John C. "The Tradition of the Hypocrite in Eighteenth-Century English Literature." *Dissertation Abstracts International* 34 (1974): 5128A (Virginia).

Ward, William S. "Three Hitherto Unnoted Contemporary Reviews of Jane Austen." *Nineteenth Century Fiction* 26 (March 1972): 469–77.

Webb, William. "The Rumford Grote." *Notes and Queries* 12 (November 1965): 425.

Weinsheimer, Joel C. "Three Essays of Jane Austen's Novels." *Dissertation Abstracts International* 34 (1974): 6002A–3A (Ohio).

Welty, Eudora. "A Note on Jane Austen." *Shenandoah* 20 (1969): 3–7.

Wilhelm, Albert E. "Word Clusters in Jane Austen's Major Novels." *Dissertation Abstracts International* 32 (1972): 5206A–7A (North Carolina).

Willis, Lesley H. "Object Association and Minor Characters in Jane Austen's Novels." *Studies in the Novel* 7 (Spring 1975): 104–19.

Wilson, Angus. "Evil in the English Novel." *Listener* (December 27, 1962): 1079–80.

Wiltshire, John. "Jane Austen: 'The Complete Artist.'" *Cambridge Quarterly* 2 (1967): 184–93.

Wood, Sally. "The Real Jane Austen." *Sewanee Review* 81 (Spring 1973): 380–86.

Woods, Sister Mary St. Francis. "Jane Austen and the Omniscient Narrative Voice." *Dissertation Abstracts* 26 (1965): 2734 (Catholic U.).

Zimmerman, Everett. "Jane Austen and Sensibility: A Study of Tradition and Technique." *Dissertation Abstracts* 27 (1967): 3476A (Temple).

Individual Works

Emma (1816)

Bennett, James R. "'Doating on You and All': Mr. George Knightley." *Studies in the Novel* 5 (Summer 1973): 248–53.

Booth, Wayne C. "Point of View and the Control of Distance in *Emma*." *Nineteenth Century Fiction* 16 (June 1961): 95–116.

Bradbury, Malcolm. "Jane Austen's *Emma*." *Critical Quarterly* 4 (Winter 1962): 335–46.

Bramer, George R. "The Setting in *Emma*." *College English* 22 (December 1960): 150–56.

Burrows, J.F. "Jane Austen's *Emma*." *Sydney Studies in Literature* 4 (1968): 7–132.

Collins, Thomas J. "Some Mutual Sets of Friends: Moral Monitors in *Emma* and *Our Mutual Friend*." *Dickensian* 65 (January 1969): 32–34.

Corsa, Helen S. "A Fair but Frozen Maid: A Study of Jane Austen's *Emma*." *Literature and Psychology* 19 (1969): 101–24.

Halperin, John W. "The Language of Meditation: Four Studies in Nineteenth Century Fiction." *Dissertation Abstracts International* 32 (1972): 6976A–77A (Johns Hopkins).

Hamouchene, Ulla, Gerd Lemvig, and Else Thomsen. "Aspects of Three Novels by Jane Austen, Part Two: *Emma*. Love and Marriage, or How the Rigid Class Division Should Be Mollified a Little." *Language and Literature* 2 (1973): 56–71.

Harris, Harold J. "A Note on Snobbishness in *Emma*." *Ball State Teachers College Forum* 5 (Spring 1964): 55–57.

Harvey, W.J. "The Plot of *Emma*." *Essays in Criticism* 17 (January 1967): 48–63.

Hellstrom, Ward. "Francophobia in *Emma*." *Studies in English Literature, 1500–1900* 5 (Autumn 1965): 607–17.

Higuchi, Kinzo. "The Comic Structure of *Emma*." *Studies in English Literature,* English Number (1972): 191–92.

Hough, Graham. "Morality and the Novel." *Listener* (May 2, 1963): 747–48.

Hughes, R.E. "The Education of Emma Woodhouse." *Nineteenth Century Fiction* 16 (June 1961): 69–74.

Jones, Evan. "Characters and Values: *Emma* and *Mansfield Park*." *Quadrant* 12 (1968): 35–45.

Kissane, Joseph M. "Comparison's Blessed Felicity: Character Arrangement in *Emma*." *Studies in the Novel* 2 (Summer 1970): 173–84.

Knight, Charles A. "Irony and Mr. Knightley." *Studies in the Novel* 2 (Summer 1970): 185–93.

Knoepflmacher, U.C. "Importance of Being Frank: Character and Letter-Writing in *Emma*." *Studies in English Literature, 1500–1900* 7 (Autumn 1967): 639–58.

Latham, Jacqueline E.M. "Head versus Heart: The Role of Miss Bates in *Emma*." *English* 15 (Spring 1965): 140–43.

Lawry, J.S. "Decided and Open: Structure in *Emma*." *Nineteenth Century Fiction* 24 (June 1969): 1–15.

Marshall, Sarah Latimer. "Rationality and Delusion in Jane Austen's *Emma*." *University of Mississippi Studies in English* 9 (1968): 57–67.

Martin, W.R. "*Emma*: A Definition of Virtue." *English Studies in Africa* 3 (March 1960): 21–30.

Minter, David Lee. "Aesthetic Vision and the World of *Emma*." *Nineteenth Century Fiction* 21 (June 1966): 49–59.

Moore, E. Margaret. "*Emma* and Miss Bates: Early Experience of Separation and the Theme of Dependency in Jane Austen's Novels." *Studies in English Literature, 1500–1900* 9 (Autumn 1969): 573–85.

Morgan, Alice. "On Teaching *Emma*." *Journal of General Education* 24 (July 1972): 103–8.

Morgan, Susan J. "Emma Woodhouse and the Charms of Imagination." *Studies in the Novel* 7 (Spring 1975): 33–48.

Nardin, Jane. "Charity in *Emma*." *Studies in the Novel* 7 (Spring 1975): 61–72.

Ross, Mary Beth. "Jane Austen as a Political Novelist: Class Consciousness in *Emma*." *Mary Wollstonecraft Newsletter* 1 (July 1972): 8–12.

Sharma, S.S. "Jane Austen's Ironic View in the Letters of *Emma*." *Rajasthan University Studies in English* 6 (1972): 18–25.

Siefert, Susan Elizabeth. "The Dilemma of the Talented Woman: A Study in Nineteenth Century Fiction." *Dissertation Abstracts International* 36 (1975) 285A–86A (Marquette).

Tomlinson, T.B. "Jane Austen's Originality: *Emma*." *Critical Review* 9 (1966): 22–37.

Watson, J. "Mr. Perry's Patients: A View of *Emma*." *Essays in Criticism* 20 (July 1970): 334–43.

Weinsheimer, J.C. "In Praise of Mr. Woodhouse: Duty and Desire in *Emma*." *Ariel* 6 (1975): 81–95.

White, Edward M. "*Emma* and the Parodic Point of View." *Nineteenth Century Fiction* 18 (June 1963): 55–63.

Wilhelm, Albert E. "Three Word Clusters in *Emma*." *Studies in the Novel* 7 (Spring 1975): 49–60.

The History of England (c. 1793) Mansell, Darrel, Jr. "Another Source of Jane Austen's *The History of England*." *Notes and Queries* 14 (August 1967): 305.

Jack and Alice (c. 1793) Moler, Kenneth L. "Fanny Burney's *Cecilia* and Jane Austen's *Jack and Alice*." *English Language Notes* 3 (September 1965): 40–42.

Juvenilia (c. 1793)

Bradbrook, Frank W. "Jane Austen's Juvenilia." *Times Literary Supplement* (January 28, 1965): 72.

Chillman, Dawes. "Jane Austen's Juvenilia as a Key to the Structure of Her First Three Mature Novels." *Dissertation Abstracts* 24 (1963): 724–25 (Texas).

Southam, B.C. "Jane Austen's Juvenilia: The Question of Completeness." *Notes and Queries* 11 (May 1964): 180–81.

Lady Susan (c. 1805)

Levine, Jay A. "*Lady Susan:* Jane Austen's Character of the Merry Widow." *Studies in English Literature, 1500–1900* 1 (Autumn 1961): 23–34.

Mansfield Park (1814)

Ames, Carol. "Fanny and Mrs. Norris: Poor Relations in *Mansfield Park*." *Dalhousie Review* 54 (Autumn 1974): 491–98.

Anderson, Walter E. "The Plot of *Mansfield Park*." *Modern Philology* 71 (August 1973): 16–27.

Banfield, Ann. "The Moral Landscape of *Mansfield Park*." *Nineteenth Century Fiction* 26 (June 1971): 1–24.

Bradbrook, Frank W. "Sources of Jane Austen's

Ideas about Nature in *Mansfield Park*." *Notes and Queries* 8 (June 1961): 222–24.

Brenner, Gerry. "*Mansfield Park*: Reading for 'Improvement.'" *Studies in the Novel* 7 (Spring 1975): 24–32.

Brogan, Hugh. "*Mansfield Park*." *Times Literary Supplement* (December 19, 1968): 1440.

Brown, Lloyd W. "The Comic Conclusion in Jane Austen's Novels." *Publications of the Modern Language Association* 84 (1969): 1582–87.

Brown, Lloyd W. "Jane Austen and the Sublime: A Note on *Mansfield Park*." *Studies in Burke and His Time* 10 (Fall 1968): 1041–43.

Burroway, Janet. "The Irony of the Insufferable Prig: *Mansfield Park*." *Critical Quarterly* 9 (Summer 1967): 127–38.

Carroll, D.R. "*Mansfield Park, Daniel Deronda* and Ordination." *Modern Philology* 62 (February 1965): 217–26.

Chanda, S.M. "The New Vein in *Mansfield Park*." *Indian Journal of English Studies* 1 (1960): 96–99.

Devlin, David D. "*Mansfield Park*." *Ariel* 2 (1971): 30–44.

Donohue, Joseph W., Jr. "Ordination and the Divided House at *Mansfield Park*." *English Literary History* 32 (June 1965): 169–78.

Draffan, Robert A. "*Mansfield Park*: Jane Austen's Bleak House." *Essays in Criticm* 19 (October 1969): 371–84.

Duckworth, Alistair M. "*Mansfield Park* and Estate Improvements: Jane Austen's Grounds of Being." *Nineteenth Century Fiction* 26 (June 1971): 25–48.

Edge, Charles E. "*Mansfield Park* and Ordination." *Nineteenth Century Fiction* 16 (December 1961): 269–74.

Edwards, Thomas R., Jr. "*The Difficult Beauty of Mansfield Park*." *Nineteenth Century Fiction* 20 (June 1965): 51–67.

Ellis, David. "The Irony of *Mansfield Park*." *Melbourne Critical Review* 12 (1969): 107–19.

Fleishman, Avrom. "*Mansfield Park* in Its Time." *Nineteenth Century Fiction* 22 (June 1967): 1–18.

Fowler, Marian E. "The Courtesy Book: Heroine in *Mansfield Park*." *University of Toronto Quarterly* 44 (Fall 1974): 31–46.

Fryxell, Donald R. "*Lovers' Vows* in *Mansfield Park*." *Midwest Review* (Spring 1961): 75–78.

Goldberg, Annemette, Margit Mortensen, and Marianne Sorensen. "*Aspects of Three Novels by Jane Austen, Part One: Mansfield Park.* Love and Marriage, or How to Catch a Husband Without Really Trying." *Language and Literature* 2 (1973): 39–56.

Gould, Gerald L. "The Gate Scene at Sotherton in *Mansfield Park*." *Literature and Psychology* 20 (1970): 75–78.

Gullans, C.B. "Jane Austen's *Mansfield Park* and Dr. Johnson." *Nineteenth Century Fiction* 27 (September 1972): 206–8.

Halperin, John. "Trouble with *Mansfield Park*." *Studies in the Novel* 7 (Spring 1975): 6–23.

Henfrey, Norman. "*Mansfield Park*." *Delta*, no. 39 (Summer 1966): 4–11.

Hirst, Clinton S. "Jane Austen's *Mansfield Park*." *Dissertation Abstracts International* 34 (1973): 1858A (Notre Dame).

Hummel, Madeline. "Emblematic Charades and the Observant Woman in *Mansfield Park*." *Texas Studies in Literature and Language* 15 (Summer 1973): 251–65.

Jones, Evan. "Characters and Values: *Emma* and *Mansfield Park*." *Quadrant* 12 (1968): 35–45.

Jordan, Ellen. "*Mansfield Park*." *Times Literary Supplement* (June 23, 1972): 719.

Kirkham, M. "Theatricals in *Mansfield Park* and Frederick in *Lovers' Vows*." *Notes and Queries* 22 (September 1975): 388–89.

Lauber, John. "Minds Bewildered and Astray: The Crawfords in *Mansfield Park*." *Studies in the Novel* 2 (Summer 1970): 194–210.

Litz, Walton. "The Chronology of *Mansfield Park*." *Notes and Queries* 8 (June 1961): 221–22.

Lodge, David. "A Question of Judgment: The Theatricals at Mansfield Park." *Nineteenth Century Fiction* 17 (December 1962): 275–82.

Lynch, P.R. "Speculation at Mansfield Parsonage." *Notes and Queries* 14 (January 1967): 21–22.

Magee, William H. "Romanticism on Trial in *Mansfield Park*." *Bucknell Review* 14 (March 1966): 44–59.

"*Mansfield Park*." *Times Literary Supplement* (October 21, 1966): 946; (October 28, 1966): 966; (November 11, 1966): 1003.

Martin, W.R. "Ordination in *Mansfield Park*." *English Studies in Africa* 9 (September 1966): 146–57.

Porteous, Alexander. "The Beast in the Park: Some Features of Jane Austen's Work." *Melbourne Critical Review* 7 (1964): 66–77.

Riley, Michael D. "Reduction and Redemption: The Meaning of *Mansfield Park*." *Dissertation Abstracts International* 34 (1974): 5926A (Ohio).

Ryals, Clyde De L. "Being and Doing in *Mansfield Park*." *Archiv* 5 (March 1970): 345–60.

Schneider, Sister M. Lucy. "The Little White Attic and the East Room: Their Function in *Mansfield Park*." *Modern Philology* 63 (February 1966): 227–35.

Southam, Brian. "*Mansfield Park*." *Times Literary Supplement* (January 2, 1969): 22; (January 9, 1969): 39; (January 16, 1969): 62; (January 30, 1969): 111.

Weinsheimer, Joel C. "*Mansfield Park*: Three Problems." *Nineteenth Century Fiction* 29 (September 1974): 185–205.

White, Edward M. "A Critical Theory of *Mansfield Park*." *Studies in English Literature, 1500–1900* 7 (Autumn 1967): 659–77.

Wiltshire, John. "*Mansfield Park* and Fanny Price." *Melbourne Critical Review* 8 (1965): 121–28.

Zimmerman, Everett. "Jane Austen and *Mansfield Park*: A Discrimination of Ironies." *Studies in the Novel* 1 (Fall 1969): 347–56.

Northanger Abbey (1818)

Baker, Sheridan. "The Comedy of Illusion in *Northanger Abbey*." *Papers of the Michigan Academy of Science, Arts and Letters* 51 (1965): 547–58.

Chard, Leslie F., II. "Jane Austen and the Obituaries: The Names of *Northanger Abbey*." *Studies in the Novel* 7 (Spring 1975): 133–36.

Chillman, Dawes. "Miss Morland's Mind: Sentiment, Reason, and Experience in *Northanger Abbey*." *South Dakota Review* 1 (December 1963): 37–47.

Ehrenpreis, Anne Henry. "*Northanger Abbey*: Jane Austen and Charlotte Smith." *Nineteenth Century Fiction* 25 (December 1970): 343–48.

Emden, Cecil S. "The Composition of *Northanger Abbey*." *Review of English Studies* 19 (August 1968): 279–87.

Fleishman, Avrom. "Socialization of Catherine Morland." *English Literary History* 41 (Winter 1974): 649–67.

Gallon, D.N. "Comedy in *Northanger Abbey*." *Modern Language Review* 63 (October 1968): 802–9.

Kearful, Frank J. "Satire and the Form of the Novel: The Problem of Aesthetic Unity in *Northanger Abbey*." *English Literary History* 32 (December 1965): 511–27.

Mansell, Darrel, Jr. "The Date of Jane Austen's

Revision of *Northanger Abbey*." *English Language Notes* 7 (September 1969): 40–41.

Morkam, R.C. "Austen Editions." *Times Literary Supplement* (November 18, 1965): 1023.

Rawson, C.J. " 'Nice' and 'Sentimental': A Parallel between *Northanger Abbey* and Richardson's *Correspondence*." *Notes and Queries* 11 (May 1964): 180.

Rothstein, Eric. "The Lessons of *Northanger Abbey*." *University of Toronto Quarterly* 44 (Fall 1974): 14–30.

Rubinstein, E. "*Northanger Abbey*: The Elder Morlands and 'John Homespun.' " *Papers on Language and Literature* 5 (1969): 434–40.

Sorensen, Knud. "Johnsonese in *Northanger Abbey*: A Note on Jane Austen's Style." *English Studies* 50 (1969): 390–97.

Southam, B.C. "*Northanger Abbey*." *Times Literary Supplement* (October 12, 1962): 800.

Speakman, James S. "Wit, Humor and Sensibility in *Evelina, Belinda* and *Northanger Abbey*." *Dissertation Abstracts International* 34 (1973): 791A–92A (California, Davis).

Zimmerman, Everett. "Function of Parody in *Northanger Abbey*." *Modern Language Quarterly* 30 (March 1969): 53–63.

Persuasion (1818)

Auerbach, Nina. "O Brave New World: Evolution and Revolution in *Persuasion*." *English Literary History* 39 (March 1972): 112–28.

Bogh, Kirsten. "Aspects of Three Novels by Jane Austen, Part Three: *Persuasion*, Love and Marriage, or 'Bad Morality to Conclude With.' " *Language and Literature* 2 (1973): 72–94.

Bradbury, Malcolm. "*Persuasion* Again." *Essays in Criticism* 18 (October 1968): 383–96.

Erickson, E. Joyce Q. "The Significance of *Persuasion*." *Dissertation Abstracts International* 31 (1971): 3501A (Washington).

Gomme, Andor. "On Not Being Persuaded." *Essays in Criticism* 16 (April 1966): 170–84.

Gooneratne, Yasmine. " 'The Loveliest Medium': The New Element in Jane Austen's *Persuasion*." *University of Ceylon Review* 24 (April–October 1966): 1–28.

Helms, Alan E. "1. Visual Prosody and the Sound of Punctuation. 2. Sensibility and Sense in Jane Austen's *Persuasion*. 3. The Mower Poems of Andrew Marvell." *Dissertation Abstracts International* 32 (1971): 3305A (Rutgers).

Lading, Ase. "Love and Marriage, or How Sexuality Becomes Integrated in the Family." *Language and Literature* 2 (1973): 94–103.

Laski, M. "Sensibility and Sense: A Reading of *Persuasion*." *English Studies in Africa* 3 (September 1960): 119–30.

Monaghan, David M. "The Decline of the Gentry: A Study of Jane Austen's Attitude to Formality in *Persuasion*." *Studies in the Novel* 7 (Spring 1975): 73–87.

Morkam, R.C. "Austen Editions." *Times Literary Supplement* (November 18, 1965): 1023.

Page, Norman. "Categories of Speech in *Persuasion*." *Modern Language Review* 64 (October 1969): 734–41.

Whitten, Benjamin G., Jr. "Jane Austen's 'Comedy of Feeling': A Critical Analysis of *Persuasion*." *Dissertation Abstracts International* 32 (1972): 4031A (California, Davis).

Wiesenfarth, Joseph. "*Persuasion*: History and Myth." *Wordsworth Circle* 2 (Autumn 1971): 160–68.

Wiltshire, John. "A Romantic Persuasion?" *Critical Review* 14 (1971): 3–16.

Wolfe, Thomas P., II. "The Achievement of *Persuasion*." *Studies in English Literature, 1500–1900* 11 (Autumn 1971): 687–700.

Zeitlow, Paul N. "Luck and Fortuitous Circumstance in *Persuasion*: Two Interpretations." *English Literary History* 32 (June 1965): 179–95.

Pride and Prejudice (1813, original title *First Impressions*).

Andrews, P.B.S. "The Date of *Pride and Prejudice*." *Notes and Queries* 15 (September 1968): 338–42.

Copeland, Catherine H. "*Pride and Prejudice*: A Neo-Classical Work in a Romantic Age." *College Language Association Journal* 14 (December 1970): 156–62.

Davie, John, Duncan Isles, and Alastair Stead. "Pride and Prejudice." *Notes and Queries* 11 (May 1964): 181–82.

Dooley, D.J. "Pride, Prejudice and Vanity in Elizabeth Bennet." *Nineteenth Century Fiction* 20 (September 1965): 185–88.

Ebiike, Shunji. "*Pride and Prejudice* and *First Impressions*." *Studies in English Literature*, English Number (1965): 31–45.

Ferns, John. "Neo-Classical Structure: *The Rape of the Lock* and *Pride and Prejudice*." *Queen's Quarterly* 75 (1968): 685–90.

Fox, Robert C. "Elizabeth Bennet: Prejudice or Vanity?" *Nineteenth Century Fiction* 17 (September 1962): 185–87.

Halliday, E.M. "Narrative Perspective in *Pride and Prejudice*." *Nineteenth Century Fiction* 15 (June 1960): 65–71.

Halperin, John W. "The Language of Meditation: Four Studies in Nineteenth Century Fiction." *Dissertation Abstracts International* 32 (1972): 6976A–77A (Johns Hopkins).

Katz, Judith N. "Rooms of Their Own: Forms and Images of Liberation in Five Novels." *Dissertation Abstracts International* 34 (1973): 1283A (Penn. State).

Laski, Marghanita. "Some Words from *Pride and Prejudice*." *Notes and Queries* 7 (September 1960): 312.

Marcus, Mordecai. "A Major Thematic Pattern in *Pride and Prejudice*." *Nineteenth Century Fiction* 16 (December 1961): 274–79.

McCann, Charles J. "Setting and Character in *Pride and Prejudice*." *Nineteenth Century Fiction* 19 (June 1964): 65–75.

Moler, Kenneth L. "The Bennet Girls and Adam Smith on Vanity and Pride." *Philological Quarterly* 46 (October 1967): 567–69.

Moler, Kenneth L. "*Pride and Prejudice*: Jane Austen's 'Patrician Hero.' " *Studies in English Literature, 1500–1900* 7 (Summer 1967): 491–508.

Moler, Kenneth L. "*Pride and Prejudice* and Edward Cooper's *Sermons*." *Notes and Queries* 13 (May 1966): 182.

Morgan, Susan J. "Intelligence in *Pride and Prejudice*." *Modern Philology* 73 (August 1975): 54–68.

Nash, Ralph. "The Time Scheme for *Pride and Prejudice*." *English Language Notes* 4 (March 1967): 194–98.

Orum, Tania. "Love and Marriage, or How Economy Becomes Internalized: A Study of *Pride and Prejudice*." *Language and Literature* 2 (1973): 3–37.

Phare, E.E. "Lydia Languish, Lydia Bennet, and Dr. Fordyce's Sermons." *Notes and Queries* 11 (May 1964): 182–83.

Pikoulis, John. "Jane Austen: The Figure in the Carpet." *Nineteenth Century Fiction* 27 (June 1972): 38–60.

Siefert, Susan Elizabeth. "The Dilemma of the Talented Woman: A Study in Nineteenth Century Fiction." *Dissertation Abstracts International* 36 (1975): 285A–86A (Marquette).

Southam, B.C. "Jane Austen and *Clarissa*." *Notes and Queries* 10 (May 1963): 191–92.

Ten Harmsel, Henrietta. "The Villain-Hero in *Pamela* and *Pride and Prejudice*." *College English* 23 (November 1961): 104–8.

Weinsheimer, Joel. "Chance and the Hierarchy of Marriages in *Pride and Prejudice*." *English Literary History* 39 (September 1972): 404–19.

Weinstein, M.A. "Echo of Mrs. Bennet in *Waverley*." *Notes and Queries* 22 (February 1975): 63–64.

Zimmerman, Everett. "Pride and Prejudice in *Pride and Prejudice*." *Nineteenth Century Fiction* 23 (June 1968): 64–73.

Sanditon (1817)

Lauber, John. "*Sanditon*: The Kingdom of Folly." *Studies in the Novel* 4 (Fall 1972): 353–63.

Lock, F.P. " 'The Neighborhood of Tombuctoo': A Note on *Sanditon*." *Notes and Queries* 19 (March 1972): 97–99.

Martin, W.R. "The Subject of Jane Austen's *Sanditon*." *English Studies in Africa* 10 (March 1967): 87–93.

Southam, B.C. "The Text of *Sanditon*." *Notes and Queries* 8 (January 1961): 23–24.

Sense and Sensibility (1811)

Metcalfe, Alvin C. "*Sense and Sensibility*: A Study of Its Similarity to the History of Sir Charles Grandison." *Dissertation Abstracts International* 31 (1971): 4129A (Kent State).

Moler, Kenneth L. "*Sense and Sensibility* and Its Sources." *Review of English Studies* 17 (November 1966): 413–19.

Phillipps, K.C. "Lucy Steele's English." *English Studies,* Anglo-American Supplement (1969): 15–16.

Stone, Donald D. "Sense and Semantics in Jane Austen." *Nineteenth Century Fiction* 25 (June 1970): 31–50.

Volume the First (1925)

Southam, B.C. "The Manuscript of Jane Austen's *Volume the First*." *Library* 17 (September 1962): 231–37.

Southam, B.C. "A Note on Jane Austen's *Volume the First*." *Notes and Queries* 9 (November 1962): 422.

Volume the Third (1951)

Southam, B.C. "Interpolations to Jane Austen's *Volume the Third*." *Notes and Queries* 9 (May 1962): 185–87.

Mary Austin, née Hunter (1868–1934) U.S.
Bibliography
Berry, J. Wilkes. "Mary Hunter Austin (1868–1934)." *American Literary Realism* 2 (1969): 125–31.
General Works
Anderson, Barbara. "Thoreau and Mary Austin." *Thoreau Society Bulletin* 126 (Winter 1974): 7.
Berry, J. Wilkes. "Characterization in Mary Austin's Southwest Works." *Southwestern American Literature* 2 (1972): 119–24.
Berry, J. Wilkes. "Mary Austin: Sibylic Gourmet of the Southwest." *Western Review* 9 (Winter 1972): 3–8.
Ford, Thomas W. "The American Rhythm: Mary Austin's Poetic Principle." *Western American Literature* 5 (Spring 1970): 3–14.
Forman, H.J. "On a Letter from Mary Austin." *New Mexico Quarterly* 31 (Winter 1961–1962): 339–44.
Johnson, Lee Ann. "Western Literary Realism: The California Tales of Norris and Austin." *American Literary Realism* 7 (1974): 278–80.
Powell, Laurence Clark. "A Dedication to the Memory of Mary Hunter Austin, 1868–1934." *Arizona and the West* 10 (Spring 1968): 1–4.
Powell, Laurence Clark. "Southwest Classics Reread: A Prophetic Passage." *Westways* 65 (February 1973): 60–65.
Powell, Laurence Clark. "Strickly Local." *Southern California Quarterly* 47 (December 1965): 347–55.
Ringler, Donald P. "Mary Austin: Kern County Days, 1888–1892." *Southern California Quarterly* 45 (March 1963): 25–63.
Robbins, Millie. "Her Pen Made the Desert Bloom." *San Francisco Chronicle* (December 28, 1967): 19.
Robinson, Frank K. "From Mary Austin to Edgar Lee Masters: A Book Inscription." *Library Chronicle of the University of Texas*, n.s. 6 (December 1973): 82–85.
Waters, Lena W. "Mary Austin as Nature Essayist." *Dissertation Abstracts International* 35 (1975): 895A–96A (Texas Tech).

Margaret Avison (1918–) Canada
General Works
Bowering, George. "Avison's Imitation of Christ the Artist." *Canadian Literature*, no. 54 (Autumn 1972): 56–69.
Columbo, John Robert. "Avison and Wevill." *Canadian Literature*, no. 34 (Autumn 1967): 72–76.
Doerksen, D.W. "Search and Discovery: Margaret Avison's Poetry." *Canadian Literature*, no. 60 (Spring 1974): 7–20.
Jones, Lawrence M. "A Core of Brilliance: Margaret Avison's Achievement." *Canadian Literature*, no. 38 (Autumn 1968): 50–57.
MacCallum, Hugh. "Poetry." *University of Toronto Quarterly* 36 (July 1967): 354–79.
New, William H. "The Mind's Eyes (I's) (Ice): The Poetry of Margaret Avison." *Twentieth Century Literature* 16 (July 1970): 185–202.
Wilson, Milton. "The Poetry of Margaret Avison." *Canadian Literature*, no. 2 (Autumn 1960): 47–57.

B

NATALIE BABBITT (1932–) U.S.
General Works
Mercier, J. "Natalie Babbitt." *Publishers Weekly* (July 28, 1975): 66–67.

PEGGY BACON (1895–) U.S.
General Works
Munson, Gorham. "Peggy Bacon." *Literary Review* 6 (Spring 1963): 279–82.

MARGARET JEWETT BAILEY (1812–1882) U.S.
Individual Works
The Grains, or, Passages in the Life of Ruth Rover with Occasional Pictures of Oregon, Natural and Moral (1954)
Duncan, Janice K. " 'Ruth Rover'—Indictive Falsehood or Historical Truth." *Journal of the West* 12 (April 1973): 240–53.

JOANNA BAILLIE (1762–1851) Scotland
General Works
Lambertson, C.L., ed. "Speaking of Byron, Part I." *Malahat Review* 12 (October 1969): 18–42; Part II, 13 (January 1970): 24–46.
Marshall, George O., Jr. "Giftbooks, Tennyson and *The Tribute* (1837)." *Georgia Review* 16 (Winter 1962): 459–64.
Individual Works
De Monfort (1798)
Insch, A.G. "Joanna Baillie's *De Monfort* in Relation to Her Theory of Tragedy." *Durham University Journal* 54 (June 1962): 114–20.
Plays on the Passions (1798)
Lamb, Virginia B. "Joanna Baillie's *Plays on the Passions* Viewed in Relation to Her Dramatic Theories." *Dissertation Abstracts International* 35 (1974): 406A (Kent State).

DOROTHY BAKER (1903–1968) U.S.
General Works
Kazin, Alfred. "The Story as Manner." *Reporter* (March 14, 1962): 44–46.
Individual Works
Cassandra at the Wedding (1962)
Johnson, S.F. "Identities of Cassandra." *Novel* 1 (Fall 1967): 71–74.

MARILYN BAKER (1929–) U.S.
General Works
Waters, H., and G.C. Lubenow. "Hearst Sleuth." *Newsweek* (May 19, 1975): 94–95.

Mrs. George Linnaeus Banks, née Isabella Varley (1821–1897) Great Britain
General Works
Burney, E.L. "Mrs. George Linnaeus Banks (née Isabella Varley), 1821–1897: An Address to the Manchester Society of Book Collectors, on Thursday 21st November 1968." *Manchester Review* 11 (1968–1969): 221–24.

HELEN BANNERMAN (1862/3–1946) Great Britain
Individual Works
Little Black Sambo (1899)
Schiller, Justin G. "The Story of *Little Black Sambo*." *Book Collector* 23 (Autumn 1974): 381–86.

MARGARET CULKIN BANNING (1891–) U.S.
General Works
Baker, J.F. "On Being a Writer in the Midwest." *Publishers Weekly* (October 22, 1973): 71.

ANNA BARBAULD, née Aikin (1743–1825) Great Britain
General Works

Zall, Paul M. "Mrs. Barbauld's Crew and the Building of a Mass Reading Class." *Wordsworth Circle* 2 (Summer 1971): 74–79.

Individual Works

Hymns in Prose (c. 1773)

Pickering, Samuel F., Jr. "Mrs. Barbauld's *Hymns in Prose*: An Air-Blown Particle of Romanticism." *Southern Humanities Review* 9 (Summer 1975): 259–67.

Zall, Paul M. "Wordsworth's 'Ode' and Mrs. Barbauld's Hymns." *Wordsworth Circle* 1 (Autumn 1970): 177–79.

MARY BARBER (1690–1757) Ireland (?)
Individual Works

Poems on Several Occasions (1714) Authorship disputed

Isdell-Carpenter, Andrew P. "On a Manuscript of Poems Catalogued as by Mary Barber in the Library of TCD." *Hermathena* 109 (Autumn 1969): 54–64.

MARJORIE BARNARD (1897–) Australia
Bibliography

Brown, Lyn. "Marjorie Barnard: A Checklist, 1919–1920." *Biblionews and Australian Notes and Queries* 4 (1970): 5–9.

DJUNA BARNES (1892–) U.S.
Bibliography

Hipkiss, Robert A. "Djuna Barnes (1892–)—A Bibliography." *Twentieth Century Literature* 14 (October 1968): 161–63.

General Works

Ferguson, Suzanne C. "Djuna Barnes' Short Stories: An Estrangement of the Heart." *Southern Review* (U.S.) 5 (1969): 26–41.

Hirschman, Jack Aaron. "The Orchestrated Novel: A Study of Poetic Devices in Novels of Djuna Barnes and Hermann Broch, and the Influences of the Works of James Joyce upon Them." *Dissertation Abstracts* 22 (1962): 3220 (Indiana).

Williamson, Alan. "The Divided Image: The Quest for Identity in the Works of Djuna Barnes." *Critique* 7 (1964): 58–74.

Individual Works

Nightwood (1936)

Baxter, Charles. "A Self-Consuming Light: *Nightwood* and the Crisis of Modernism." *Journal of Modern Literature* 3 (1974): 1175–87.

Greiner, D.J. "Djuna Barnes' *Nightwood* and the American Origins of Black Humor." *Critique* 17 (1975): 41–54.

Gunn, Edward. "Myth and Style in Djuna Barnes' *Nightwood*." *Modern Fiction Studies* 19 (Winter 1973–1974): 545–55.

Johnsen, William A. "Modern Women Novelists: *Nightwood* and the Novel of Sensibility." *Bucknell Review* 21 (Spring 1973): 29–42.

Nelson, Paula K. "The Functions of Figures of Speech in Selected Anti-Realistic Novels." *Dissertation Abstracts International* 33 (1972): 1736A–37A (N.Y.U.).

Weisstein, Ulrich. "Beast, Doll, and Woman: Djuna Barnes' Human Bestiary." *Renascence* 15 (Fall 1962): 3–11.

AMELIA EDITH BARR, née Huddleston (1831–1919) U.S. (Born in Great Britain)
General Works

Bargard, Robert. "Amelia Barr, Augusta Evans Wilson and the Sentimental Novel." *Marab* 1 (Winter 1965–1966): 13–25.

CLARA BARRUS (1864–1931) U.S.
General Works

Wordan, J. D. "Doctors as Men of Letters." *Bulletin of the New York Public Library* 68 (November 1964): 594.

CHARLOTTE FISKE BATES (1838–1916) U.S.
General Works

Cary, Richard. "Charlotte Fiske Bates: Cupbearer to the Gods." *Colby Library Quarterly* 6 (March 1964): 385–98.

Cary, Richard. "Whittier Regained." *New England Quarterly* 34 (September 1961): 370–75.

BLANCHE EDITH BAUGHAN (1870–1958) New Zealand

General Works

Alcock, P.C.M. "A True Colonial Voice: Blanche Edith Baughan." *Landfall* 26 (June 1972): 162–76.

BARBARA BAYNTON, née Kilpatrick (1862–1929) Australia

General Works

Phillips, A.S. "Barbara Baynton and the Dissidence of the Nineties." *Overland* no. 22 (1961): 15–20.

Sylvia Beach (1887–1962) U.S.
Bibliography
Mathews, Jackson, and Maurice Saillet, eds. "Sylvia Beach (1887–1962)." *Mercure de France* 349 (August–September 1963): 7–169.
General Works
Fitch, Noel. "Sylvia Beach's Shakespeare and Company: Port of Call for American Expatriates." *Research Studies* 33 (1965): 197–207.
Rice, Howard C., Jr. "The Sylvia Beach Collection." *Princeton University Library Chronicle* 26 (Autumn 1964): 7–13.

Sybille Bedford (1911–) Great Britain
General Works
Baker, J.F. "Sybille Bedford." *Publishers Weekly* (December 16, 1974): 6–7.

Catherine Beecher (1800–1878) U.S.
General Works
Bacon, Martha. "Miss Beecher in Hell." *American Heritage* 14 (December 1962): 28.
Burstyn, J. N. "Catherine Beecher and the Education of American Woman." *New England Quarterly* 47 (September 1974): 386–403.

Aphra Behn (1640–1689) Great Britain
General Works
Barrett, Alberta Gregg. "Plot, Characterization and Theme in the Plays of Aphra Behn." *Dissertation Abstracts* 26 (1965): 7294 (Penn.).
Day, Robert Adams. "Aphra Behn's First Biography." *Studies in Bibliography* 22 (1969): 227–40.
Hargreaves, Henry Allen. "The Birth of Mrs. Behn." *Humanities Association Bulletin* 16 (Spring 1965): 19–20.
Hargreaves, Henry Allen. "A Case for Mister Behn." *Notes and Queries* 9 (June 1962): 203–5.
Hargreaves, Henry Allen. "The Life and Plays of Mrs. Aphra Behn." *Dissertation Abstracts* 21 (1961): 2774–75 (Duke).
Hargreaves, Henry Allen. "Mrs. Behn's Warning of the Dutch 'Thames Plot.'" *Notes and Queries* 9 (February 1962): 61–63.
Jordan, Robert. "Mrs. Behn and *Sir Anthony Love*." *Restoration and Eighteenth Century Theatre Research* 12 (1973): 58–59.
Kramer, Rita. "Aphra Behn: Novelist, Spy, Libertine." *Ms.* (February 1973): 16.
Leja, Alfred Eric. "Aphra Behn—Tory." *Dissertation Abstracts* 23 (1962): 1686–87 (Texas).
Lindquist, Carol A. "The Prose Fiction of Aphra Behn." *Dissertation Abstracts International* 31 (1971): 4126A (Maryland).
Quaintance, Richard E. "French Sources of the Restoration 'Imperfect Enjoyment' Poem." *Philological Quarterly* 42 (April 1963): 190–99.
Scott, Clayton S., Jr. "Aphra Behn: A Study in Dramatic Continuity." *Dissertation Abstracts International* 33 (1972): 2344A (Texas Christian).
Seward, Patricia M. "Calderón and Aphra Behn: Spanish Borrowings in *The Young King*." *Bulletin of Hispanic Studies* 49 (1972): 149–64.
Shea, P.K. "Alexander Pope and Aphra Behn on Wit." *Notes and Queries* 22 (January 1975): 12.
Simpson, Joan Murray. "The Incomparable Aphra." *Cornhill Magazine*, no. 1067 (Spring 1971): 368–71.
Stephenson, Peter Stansfield. "Three Playwright-Novelists: The Contribution of Dramatic Techniques to Restoration and Early Eighteenth Century Prose Fiction." *Dissertation Abstracts International* 30 (1970): 3920A (California, Davis).
Vernon, P.F. "Marriage of Convenience and the Moral Code of Restoration Comedy." *Essays in Criticism* 12 (October 1962): 370–87.
Individual Works
Oroonoko, or the History of the Royal Slave (c. 1678)
Duchovnay, Gerald C. "Aphra Behn's *Oroonoko*: A Critical Edition." *Dissertation Abstracts International* 32 (1972): 4559A–60A (Indiana).
Hargreaves, Henry Allen. "New Evidence of the Realism of Mrs. Behn's *Oroonoko*." *Bulletin of the New York Public Library* 74 (September 1970): 437–44.
Ramsaran, J.A. "*Oroonoko*: A Study of Factual Elements." *Notes and Queries* 7 (April 1960): 142–45.
Sheffey, Ruthe T. "Some Evidence for a New Source of Aphra Behn's *Oroonoko*." *Studies in Philology* 59 (1962): 52–63.
The Rover, or The Banished Cavaliers, Parts I and II (1677, 1680)
Langhans, Edward A. "Three Early Eighteenth Century Promptbooks." *Theatre Notebook* 20 (Summer 1966): 142–50.
The Widow Ranter, or the History of Bacon in Virginia (1690)
Batten, Charles L., Jr. "The Source of Aphra Behn's *The Widow Ranter*." *Restoration and Eighteenth*

Century Theatre Research 13 (1974): 12–18.
Witmer, Anne, and John Freehafer. "Aphra Behn's Strange News from Virginia." *Library Chronicle* (Penn.) 34 (1968): 7–23.

ACTON BELL [pseud.]. *See* Anne Brontë

CURRER BELL [pseud.]. *See* Charlotte Brontë

ELLIS BELL [pseud.]. *See* Emily Brontë

ELEANOR BERGSTEIN (1938–) U.S.
General Works
Martin, Wendy. "Eleanor Bergstein, Novelist—An Interview." *Women's Studies* 2 (1974): 91–97.

JULIANA BERNERS (b. 1388?) Great Britain
Individual Works
The Boke of St. Albans (1486)
Hands, Rachel. "Juliana Berners and *The Boke of St. Albans*." *Review of English Studies* 18 (November 1967): 373–86.

DORIS BETTS, née Waugh (1932–) U.S.
General Works
Betts, Doris. "Fiction, Induction and Deduction." *Arts in Society* 2 (Summer–Fall 1974): 274–78.
Evans, Elizabeth. "Negro Characters in the Fiction of Doris Betts." *Critique* 17 (1975): 59–76.
Individual Works
River to Pickle Beach (1972)
Moose, Ruth. "Superstition in Doris Betts' New Novel." *North Carolina Folklore* 21 (May 1973): 61–62.

ELIZABETH BISHOP (1911–) U.S.
Bibliography
McNally, Nancy L. "Checklist of Elizabeth Bishop's Published Writings." *Twentieth Century Literature* 11 (January 1966): 201.
General Works
Brown, Ashley. "An Interview with Elizabeth Bishop." *Shenandoah* 17 (1966): 3.
Bryan, Nancy L. "A Place for the Genuine Elizabeth Bishop and the Factual Tradition in Modern American Poetry." *Dissertation Abstracts International* 34 (1974): 4245A (Claremont).
Emig, J.A. "The Poem as Puzzle." *English Journal* 52 (April 1963): 222–24.
Gordon, Jan B. "Days and Distances: The Car-

tographic Imagination of Elizabeth Bishop." *Salmagundi* 22–23 (1973): 294–305.
Kirby-Smith, H.T., Jr. "Miss Bishop and Others." *Sewanee Review* 80 (Summer 1972): 483–93.
Mazzaro, Jerome. "Elizabeth Bishop and the Poetics of Impediment." *Salmagundi* 27 (1974): 118–44.
Mazzocco, Robert. "A Poet of Landscape." *New York Review of Books* (October 12, 1967): 4–6.
McNally, Nancy L. "Elizabeth Bishop: The Discipline of Description." *Twentieth Century Literature* 11 (January 1966): 189–201.
Newman, Anne Royall. "Elizabeth Bishop: A Study of Form and Theme." *Dissertation Abstracts International* 35 (1975): 891A–92A (South Carolina).
Spiegelman, Willard. "Landscape and Knowledge: The Poetry of Elizabeth Bishop." *Modern Poetry Studies* 6 (Winter 1975): 203–24.
Stevenson, Anne. "The Poetry of Elizabeth Bishop." *Shenandoah* 17 (1966): 45–54.
Warnke, Frank J. "The Voyages of Elizabeth Bishop." *New Republic* (April 19, 1966): 19–21.

NORA SCHELTER BLAIR (fl. 1890s) U.S.
General Works
Myerson, Joel. "Two Unpublished Reminiscences of Brook Farm." *New England Quarterly* 48 (June 1975): 253–60.

MARGUERITE POWER LADY BLESSINGTON (1789–1849) Great Britain
General Works
Earle, Kathleen. "Portrait of Marguerite Lady Blessington." *Queen's Quarterly* 77 (1970): 236–51.
Lambert, Cecily. "Most Gorgeous Lady Blessington." *Keats-Shelley Memorial Bulletin* 25 (1970): 26–30.
Tomalin, Claire. "Miledis Birron." *New Statesman* (January 16, 1970): 86–87.

KAREN BLIXEN. *See* Isak Dinesen

LOUISE BOGAN (1897–1970) U.S.
General Works
Carruth, Hayden. "A Balance Exactly Struck." *Poetry* 114 (August 1969): 330–31.
Ciardi, J. "A Manner of Speaking." *Saturday Review* (February 21, 1970): 20.
Ramsey, Paul. "Louise Bogan." *Iowa Review* 1 (Summer 1970): 116–24.

Roethke, Theodore. "The Poetry of Louise Bogan." *Critical Quarterly* 3 (Summer 1961): 142–50.

Roethke, Theodore. "The Poetry of Louise Bogan." *Michigan Alumni Quarterly Review* 67 (Autumn 1960): 13–20.

Roethke, Theodore. "The Poetry of Louise Bogan: The Work of a True Inheritor." *Michigan Quarterly Review* 6 (Summer 1967): 246–51.

SHERWOOD BONNER [pseud.]. *See* Katherine Sherwood MacDowell

CHARLOTTE BOOKMAN [pseud.]. *See* Charlotte Zolotow

ELISABETH MANN BORGESE (1930?–) U.S.
General Works
Nichols, L. "Youngest Mann." *New York Times Book Review* (October 30, 1960): 8.

THEODORA BOSANQUET (1887?–1961) Great Britain
General Works
Hyde, H.M. "Henry James and Theodora Bosanquet." *Encounter* 39 (October 1972): 6–12.

ELIZABETH DOROTHEA COLE BOWEN (1899–1973) Great Britain
Bibliography
Sellery, J'Nan. "Elizabeth Bowen: A Check List." *Bulletin of the New York Public Library* 74 (April 1970): 219–74.
General Works
Abrahams, William. "Elizabeth Bowen: On the Mark." *Atlantic Monthly* (March 1975): 133–36.

Blodgett, Harriet H. "Circles of Reality: A Reading of the Novels of Elizabeth Bowen." *Dissertation Abstracts* 29 (1969): 2250A–51A (California, Davis).

Davenport, Gary T. "Elizabeth Bowen and the Big House." *Southern Humanities Review* 8 (Winter 1974): 27–34.

Davis, Robert Murray. "Contributions to *Night and Day* by Elizabeth Bowen, Graham Greene, and Anthony Powell." *Studies in the Novel* 3 (Winter 1971): 401–4.

Dostal, Sister Rose Margaret. "Innocence and Knowledge in the Novels of Elizabeth Bowen." *Dissertation Abstracts* 25 (1964): 2509–10 (Notre Dame).

Greene, George. "Elizabeth Bowen: Imagination as

Therapy." *Perspective* 14 (Spring 1965): 42–52.

Hanna, John Greist. "Elizabeth Bowen and the Art of Fiction: A Study of Her Theory and Practice." *Dissertation Abstracts* 22 (1961): 1175–76 (Boston).

Kendris, Thomas. "The Novels of Elizabeth Bowen." *Dissertation Abstracts* 26 (1965): 1648 (Columbia).

Kirkpatrick, Larry James. "Elizabeth Bowen and Company: A Comparative Essay in Literary Judgment." *Dissertation Abstracts* 26 (1966): 6044 (Duke).

McDowell, Alfred B. "Identity and the Past: Major Themes in the Fiction of Elizabeth Bowen." *Dissertation Abstracts* 32 (1972): 4621A (Bowling Green).

Miller, Donald W. "Scene and Image in Three Novels by Elizabeth Bowen." *Dissertation Abstracts* 28 (1967): 637A–38A (Columbia).

Mitchell, Edward. "Themes in Elizabeth Bowen's Short Stories." *Critique* 8 (1966): 41–54.

Moss, Howard. "Elizabeth Bowen, 1899–1973." *New York Times Book Review* (April 8, 1973): 2–3.

Nardella, Anna Gayle Ryan. "Feminism, Art, and Aesthetics: A Study of Elizabeth Bowen." *Dissertation Abstracts International* 35 (1975): 2851A–52A (S.U.N.Y., Stony Brook).

Nichols, L. "Miss Bowen." *New York Times Book Review* (January 26, 1964): 8.

Pritchett, V.S. "Elizabeth Bowen." *New Statesman* (March 9, 1973): 350.

Rupp, Richard Henry. "The Achievement of Elizabeth Bowen: A Study of Her Fiction and Criticism." *Dissertation Abstracts* 25 (1965): 5286 (Indiana).

Rupp, Richard Henry. "The Post-War Fiction of Elizabeth Bowen." *Xavier University Studies* 4 (March 1965): 55–67.

Saul, George Brandon. "The Short Stories of Elizabeth Bowen." *Arizona Quarterly* 21 (Spring 1965): 53–59.

Sharp, Sister M. Corona. "The House as Setting and Symbol in Three Novels by Elizabeth Bowen." *Xavier University Studies* 2 (December 1963): 93–103.

Stern, Joan O. "A Study of Problems in Values and the Means by Which They Are Presented in the Novels of Elizabeth Bowen." *Dissertation Abstracts International* 35 (1974): 3012A–13A (N.Y.U.).

Van Duyn, Mona. "Review of *Elizabeth Bowen: An Introduction to Her Novels*, by William Heath." *Critique* 5 (1962): 89–92.

Wagner, G. "Elizabeth Bowen and the Artificial Novel." *Essays in Criticism* 13 (April 1963): 155–63.

Wild, Rebecca Smith. "Studies in the Shorter Fiction of Elizabeth Bowen and Eudora Welty." *Dissertation Abstracts* 27 (1966): 490A (Michigan).

Individual Works
The Death of the Heart (1938)

Heinemann, Alison. "The Indoor Landscape in Bowen's *The Death of the Heart*." *Criticism* 10 (1969): 5–12.

Parrish, Paul A. "The Loss of Eden: Four Novels of Elizabeth Bowen." *Critique* 15 (1973): 86–100.

Van Duyn, Mona. "Pattern and Pilgrimage: A Reading of *The Death of the Heart*." *Critique* 4 (1961): 52–66.

The Demon Lover (1945)

Hughes, Douglas A. "Cracks in the Psyche: Elizabeth Bowen's *The Demon Lover*." *Studies in Short Fiction* 10 (Fall 1973): 411–13.

Eva Trout (1968)

"Elizabeth Bowen's New Novel." *Times Literary Supplement* (January 30, 1969): 101.

Moss, Howard. "The Heiress Is an Outsider." *New York Times Book Review* (October 13, 1968): 1.

Parrish, Paul A. "The Loss of Eden: Four Novels of Elizabeth Bowen." *Critique* 15 (1973): 86–100.

Taylor, Elizabeth. "The Progress of Eva." *New Statesman* (January 24, 1969): 119.

Wyndham, Francis. "*Eva Trout*." *London Magazine* 8 (March 1969): 89–91.

The Heat of the Day (1949)

Dorenkamp, Angela G. " 'Fall of Leap': Bowen's *The Heat of the Day*." *Criticism* 10 (1969): 13–21.

The House in Paris (1935)

Parrish, Paul A. "The Loss of Eden: Four Novels of Elizabeth Bowen." *Critique* 15 (1973): 86–100.

Sharp, Sister M. Corona. "The House as Setting and Symbol in Three Novels by Elizabeth Bowen." *Xavier University Studies* 2 (December 1963): 93–103.

The Last September (1929)

Sharp, Sister M. Corona. "The House as Setting and Symbol in Three Novels by Elizabeth Bowen." *Xavier University Studies* 2 (December 1963): 93–103.

The Little Girls (1964)

Burgess, Anthony. "Treasures and Fetters." *Spectator* (February 21, 1964): 254.

McDowell, Frederick P. W. "Elizabeth Bowen's *The Little Girls*." *Critique* 7 (1964): 139–43.

JANE BOWLES, née Sydney (1917–1973) U.S.
General Works
Capote, Truman. "Truman Capote Introduces Jane Bowles." *Mademoiselle* (December 1966): 115–16.

Kraft, James. "Jane Bowles as Serious Lady." *Novel* 1 (Spring 1968): 273–77.

Nichols, L. "Up from the Underground." *New York Times Book Review* (February 12, 1967): 8.

NANCY BOYD [pseud.]. *See* Edna St. Vincent Millay

KAY BOYLE (1903–) U.S.
General Works
Carpenter, R.C. "Kay Boyle: The Figure in the Carpet." *Critique* 7 (1965): 65–78.

Centing, Richard R. "Kay Boyle: The Cincinnati Years." *Ohioana Quarterly* 15 (Spring 1972): 11–13.

Gado, Frank. "Kay Boyle: From the Aesthetics of Exile to the Politics of Return." *Dissertation Abstracts* 29 (1968): 4485A (Duke).

Nichols, L. "Miss Boyle." *New York Times Book Review* (January 17, 1960): 8.

"Talk with the Author." *Newsweek* (January 25, 1960): 92–93.

Individual Works
Nothing Ever Breaks Except the Heart (1967)

Stuckey, W.J. "Review of *Nothing Ever Breaks Except the Heart*." *Critique* 9 (1967): 85–88.

The Smoking Mountain (1951)

Alter, Robert. "Review of *The Smoking Mountain*." *Critique* 6 (1964): 181–84.

MARY ELIZABETH BRADDON, Mrs. Maxwell (1837–1915) Great Britain
General Works
Heywood, C. "Flaubert, Miss Braddon, and George Moore." *Comparative Literature* 12 (1960): 151–58.

Individual Works
The Doctor's Wife (1864)

Heywood, C. "Miss Braddon's *The Doctor's Wife*: An Intermediary between *Madame Bovary* and *The Return of the Native*." *Revue de Littérature*

Comparée 38 (1964): 255–61.

Heywood, C. "Somerset Maugham's Debt to *Madame Bovary* and Miss Braddon's *The Doctor's Wife.*" *Etudes Anglaises* 19 (1966): 64–69.

Heywood, C. "A Source for *Middlemarch*: Miss Braddon's *The Doctor's Wife* and *Madame Bovary.*" *Revue de Littérature Comparée* 44 (1970): 184–94.

Lady Audley's Secret (1862)

Nyberg, Benjamin Matthew. "The Novels of Mary Elizabeth Braddon (1837–1915): A Reappraisal of the Author of *Lady Audley's Secret.*" *Dissertation Abstracts* 26 (1965): 6047–48 (Colorado).

ANNE BRADSTREET, née Dudley (c. 1612–1672) U.S.
Bibliography
Stanford, Ann. "Anne Bradstreet: An Annotated Checklist." *Bulletin of Bibliography* 27 (April–June 1970): 34–37.

Stanford, Ann. "Anne Bradstreet: An Annotated Checklist." *Early American Literature* 3 (Winter 1968–1969): 118–23.

General Works
Baldwin, Lewis M., II. "Moses and Mannerism: An Aesthetic for the Poetry of Colonial New England." *Dissertation Abstracts International* 35 (1974): 1035A (Syracuse).

Ball, Kenneth R. "Puritan Humility in Anne Bradstreet's Poetry." *Cithara* 13 (1973): 29–41.

"Benevolent Phantom." *Time* (July 7, 1967): 84.

Eby, Cecil D., Jr. "Anne Bradstreet and Thomas Gray: A Note on Influence." *Essex Institute Historical Collections* 97 (1961): 292–93.

Hamblen, Abigail Ann. "Anne Bradstreet: Portrait of a Puritan Lady." *Cresset* 32 (November 1968): 11–13.

Johnson, Carol. "John Berryman and Mistress Bradstreet." *Essays in Criticism* 14 (October 1964): 388–96.

Johnston, Thomas E., Jr. "American Puritan Poetic Voices: Essays on Anne Bradstreet, Edward Taylor, Roger Williams, and Philip Pain." *Dissertation Abstracts* 29 (1968): 3141A–42A (Ohio).

Johnston, Thomas E., Jr. "A Note on the Voices of Anne Bradstreet, Edward Taylor, Roger Williams, and Philip Pain." *Early American Literature* 3 (Winter 1968–1969): 125–26.

Keeble, Neil H. "Anne Bradstreet: The First Colonial Poet." *Literary Half-Yearly* 13 (January 1972): 13–28.

Laughlin, Rosemary M. "Anne Bradstreet: Poet in Search of Form." *American Literature* 42 (March 1970): 1–17.

McMahon, Helen. "Anne Bradstreet, Jean Bertault, and Dr. Crooke," *Early American Literature* 3 (Fall 1968): 118–23.

Requa, Kenneth A. "Anne Bradstreet's Poetic Voices." *Early American Literature* 9 (Spring 1974): 3–18.

Requa, Kenneth A. "Public and Private Voices in the Poetry of Anne Bradstreet, Michael Wigglesworth and Edward Taylor." *Dissertation Abstracts International* 32 (1972): 5802A–3A (Indiana).

Richardson, R.D. "The Puritan Poetry of Anne Bradstreet." *Texas Studies in Literature and Language* 9 (Autumn 1967): 317–31.

Rowlette, Edith Jeannine Hensley. "The Works of Anne Bradstreet." *Dissertation Abstracts* 25 (1965): 4707–8 (Boston).

Stanford, Ann. "Anne Bradstreet: Dogmatist and Rebel." *New England Quarterly* 39 (September 1966): 373–89.

Stanford, Ann. "Anne Bradstreet as a Meditative Writer." *College English Journal* 2 (1966): 24–31.

Stanford, Ann. "Anne Bradstreet's Portrait of Sir Philip Sidney." *Early American Literature* 1 (Winter 1966–1967): 11–13.

Waller, Jennifer R. " 'My Hand a Needle Better Fits': Anne Bradstreet and Women Poets of the Renaissance." *Dalhousie Review* 54 (Autumn 1974): 436–50.

Individual Works
Contemplations (c. 1650)

Hildebrand, Anne. "Anne Bradstreet's *Quaternions* and 'Contemplations.' " *Early American Literature* 8 (Fall 1973): 117–25.

Requa, Kenneth A. "Anne Bradstreet's Use of Du Bartas in 'Contemplations.' " *Essex Institute Historical Collections* 110 (1974): 64–69.

Rosenfeld, Alvin H. "Anne Bradstreet's 'Contemplations': Patterns of Form and Meaning." *New England Quarterly* 43 (March 1970): 79–96.

Quaternions (c. 1650)

Eberwein, Jane. "The 'Unrefined Ore' of Anne Bradstreet's *Quaternions.*" *Early American Literature* 9 (Spring 1974): 19–26.

Hildebrand, Anne. "Anne Bradstreet's *Quaternions* and 'Contemplations.' " *Early American Literature* 8 (Fall 1973): 117–25.

Several Poems (c. 1650)

Hensley, Edith Jeannine. "The Editor of Anne Bradstreet's *Several Poems.*" *American Literature* 35 (January 1964): 502–4.

DOROTHY BRETT (1891–) U.S. (Born in Great Britain)

General Works

Manchester, John. "Thoughts on Brett: 1967." *South Dakota Review* 5 (Summer 1967): 3–9.

Morrill, Claire. "Three Women of Taos: Frieda Lawrence, Mabel Luhan, and Dorothy Brett." *South Dakota Review* 2 (Spring 1965): 3–22.

Zytaruk, George J., ed. "Dorothy Brett's Letters to S.S. Kateliansky." *D.H. Lawrence Review* 7 (1974): 240–74.

LUCY BREWER (fl. 1810–1819) U.S.

Individual Works

A Female Marine (1814)

Medlicott, Alexander. "The Legend of Lucy Brewer: An Early American Novel." *New England Quarterly* 39 (December 1966): 461–73.

ELIZABETH BREWSTER (1922–) Canada

General Works

Gibbs, Robert. "Next Time from a Different Country." *Canadian Literature* no. 62 (Autumn 1974): 17–32.

Pacey, Desmond. "The Poetry of Elizabeth Brewster." *Ariel* 4 (1973): 58–69.

Individual Works

Passage of Summer (1969)

Brewster, Elizabeth. "Chronology of Summer." *Humanities Association Bulletin* 21 (Winter 1970): 34–39.

THE BRONTËS

Bibliography

Cross, B. Gilbert. "A Brontë Reading List, 1969." *Brontë Society Transactions* 15 (1970): 424–26.

Cross, B. Gilbert. "A Brontë Reading List, 1970." *Brontë Society Transactions* 16 (1971): 52–54.

Cross, B. Gilbert. "A Brontë Reading List, 1971." *Brontë Society Transactions* 16 (1972): 146–50.

Cross, B. Gilbert. "A Brontë Reading List, 1972." *Brontë Society Transactions* 16 (1973): 228–31.

Cross, B. Gilbert. "A Brontë Reading List, 1973." *Brontë Society Transactions* 16 (1974): 299–302.

Millgate, Jane. "Recent Work on the Brontës." *Victorian Studies* 11 (June 1968): 523–28.

General Works

"An American Visitor for Mr. Brontë." *Brontë Society Transactions* 15 (1969): 327–30.

Bentley, Phyllis. "Love among the Brontës." *Contemporary Review* 217 (1970): 225–30.

Branch, James W. "Concerning the Last of the Brontës." *Books Abroad* 41 (Spring 1967): 286–88.

"Brontë Letters Purchased." *Brontë Society Transactions* 16 (1971): 19–21.

Butterfield, Herbert. "Charlotte Brontë and Her Sisters in the Crucial Year (1845)." *Brontë Society Transactions* 14 (1963): 3–17.

Cecil, Lord David. "Fresh Thoughts on the Brontës." *Brontë Society Transactions* 16 (1973): 169–76.

Chernaik, Judith. "All Roads Lead to the Moor." *Saturday Review* (January 1973): 62–63.

Cockerill, Timothy. "A Brontë at Broughton-in-Furness." *Brontë Society Transactions* 15 (1966): 34–35.

Copley, J. "An Early Visitor to Haworth. *Brontë Society Transactions* 16 (1973): 219–21.

Crandall, Norma. "Charlotte, Emily and Branwell Brontë." *American Book Collector* 13 (February 1963): 21–22.

Curry, Catherine. "Marie Brontë and the Brontës' View of Death." *Dublin Magazine* 10 (Winter 1973): 46–55.

Dewhirst, Jan. "The Reverend Patrick Brontë and The Keighley Mechanics' Institute." *Brontë Society Transactions* 14 (1965): 35–37.

Dodds, M.H. "George Hudson and the Brontës." *Brontë Society Transactions* 14 (1962): 56–57.

Dodds, M. Hope. "Daughters of the Clergy." *Brontë Society Transactions* 14 (1965): 20–24.

Drabble, Margaret. "The Writer as Recluse: The Theme of Solitude in the Works of the Brontës." *Brontë Society Transactions* 16 (1974): 259–69.

Earle, Kathleen, "Haworth, Home of the Brontës." *Queen's Quarterly* 75 (1968): 340–46.

"Further Thoughts on Branwell Brontë's Story: A Discussion." *Brontë Society Transactions* 14 (1962): 3–16.

Gerin, Winifred. "Byron's Influence on the Brontës." *Essays by Divers Hands* 37 (1972): 47–62.

Gerin, Winifred. "Byron's Influence on the Brontës." *Keats-Shelley Memorial Bulletin* 17

(1966): 1–19.

Gerin, Winifred. "The Effects of Environment on the Brontë Writings." *Essays by Divers Hands* 36 (1970): 67–83.

Gill, Stephen. "A Manuscript of Branwell Brontë, with Letters of Mrs. Gaskell." *Brontë Society Transactions* 15 (1970): 408–11.

Hargreaves, G.D. "The Publishing of Poems by Currer, Ellis and Acton Bell." *Brontë Society Transactions* 15 (1969): 294–300.

Hargreaves, G.D. "The Publishing of Poems by Currer, Ellis and Acton Bell." *Library Review* 22 (1970): 353–56.

"The Hégers and a Yorkshire Family." *Brontë Society Transactions* 14 (1963): 32.

Hoar, Nancy Cowley. "The Brontës' Floral Year." *Brontë Society Transactions* 16 (1971): 40–42.

Holgate, Ivy. "A Pilgrim at Haworth, 1879." *Brontë Society Transactions* 14 (1961): 29–37.

Hopkins, A.B. "Biographer's Postscript." *Brontë Society Transactions* 14 (1961): 8–12.

Hutton, Joanna. "Items from the Museum's Cuttings Book." *Brontë Society Transactions* 14 (1963): 26–30.

Hutton, Joanna. "The Sale at Haworth Parsonage on October 1st and 2nd, 1861." *Brontë Society Transactions* 14 (1965): 46–50.

"In Haworth a Century Ago." *Brontë Society Transactions* 16 (1973): 219.

Isenberg, David R. "A Gondal Fragment." *Brontë Society Transactions* 14 (1962): 24–26.

Langlois, Emile. "A Frenchman's Visit to Haworth." *Brontë Society Transactions* 16 (1973): 222–23.

Larkin, Geoffrey. "The Shuffing Scamp." *Brontë Society Transactions* 15 (1970): 400–407.

"A Letter from Mrs. Gaskell." *Brontë Society Transactions* 14 (1965): 50.

Marks, William S., III. "The Novel as Puritan Romance: A Comparative Study of Samuel Richardson, the Brontës, Thomas Hardy, and D.H. Lawrence." *Dissertation Abstracts* 25 (1964): 1214 (Stanford).

Nelson, Jane Gray. "Sicily and the Brontë Name." *Brontë Society Transactions* 16 (1971): 43–45.

Nussey, J.T.M. "Notes on the Background of Three Incidents in the Lives of the Brontës." *Brontë Society Transactions* 15 (1969): 331–36.

Nussey, J.T.M. "Rydings—Home of Ellen Nussey." *Brontë Society Transactions* 15 (1968): 244–49.

Odom, Keith C. "The Brontës and Romantic Views of Personality." *Dissertation Abstracts* 22 (1961): 2004–5 (Wisconsin).

Oram, Eanne. "Brief for Miss Branwell." *Brontë Society Transactions* 14 (1964): 28–38.

Pruntz, Maura. "Father of the Brontë Sisters." *Irish Digest* 73 (December 1961): 52–54.

Quertermous, Harry Maxwell. "The Byronic Hero in the Writings of the Brontës." *Dissertation Abstracts* 21 (1960): 191–92 (Texas).

Randall, David A. "The First American Edition of the Brontës' Poems." *Book Collector* 9 (Summer 1960): 122–201.

Rauth, Heidemarie. "A Survey of Brontë Plays." *Brontë Society Transactions* 16 (1974): 288–90.

"The Reverend Arthur Bell Nicholls." *Brontë Society Transactions* 15 (1969): 345–50.

Rhodes, Margaret G. "A Brief Interlude . . . the Brontës at Silverdale." *Brontë Society Transactions* 14 (1964): 44–45.

Rhodes, Philip. "A Medical Appraisal of the Brontës." *Brontë Society Transactions* 16 (1972): 101–9.

Spark, Muriel, "The Brontës as Teachers." *New Yorker* (January 22, 1966): 30–33.

St. John-Stevas, Norman. "The Author's Struggles with the Law." *Catholic World* (March 1962): 345–50.

Stanley, B.E. "Patrick Brontë's Notebook." *Brontë Society Transactions* 14 (1962): 17–19.

Stedman, Jane W. "The Genesis of the Genii." *Brontë Society Transactions* 14 (1965): 16–19.

Stephens, F.C. "Hartley Coleridge and the Brontës." *Times Literary Supplement* (May 14, 1970): 544.

Stevens, Joan. "Her Own Landmarks . . . Mary Taylor's Shop in New Zealand." *Brontë Society Transactions* 15 (1969): 314–22.

Stevens, Joan. "A Note on Mossmans." *Brontë Society Transactions* 16 (1971): 47–50.

"Three Brontë Letters." *Brontë Society Transactions* 14 (1964): 46–49.

Tillotson, Kathleen. "*Haworth Churchyard*: The Making of Arnold's Elegy." *Brontë Society Transactions* 15 (1967): 105–22.

Timings, E.K. "A Great Fancy for Arms." *Brontë Society Transactions* 14 (1961): 13–17.

"A Visit to Haworth in 1866." *Brontë Society Transactions* 15 (1968): 255–57.

Wilson, F.A.C. "The Primrose Wreath: The Heroes of the Brontë Novels (Concept of the Androgyne)." *Nineteenth Century Fiction* 29 (June 1974): 40–57.

ANNE BRONTË [pseud. Acton Bell] (1820–1849) Great Britain
General Works
Bell, A. Craig. "Anne Brontë: A Re-Appraisal." *Quarterly Review* 304 (July 1966): 315.

Nelson, Jane Gray. "First American Reviews of the Works of Charlotte, Emily, and Anne Brontë." *Brontë Society Transactions* 14 (1964): 39–44.

Neufeldt, Victor A. "The Shared Vision of Anne and Emily Brontë: The Context for *Wuthering Heights.*" *Dissertation Abstracts* 31 (1970: 764A–65A (Illinois).

Platt, Carolyn Virginia. "The Female Quest in the Works of Anne, Charlotte, and Emily Brontë." *Dissertation Abstracts International* 35 (1975): 4450A (Illinois).

Schofield, Guy. "The Gentle Anne." *Brontë Society Transactions* 16 (1971): 1–10.

Tiffany, Lewis K. "Charlotte and Anne's Literary Reputation." *Brontë Society Transactions* 16 (1974): 284–87.

Tompkins, J.M.S. "Caroline Helstone's Eyes." *Brontë Society Transactions* 14 (1961): 18–28.
Individual Works
The Narrow Way (1848)
Pacey, Desmond. " 'The Narrow Way.' " *Times Literary Supplement* (August 18, 1966): 743.

The Tenant of Wildfell Hall (1848)
Andrews, Sir Linton. "A Challenge by Anne Brontë." *Brontë Society Transactions* 14 (1965): 25–30.

Ekeblad, Inga-Stina. "*The Tenant of Wildfell Hall* and *Women Beware Women.*" *Notes and Queries* 10 (December 1963): 449–50.

Hargreaves, G.D. "Incomplete Texts of *The Tenant of Wildfell Hall.*" *Brontë Society Transactions* 16 (1972): 113–17.

Meier, T.K. "*The Tenant of Wildfell Hall*: Morality as Art." *Revue des Langues Vivantes* 39 (1973): 59–62.

CHARLOTTE BRONTË [pseud. Currer Bell] (1816–1855) Great Britain
Bibliography
Passel, Anne. "Charlotte Brontë: A Bibliography of the Criticism of Her Novels." *Bulletin of Bibli-* *ography* 26 (October–December 1969): 118–20.

Passel, Anne. "Charlotte Brontë: A Bibliography of the Criticism of Her Novels." *Bulletin of Bibliography* 27 (January–March 1970): 13–20.
General Works
Auerbach, Nina. "Charlotte Brontë: The Two Countries." *University of Toronto Quarterly* 42 (Spring 1973): 328–42.

Blom, M. A. "Charlotte Brontë, Feminist *Manquée.*" *Bucknell Review* 21 (Spring 1973): 87–102.

Brayfield, Peggy L. "A New Feminist Approach to the Novels of Charlotte Brontë." *Dissertation Abstracts International* 34 (1973): 1850A (Southern Illinois).

Butterfield, Herbert. "Charlotte Brontë and Her Sisters in the Crucial Year (1845)." *Brontë Society Transactions* 14 (1963): 3–17.

"Charlotte Brontë Manuscript and Letters Purchased." *Brontë Society Transactions* 16 (1972): 110–12.

Chernaik, Judith. "An Unpublished Tale by Charlotte Brontë." *Times Literary Supplement* (November 23, 1973): 1453–54.

Corrigan, Eileen M. "Charlotte Brontë and Scotland." *Brontë Society Transactions* 14 (1965): 31–34.

Corrigan, Eileen M. "Charlotte Brontë's Brussels: Does Anything Remain?" *Brontë Society Transactions* 15 (1970): 421–23.

Cross, B.G. "Charlotte Had No Profession." *Brontë Society Transactions* 15 (1968): 252–54.

Dessner, Laurence J. " 'The Homely Web of Truth': A Study of Charlotte Brontë's Novels." *Dissertation Abstracts International* 31 (1971): 3500A (N.Y.U.).

Diskin, Patrick. "Joyce and Charlotte Brontë." *Notes and Queries* 13 (March 1966): 94–95.

Dodds, M. Hope. "Daughters of the Clergy." *Brontë Society Transactions* 14 (1965): 20–24.

Drew, Philip. "Charlotte Brontë as a Critic of *Wuthering Heights.*" *Nineteenth Century Fiction* 18 (March 1964): 365–81.

Eagleton, Terry. "Class, Power, and Charlotte Brontë." *Critical Quarterly* 14 (Autumn 1972): 225–35.

Flahill, Frederick T.C. "Formative Ideas in the Novels of Charlotte and Emily Jane Brontë." *Dissertation Abstracts* 27 (1966): 746A–47A (Toronto).

Heilman, Robert B. "Charlotte Brontë, Reason, and

the Moon." *Nineteenth Century Fiction* 14 (December 1960): 283–302.

Hopewell, Donald G. "The 150th Anniversary of the Birth of Charlotte Brontë." *Brontë Society Transactions* 15 (1966): 1–10.

Hoult, W. Hartmann. "Charlotte Brontë's Holiday in the Peak District." *Brontë Society Transactions* 14 (1964): 19–27.

Howard, Margaret Adelia. "Charlotte Brontë's Novels: An Analysis of Their Thematic and Structural Patterns." *Dissertation Abstracts* 24 (1963): 728 (Washington).

Isenberg, David R. "Charlotte Brontë and the Theatre." *Brontë Society Transactions* 15 (1968): 237–41.

Jack, Ian. "Phrenology, Physiognomy and Characterization in the Novels of Charlotte Brontë." *Brontë Society Transactions* 15 (1970): 377–91.

Jackson, Robert J. "Charlotte Brontë to Lady Kay-Shuttleworth: An Unpublished Letter." *Brontë Society Transactions* 16 (1974): 274–75.

Kay, Brian, and James Knowles. "The *Twelfth Night* Charlotte Saw." *Brontë Society Transactions* 15 (1968): 241–43.

Knies, Earl Allen. "The Art of Charlotte Brontë: A Study of Point of View in Her Fiction." *Dissertation Abstracts* 25 (1965): 6596 (Illinois).

Knies, Earl Allen. "The Artistry of Charlotte Brontë: A Reassessment." *Ohio University Review* 7 (1965): 21–39.

Kumar, A.S. "Charlotte Brontë: A Study in Feminine Sensibility." *Osmania Journal of English Studies* 2 (1962): 49–53.

Lambert, Diana E.D. "The Shaping Spirit: A Study of the Novels of Emily and Charlotte Brontë." *Dissertation Abstracts* 28 (1968): 4634A–35A (Stanford).

Laski, Marghanita. "Crazy Windows." *Notes and Queries* 10 (May 1963): 229.

Lerner, L. "Tremulous Homely-Faced Creature: Charlotte Brontë and Her Critics." *Encounter* 45 (July 1975): 60–64.

"A Letter from Charlotte Brontë to Ellen Nussey, Returns to Haworth." *Brontë Society Transactions* 16 (1973): 203–4.

Lever, Tresham. "Charlotte Brontë and Kitty Bell." *Times Literary Supplement* (March 13, 1969): 267; (April 3, 1969): 369; (April 17, 1969): 414–15.

Linder, C. A. "The Ideal Marriage as Depicted in the Novels of Jane Austen and Charlotte Brontë."

Standpunte 24 (1971): 20–30.

Maddox, James H., Jr. "The Survival of Gothic Romance in the Nineteenth Century Novel: A Study of Scott, Charlotte Brontë, and Dickens." *Dissertation Abstracts International* 32 (1971): 442A (Yale).

Momberger, Philip. "Self and World in the Works of Charlotte Brontë." *English Literary History* 32 (September 1965): 349–69.

Moss, Frederick K. "Characterization in Charlotte Brontë's Fiction." *Dissertation Abstracts* 31 (1970): 363A (Wisconsin).

Nelson, Jane Gray. "First American Reviews of the Works of Charlotte, Emily, and Anne Brontë." *Brontë Society Transactions* 14 (1964): 39–44.

Newton-De Molina, David. "A Note on an Early French View of Charlotte Brontë: Charles De Mouy's *Romanciers Anglais Contemporarians—Miss Brontë (Currer Bell)*, *Revue Européenne*, Vol. 12 (Paris, 1860)." *Brontë Society Transactions* 15 (1970): 417–20.

Nussey, J.T.M. "Rydings—Home of Ellen Nussey." *Brontë Society Transactions* 15 (1968): 244–49.

Oram, Eanne. "Charlotte Brontë's Honeymoon." *Brontë Society Transactions* 15 (1969): 343–44.

Passel, Anne W. "Charlotte Brontë's Novels: The Artistry of Their Construction." *Dissertation Abstracts* 28 (1968): 1444A (University of the Pacific).

Peters, Margot M. "Four Essays on the Style of Charlotte Brontë." *Dissertation Abstracts* 31 (1970): 379A (Wisconsin).

Platt, Carolyn Virginia. "The Female Quest in the Works of Anne, Charlotte, and Emily Brontë." *Dissertation Abstracts International* 35 (1975): 4450A (Illinois).

Pollard, Arthur, and Albert H. Preston. "Mrs. Gaskell's *Life of Charlotte Brontë* with an Appendix on Some New Gaskell Letters." *Bulletin of the John Rylands Library* 47 (March 1965): 453–88.

Pollin, Burton R. "Two Letters concerning Charlotte Brontë in Contemporary American Journals." *Brontë Society Transactions* 16 (1973): 205–12.

"The Reverend Arthur Bell Nicholls." *Brontë Society Transactions* 15 (1969): 345–50.

Rhodes, Margaret G. "Where Are the Letters?" *Brontë Society Transactions* 15 (1968): 250–51.

Schmidt, Emily Tresselt. "From Highland to Lowland: Charlotte Brontë's Editorial Changes in Emily's Poems." *Brontë Society Transactions* 15 (1968): 221–26.

Schreiber, Annette. "The Myth in Charlotte Brontë." *Literature and Psychology* 18 (1968): 48–67.

Schwartz, Roberta C. "The Search After Happiness: A Study of Charlotte Brontë's Fiction." *Dissertation Abstracts* 29 (1969): 3587A (Wayne State).

Shapiro, Arnold. "A Study in the Development of Art and Ideas in Charlotte Brontë's Fiction." *Dissertation Abstracts* 26 (1965): 2730 (Indiana).

Sharme, P.P. "Charlotte Brontë: Champion of Woman's Economic Independence." *Brontë Society Transactions* 14 (1965): 38–40.

Sharps, John Geoffrey. "Charlotte Brontë and the Mysterious 'Miss H': A Detail in Mrs. Gaskell's *Life*." *English* 14 (Autumn 1963): 236.

Stedman, Jane W. "Charlotte Brontë and Bewick's British Birds." *Brontë Society Transactions* 15 (1966): 36–40.

Stevens, Joan. "A Brontë Letter Corrected." *Brontë Society Transactions* 16 (1971): 46.

Stevens, Joan. "A Brontë Letter Misdated." *Notes and Queries* 19 (July 1972): 254.

Stevens, Joan. "Charlotte Brontë's Mistake." *Notes and Queries* 17 (January 1970): 19.

Stevens, Joan. "Her Own Landmarks . . . Mary Taylor's Shop in New Zealand." *Brontë Society Transactions* 15 (1969): 314–22.

Stevens, Joan. "Woozles in Brontëland: A Cautionary Tale." *Studies in Bibliography* 24 (1971): 91–108.

"The 'Taste' of Charlotte Brontë." *Brontë Society Transactions* 14 (1962): 20–24.

"Three Brontë Letters." *Brontë Society Transactions* 14 (1964): 46–49.

Tiffany, Lewis K. "Charlotte and Anne's Literary Reputation." *Brontë Society Transactions* 16 (1974): 284–87.

Tillotson, Kathleen. "A Day with Charlotte Brontë in 1850." *Brontë Society Transactions* 16 (1971): 22–30.

"To That Same 'Quarterly' . . . The Gift of an Unpublished Letter by Charlotte Brontë." *Brontë Society Transactions* 16 (1974): 276.

Unger, William E., Jr. "Implied Authors and Created Readers in Thackeray, Trollope, Charlotte Brontë, and George Eliot." *Dissertation Abstracts International* 35 (1974): 2956A–57A (Ohio

State).

"An Unpublished Letter by Charlotte Brontë." *Brontë Society Transactions* 15 (1966): 20–21.

Wills, Jack C. "Charlotte Brontë's Literary Theories." *Dissertation Abstracts* 28 (1968): 1413A (Delaware).

Wills, Jack C. "The Shrine of Truth: An Approach to the Works of Charlotte Brontë." *Brontë Society Transactions* 15 (1970): 392–99.

Winnifrith, T.J. "Charlotte Brontë's Letters to *Notes and Queries* 17 (January 1970): 17–18.

Winnifrith, T.J. "Charlotte Brontë's Letters to Ellen Nussey." *Durham University Journal* 63 (December 1970): 16–18.

Individual Works

Jane Eyre (1847)

Benvenuto, Richard. "The Child of Nature, the Child of Grace, and the Unresolved Conflict of *Jane Eyre*." *English Literary History* 39 (December 1972): 620–38.

Bishop, Morchard. "*Jane Eyre*." *Times Literary Supplement* (June 11, 1971): 677; (June 18, 1971): 706–7.

Blom, M. A. "*Jane Eyre*: Mind as Law unto Itself." *Criticism* 15 (1973): 350–64.

Burkhart, Charles. "Another Key Word for *Jane Eyre*." *Nineteenth Century Fiction* 16 (September 1961): 177–79.

Bushnell, Nelson S. "Artistic Economy in *Jane Eyre*: A Contract with *The Old Manor House*." *English Language Notes* 5 (March 1968): 197–202.

Clement, Brother David. "Note the Literary Allusions." *English Journal* 54 (January 1965): 59–60.

Day, Martin S. "Central Concepts of *Jane Eyre*." *Personalist* 41 (Autumn 1960): 495–505.

Downing, Janay. "Fire and Ice Imagery in *Jane Eyre*." *Paunch*, no. 27 (October 1966): 68–78.

Eagleton, Terry. "Class, Power, and Charlotte Brontë." *Critical Quarterly* 14 (Autumn 1972): 225–35.

Ericksen, Donald H. "Imagery as Structure in *Jane Eyre*." *Victorian Newsletter* 30 (Fall 1966): 18–22.

Gribble, Jennifer. "Jane Eyre's Imagination." *Nineteenth Century Fiction* 23 (December 1968): 279–93.

Hagan, John. "Enemies of Freedom in *Jane Eyre*." *Criticism* 13 (1971): 351–76.

Harkness, Bruce. "Review of the Oxford Edition of *Jane Eyre*." *Nineteenth Century Fiction* 25 (December 1970): 355–69.

Hughes, R.E. "*Jane Eyre*: The Unbaptized Dionysos." *Nineteenth Century Fiction* 18 (March 1964): 347–64.

Jack, Ian, and Margaret Smith. "The Clarendon *Jane Eyre*: A Rejoinder." *Nineteenth Century Fiction* 26 (December 1971): 370–76.

Katz, Judith N. "Rooms of Their Own: Forms and Images of Liberation in Five Novels." *Dissertation Abstracts International* 34 (1973): 1283A (Penn. State).

Kay, Brian, and James Knowles. "Where *Jane Eyre* and *Mary Barton* Were Born." *Brontë Society Transactions* 15 (1967): 145–48.

Knies, Earl A. "The 'I' of *Jane Eyre*." *College English* 27 (April 1966): 546–56.

Kramer, Dale. "Thematic Structure in *Jane Eyre*." *Papers on Language and Literature* 4 (1968): 288–98.

Langford, Thomas. "The Three Pictures in *Jane Eyre*." *Victorian Newsletter* 31 (Spring 1967): 47–48.

Langford, Thomas A. "Prophetic Imagination and the Unity of *Jane Eyre*." *Studies in the Novel* 6 (Summer 1974): 228–35.

Langlois, Emile. "Early Critics and Translators of *Jane Eyre* in France." *Brontë Society Transactions* 16 (1971): 11–18.

Leavis, Q.D. "Dating *Jane Eyre*." *Times Literary Supplement* (May 27, 1965): 436.

Lester, John A., Jr. "The Consolations of Ecstasy." *English Literature in Transition* 6 (1963): 200–11.

Marshall, William H. "The Self, the World and the Structure of *Jane Eyre*." *Revue des Langues Vivantes* 27 (1961): 416–25.

McElrath, Joseph R., Jr. "Jane Eyre's 'Brocklehurst': Names, Sign, and Symbol." *College English Association Critic* 33 (January 1971): 23.

McLaughlin, M. B. "Past or Future Mindscapes: Pictures in *Jane Eyre*." *Victorian Newsletter* 41 (Spring 1972): 22–24.

Millgate, Jane. "Jane Eyre's Progress." *English Studies*, Anglo-American Supplement (1969): 21–29.

Millgate, Jane. "Narrative Distance in *Jane Eyre*: The Relevance of the Pictures." *Modern Language Review* 63 (April 1968): 315–19.

Moser, Lawrence E. "From Portrait to Person: A Note on the Surrealistic in *Jane Eyre*." *Nineteenth Century Fiction* 20 (December 1965): 275–81.

Oldfield, Jennifer. " 'The Homely Web of Truth': Dress as a Mirror of Personality in *Jane Eyre* and *Villette*." *Brontë Society Transactions* 16 (1973): 177–84.

Peterson, William S. "Henry James on *Jane Eyre*." *Times Literary Supplement* (July 30, 1971): 919–20.

Prescott, Joseph. "*Jane Eyre:* A Romantic Exemplum with a Difference." *Literary Half-Yearly* 3 (January 1962): 28–37.

Robertson, D. A., Jr. "Queen Victoria's Lady Novelists: The Lady Who Reviewed *Jane Eyre*." *Gazette of the Grolier Club* (February 12, 1970): 2–10.

Shapiro, Arnold. "In Defense of *Jane Eyre*." *Studies in English Literature, 1500–1900* 8 (Autumn 1968): 681–98.

Siefert, Susan Elizabeth. "The Dilemma of the Talented Woman: A Study in Nineteenth Century Fiction." *Dissertation Abstracts International* 36 (1975): 285A–86A (Marquette).

Simpson, Jacqueline. "The Function of Folklore in *Jane Eyre* and *Wuthering Heights*." *Folklore* 85 (Spring 1974): 47–61.

Smith, David J. "The Arrested Heart: Familial Love and Psychic Conflict in Five Mid-Victorian Novels." *Dissertation Abstracts* 27 (1966): 1839A (Washington).

Smith, David J. "Incest Patterns in Two Victorian Novels." *Literature and Psychology* 15 (1965): 135–62.

Solomon, Eric. "*Jane Eyre*: Fire and Water." *College English* 25 (December 1963): 215–17.

Sullivan, Paula. "Rochester Reconsidered: *Jane Eyre* in the Light of Sampson Story." *Brontë Society Transactions* 16 (1973): 192–98.

Waidner, Maralee L. "From Reason to Romance: A Progression from an Emphasis on Neoclassic Rationality to Romantic Intuition in Three English Woman Novelists." *Dissertation Abstracts International* 34 (1973): 1259A–60A (Tulsa).

Yeazell, Ruth Bernard. "More True Than Real: Jane Eyre's 'Mysterious Summons.' " *Nineteenth Century Fiction* 29 (September 1974): 127–43.

John Henry (c. 1848)

Geer, Joseph R. "An Unpublished Manuscript by Charlotte Brontë." *Brontë Society Transactions* 15 (1966): 21–27.

Le Nid (c. 1848)

Dessner, Laurence Jay. "Charlotte Brontë's *Le Nid*: An Unpublished Manuscript." *Brontë Society Transactions* 16 (1973): 213–18.

The Professor (1857)

Brammer, M.M. "The Manuscript of *The Professor.*" *Review of English Studies* 11 (May 1960): 157–70.

Shirley (1849)

Ankenbrandt, Katherine Ware. "Charlotte Brontë's *Shirley* and John Leyden's *The Cout of Keelder.*" *Victorian Newsletter* 34 (Fall 1968): 33–34.

Grayson, Laura. "*Shirley*: Charlotte Brontë's Own Evidence." *Brontë Society Transactions* 14 (1963): 31.

Holgate, Ivy. "The Structure of *Shirley.*" *Brontë Society Transactions* 14 (1962): 27–35.

Jeffares, A. Norman. "*Shirley*—A Yorkshire Novel." *Brontë Society Transactions* 15 (1969): 281–93.

Knies, Earl Allen. "Art, Death and the Composition of *Shirley.*" *Victorian Newsletter* 28 (Fall 1965): 22–24.

Passel, Anne W. "The Three Voices in Charlotte Brontë's *Shirley.*" *Brontë Society Transactions* 15 (1969): 323–26.

Shapiro, Arnold. "Public Themes and Private Lives: Social Criticism in *Shirley.*" *Papers on Language and Literature* 4 (1968): 74–84.

Stevens, Joan. "Sidelights on *Shirley*: Brontëana in New Zealand." *Brontë Society Transactions* 15 (1969): 301–13.

Todd, William B. "An Early State of Charlotte Brontë's *Shirley*, 1849." *Book Collector* 12 (Autumn 1963): 355–56.

Tompkins, J.M.S. "Caroline Helstone's Eyes." *Brontë Society Transactions* 14 (1961): 18–28.

Villette (1853)

Arndt, Frances C. "*Villette*: Another Turn of the Wheel." *Dissertation Abstracts International* 34 (1973): 718A–19A (Duke).

Brigham, Caroline. "The Panzaic Principle in *Villette.*" *Paunch*, no. 22 (January 1965): 32–46.

Burkhart, Charles. "Brontë's *Villette.*" *Explicator* 21 (September 1962): Item 8.

Burkhart, Charles. "The Nuns of Villette." *Victorian Newsletter* 44 (Fall 1973): 8–13.

Colby, Robert A. "*Villette* and the Life of the Mind." *Publications of the Modern Language Association* 75 (1960): 410–19.

Coursen, Herbert R., Jr. "Storm and Calm in *Villette.*" *Discourse* 5 (Summer 1962): 318–33.

Dunbar, Georgia S. "Proper Names in *Villette.*" *Nineteenth Century Fiction* 15 (June 1960): 77–80.

Hoar, Nancy Cowley. " 'And My Ending in Despair': *Villette*—Charlotte Brontë's Valediction."

Brontë Society Transactions 16 (1973): 185–91.

Johnson, E. D. H. " 'Daring the Dread Glance': Charlotte Brontë's Treatment of the Supernatural in *Villette.*" *Nineteenth Century Fiction* 20 (March 1966): 325–36.

Lemon, Charles. "The Origins of Ginevra Fanshawe." *Brontë Society Transactions* 16 (1971): 51.

Oldfield, Jennifer. " 'The Homely Web of Truth': Dress as a Mirror of Personality in *Jane Eyre* and *Villette.*" *Brontë Society Transactions* 16 (1973): 177–84.

Schwartz, Roberta C. "The Ambiguities of *Villette.*" *North Dakota Quarterly* 42 (1974): 40–52.

EMILY BRONTË [pseud. Ellis Bell] (1818–1848) Great Britain

Bibliography

Byers, David M. "An Annotated Bibliography of the Criticism on Emily Brontë's *Wuthering Heights*, 1847–1947." *Dissertation Abstracts International* 34 (1973): 2611A–12A (Minnesota).

General Works

Beeton, D.R. "Emily Brontë and Jan Christiaan Smuts." *Brontë Society Transactions* 15 (1968): 214–20.

Buchen, Irving H. "Emily Brontë and the Metaphysics of Childhood and Love." *Nineteenth Century Fiction* 22 (June 1967): 63–70.

Cooper, Dorothy. "Dr. Blondel Writes Again on Emily Brontë." *Brontë Society Transactions* 14 (1963): 21–22.

Cross, B. Gilbert, and Peggy L. Cross. "Farewell to Hoffman?" *Brontë Society Transactions* 15 (1970): 412–16.

Day-Lewis, C. "Emily Brontë." *Brontë Society Transactions* 15 (1968): 206.

Flahill, Frederick T.C. "Formative Ideas in the Novels of Charlotte and Emily Jane Brontë." *Dissertation Abstracts* 27 (1966): 746A–47A (Toronto).

Friesner, Donald Neil. "Ellis Bell and Israfel." *Brontë Society Transactions* 14 (1964): 11–18.

Kelly, Charlotte M. "What I Saw at Haworth." *Irish Digest* 78 (October 1963): 83–85.

Lambert, Diana E. D. "The Shaping Spirit: A Study of the Novels of Emily and Charlotte Brontë." *Dissertation Abstracts* 28 (1968): 4634A–35A (Stanford).

Landor, Mikail, "Emily Brontë in Russia (On the 150th Anniversary of Her Birth)." *Soviet Litera-*

ture 11 (1968): 180–85.

Levin, Harry. "Janes and Emilies, or the Novelist as Heroine." *Southern Review* (U.S.) 1 (1965): 735–53.

Livermore, Ann Lapraik. "Byron and Emily Brontë." *Quarterly Review* 300 (July 1962): 337–44.

Manley, Sandra M. " 'Pal T-Guilp Off.' " *Transactions of the Yorkshire Dialect Society* 13 (1971): 25–28.

Nelson, Jane Gray. "First American Reviews of the Works of Charlotte, Emily, and Anne Brontë." *Brontë Society Transactions* 14 (1964): 39–44.

Neufeldt, Victor A. "Emily Brontë and the Responsible Imagination." *Victorian Newsletter* 43 (Spring 1973): 15–21.

Odumu, Ocheibi. "Women Talk about Women: The Image of Women in the Novels of Jane Austen and Emily Brontë." *Horizon* (Ibadan) 9 (1973): 47–54.

Ohmann, Carol. "Emily Brontë in the Hands of Male Critics." *College English* 32 (April 1971): 906–13.

"The 150th Anniversary of the Birth of Emily Jane Brontë." *Brontë Society Transactions* 15 (1968): 201–5.

Platt, Carolyn Virginia. "The Female Quest in the Works of Anne, Charlotte, and Emily Brontë." *Dissertation Abstracts International* 35 (1975): 4450A (Illinois).

Stephens, Margaret A. W. "Mysticism in the Works of Emily Jane Brontë." *Dissertation Abstracts* 31 (1970): 2890A (Case Western Reserve).

Widdowson, Peter. "Emily Brontë: The Romantic Novelist." *Moderna Sprak* 66 (1972): 1–19.

Wilson, Craeme. "Emily Brontë." *Cornhill Magazine,* no. 1061 (Autumn 1969): 414.

Individual Works

Collected Poems (1906)

Dingle, Herbert. "An Examination of Emily Brontë's Poetry from an Unaccustomed Angle." *Brontë Society Transactions* 14 (1964): 5–10.

Drew, David P. "Emily Brontë and Emily Dickinson as Mystic Poets." *Brontë Society Transactions* 15 (1968): 227–32.

Hartley, L. P. "Emily Brontë in Gondal and Gaaldine." *Brontë Society Transactions* 14 (1965): 1–15.

Isenberg, David R. "A Gondal Fragment." *Brontë Society Transactions* 14 (1962): 24–26.

Pearsall, Robert Brainard. "The Presiding Tropes of Emily Brontë." *College English* 27 (January 1966): 267–73.

Schmidt, Emily Tresselt. "From Highland to Lowland: Charlotte Brontë's Editorial Changes in Emily's Poems." *Brontë Society Transactions* 15 (1968): 221–26.

Starzyk, Laurence J. "Emily Brontë: Poetry in a Mingled Tone." *Criticism* 14 (1972): 119–36.

Starzyk, Laurence J. "The Faith of Emily Brontë's Immortality Creed." *Victorian Poetry* 11 (Winter 1973): 295–305.

Wordsworth, Jonathan. "Wordsworth and the Poetry of Emily Brontë." *Brontë Society Transactions* 16 (1972): 85–100.

The Palace of Death (1842)

Maxwell, J. C. "Emily Brontë's *The Palace of Death.*" *Brontë Society Transactions* 15 (1967): 139–40.

Le Papillon or The Butterfly (1842)

Wilson, Jo Anne A. *"The Butterfly* and *Wuthering Heights:* A Mystic's Eschatology." *Victorian Newsletter* 33 (Spring 1968): 22–25.

Second Novel (c. 1848)

Braco, Edgar Jean, et al. "Emily Brontë's Second Novel." *Brontë Society Transactions* 15 (1966): 28–33.

Hewish, John. "Emily Brontë's Missing Novel." *Times Literary Supplement* (March 10, 1966): 197; (March 17, 1966): 223.

Wuthering Heights (1846)

Ankenbrandt, Katherine W. "Songs in *Wuthering Heights.*" *Southern Folklore Quarterly* 33 (1969): 92–115.

Arnold, J.V. "George Sand's *Mauprat* and Emily Brontë's *Wuthering Heights.*" *Revue de Littérature Comparée* 46 (1972): 209–18.

Basco, Ronald A. "Heathcliff: Societal Victim or Demon?" *Gypsy Scholar* 2 (1974): 21–39.

Bell, Vereen M. *"Wuthering Heights* and the Unforgivable Sin." *Nineteenth Century Fiction* 17 (September 1962): 188–91.

Bell, Vereen M. *"Wuthering Heights* as Epos." *College English* 25 (December 1963): 199–208.

Brick, Allan R. "Lewes's Review of *Wuthering Heights.*" *Nineteenth Century Fiction* 14 (June 1960): 355–59.

Buchen, Irving H. "Emily Brontë and the Metaphysics of Childhood and Love." *Nineteenth Century Fiction* 22 (June 1967): 63–70.

Buchen, Irving H. "Metaphysical and Social Evolution in *Wuthering Heights.*" *Victorian News-*

letter 31 (Spring 1967): 15–20.

Buckley, Vincent. "Passion and Control in *Wuthering Heights*." *Southern Review* (Australia) 1 (1964): 5–23.

Burkhart, Robert E. "The Structure of *Wuthering Heights*." *Publications of the Modern Language Association* 87 (1972): 104–5.

Burns, Wallace. "On *Wuthering Heights*." *Recovering Literature* 1 (1972): 5–25.

Champion, Larry S. "Heathcliff: A Study in Authorial Technique." *Ball State University Forum* 9 (Spring 1968): 19–25.

Cott, Jeremy. "Structure of Sound: The Last Sentence of *Wuthering Heights*." *Texas Studies in Literature and Language* 6 (Summer 1964): 280–89.

Cowhig, Ruth M. "*Wuthering Heights*: An Amoral Book?" *Use of English* 17 (Winter 1965): 123–26.

Daley, A. Stuart. "The Moons and Almanacs of *Wuthering Heights*." *Huntington Library Quarterly* 37 (August 1974): 337–53.

Davies, Cecil W. "A Reading of *Wuthering Heights*." *Essays in Criticism* 19 (July 1969): 254–72.

Dean, Christopher. "Joseph's Speech in *Wuthering Heights*." *Notes and Queries* 7 (February 1960): 73–76.

Devlin, James E. "*Wuthering Heights*: The Dominant Image." *Discourse* 5 (Summer 1962): 337–46.

Dingle, Herbert. "The Origin of Heathcliff." *Brontë Society Transactions* 16 (1972): 131–38.

Doheny, John. "From *PMLA* to *Wuthering Heights*." *Paunch*, no. 17 (January 1964): 21–34.

Drew, Philip. "Charlotte Brontë as a Critic of *Wuthering Heights*." *Nineteenth Century Fiction* 18 (March 1964): 365–81.

Fike, Francis. "Bitter Herbs and Wholesome Medicines: Love as Theological Affirmation in *Wuthering Heights*." *Nineteenth Century Fiction* 23 (September 1968): 127–49.

Fine, Ronald E. "Lockwood's Dreams and the Key to *Wuthering Heights*." *Nineteenth Century Fiction* 24 (June 1969): 16–30.

Fraser, John. "The Name of Action: Nelly Dean and *Wuthering Heights*." *Nineteenth Century Fiction* 20 (December 1965): 223–36.

Gose, Elliott B., Jr. "*Wuthering Heights*: The Heath and the Hearth." *Nineteenth Century Fiction* 21 (June 1966): 1–19.

Gould, Gerald L. "Emily Brontë's Relation to Gondal as Subject of *Wuthering Heights*." *Dissertation Abstracts International* 35 (1974): 1655A–56A (C.U.N.Y.).

Grove, Robin. "*Wuthering Heights*." *Critical Review* 8 (1965): 70–87.

Grudin, P.D. "*Wuthering Heights*: The Question of Unquiet Slumbers." *Studies in the Novel* 6 (Winter 1974): 389–407.

Hagan, John. "Control of Sympathy in *Wuthering Heights*." *Nineteenth Century Fiction* 21 (March 1967): 305–23.

Hatch, Ronald B. "Heathcliff's 'Queer End' and Schopenhauer's Denial of the Will." *Canadian Review of Comparative Literature* 1 (1974): 49–64.

Jordan, John E. "The Ironic Vision of Emily Brontë." *Nineteenth Century Fiction* 20 (June 1965): 1–18.

Junkin-Hill, Margaret. "Myths and Fallacies in *Wuthering Heights*." *Lakehead University Review* 3 (1970): 46–55.

Justus, James. "Beyond Gothicism: *Wuthering Heights* and an American Tradition." *Tennessee Studies in Literature* 5 (1960): 25–33.

Kenney, Blair G. "Nelly Dean's Witchcraft." *Literature and Psychology* 18 (1968): 225–32.

Kermode, F. "Modern Way with the Classic." *New Literary History* 5 (Spring 1974): 415–34.

Krupat, Arnold. "The Strangeness of *Wuthering Heights*." *Nineteenth Century Fiction* 25 (December 1970): 269–80.

Lane, Margaret. "Emily Brontë in a Cold Climate." *Brontë Society Transactions* 15 (1968): 187–200.

Langman, F.H. "*Wuthering Heights*." *Essays in Criticism* 15 (July 1965): 294–312.

Lavers, Norman. "The Action of *Wuthering Heights*." *South Atlantic Quarterly* 72 (Winter 1973): 43–52.

Lemon, C.H. "Balthus and *Wuthering Heights*." *Brontë Society Transactions* 15 (1969): 341–42.

Lemon, Charles. "Sickness and Health in *Wuthering Heights*." *Brontë Society Transactions* 14 (1963): 23–25.

Loe, Thomas B. "The Gothic Strain in the Victorian Novel: Four Studies." *Dissertation Abstracts International* 35 (1974): 2231A (Iowa).

Loxterman, Alan S. "The Giant's Foot: A Reading of *Wuthering Heights*." *Dissertation Abstracts International* 32 (1972): 4007A–8A (Ohio State).

MacKay, Ruth M. "Irish Heaths and German Cliffs: A Study of the Foreign Sources of *Wuthering*

Heights." *Brigham Young University Studies* 7 (Autumn 1965): 28–39.

Madden, David. "Chapter 17 of *Wuthering Heights*." *English Record* 17 (February 1967): 2–8.

Madden, William A. "*Wuthering Heights*: The Binding of Passion." *Nineteenth Century Fiction* 27 (September 1972): 127–54.

Marshall, William H. "Hareton Earnshaw: Natural Theology on the Moors." *Victorian Newsletter* 21 (Spring 1962): 14–15.

Mayne, Isobel. "Emily Brontë's Mr. Lockwood." *Brontë Society Transactions* 15 (1968): 207–13.

McCaughey, G. S. "An Approach to *Wuthering Heights*." *Humanities Association Bulletin* 15 (Autumn 1964): 28–34.

McKibben, Robert C. "The Image of the Book in *Wuthering Heights*." *Nineteenth Century Fiction* 15 (September 1960): 159–69.

Meier, T.K. "*Wuthering Heights* and Violation of Class." *Brontë Society Transactions* 15 (1968): 233–36.

Merry, Bruce. "An Unknown Italian Dramatisation of *Wuthering Heights*." *Brontë Society Transactions* 16 (1971): 31–39.

Mitchell, Giles. "Incest, Demonism, and Death in *Wuthering Heights*." *Literature and Psychology* 23 (1973): 27–36.

Moglen, Helene. "The Double Vision of *Wuthering Heights*: A Clarifying View of Female Development." *Centennial Review of Arts and Sciences* 15 (1971): 391–405.

Moody, Philippa. "The Challenge to Maturity in *Wuthering Heights*." *Melbourne Critical Review* 5 (1962): 27–39.

Moser, Thomas. "What Is the Matter with Emily Jane? Conflicting Impulses in *Wuthering Heights*." *Nineteenth Century Fiction* 17 (June 1962): 1–19.

Neufeldt, Victor A. "The Shared Vision of Anne and Emily Brontë: The Context for *Wuthering Heights*." *Dissertation Abstracts* 31 (1970): 764A–65A (Illinois).

Nicolai, Ralf R. "*Wuthering Heights*: Emily Brontë's Kleistian Novel." *South Atlantic Bulletin* 38 (1973): 23–32.

Nixon, Ingeborg. "A Note on the Pattern of *WutheringHeights*." *English Studies* 45, Supplement (1964): 235–42.

Petyt, K. M. " 'Thou' and 'You' in *Wuthering Heights*." *Brontë Society Transactions* 16 (1974): 291–93.

Power, S.A. "The Chronology of *Wuthering Heights*." *Brontë Society Transactions* 16 (1972): 139–43.

Reynolds, Thomas. "Division and Unity in *Wuthering Heights*." *University Review* (Kansas) 32 (1965): 31–37.

Scheuerle, William H. "Brontë's *Wuthering Heights*." *Explicator* 33 (May 1975): Item 69.

Scrivner, Buford, Jr. "The Ethos of *Wuthering Heights*." *Dalhousie Review* 54 (Autumn 1974): 451–62.

Shapiro, Arnold. "*Wuthering Heights* as a Victorian Novel." *Studies in the Novel* 1 (Fall 1969): 284–96.

Shunami, G. "The Unreliable Narrator in *Wuthering Heights*." *Nineteenth Century Fiction* 27 (March 1973): 449–68.

Simpson, Jacqueline. "The Function of Folklore in *Jane Eyre* and *Wuthering Heights*." *Folklore*, 85 (Spring 1974): 47–61.

Smith, David. "The Panelled Bed and the Unrepressible Wish of *Wuthering Heights*." *Paunch*, no. 30 (December 1967): 40–46.

Smith, David J. "The Arrested Heart: Familial Love and Psychic Conflict in Five Mid-Victorian Novels." *Dissertation Abstracts* 27 (1966): 1839A (Washington).

Sonstroem, David. "*Wuthering Heights* and the Limits of Vision." *Publications of the Modern Language Association* 86 (1971): 51–62.

Stone, Roy de Montpensier. "Re *Wuthering Heights* and Re 'Thurshcross Grange' Case for the Opinion of Counsel." *Brontë Society Transactions* 16 (1972): 118–30.

Sucksmith, Harvey P. "The Theme of *Wuthering Heights* Reconsidered." *Dalhousie Review* 54 (Autumn 1974): 418–28.

Thompson, Wade. "Infanticide and Sadism in *Wuthering Heights*." *Publications of the Modern Language Association* 78 (1963): 69–74.

Thomson, Patricia. "*Wuthering Heights* and *Mauprat*." *Review of English Studies* 24 (February 1973): 26–37.

Tough, A.J. "*Wuthering Heights* and *King Lear*." *English* 21 (Spring 1972): 1–5.

Vancura, Zdenek, "The Stones of *Wuthering Heights*." *Philologica Pragensia* 13 (1970): 1–15.

Vargish, Thomas. "Revenge and *Wuthering Heights*." *Studies in the Novel* 3 (Spring 1971): 7–17.

Viswanathan, Jacqueline. "Point of View and Unreliability in Brontë's *Wuthering Heights*, Conrad's *Under Western Eyes*, and Mann's *Doktor Faustus.*" *Orbis Litterarum* 29 (1974): 42–60.

Von Frank, Albert J. "An American Defence of *Wuthering Heights*—1848." *Brontë Society Transactions* 16 (1974): 277–80.

Waddington-Feather, John B. "Emily Brontë's Use of Dialect in *Wuthering Heights*." *Brontë Society Transactions* 15 (1969): 12–19.

Waidner, Maralee L. "From Reason to Romance: A Progression from an Emphasis on Neoclassic Rationality to Romantic Intuition in Three English Woman Novelists." *Dissertation Abstracts International* 34 (1973): 1259A–60A (Tulsa).

Williams, Gordon. "The Problem of Passion in *Wuthering Heights*." *Trivium* 7 (May 1972): 41–53.

Willis, Irene Cooper. "Looking for a Key to *Wuthering Heights*." *Brontë Society Transactions* 14 (1965): 20–24.

Wilson, Jo Anne A. "*The Butterfly* and *Wuthering Heights*: A Mystic's Eschatology." *Victorian Newsletter* 33 (Spring 1968): 22–25.

FRANCES MORE BROOKE (1724?–1789) Canada (Born in Great Britain)
General Works
Needham, Gwendolyn B. "Mrs. Frances Brooke: Dramatic Critic." *Theatre Notebook* 15 (Winter 1960–1961): 47–55.
Individual Works
History of Emily Montague (1769)
New, William H. "Frances Brooke's Chequered Gardens." *Canadian Literature*, no. 52 (Spring 1972): 24–38.

GWENDOLYN BROOKS (1917–) U.S.
Bibliography
Loff, Jon N. "Gwendolyn Brooks: A Bibliography." *College Language Association Journal* 17 (September 1973): 21–32.

Mahoney, Heidi L. "Selected Checklist of Material by and about Gwendolyn Brooks." *Negro American Literature Forum* 8 (1974): 210–11.
General Works
Baker, Houston A. "The Achievement of Gwendolyn Brooks." *College Language Association Journal* 16 (September 1972): 23–31.

Bambara, T. C. "Report from Part One." *New York Times Book Review* (January 7, 1973): 1.

Baumgaertner, Jill. "Gwendolyn Brooks: Tintinnabulation." *Cresset* 37 (January 1974): 12–15.

Beja, Morris. "It Must Be Important: Negroes in Contemporary American Fiction." *Antioch Review* 24 (Fall 1964): 323–36.

Bird, G. Leonard. "Gwendolyn Brooks: Educator Extraordinaire." *Discourse* 12 (Summer 1969): 158–66.

Dana, Robert Patrick. "Double Martini and Broken Crank Shaft." *Prairie Schooner* 35 (Winter 1961–1962): 357–362.

Davis, Arthur P. "The Black-and-Tan Motif in the Poetry of Gwendolyn Brooks." *College Language Association Journal* 6 (December 1962): 90–97.

Davis, Arthur P. "Gwendolyn Brooks: Poet of the Unheroic." *College Language Association Journal* 7 (December 1963): 114–25.

Furman, Marva Riley. "Gwendolyn Brooks, the 'Unconditioned' Poet." *College Language Association Journal* 17 (September 1973): 1–10.

Garland, P. "Gwendolyn Brooks: Poet Laureate." *Ebony* (July 1968): 48–50.

Hansell, W. H. "Role of Violence in Recent Poems of Gwendolyn Brooks." *Studies in Black Literature* 5 (Summer 1974): 21–27.

Kent, George E. "The Poetry of Gwendolyn Brooks: Part I." *Black World* 20 (September 1971): 30–43; Part II, 20 (October 1971): 36.

Lee, Don L. "The Achievement of Gwendolyn Brooks." *Black Scholar* 3 (1972): 32–41.

Lewis, Ida. "Conversation: Gwen Brooks and Ida Lewis." *Essence* (April 1971): 27–31.

Shands, Annette Oliver. "Gwendolyn Brooks as Novelist." *Black World* 22 (June 1973): 22–30.

Shaw, Harry B. "Social Themes in the Poetry of Gwendolyn Brooks." *Dissertation Abstracts International* 34 (1973): 740A (Illinois).

Starves, George. "An Interview with Gwendolyn Brooks." *Contemporary Literature* 11 (Winter 1970): 1–20.
Individual Works
In the Mecca (1968)
Hansell, William H. "Aestheticism versus Political Militancy in Gwendolyn Brooks's 'The Chicago Picasso' and 'The Wall.' " *College Language Association Journal* 17 (September 1973): 11–15.

Hansell, William H. "Gwendolyn Brooks's *In the Mecca*: A Rebirth into Blackness." *Negro American Literature Forum* 8 (1974): 199–207.

McCluskey, John. "*In the Mecca*." *Studies in Black*

Literature 4 (Autumn 1973): 25–30.

Report from Part One (1972)

Brooks, Gwendolyn. "*Report from Part One*: The Autobiography of Gwendolyn Brooks." *Black World* 21 (September 1972): 4–12.

Washington, Mary Helen. "Review of *Report from Part One*." *Black World* 22 (March 1973): 51–52.

Selected Poems (1963)

Hudson, Clenora F. "Racial Themes in the Poetry of Gwendolyn Brooks." *College Language Association Journal* 17 (September 1973): 16–20.

RHODA BROUGHTON (1840–1920) Great Britain
General Works

Watters, Tamie. "An Oxford Provocation and Caricature: Rhoda Broughton and Mark Pattison." *Encounter* 36 (April 1971): 34–42.

ALICE BROWN (1857–1948) U.S.
Bibliography

Toth, Susan A. "Alice Brown (1857–1948)." *American Literary Realism* 5 (1972): 134–43.
General Works

Toth, Susan A. "A Forgotten View from Beacon Hill: Alice Brown's New England Short Stories." *Colby Library Quarterly* 10 (March 1972): 1–17.

Toth, Susan A. "More than Local-Color: A Reappraisal of Rose Terry Cooke, Mary Wilkins Freeman and Alice Brown." *Dissertation Abstracts* 30 (1969): 3004A (Minnesota).

HELEN GURLEY BROWN (1922–) U.S.
General Works

Ephron, N. "Helen Gurley Brown Only Wants to Help." *Esquire* (February 1970): 75.

Harrington, S. "Two Faces of the Same Eve." *New York Times Magazine* (August 11, 1974): 10–11.

RITA MAE BROWN (1944?–) U.S.
General Works

Alexander, D. "Rita Mae Brown: The Issue for the Future Is Power." *Ms.* (September 1974): 110–13.

ELIZABETH BARRETT BROWNING (1806–1861) Great Britain
Bibliography

Abbott, Nedah. "A Bibliography of the Brownings (1968–First Quarter 1972)." *Studies in Browning and His Circle* 1 (Spring 1973): 63–91.

Barnes, Warner. "The Browning Collection." *Library Bibliographic Society* 7 (Summer 1963): 12–13.

Barnes, Warner. "Money, Metaphor and the Machine: Some Remarks on a Bibliography of Elizabeth Barrett Browning." *Browning Newsletter* 8 (Spring 1972): 33–41.

Freeman, Ronald E. "A Checklist of Publications (July 1970–December 1970)." *Browning Newsletter* 6 (Spring 1971): 63–67.

Freeman, Ronald E. "A Checklist of Publications (January 1971–July 1971)." *Browning Newsletter* 7 (Fall 1971): 63–68.

Freeman, Ronald E. "A Checklist of Publications (July 1971–December 1971)." *Browning Newsletter* 8 (Spring 1972): 68–72.

Freeman, Ronald E. "A Checklist of Publications (July–December 1973)." *Studies in Browning and His Circle* 2 (Spring 1974): 71–77.

Freeman, Ronald E. "A Checklist of Publications (January 1974–July 1974)." *Studies in Browning and His Circle* 2 (Fall 1974): 49–54.

Kelley, Philip. "Collection: The Moulton-Barrett Papers in the New York Public Library." *Browning Newsletter* 2 (Spring 1969): 10–12.

Luedecke, Margaret A. "A Bibliography of the Brownings: 1965–68." *Browning Newsletter* 2 (Spring 1969): 13–24.

Luedecke, Margaret A. "A Checklist of Publications (June 1968–December 1968)." *Browning Newsletter* 2 (Spring 1969): 48–51.

Munich, Adrienne. "The Browning Collection in the New York Public Library." *Studies in Browning and His Circle* 1 (Fall 1973): 23–25.

Munich, Adrienne. "The Yale Browning Collection: The Beinecke Library." *Browning Newsletter* 8 (Spring 1972): 21–25.

Peterson, William S. "Robert and Elizabeth Barrett Browning: An Annotated Bibliography for 1972." *Browning Institute Studies* 2 (1974): 181–202.

Peterson, William S., and Richard C. Keenan. "Robert and Elizabeth Barrett Browning: An Annotated Bibliography for 1971." *Browning Institute Studies* 1 (1973): 173–86.

"A Reprint of the Dobell Browning Catalogue." *Browning Institute Studies* 2 (1974): 77–118.

Szladits, Lola L. "New in the Berg Collection: 1965–1969." *Bulletin of the New York Public Library* 75 (January 1971): 9–29.

Taplin, Gardner B. "Elizabeth Barrett Browning."

Victorian Poetry 12 (Autumn 1974): 241–44.

Tennison, James E. "Elizabeth Barrett Browning: Index to the NCBEL." *Browning Newsletter* 8 (Spring 1972): 42–43.

Timko, Michael. "Elizabeth Barrett Browning: A Review of the Year's Research." *Browning Newsletter* 1 (October 1968): 3–6.

Williams, Marvin L., Jr. "The Fannie Barrett Browning Collection at the University of Texas." *Browning Newsletter* 9 (Fall 1972): 3–7.

General Works

Agosta, Lucien L. "The Annotations in Fannie Barrett Browning's Copy of the May 1913 Sotheby Auction Catalogue."*Browning Newsletter* 9 (Fall 1972): 38–47.

Baly, Elaine. "Talking of the Brownings." *Browning Newsletter* 11 (Fall 1973): 2–19.

Barnes, Warner. "Query: On a Poem by E.B.B." *Browning Newsletter* 1 (October 1968): 29–30.

Berridge, Elizabeth. "Hope End Revisited." *Browning Society Notes* 4 (December 1974): 3–9.

Bishop, Morchard. "Towards a Biography of Flush." *Times Literary Supplement* (December 15, 1966): 1180.

Bultman, Sandra. "Hope End, Herefordshire: Childhood Home of Elizabeth Barrett Browning." *Country Life* 144 (1968): 715.

Delaura, David J. "Ruskin and the Brownings: Twenty-Five Unpublished Letters." *Bulletin of the John Rylands Library* 54 (Spring 1972): 314–56.

"E.B.B." *Times Literary Supplement* (June 2, 1961): 348.

Faverty, Frederic E. "Review Essay: The Brownings and Their Contemporaries." *Browning Institute Studies* 2 (1974): 161–80.

Gladish, Robert W. "Mrs. Browning's Contributions to the *New York Independent*." *Bulletin of the New York Public Library* 71 (January 1967): 47–54.

Green, David Bonnell. "Elizabeth Barrett and R. Shelton Mackenzie." *Studies in Bibliography* 14 (1961): 245–50.

Green, David Bonnell. "Elizabeth Barrett to Hugh Stuart Boyd: An Additional Letter." *Publications of the Modern Language Association* 76 (1961): 154–55.

Hayter, Alethea. "Windows Toward the Future." *Browning Institute Studies* 1 (1973): 31–36.

Hope, Emily Blanchard. "Saving Casa Guidi."

Browning Institute Studies 1 (1973): 1–30.

Hudson, Ronald. "Elizabeth Barrett Browning and Her Brother Alfred: Some Unpublished Letters." *Browning Institute Studies* 2 (1974): 135–60.

Hunt, Martha Caskey. "Note: Elizabeth's Writing Table." *Browning Newsletter* 8 (Spring 1972): 53.

Kimball, Jim C. "A Ruskin Letter to Mrs. Browning." *Browning Newsletter* 8 (Spring 1972): 47–49.

Lewis, Naomi. "The Genius of Elizabeth Barrett Browning." *Listener* (July 20, 1961): 91–92.

Lohrli, Anne. "Greek Slave Mystery." *Notes and Queries* 13 (February 1966): 58–60.

Moll, June. "Note: 'Robert and Elizabeth Browning,' a Painting by Anna de L'Epinois." *Browning Newsletter* 2 (Spring 1969): 33–34.

Mouton-Barrett, Edward. "Talking of the Barretts, I (1655–1800)." *Browning Society Notes* 2 (March 1972): 4–5; Part II (1800–1837), 2 (July 1972): 3–4; Part III (1837–1910), 2 (December 1972): 3–4.

Paroissien, David. "Mrs. Browning's Influence on and Contribution to *A New Spirit of the Age* (1844)." *English Language Notes* 8 (June 1971): 274–81.

Pearsall, Robert B. "Elizabeth Barrett Meets Wolf Larsen." *Western American Literature* 4 (Spring 1969): 3–13.

Peattie, D., and L. Peattie. "Immortal Romance." *Reader's Digest* (November 1961): 304–9.

Peterson, William S. "Robert Browning and Mrs. Humphry Ward." *Browning Newsletter* 7 (Fall 1971): 13–14.

Raymond, Meredith B. "A Report on the Published and Unpublished Letters of Elizabeth Barrett Browning to Mary Russell Mitford." *Browning Institute Studies* 1 (1973): 37–62.

Raymond, William O. "Browning and the Harriet Westbrook Shelley Letters." *University of Toronto Quarterly* 32 (January 1963): 184–92.

Rothenberg, Albert. "The Flesh-and-Blood Face on the Commemorative Stamp." *Saturday Review* (September 11, 1971): 33–38.

Ryals, Clyde De L. "The Poet as Critic: Appraisals of Tennyson by His Contemporaries." *Tamarack Review* 23 (Spring 1962): 113–25.

Thale, Mary. "T. S. Eliot and Mrs. Browning on the Metaphysical Poets." *College Language Association Journal* 11 (March 1968): 255–58.

Thomson, Fred C. "Elizabeth Barrett Browning on

Spiritualism: A New Letter." *Victorian Newsletter* 31 (Spring 1967): 49–52.

Thomson, Patricia. "Elizabeth Barrett and George Sand." *Durham University Journal* 64 (June 1972): 205–19.

"Two Autobiographical Essays by Elizabeth Barrett." *Browning Institute Studies* 2 (1974): 119–34.

Wiggins, Genevieve E. "The Brownings and Napoleon III: A Study in Political Poetry." *Dissertation Abstracts International* 34 (1974): 7206A–7A (Tennessee).

Individual Works

Aurora Leigh (1857)

Thomson, Patricia. "Elizabeth Barrett and George Sand." *Durham University Journal* 64 (June 1972): 205–19.

Casa Guidi Windows (1851)

Hayter, Alethea. "Windows Toward the Future." *Browning Institute Studies* 1 (1973): 31–36.

Hope, Emily Blanchard. "Saving Casa Guidi." *Browning Institute Studies* 1 (1973): 1–30.

A Curse for a Nation (1860)

Arinshtein, Leonid N. "*A Curse for a Nation*: A Controversial Episode in Elizabeth Barrett Browning's Political Poetry." *Review of English Studies* 20 (February 1969): 33–42.

Delaura, David J. "A Robert Browning Letter: The Occasion of Mrs. Browning's *A Curse for a Nation*." *Victorian Poetry* 4 (Summer 1966): 210–12.

Gladish, Robert W. "Mrs. Browning's *A Curse for a Nation*: Some Further Comments." *Victorian Poetry* 7 (Autumn 1969): 275–80.

A Drama of Exile (1845)

Boos, Florence, and William Boos. "A Source for the Rimes of Poe's 'The Raven': Elizabeth Barrett Browning's 'A Drama of Exile.'" *Mary Wollstonecraft Journal* 2 (1974): 30–31.

The Runaway Slave (1848)

Carter, John. "A Unique Copy of *The Runaway Slave*, 1849." *Book Collector* 12 (Summer 1963): 68–71.

Sonnets from the Portuguese (1850)

Kay, Carol M. "An Analysis of Sonnet 6 in *Sonnets from the Portuguese*." *Concerning Poetry* 4 (1971): 17–21.

Phillipson, John S. " 'How Do I Love Thee?' An Echo of St. Paul." *Victorian Newsletter* 22 (Fall 1962): 22.

Zimmerman, Susan. "*Sonnets from the Portuguese*: A Negative and Positive Context." *Mary*

Wollstonecraft Newsletter 2 (December 1973): 7–20.

The Sorrows of the Muses (1824)

Barnes, Warner. "*The Sorrows of the Muses*: An Early Poem by Elizabeth Barrett." *Books at Iowa*, no. 4 (1966): 19–35.

CORALIE BUARD (fl. 1860s) U.S.
General Works

Williams, Ora G. "Muskets and Magnolias: Four Civil War Diaries by Louisiana Girls." *Louisiana Studies* 4 (Fall 1965): 187–99.

CYNTHIA BUCHANAN (1942–) U.S.
General Works

Durham, Michael. "Cinderella of the Swingles." *Life* (April 7, 1972): 45.

"Ten Super Women Achievers." *Mademoiselle* (February 1973): 119.

PEARL BUCK, née Sydenstricker (1892–1973) U.S.
General Works

"At Home with Pearl Buck." *Ladies' Home Journal* (July 1965): 36.

Cerbasco, G. A. "The Image of the Chinese Family in Pearl Buck's Novels." *Chinese Culture* 6 (1966): 107–9.

Doyle, Paul A. "Pearl S. Buck's Short Stories: A Survey." *English Journal* 55 (January 1966): 62–68.

"Earth to Earth." *Time* (March 19, 1973): 81.

McConathy, D. "What I Learned from Chinese Women: Interview." *Vogue* (June 1972): 136–37.

Snow, Helen F. "Pearl S. Buck, 1892–1973." *New Republic* (March 24, 1973): 28–29.

Venne, Peter. "Pearl Buck's Literary Portrait of China and the Chinese." *Fu Jen Studies* (Republic of China) 1 (1968): 71–86.

"We Visit Pearl Buck." *Saturday Evening Post* (May 14, 1960): 136.

Individual Works

All Men Are Brothers (1933)

Hunting, Robert. "The Morals of *All Men Are Brothers*." *Western Humanities Review* 17 (Winter 1963): 86–88.

The Good Earth (1931)

Langlois, Walter G. "*The Dream of the Red Chamber, The Good Earth* and *Man's Fate*: Chronicles of Social Change in China." *Literature East and West* 11 (March 1967): 1–10.

Shimizu, Mamoru. "On Some Stylistic Features, Chiefly Biblical, of *The Good Earth*." *Studies in English Literature*, English Number (1964): 117–34.

KATHRYN BURKHART (1942–) U.S.
General Works
"Twelve Women Who Did Something: Mademoiselle Awards." *Mademoiselle* (February 1974): 103.
"Young Hopefuls." *Saturday Review/World* (December 14, 1974): 104.

CHARLOTTE BURNE (fl. 1880s) Great Britain
Individual Works
Shropshire Folklore (1885)
Burne, J. C. "Young Charlotte Burne: Author of *Shropshire Folklore*." *Folklore* 86 (Autumn–Winter 1975): 167–74.

FRANCES HODGSON BURNETT (1849–1924) U.S. (Born in Great Britain)
Bibliography
Molson, Frances J. "Frances Hodgson Burnett (1849–1924)." *American Literary Realism* 8 (1975): 35–42.
General Works
Burnett, Constance Buell. "Frances Hodgson Burnett: Episodes in Her Life." *Horn Book Magazine* 41 (1965): 86–94.
McCarthy, T. "Real Little Lord Fauntleroy." *American Heritage* 21 (February 1970): 50–55.
Thwaite, Anne. "The Life of a Great Storyteller." *Country Life* 156 (1974): 1564–65.
Individual Works
The Secret Garden (1911)
White, Alison. "Tap-Roots into a Rose Garden." *Children's Literature* 1 (1972): 74–76.

FANNY BURNEY, Madame d'Arblay (1752–1840) Great Britain
General Works
Blakeney, T. S. "Queen Charlotte: Fanny Burney's Employer: Part I." *New Rambler*, no. 104 (1968): 24–36.; Part II, no. 105 (1968): 3–15.
"The Butterfly Becomes a Moth." *Times Literary Supplement* (December 15, 1972): 1531–32.
Kvernes, David M. "A Critical Study of Fanny Burney." *Dissertation Abstracts* 28 (1967): 634A–35A (Minnesota).

Mulliken, Elizabeth Yost. "The Influence of the Drama on Fanny Burney's Novels." *Dissertation Abstracts* 30 (1970): 3913A (Wisconsin).
"The Real Fanny Burney." *Times Literary Supplement* (March 9, 1962): 160.
Rudolf, Jo-Ellen S. "The Novels That Taught the Ladies: A Study of Popular Fiction Written by Women, 1702–1834." *Dissertation Abstracts International* 33 (1972): 1695A (California, San Diego).
Sambrook, A. J. "Fanny Burney's First Letter to Dr. Johnson." *Review of English Studies* 14 (August 1963): 273–75.
Spacks, Patricia M. " 'Ev'ry Woman Is at Heart a Rake.' " *Eighteenth Century Studies* 8 (1974): 27–46.
Strauch, Gerard. "Jane Austen's Response to Fanny Burney." *Bulletin de la Faculté des Lettres de Strasbourg* 47 (1969): 217–32.
Individual Works
Cecilia, or Memoirs of an Heiress (1782)
Moler, Kenneth L. "Fanny Burney's *Cecilia* and Jane Austen's *Jack and Alice*." *English Language Notes* 3 (September 1965): 40–42.
Evelina, or The History of a Young Lady's Entrance into the World (1778)
Davie, John, Duncan Isles, and Alastair Stead. "Pride and Prejudice." *Notes and Queries* 11 (May 1964): 181–82.
Erickson, James P. "*Evelina* and *Betsy Thoughtless*." *Texas Studies in Literature and Language* 6 (Spring 1964): 96–103.
Glock, Waldo S. "Appearance and Reality: The Education of *Evelina*." *Essays in Literature* 2 (Spring 1975): 32–41.
Katz, Judith N. "Rooms of Their Own: Forms and Images of Liberation in Five Novels." *Dissertation Abstracts International* 34 (1973): 1283A (Penn. State).
Laski, Marghanita. "Antedatings of O.E.D. in *Evelina*." *Notes and Queries* 9 (August 1962): 269–70.
Malone, Kemp. "*Evelina* Revisited." *Papers on Language and Literature* 1 (1965): 3–19.
Patterson, E.H. "Unearned Irony in Fanny Burney's *Evelina*." *Durham University Journal* 67 (June 1975): 200–204.
Rubenstein, Jill. "The Crisis of Identity in Fanny Burney's *Evelina*." *New Rambler*, no. 112 (1972): 45–50.
Speakman, James S. "Wit, Humor and Sensibility in

Evelina, Belinda and *Northanger Abbey.*" *Dissertation Abstracts International* 34 (1973): 791A–92A (California, Davis).

Vopat, James B. "*Evelina*: Life as Art-Notes Toward Becoming a Performer on the Stage of Life." *Essays in Literature* 2 (Spring 1975): 42–52.

Lady Charlotte Campbell Bury (fl. 1820s–1830s)
Great Britain
General Works

White, Edward M. "Thackeray, 'Dolly Duster,' and Lady Charlotte Campbell Bury." *Review of English Studies* 16 (February 1965): 35–43.

C

ROANE FLEMING BYRNES (1890–1970) U.S.
General Works
Prevost, Verbie Lovorn. "Roane Fleming Byrnes: A Critical Biography." *Dissertation Abstracts International* 35 (1975): 4548A (Mississippi).

MARGUERITE CAETANI (1920s) U.S.
General Works
Origo, Iris. "Marguerite Caetani." *Atlantic Monthly* (February 1965): 81–88.

JANET TAYLOR CALDWELL [pseud. Max Reiner] (1900–) U.S.
General Works
Nichols, L. "Shedunit." *New York Times Book Review* (July 14, 1963): 8.

LADY MARIA GRAHAM CALLCOTT, née Dundas (1786–1844) Great Britain
General Works
Marchant, A. "Captain's Widow: Maria Graham and the Independence of South America." *Americas* 20 (October 1963): 127–42.

ADA CAMBRIDGE (1844–1926) Australia
General Works
Roe, Jill. "The Scope of Women's Thoughts Is Necessarily Less: The Case of Ada Cambridge." *Australian Literary Studies* 5 (1972): 388–403.

JANE WELSH CARLYLE (1801–1866) Great Britain
General Works
Hardwick, Elizabeth. "Amateurs: Jane Carlyle." *New York Review of Books* (December 14, 1972): 32–63.
Kmetz, Gail. "The Other Carlyle: Jane." *Mas-*sachusetts *Studies in English* 4 (1974–1975): 50–54.
Lochhead, Marion. "Jane Welsh Carlyle." *Quarterly Review* 298 (July 1960): 321–32.

MARY AITKEN CARLYLE (1771–1853) Great Britain
General Works
Tarr, Rodger L. "Mary Aitken Carlyle: An Unpublished Letter to Her Son." *English Language Notes* 8 (June 1971): 281–83.

SARAH ELIZABETH CARMICHAEL (fl. 1840s–1850s) U.S.
General Works
Murphy, Miriam B. "Sarah Elizabeth Carmichael: Poetic Genius of Pioneer Utah." *Utah Historical Quarterly* 43 (Winter 1975): 52–66.

EMILY CARR (1871–1945) Canada
General Works
Blissett, W. F. "Letters from Emily Carr." *University of Toronto Quarterly* 41 (Winter 1972): 93–150.

ELIZABETH CARTER (1717–1806) Great Britain
General Works
Ewert, Leonore H. "Elizabeth Montagu to Elizabeth Carter: Literary Gossip and Critical Opinions from the Pen of the Queen of the Blues." *Dissertation Abstracts* 29 (1968): 566A–67A (Claremont).
Hampshire, G. "Johnson, Elizabeth Carter and Pope's Garden." *Notes and Queries* 19 (June 1972): 221–22.
Sena, John F. "Melancholy in Anne Finch and Elizabeth Carter: The Ambivalence of an Idea." *Yearbook of English Studies* 1 (1971): 108–19.

BARBARA CARTLAND (1904–) Great Britain
General Works
Pitman, John. "My Wonderful Daughter." *Listener* (March 22, 1973): 375–76.

ALICE CARY (1820–1871) U.S.
General Works
Pulsifer, Janice G. "Alice and Phoebe Cary, Whittier's Sweet Singers of the West." *Essex Institute Historical Collections* 109 (1973): 9–59.

PHOEBE CARY (1824–1871) U.S.
General Works
Pulsifer, Janice G. "Alice and Phoebe Cary, Whittier's Sweet Singers of the West." *Essex Institute Historical Collections* 109 (1973): 9–59.

LINDA TY CASPER (fl. 1960s) U.S.
Individual Works
The Peninsulars (1964)
Hidalgo, Perca R. "The Art of *The Peninsulars* by Linda Casper." *St. Louis University Research Journal* 2 (June 1971): 267–92.

WILLA CATHER, née Sibert (1873–1947) U.S.
Bibliography
Bennett, J.Q. "Bibliographical Points on Cather and Fisher." *American Notes and Queries* 2 (February 1964): 85.
Bennett, Mildred R. "Two Cather Collections." *Prairie Schooner* 42 (Summer 1968): 178–81.
Cary, Richard. "A Willa Cather Collection." *Colby Library Quarterly* 8 (December 1969): 82–95.
General Works
Adams, Theodore Stanford. "Six Novels of Willa Cather: A Thematic Study." *Dissertation Abstracts* 22 (1961): 570–71 (Ohio).
Allen, David A. "Willa Cather: A Critical Study." *Dissertation Abstracts International* 33 (1973): 4397A–98A (Denver).
"American Woman: Willa Cather Centennial." *Vogue* (June 1973): 113.
Anderson, Quentin. "Willa Cather: Her Masquerade." *New Republic* (November 27, 1965): 28–31.
Arnold, Marilyn. "Self-Division and Self-Unity in the Novels of Willa Cather." *Dissertation Abstracts* 29 (1969): 3089A–90A (Wisconsin).
Baker, Bruce. "Image and Symbol in Selected Writings of Willa Cather." *Dissertation Abstracts* 29

(1969): 3604A (Texas Christian).
Baker, Bruce. "Nebraska Regionalism in Selected Works of Willa Cather." *Western American Literature* 3 (Spring 1968): 19–35.
Barba, Sharon R. "Willa Cather: A Feminist Study." *Dissertation Abstracts International* 34 (1973): 2605A (New Mexico).
Bash, James R. "Willa Cather and the Anathema of Materialism." *Colby Library Quarterly* 10 (September 1973): 157–68.
Bennett, Mildred R. "How Willa Cather Chose Her Names." *Names* 10 (1962): 29–37.
Bennett, S.M. "Ornament and Environment: Uses of Folklore in Willa Cather's Fiction." *Tennessee Folklore Society Bulletin* 40 (1974): 95–102.
Borgman, P. "Dialectic of Willa Cather's Moral Vision." *Renascence* 27 (Spring 1975): 145–59.
Brennan, Joseph X. "Willa Cather and Music." *University Review* (Kansas) 31 (1965): 175–83.
Bryden, Ronald. "The American Sublime." *Spectator* (May 26, 1961): 767.
Cary, Richard. "The Sculptor and the Spinster: Jewett's Influence on Cather." *Colby Library Quarterly* 10 (September 1973): 168–78.
Charles, Sister Peter Damian. "Love and Death in the Novels of Willa Cather." *Dissertation Abstracts* 26 (1965): 2205–6 (Notre Dame).
Chase, Mary Ellen. "Five Literary Portraits." *Massachusetts Review* 3 (Spring 1962): 511–16.
Clark, Harry Hayden. "Willa Cather." *Contemporary Literature* 13 (Spring 1972): 258–60.
Cooper, Clara B. "Willa Cather: The Nature of Evil and Its Purgation." *Dissertation Abstracts International* 32 (1972): 6420A (Florida State).
Curtin, William M. "Willa Cather: Individualism and Style." *Colby Library Quarterly* 8 (December 1969): 37–55.
Curtin, William M. "Willa Cather and *The Varieties of Religious Experience*." *Renascence* 27 (Spring 1975): 115–23.
Danielson, Jeannette C. "'A Sense of a Sense' of Place in the Works of Willa Cather." *Dissertation Abstracts* 30 (1969): 718A–19A (Bowling Green).
Dinn, James M. "'Only Two or Three Human Stories': Recurrent Patterns of Action in the Major Fiction of Willa Cather." *Dissertation Abstracts International* 33 (1973): 6351A–52A (Notre Dame).
Ditsky, John. "Nature and Character in the Novels

of Willa Cather." *Colby Library Quarterly* 10 (September 1974): 391–412.

Donohue, J.W., Jr. "Two Women: A Centennial." *America* (March 31, 1973): 276–80.

Duffy, M. "The Old Sod" *Time* (August 13, 1973): 80.

Durham, Philip. "Willa Cather's 'There-about.'" *Neuphilologische Mitteilungen* 73 (1972): 83–89.

Eichorn, Harry B. "Willa Cather: Stranger in Three Worlds." *Dissertation Abstracts* 29 (1969): 4002A (Stanford).

Ferguson, J. M. " 'Vague Outlines': Willa Cather's Enchanted Bluffs." *Western Review* 7 (Spring 1970): 61–64.

Fetty, Audrey M.S. "Biblical Allusions in the Fiction of Willa Cather." *Dissertation Abstracts International* 34 (1973): 2621A–22A (Nebraska).

Fleming, Patricia J. "The Integrated Self: Sexuality and the Double in Willa Cather's Fiction." *Dissertation Abstracts International* 35 (1974): 1653A (Boston).

Forman, Henry James. "Willa Cather: A Voice from the Prairie." *Southwest Review* 47 (Summer 1962): 248–58.

Fox, Clyde Maynard. "Revelation of Character in Five Cather Novels." *Dissertation Abstracts* 24 (1964): 4699–4700 (Colorado).

Frank, John. "Cather and the Pursuit of Beauty." *Analects* 1 (October 1960): 12–15.

Freydberg, Margaret Howe. "Willa Cather: The Light behind Her Books." *American Scholar* 43 (Spring 1974): 282–87.

"The Frontier Dream." *Times Literary Supplement* (July 27, 1962): 540.

Furness, Edna. "Image of the Schoolteacher in Western Literature." *Arizona Quarterly* 18 (Winter 1962): 346–57.

Gale, Robert. "Manuel Lujon, Another Name by Willa Cather." *Names* 11 (1963): 210–11.

Gale, Robert. "Willa Cather and the Usable Past." *Nebraska History* 42 (1961): 181–90.

Giannone, Richard. "Music in Willa Cather's Fiction." *Dissertation Abstracts* 25 (1964): 2980–81 (Notre Dame).

Harper, Marion. "The West of Twain and Cather." *Diliman Review* 14 (January 1966): 60–80.

Harris, Richard C. "Energy and Order in Willa Cather's Novels." *Dissertation Abstracts International* 35 (1974): 3742A (North Carolina).

Helmick, Evelyn Thomas. "Myth in the Works of

Willa Cather." *Midcontinent American Studies Journal* 9 (1968): 63–69.

Hinz, Evelyn. "Willa Cather's Technique and the Ideology of Populism." *Western American Literature* 7 (Spring 1972): 47–61.

"The Incomparable Opera House." *Nebraska History* 49 (1968): 373–78.

Jacks, L.V. "The Classics and Willa Cather." *Prairie Schooner* 35 (Winter 1961–1962): 289–96

Janeway, E. "An Epic Was Around Her." *New York Times Book Review* (September 5, 1965): 1.

Johnson, Edward R. "Evil, Vision, and Artistic Purity: The Existential Implications of Willa Cather." *Newsletter: Willa Cather Pioneer Memorial and Educational Foundation* 12 (Fall 1968): 1–2.

Karita, Motoshi. "The Genteel Tradition at Bay." *Sophia* 2 (Winter 1962): 24–46.

Keeler, Clinton. "Narrative without Accent: Willa Cather and Puvis de Chavannes." *American Quarterly* 17 (Spring 1965): 119–26.

Klotman, P.R. "Musical Soul of Willa Cather." *Music Journal* 28 (March 1970): 42–43.

Knopf, A. A. "Random Recollections of a Publisher." *Proceedings of the Massachusetts Historical Society* 74 (1962): 92–103.

La Hood, Marvin. "Conrad Richter and Willa Cather: Some Similarities." *Xavier University Studies* 9 (Spring 1970): 33–44.

Lambert, Maude Eugenie. "Theme and Craftsmanship in Willa Cather's Novels." *Dissertation Abstracts* 26 (1965): 3925 (North Carolina).

Lauerman, David A. "The Garden and the City in the Fiction of Willa Cather." *Dissertation Abstracts International* 33 (1973): 4421A–22A (Indiana).

McAlpin, Sister Sara. "Enlightening the Commonplace: The Art of Sarah Jewett, Willa Cather and Ruth Suckow." *Dissertation Abstracts International* 32 (1971): 2061A (Penn.).

McLaw, Catherine M. "Religion in the Novels of Willa Cather." *Renascence* 27 (Spring 1975): 125–44.

Miller, James E., Jr. "The Nebraska Encounter: Willa Cather and Wright Morris." *Prairie Schooner* 41 (Summer 1967): 165–67.

Moers, Ellen. "The Angry Young Women." *Harper's* (December 1963): 88–95.

Moseley, Ann. "The Voyage Perilous: Willa Cather's Mythic Quest." *Dissertation Abstracts International* 35 (1975): 6102A (Oklahoma).

Mukoyama, Yasuko. "Cather's Love of Place." *Thought Currents in English Literature* 35 (February 1963): 71–82.

Murphy, J. J. "Willa Cather and Hawthorne: Significant Resemblances." *Renascence* 27 (Spring 1975): 161–75.

Murphy, Michael W. "The Complex Past in Willa Cather's Novels of the Twenties." *Dissertation Abstracts International* 35 (1974): 3001A (Texas).

O'Connor, Margaret Anne. "A Guide to the Letters of Willa Cather." *Resources for American Literary Studies* 4 (1974): 145–72.

O'Connor, Margaret Anne. "Willa Cather and the Short Story." *Dissertation Abstracts International* 32 (1972): 5240A (California, Davis).

Okita, Hagime. "From Henry James to Willa Cather." *Albion* 8 (November 1961): 132–45.

Omori, Mamoru. "Some Problems on Cather's Works, Part II." *Studies in English Literature and Language* 3 (Summer 1962): 23–43.

"One-Hundredth Anniversary of Willa S. Cather." *Colby Library Quarterly* 10 (September 1973).

Parker, Jeraldine. " 'Uneasy Survivors': Five Women Writers, 1896–1923." *Dissertation Abstracts International* 34 (1973): 1927A (Utah).

Randall, John H., III. "Willa Cather's Search for Value: A Critical and Historical Study of Her Fiction." *Dissertation Abstracts* 20 (1960): 4115 (Minnesota).

Reynard, Grant. "Willa Cather's Advice to a Young Artist." *Prairie Schooner* 46 (Summer 1972): 111–24.

Ross, Janet. "Willa Cather and the Realistic Movement in American Fiction." *Dissertation Abstracts* 21 (1960): 1571–72 (Iowa).

Schmittlein, Albert Edward. "Willa Cather's Novels: An Evolving Art." *Dissertation Abstracts* 24 (1963): 2041 (Pittsburgh).

Schneider, Sister M. Lucy. "Artistry and Instinct: Willa Cather's 'Land-Philosophy.' " *College Language Association Journal* 16 (June 1973): 485–504.

Schneider, Sister M. Lucy. "Artistry and Intuition: Willa Cather's 'Land-Philosophy.' " *South Dakota Review* 6 (Winter 1968): 53–64.

Schneider, Sister M. Lucy. "Willa Cather's Early Stories in the Light of her 'Land-Philosophy.' " *Midwest Quarterly* 9 (Summer 1967): 75–93.

Schneider, Sister M. Lucy. "Willa Cather's 'Land-Philosophy' in Her Novels and Short Stories." *Dissertation Abstracts* 28 (1967): 3683A (Notre Dame).

Seibel, George. "Willa Cather and the Village Atheist." *Prairie Schooner* 41 (Summer 1967): 168–71.

Shelton, Frank W. "The Family in the Novels of Wharton, Faulkner, Cather, Lewis and Dreiser." *Dissertation Abstracts International* 32 (1972): 5244A (North Carolina).

Slote, Bernice. "Willa Cather and Walt Whitman." *Walt Whitman Review* 12 (March 1966): 3–5.

Slote, Bernice. "Willa Cather Reports Chautauqua, 1894." *Prairie Schooner* 43 (Spring 1969): 117–28.

Smith, Anneliese H. "The Persistent Hardness of Life in Willa Cather's Major Fiction: A Study of Her Dominant Stays against the Hard Realities." *Dissertation Abstracts International* 33 (1972): 2953A (S.U.N.Y., Albany).

Stouck, David. "Willa Cather's Last Four Books." *Novel* 7 (Fall 1973): 41–53.

Stouck, David. "Willa Cather's Unfinished Novel: Narrative in Perspective." *Wascana Review* 6 (1972): 41–51.

Stouck, Mary-Ann. "Chaucer's Pilgrims and Cather's Priests." *Colby Library Quarterly* 9 (December 1972): 531–37.

Strozier, Robert. "Willa Cather, Story Teller." *Descant* 8 (1964): 41–48.

Sullivan, Patrick J. "Willa Cather's Southwest." *Western American Literature* 7 (Spring 1972): 25–37.

Sutherland, Raymond C. "The Kentucky Girl in Two Literary Classics." *Kentucky Historical Society Register* 65 (April 1967): 134–43.

Thomas, Clara. "Proud Lineage: Willa Cather and Margaret Laurence." *Canadian Review of American Studies* 2 (Spring 1971): 3–12.

Thompson, Bernita L. A. "Continuity in the Work of Willa Cather." *Dissertation Abstracts International* 35 (1974): 3013A–14A (Nebraska).

Thorberg, Raymond. "Willa Cather: From *Alexander's Bridge* to *My Ántonia*." *Twentieth Century Literature* 7 (January 1962): 147–58.

Toler, Sister Colette. "Man as Creator of Art and Civilization in the Works of Willa Cather." *Dissertation Abstracts* 26 (1965): 2226 (Notre Dame).

Toler, Sister Colette. "Willa Cather's Vision of the Artist." *Personalist* 45 (Autumn 1964): 503–23.

Tressin, Deanna. "Toward Understanding." *English Journal* 55 (December 1966): 1170–74.

Vigil, Ralph H. "Willa Cather and Historical Reality." *New Mexico Historical Review* 50 (April 1975): 123–38.

Walker, D.D. "The Western Humanism of Willa Cather." *Western American Literature* 1 (Summer 1966): 75–90.

Walters, R., Jr. "Not Quite Lost Lady." *New York Times Book Review* (September 5, 1965): 8.

Weales, Gerald. "Willa Cather, Girl Reporter." *Southern Review* (U.S.) 8 (1972): 681–88.

Welborn, Grace Pleasant. "Willa Cather and the Southwest." *Forum* 4 (Winter 1963): 38–41.

Welty, Eudora. "The Physical World of Willa Cather." *New York Times Book Review* (January 27, 1974): 19.

Whittington, Curtis, Jr. "The Burden of Narration: Democratic Perspective." *Southern Humanities Review* 2 (Spring 1968): 236–45.

Whittington, Curtis C., Jr. "The Use of Inset Narratives in the Novels of Willa Cather." *Dissertation Abstracts International* 33 (1973): 4440A (Vanderbilt).

"Willa Cather: A Portfolio." *Prairie Schooner* 38 (Winter 1964–1965): 321–61.

"Willa Cather on Shakespeare." *Prairie Schooner* 38 (Spring 1964): 65–74.

Woodress, James. "Willa Cather Seen Clear." *Papers on Language and Literature* 7 (1971): 96–109.

Wright, Robert C. "Hardy's Heath and Cather's Prairie as Naturalistic Symbols." *Mankato State College Studies* 1 (May 1966): 55–68.

Yongue, Patricia L. "The Immense Design: A Study of Willa Cather's Creative Process." *Dissertation Abstracts International* 33 (1973): 5207A–8A (California, Los Angeles).

Zeigel, John Stoufer. "The Romanticism of Willa Cather." *Dissertation Abstracts* 29 (1968): 280A (Claremont).

Individual Works
Alexander's Bridge (1912)

Thorberg, Raymond. "Willa Cather: From *Alexander's Bridge* to *My Ántonia*." *Twentieth Century Literature* 7 (January 1962): 147–58.

The Best Years (1948)

Bush, Sargent, Jr. "*The Best Years*: Willa Cather's Last Story and Its Relation to Her Canon." *Studies in Short Fiction* 5 (Spring 1968): 269–74.

Schneider, Sister M. Lucy. "Willa Cather's *The Best Years*: The Essence of her 'Land-Philosophy.'" *Midwest Quarterly* 15 (Autumn 1973): 61–69.

The Clemency of the Court (1893)

Bohlke, L. Brent. "Beginnings: Willa Cather and 'The Clemency of the Court.'" *Prairie Schooner* 48 (Summer 1974): 134–44.

Death Comes for the Archbishop (1927)

Charles, Sister Peter Damian. "*Death Comes for the Archbishop*: A Novel of Love and Death." *New Mexico Quarterly* 36 (Winter 1966–1967): 389–403.

Dinn, James M. "A Novelist's Miracle: Structure and Myth in *Death Comes for the Archbishop*." *Western American Literature* 7 (Spring 1972): 39–46.

Gale, Robert L. "Cather's *Death Comes for the Archbishop*." *Explicator* 22 (May 1963): Item 75.

Giannone, Richard. "The Southwest's Eternal Echo: Music in *Death Comes for the Archbishop*." *Arizona Quarterly* 22 (Spring 1966): 5–18.

Keeler, Clinton. "Narrative without Accent: Willa Cather and Puvis de Chavannes." *American Quarterly* 17 (Spring 1965): 119–26.

Motoyanagi, Fumiko. "Willa Cather's *Death Comes for the Archbishop* and Its Epic Trend." *Kyushu American Literature* 8 (1965): 36–40.

Schneider, Sister M. Lucy. "Cather's Land-Philosophy in *Death Comes for the Archbishop*." *Renascence* 22 (Winter 1970): 78–86.

Shults, Donald. "Willa Cather: Style in *Death Comes for the Archbishop*." *Kyushu American Literature* 15 (1974): 75–83.

Stewart, D.H. "Cather's Mortal Comedy." *Queen's Quarterly* 73 (1966): 244–59.

Stouck, Mary-Ann and David. "Art and Religion in *Death Comes for the Archbishop*." *Arizona Quarterly* 29 (Winter 1973): 293–302.

Stouck, Mary-Ann and David. "Hagiographical Style in *Death Comes for the Archbishop*." *University of Toronto Quarterly* 41 (Summer 1972): 293–307.

Whittington, Curtis, Jr. "'The Stream and the Broken Pottery': The Form of Willa Cather's *Death Comes for the Archbishop*." *McNeese Review* 16 (1965): 16–24.

Ghost Town on the River (1894)

Cather, Willa. "Ghost Town on the River." *American Heritage* 21 (October 1970): 68–115.

A Lost Lady (1923)

Brunauer, Dalma H. "The Problem of Point of View in *A Lost Lady*." *Renascence* 28 (Autumn 1975): 47–52.

Helmick, Evelyn Thomas. "The Broken World: Medievalism in *A Lost Lady*." *Renascence* 28 (Autumn 1975): 39–46.

Ikuta, Toshiko. "*A Lost Lady*: The Problem of Point of View." *Kyushu American Literature* 15 (1974): 85–87.

Miller, Bruce E. "The Testing of Willa Cather's Humanism: *A Lost Lady* and Other Cather Novels." *Kansas Quarterly* 5 (Fall 1973): 43–50.

Yongue, Patricia. "*A Lost Lady*: The End of the First Cycle." *Western American Literature* 7 (Spring 1972): 3–12.

Lucy Gayheart (1935)

Schneider, Sister M. Lucy. "Of Land and Light: Willa Cather's *Lucy Gayheart*." *Kansas Quarterly* 5 (Fall 1973): 51–62.

My Ántonia (1918)

Charles, Sister Peter Damian. "*My Ántonia*: A Dark Dimension." *Western American Literature* 2 (Summer 1967): 91–108.

Ferger, Lois. "The Dark Dimension of Willa Cather's *My Ántonia*." *English Journal* 59 (September 1970): 774–79.

Gelfant, Blanche H. "The Forgotten Reaping-Hook: Sex in *My Ántonia*." *American Literature* 43 (March 1971): 60–82.

Giannone, Richard. "Music in *My Ántonia*." *Prairie Schooner* 38 (Winter 1964–1965): 346–61.

Martin, Terence. "The Drama of Memory in *My Ántonia*." *Publications of the Modern Language Association* 84 (1969): 304–11.

Miller, James E., Jr. "*My Ántonia* and the American Dream." *Prairie Schooner* 48 (Summer 1974): 112–23.

Miyake, Tsuneo. "On Willa Cather's Pioneer Novels: Referring to *O Pioneers!* and *My Ántonia*." *Kyushu American Literature* 15 (1974): 83–84.

Murphy, John J. "The Respectable Romantic and the Unwed Mother: Class Consciousness in *My Ántonia*." *Colby Library Quarterly* 10 (September 1973): 149–56.

Nyquist, Edna. "The Significance of the Locale in the Nebraska Fiction of Willa Cather, Especially in *My Ántonia*." *Wisconsin Studies in Literature* 2 (1965): 81–89.

Quinn, James. "Cather's *My Ántonia* and the Critics: An Annotated Bibliography." *Kansas English* 59 (1974): 20–21.

Rucker, M.E. "Prospective Focus in *My Ántonia*." *Arizona Quarterly* 29 (Winter 1973): 303–16.

Scholes, Robert E. "Hope and Memory in *My Ántonia*." *Shenandoah* 14 (1962): 24–29.

Slote, Bernice. "Willa Cather as a Regional Writer."

Kansas Quarterly 2 (Spring 1970): 7–15.

Stouck, David. "Perspective as Structure and Theme in *My Ántonia*." *Texas Studies in Literature and Language* 12 (Summer 1970): 285–94.

Stuckey, William J. "*My Ántonia*: A Rose for Miss Cather." *Studies in the Novel* 4 (Fall 1972): 473–83.

Suderman, Elmer F. "Perceptions of the Prairie in *My Ántonia*." *Iowa English Bulletin: Yearbook* 24 (1974): 49–56.

Thorberg, Raymond. "Willa Cather: From *Alexander's Bridge* to *My Ántonia*." *Twentieth Century Literature* 7 (January 1962): 147–58.

Thornton, Ella M. "The Mystery of Blind Tom." *Georgia Review* 15 (Winter 1961): 395–400.

My Mortal Enemy (1926)

Adams, Theodore S. "Willa Cather's *My Mortal Enemy*: The Concise Presentation of Scene, Character, and Theme." *Colby Library Quarterly* 10 (September 1973): 138–48.

Eichorn, Harry B. "A Falling Out with Love: *My Mortal Enemy*." *Colby Library Quarterly* 10 (September 1973): 121–38.

Giannone, Richard. "Willa Cather's *My Mortal Enemy* and Bellini's *Norma*." *Neueren Sprachen* 14 (1965): 401–11.

Whaley, Elizabeth G. "Cather's *My Mortal Enemy*." *Prairie Schooner* 48 (Summer 1974): 124–33.

Neighbour Rosicky (1956)

Andes, Cynthia J. "The Bohemian Folk Practice in Neighbour Rosicky." *Western American Literature* 7 (Spring 1972): 63–64.

O Pioneers! (1913)

Charles, Sister Peter Damian. "Love and Death in Willa Cather's *O Pioneers!*" *College Language Association Journal* 9 (December 1965): 140–50.

Fox, Clyde Maynard. "Symbolic Representation in Willa Cather's *O Pioneers!*" *Western American Literature* 9 (November 1974): 187–97.

Giannone, Richard. "*O Pioneers!*: Song of the Earth and Youth." *South Dakota Review* 2 (Spring 1965): 52–68.

Harris, Celia. "*O Pioneers!* . . . An Early Nebraska Review." *Willa Cather Pioneer Memorial* 16 (1972): 2–4.

Miyake, Tsuneo. "On Willa Cather's Pioneer Novels: Referring to *O Pioneers!* and *My Ántonia*." *Kyushu American Literature* 15 (1974): 83–84.

Reaver, J. Russell. "Mythic Motivation in Willa Cather's *O Pioneers!*" *Western Folklore* 27 (January 1968): 19–25.

Schneider, Sister M. Lucy. "*O Pioneers!*: In the Light of Willa Cather's 'Land-Philosophy.'" *Colby Library Quarterly* 8 (June 1968): 55–70.

Slote, Bernice. "Willa Cather as a Regional Writer." *Kansas Quarterly* 2 (Spring 1970): 7–15.

Stouck, David. "*O Pioneers!*: Willa Cather and the Epic Imagination." *Prairie Schooner* 46 (Spring 1972): 23–34.

Thorberg, Raymond. "Willa Cather: From *Alexander's Bridge* to *My Ántonia*." *Twentieth Century Literature* 7 (January 1962): 147–58.

Obscure Destinies (1932)

Randall, John H., III. "Willa Cather: The Middle West Revisited." *New Mexico Quarterly* 31 (Spring 1961): 25–36.

One of Ours (1922)

Cooperman, Stanley. "Willa Cather and the Bright Face of Death." *Literature and Psychology* 3 (1963): 81–87.

Giannone, Richard. "*One of Ours*: Willa Cather's Suppressed, Bitter Melody." *South Atlantic Quarterly* 64 (Winter 1965): 72–86.

Prendergast, Arline F. "*One of Ours*: Willa Cather's Successful Failure." *Dissertation Abstracts International* 32 (1971): 242A (Pittsburgh).

Paul's Case (1905)

Rubin, Larry. "The Homosexual Motif in Willa Cather's *Paul's Case*." *Studies in Short Fiction* 12 (Spring 1975): 127–32.

The Professor's House (1925)

Cecil, L. Moffitt. "Anti-Intellectualism as Theme in Willa Cather's *The Professor's House*." *Research Studies* 37 (1969): 235–41.

Charles, Sister Peter Damian. "*The Professor's House*: An Abode of Love and Death." *Colby Library Quarterly* 8 (June 1968): 70–82.

Fleischmann, Wolfgang Bernard. "Willa Cather's *The Professor's House* and Anatole France's *Le Mannequin d'Osier*." *Romance Notes* 1 (Spring 1960): 92–93.

Fox, Clyde Maynard. "Proponents of Order: Tom Outland and Bishop Latour." *Western American Literature* 4 (Summer 1969): 107–15.

Fox, Clyde Maynard. "Two Primitives: Huck Finn and Tom Outland." *Western American Literature* 1 (Spring 1966): 26–33.

Giannone, Richard. "Music in *The Professor's House*." *College English* 26 (March 1965): 464–69.

Giannone, Richard. "*The Professor's House*: A Novel in Sonata Form." *Colby Library Quarterly* 7 (June 1965): 53–60.

Hart, Clive. "*The Professor's House*: A Shapely Story." *Modern Language Review* 67 (April 1972): 271–81.

Jobes, Lavon Mattes. "Willa Cather's *The Professor's House*." *University Review* (Kansas) 34 (1967): 154–60.

Schroeter, James. "Willa Cather and *The Professor's House*." *Yale Review* 54 (Summer 1965): 494–512.

Stineback, D.C. "Willa Cather's Ironic Masterpiece." *Arizona Quarterly* 29 (Winter 1973): 317–30.

Stouck, David. "Willa Cather and *The Professor's House*: 'Letting Go with the Heart.'" *Western American Literature* 7 (Spring 1972): 13–24.

Sapphira and the Slave Girl (1940)

Jobes, Lavon Mattes. "Willa Cather's Last Novel." *University Review* (Kansas) 34 (1967): 77–80.

Shadows on the Rock (1931)

Bush, Sargent, Jr. "*Shadows on the Rock* and Willa Cather's View of the Past." *Queen's Quarterly* 76 (1969): 269–85.

Murphy, John J. "*Shadows on the Rock*: Cather's Medieval Refuge." *Renascence* 15 (Winter 1963): 76–78.

Schneider, Sister M. Lucy. "Permanence and Promise: Cather's *Shadows on the Rock*." *Renascence* 26 (Winter 1974): 83–94.

The Song of the Lark (1915)

Creutz, Kathleen E. "The Genesis of Willa Cather's *The Song of the Lark*." *Dissertation Abstracts* 29 (1969): 3130A (California, Los Angeles).

Olson, Laurence. "Reconsideration: Willa Cather's *Song of the Lark*." *New Republic* (July 7, 1973): 28–31.

Thorberg, Raymond. "Willa Cather: From *Alexander's Bridge* to *My Ántonia*." *Twentieth Century Literature* 7 (January 1962): 147–58.

MARY CATHERWOOD (1847–1902) U.S.
Bibliography

Blanck, Jacob. "BAL Addenda." *Papers of the Bibliographical Society of America* 55 (1961): 46–47.
General Works

Haworth, C.V. "H. Thompson Home, Oakford, Indiana." *Indiana History Bulletin* 38 (January 1961): 13–15.

SUSANNAH CENTLIVRE (1667?–1723) Great Britain
General Works

Bennett, Gilbert. "Conventions of the Stage Villain." *Anglo-Welsh Review* 14 (1964): 92–102.

Dunkley, John. "An English Version of Régnard's *Joueur*." *Revue de Littérature Comparée* 48 (1974): 107–13.

Faure, Jacqueline. "Two Poems by Susannah Centlivre." *Book Collector* 10 (Spring 1961): 68–69.

Stathas, Thalia. "A Critical Edition of Three Plays by Susannah Centlivre." *Dissertation Abstracts* 26 (1966): 6726 (Stanford).

Stratman, Carl J. "Scotland's First Dramatic Period: *The Edinburgh Theatrical Censor*." *Theatre Notebook* 17 (Spring 1963): 83–86.

Strozier, Robert. "A Short View of Some of Mrs. Centlivre's Celebrat'd Plays, Including a Close Accounting of the Plots, Subplots, Asides, Soliloquies, Etcetera, Contain'd Therein." *Discourse* 7 (Winter 1964): 62–80.

Ten Hoor, Henry. "A Re-Examination of Susannah Centlivre as a Comic Dramatist." *Dissertation Abstracts* 25 (1964): 1928 (Michigan).

White, Robert Benjamin, Jr. "A Study of the *Female Tatler* (1709–1710)." *Dissertation Abstracts* 27 (1967): 3021A (North Carolina).

Individual Works

A Bold Stroke for a Wife (1718)

Burke, Terrence W. "Susannah Centlivre's *A Bold Stroke for a Wife*: A Re-evaluation." *Dissertation Abstracts International* 32 (1972): 4555A (Case Western Reserve).

MARY CHALLANS. *See* Mary Renault

CHARLOTTE CHARKE (fl. 1760s) Great Britain
General Works

Peary, Charles D. "The Chimerical Career of Charlotte Charke." *Restoration and Eighteenth Century Theatre Research* 8 (1969): 1–12.

GERDA CHARLES (fl. 1960s) Great Britain
Individual Works

The Crossing Point (1960)

McDowell, Frederick P. W. "Review of *The Crossing Point* by Gerda Charles and *The Limits of Love* by Frederick Raphael." *Critique* 6 (1963): 143–50.

Logical Girl (1967)

Winegarten, Renee. "The World of Gerda Charles." *Jewish Quarterly* 17 (Summer 1967): 37–40.

A Slanting Light (1963)

McDowell, Frederick P. W. "Review of *A Slanting Light*." *Critique* 7 (1964): 172–75.

MARY ELLEN CHASE (1887–1973) U.S.
Bibliography

Cary, Richard. "A Bibliography of the Published Writings of Mary Ellen Chase." *Colby Library Quarterly* 6 (March 1962): 34–45.

General Works

Chase, Mary Ellen. "Five Literary Portraits." *Massachusetts Review* 3 (Spring 1962): 511–16.

Chase, Mary Ellen. "My Novels about Maine." *Colby Library Quarterly* 6 (March 1962): 14–20.

Dodge, Evelyn Caldwell. "A Critical Study of the Writings of Mary Ellen Chase." *Dissertation Abstracts* 24 (1963): 1614 (Boston).

Duckett, Eleanor S. "Mary Ellen Chase: A Portrait, 1962." *Colby Library Quarterly* 6 (March 1962): 1–4.

Iorio, J.J. "Mary Ellen Chase and the Novel of Regional Crisis." *Colby Library Quarterly* 6 (March 1962): 21–34.

Millbank, Helen Kirkpatrick. "Mary Ellen Chase: Teacher, Writer, Lecturer." *Colby Library Quarterly* 6 (March 1962): 5–13.

"Where Are They Now?" *Newsweek* (February 4, 1963): 8.

LYDIA MARIA CHILD (1802–1880) U.S.
General Works

Hornick, Nancy S., ed. "The Last Appeal: Lydia Maria Child's Antislavery Letters to John C. Underwood." *Virginia Magazine of History and Biography* 79 (January 1971): 45–54.

Tarr, Rodger L. "Emerson's Transcendentalism in Lydia Maria Child's Letter to Carlyle." *Emerson Society Quarterly* 58 (1970): 112–15.

Taylor, Lloyd C., Jr. "Lydia Maria Child: Biographer." *New England Quarterly* 34 (June 1961): 211–27.

Taylor, Lloyd C., Jr. "Lydia Maria Child and the Indians." *Boston Public Library Quarterly* 12 (January 1960): 51–56.

Individual Works

Brackett's Bust of John Brown (1863)

Swennes, Robert H. "Lydia Maria Child: Holographs of *The Hero's Heart* and *Brackett's Bust of John Brown*." *American Literature* 40 (January 1969): 539–42.

The Hero's Heart (1860)

Swennes, Robert H. "Lydia Maria Child: Holographs of *The Hero's Heart* and *Brackett's Bust of John Brown*." *American Literature* 40 (January 1969): 539–42.

Philothea or Plato Against Epicurus: A Novel of the Transcendental Movement in New England (1970)

Child, Lydia Maria. "Philothea or Plato Against Epicurus." *American Transcendental Quarterly* 6 (1970): 1–284.

MARY CHOLMONDELEY [pseud. Pax] (1858?–1925) Great Britain
Individual Works
Red Pottage (1899)

Colby, Vineta. "Devoted Amateur: Mary Cholmondeley and *Red Pottage*." *Essays in Criticism* 20 (April 1970): 213–28.

KATE CHOPIN, née O'Flaherty (1851–1904) U.S.
Bibliography
Bonner, T., Jr. "Kate Chopin: An Annotated Bibliography." *Bulletin of Bibliography* 32 (July–September 1975): 101–5.

Potter, Richard H. "Kate Chopin and Her Critics: An Annotated Checklist." *Missouri Historical Society Bulletin* 26 (July 1970): 306–17.

Seyersted, Per. "Kate Chopin (1851–1904)." *American Literary Realism* 3 (1970): 153–59.
General Works
Arner, Robert D. "Music from a Farther Room: A Study of the Fiction of Kate Chopin." *Dissertation Abstracts International* 31 (1971): 4753A–54A (Penn. State).

Bender, B. "Kate Chopin's Lyrical Short Stories." *Studies in Short Fiction* 11 (Summer 1974): 257–66.

Butcher, Philip. "Two Early Southern Realists in Revival." *College Language Association Journal* 14 (September 1970): 91–95.

Eaton, C. "Breaking a Path for the Liberation of Women in the South." *Georgia Review* 28 (Summer 1974): 193–95.

Fletcher, Marie. "The Southern Woman in the Fiction of Kate Chopin." *Louisiana Historical Quarterly* 7 (Spring 1966): 117–32.

Frisby, James R., Jr. "New Orleans Writers and the Negro: George Washington Cable, Grace King, Ruth McEnery Stuart, Kate Chopin, and Lafcadio Hearn, 1870–1900." *Dissertation Abstracts International* 33 (1972): 2890A (Emory).

Koloski, Bernard J. "Kate Chopin and the Search for a Code of Behavior." *Dissertation Abstracts International* 33 (1972): 2382A (Arizona).

Lally, Joan M. "Kate Chopin: Four Studies." *Dissertation Abstracts International* 34 (1973): 1247A (Utah).

Leary, Lewis. "Kate Chopin and Walt Whitman." *Walt Whitman Review* 16 (December 1970): 120–21.

Leary, Lewis. "Kate Chopin, Liberationist." *Southern Literary Journal* 3 (Fall 1970): 138–44.

"Love in Louisiana—Kate Chopin: A Forgotten Southern Novelist." *Times Literary Supplement* (October 9, 1970): 1163.

Martin, Richard A. "The Fictive World of Kate Chopin." *Dissertation Abstracts International* 32 (1972): 4620A (Northwestern).

Oberbeck, S. K. "St. Louis Woman." *Newsweek* (February 23, 1970): 102B.

Petersen, Peter J. "The Fiction of Kate Chopin." *Dissertation Abstracts International* 33 (1973): 3664A (New Mexico).

Potter, Richard H. "Negroes in the Fiction of Kate Chopin." *Louisiana Historical Quarterly* 12 (Winter 1971): 41–58.

Rocks, James E. "Kate Chopin's Ironic Vision." *Revue de Louisiane/Louisiana Review* 1 (1972): 110–20.

Seyersted, Per. "Kate Chopin: A Critical Biography." *Edda* 71 (1971): 341–66.

Seyersted, Per. "Kate Chopin: An Important St. Louis Writer Reconsidered." *Missouri Historical Society Bulletin* 19 (January 1963): 89–114.

Skaggs, Peggy D. "A Woman's Place: The Search for Identity in Kate Chopin's Female Characters." *Dissertation Abstracts International* 33 (1973): 6325A–26A (Texas A & M).

Zlotnick, Joan. "A Woman's Will: Kate Chopin on Selfhood, Wifehood, and Motherhood." *Markham Review* 1 (October 1968): 1–5.
Individual Works
At the Cadian Ball (1892)

Arner, Robert D. "Kate Chopin's Realism: *At the Cadian Ball* and *The Storm*." *Markham Review* 2 (February 1970): 1–4.

At Fault (1890)

Arner, Robert D. "Landscape Symbolism in Kate Chopin's *At Fault*." *Louisiana Studies* 9 (Fall 1970): 142–53.

The Awakening (1899)

Koloski, Bernard J. "The Swinburne Lines in *The Awakening*." *American Literature* 45 (January 1974): 608–10.

Ladenson, Joyce Ruddel. "Paths to Suicide: Rebellion against Victorian Womanhood in Kate Chopin's *The Awakening*." *Intellect* 104 (July–August 1975): 52–55.

May, John R. "Local Color in *The Awakening*." *Southern Review* (U.S.) 6 (1970): 1031–40.

Milliner, Gladys W. "The Tragic Imperative: *The Awakening* and *The Bell Jar*." *Mary Wollstonecraft Newsletter* 2 (December 1973): 21–27.

Ringe, Donald A. "Romantic Imagery in Kate Chopin's *The Awakening*." *American Literature* 43 (January 1972): 580–88.

Rosen, Kenneth M. "Kate Chopin's *The Awakening*." *Journal of American Studies* 5 (August 1971): 197–99.

Spangler, George. "Kate Chopin's *The Awakening*: A Partial Dissent." *Novel* 3 (Spring 1970): 249–55.

Sullivan, Ruth, and Stewart Smith. "Narrative Stance in Kate Chopin's *The Awakening*." *Studies in American Fiction* 1 (Spring 1973): 62–75.

Wheeler, O.B. "Five Awakenings of Edna Pontellier." *Southern Review* (U.S.) 11 (1975): 118–28.

Wolff, Cynthia G. "Thanatos and Eros: Kate Chopin's *The Awakening*." *American Quarterly* 25 (October 1973): 449–71.

Désirée's Baby (1894)

Arner, Robert D. "Pride and Prejudice: Kate Chopin's *Désirée's Baby*." *Mississippi Quarterly* 25 (Spring 1972): 131–40.

The Storm (1898)

Arner, Robert D. "Kate Chopin's Realism: *At the Cadian Ball* and *The Storm*." *Markham Review* 2 (February 1970): 1–4.

Vagabonds (1895)

Arner, Robert D. "Characterization and the Colloquial Style in Kate Chopin's *Vagabonds*." *Markham Review* 2 (May 1971): 110–12.

AGATHA CHRISTIE, Dame Mallowan (1891–1976) Great Britain
Bibliography
McCarthy, Paul. "The Short Mystery Stories of Agatha Christie: A Checklist." *Armchair Detective* 6 (1972): 16–19.

General Works

Benedict, Stewart H. "Agatha Christie and Murder Most Unsportsman-like." *Claremont Quarterly* 9 (1962): 37–42.

Dueren, Fred. "Hercule Poirot: The Private Life of a Private Eye." *Armchair Detective* 7 (1974): 111–15.

"Horseman, Pass By." *Time* (July 17, 1972): 31.

"The Mallowans." *New Yorker* (October 29, 1966): 51–52.

"People." *Time* (December 10, 1973): 68.

Peters, Margot, and Agate N. Krouse. "Women and Crime: Sexism in Allingham, Sayers, and Christie." *Southwest Review* 59 (Spring 1974): 144–52.

Petschek, W. "Agatha Christie: The World's Most Mysterious Woman." *McCall's* (February 1969): 80.

LADY MARY CHUDLEIGH (fl. 1690–1700) Great Britain
Individual Works
The Ladies Defence (1701)
Coleman, Antony. "*The Provok'd Wife* and *The Ladies Defence*." *Notes and Queries* 17 (March 1970): 88–91.

BEATRICE JOY CHUTE (1913–) U.S.
General Works
"When the Writer Comes of Age." *Bulletin of the New York Public Library* 66 (September 1962): 470–78.

ANN NOLAN CLARK (1898–) U.S.
General Works
Bishop, C.H. "Ann Nolan Clark." *Catholic Library World* 34 (February 1963): 281–86.

CATHERINE ANTHONY CLARK (1892–) Canada
General Works
Selby, Joan. "The Creation of Fantasy: The Fiction of Catherine Anthony Clark." *Canadian Literature*, no. 11 (Winter 1962): 39–45.

MARY COWDEN CLARKE (1809–1898) Great Britain
General Works
Falk, Doris V. "Mary Cowden Clarke and Her East End Injun." *Journal of the Rutgers University Library* 24 (June 1961): 85–89.

McAleer, John J. "Mary Cowden Clarke: Shakespeare's First Woman Editor." *Shakespeare Newsletter* 13 (April 1963): 18.

Nethery, Wallace. "Robert Balmanno, Father-in-Love, Part II." *American Book Collector* 14 (November 1963): 15–20.

Vaughan, Dorothy M. "Celia Thaxter's Library." *Colby Library Quarterly* 6 (December 1964): 536–49.

Individual Works
The Girlhood of Shakespeare's Heroines (1850)

Gross, George C. "Mary Cowden Clarke, *The Girlhood of Shakespeare's Heroines*, and the Sex Education of Victorian Woman." *Victorian Studies* 16 (September 1972): 37–58.

SARAH CLARKE (fl. 1840s–1850s) U.S.
General Works
Myerson, Joel. "True and High-Minded Person: Transcendentalist Sarah Clarke." *Southwest Review* 59 (Spring 1974): 163–72.

MRS. MARY CLAVERS [pseud.] *See* Caroline Kirkland

CATHERINE [KITTY] CLIVE (1711–1785) Great Britain
General Works
Frushell, Richard C. "Kitty Clive as Dramatist." *Durham University Journal* 63 (March 1971): 125–32.

Frushell, Richard C. "The Textual Relationship and Biographical Significance of Two Petite Pieces by Mrs. Catherine (Kitty) Clive." *Restoration and Eighteenth Century Theatre Research* 9 (1970): 51–58.

Individual Works
Sketch of a Fine Lady's Return from a Rout (1763)

Frushell, Richard C. "The Cast of Kitty Clive's *Sketch of a Fine Lady's Return from a Rout.*" *Notes and Queries* 16 (September 1969): 350–51.

ELIZABETH COCHRANE (fl. 1730s) Scotland
General Works
Montgomerie, William A. "Bibliography of the Scottish Ballad Manuscripts 1730–1825, Part II: Elizabeth Cochrane, Her Songbook (?1730)." *Studies in Scottish Literature* 4 (October 1966): 79–88.

SARA COLERIDGE (1802–1852) Great Britain
General Works
Booth, Karen Marshall. "Two Unreported Watermarks." *Publications of the Bibliographical Society of America* 64 (1970): 338–39.

Martin, C.G. "Sara Coleridge: An Unpublished Letter." *Notes and Queries* 14 (February 1967): 51–52.

IVY COMPTON-BURNETT (1892–1969) Great Britain
General Works
"All About Ivy." *Newsweek* (April 23, 1973): 104–5.

Balutowa, Bronislawa. "The Group Dynamics in the Plots of Ivy Compton-Burnett." *Problems of Genre in Literature* (Poland) 13 (1970): 75–94.

Balutowa, Bronislawa. "Type versus Character in the Novels of Ivy Compton-Burnett." *Kwartalnik Neofilologiczny* 17 (1970): 377–98.

Bradbury, Malcolm. "Unhappy Families Are All Alike: New Views of Ivy Compton-Burnett." *Encounter* 41 (July 1973): 71–74.

Brophy, Brigid. "Sir Hereward." *New Statesman* (December 6, 1963): 842.

Curtis, Mary M. "The Moral Comedy of Miss Compton-Burnett." *Wisconsin Studies in Contemporary Literature* 5 (Autumn 1964): 213–21.

Devlin, P. "Alarming Qualities." *Vogue* (September 1965): 252.

Duffy, M. "Household Tyrants." *Time* (August 16, 1971): 73.

Fedden, Robin. "Recollection of Ivy Compton-Burnett." *Cornhill Magazine*, no. 1062 (Winter 1969–1970): 429–38.

Furbank, P.N. "Ivy Compton-Burnett: Butlers and Beliefs." *Encounter* 42 (June 1974): 71–74.

Ginger, John. "Ivy Compton-Burnett." *London Magazine* 9 (January 1970): 58–71.

Gold, Joseph. "Exit Everybody: The Novels of Ivy Compton-Burnett." *Dalhousie Review* 42 (Summer 1962): 227–38.

Hansen, Marlene R. "Victorianism of Ivy Compton-Burnett." *English Studies* 55 (1974): 516–22.

"Interview with Miss Compton-Burnett." *Review of English Literature* 3 (October 1962): 96–112.

Jefferson, D.W. "A Note on Ivy Compton-Burnett." *Review of English Literature* 1 (April 1960): 19–24.

Kermode, Frank. "The House of Fiction: Interviews

with Seven English Novelists." *Partisan Review* 29 (1963): 61–82.

Las Vergnas, Raymond. "Ivy Compton-Burnett." *Revue de Paris* 67 (1960): 114–21.

Levinsky, Ruth. "Literary Trends and Two Novelists: Nathalie Sarraute and Ivy Compton-Burnett." *Proceedings of the Conference of College Teachers of English of Texas* 37 (1972): 25–28.

MacSween, Roderick J. "Ivy Compton-Burnett: Merciless Understanding." *Antigonish Review* 7 (Autumn 1971): 39–46.

May, James Boyer. "Ivy Compton-Burnett: A Time Exposure." *Trace* 49 (Summer 1963): 92–99.

McCabe, Bernard. "Ivy Compton-Burnett: An English Eccentric." *Critique* 3 (1960): 47–63.

McCarthy, Mary. "The Inventions of Ivy Compton-Burnett." *Encounter* 28 (November 1966): 19–31.

Mitchell, J. "Green Room: On Adapting Ivy." *Plays and Players* 22 (April 1975): 8–10.

Mitchell, Julin. "Ivy Compton-Burnett." *New Statesman* (September 5, 1969): 316.

O'Reilly, William M., Jr. "Nature and Convention in the Novels of Ivy Compton-Burnett." *Dissertation Abstracts International* 33 (1972): 2946A (Connecticut).

Pittock, M. "Ivy Compton-Burnett's Use of Dialogue." *English Studies* 51 (1970): 43–46.

Preston, John. " 'The Matter in a Word.' " *Essays in Criticism* 10 (July 1960): 348–56.

Ruff, Lillian M. "Ivy Compton-Burnett: An Old Hollowegian." *Notes and Queries* 19 (September 1972): 337–38.

Shaw, Elizabeth Baird. "The Comic Novels of Ivy Compton-Burnett and Nathalie Sarraute." *Dissertation Abstracts International* 35 (1975): 7923A–24A (Colorado).

Spurling, Hilary. "The First and the Last." *New Statesman* (February 5, 1971): 182–83.

Sykes, Christopher. "The Enigma of Ivy." *New Statesman* (March 2, 1973): 308–9.

Taylor, John R. "Dolores." *Times Literary Supplement* (February 26, 1971): 244.

Individual Works

Pastors and Masters (1925)

Greenfield, Stanley B. "*Pastors and Masters*: The Spoils of Genius." *Criticism* 2 (1960): 66–80.

ROSE TERRY COOKE (1827–1892) U.S.

Bibliography

Toth, Susan A. "Rose Terry Cooke (1827–1892)."

American Literary Realism 4 (1971): 170–76.

General Works

Downey, Jean. "Atlantic Friends: Howells and Rose Terry Cooke." *American Notes and Queries* 1 (May 1963): 132–33.

Downey, Jean. "Three Unpublished Letters: Howells-Rose Terry Cooke." *American Literature* 32 (January 1961): 463–65.

Downey, Jean. "Whittier and Rose Cooke: Unpublished Letters." *Quaker History* 52 (Spring 1963): 33–36.

Toth, Susan A. "More than Local-Color: A Reappraisal of Rose Terry Cooke, Mary Wilkins Freeman and Alice Brown." *Dissertation Abstracts* 30 (1969): 3004A (Minnesota).

Wood, Ann Douglas. "The Literature of Impoverishment: The Women Local Colorists in America 1865–1914." *Women's Studies* 1 (1972): 3–40.

INA DONNA COOLBRITH (1842–1928) U.S.

General Works

Graham, Ina Agnes. "My Aunt, Ina Coolbrith." *Pacific Historian* 17 (Fall 1973): 12–19.

Hubbard, George U. "Ina Coolbrith's Friendship with John Greenleaf Whittier." *New England Quarterly* 45 (March 1972): 109–18.

SUSAN FENIMORE COOPER (1813–1894) U.S.

General Works

Bayn, Max, and Percy Matenko. "The Odyssey of *The Water Witch* and a Susan Fenimore Cooper Letter." *New York History* 51 (January 1970): 33–41.

MARIE CORELLI [pseud. of Mary Mackay] (1855–1924) Great Britain

Bibliography

Fleisher, Frederic. "Marie Corelli: The Woman and Her Works." *Moderna Språk* 60 (1966): 7–16.

Kowalczyk, Richard L. "A Bibliography of Marie Corelli." *Bulletin of Bibliography* 30 (October–December 1973): 141–42.

General Works

Glasheen, Adaline. "The Authoress of *Paradise Lost*." *A Wake Newsletter* 7 (December 1970): 83–87.

Huff, Chester C., Jr. "The Novels of Marie Corelli: Their Themes and Their Popularity as an Index to

Popular Taste." *Dissertation Abstracts* 31 (1971): 4718A–19A (Colorado).

Kowalczyk, Richard L. "In Vanished Summertime: Marie Corelli and Popular Culture." *Journal of Popular Culture* 7 (Spring 1974): 850–63.

Kowalczyk, Richard L. "Marie Corelli and Arthur Severn's Reputation as an Artist." *Modern Philology* 66 (May 1969): 322–27.

Kowalczyk, Richard L. "New Evidence on Marie Corelli and Arthur Severn: Some Unpublished Letters." *English Literature in Transition* 13 (1970): 27–36.

CHARLES EGBERT CRADDOCK [pseud.]. *See* Mary Noailles Murfree

ADELAIDE CRAPSEY (1878–1914) U.S.
Bibliography
Slater, John Rothwell. "The Adelaide Crapsey Collection." *University of Rochester Library Bulletin* 16 (Spring 1961): 37–40.
General Works
Goodwin, K. L. "William Soutar, Adelaide Crapsey, and Imagism." *Studies in Scottish Literature* 3 (October 1965): 96–100.

Smith, Susan S. "The Poems of Adelaide Crapsey: A Critical Edition with an Introduction and Notes." *Dissertation Abstracts International* 33 (1972): 331A (Rochester).

FRANCES CRARY (fl. 1960s) U.S.
General Works
Linenthal, Mark. "The Poetry of Frances Crary." *Contact* 3 (September 1961): 129.

ELIZABETH LADY CRAVEN (fl. 1780s) Great Britain
General Works
Franke, Wolfgang. "Elizabeth Lady Craven on Lady

Mary Wortley Montagu: Some Eighteenth-Century Hints on the Authorship of the Five Spurious Letters." *Notes and Queries* 20 (November 1973): 417–20.

MARGARET CRAVEN (1901?–) U.S.
General Works
Foote, T. "A Swimmer's Tale." *Time* (January 28, 1974): 73.

ISABELLA VALANCY CRAWFORD (1850–1886) Canada (Born in Ireland)
General Works
Livesay, Dorothy. "Tennyson's Daughter or Wilderness Child? The Factual and the Literary Background of Isabella Valancy Crawford." *Journal of Canadian Fiction* 2 (1973): 161–67.

Martin, Mary F. "The Short Life of Isabella Valancy Crawford." *Dalhousie Review* 52 (Autumn 1972): 390–400.
Individual Works
The Canoe (1884)
Ower, John B. "Isabella Valancy Crawford: *The Canoe.*" *Canadian Literature*, no. 34 (Autumn 1967): 54–62.

Malcolm's Katie (1884)
Hughes, Kenneth J., and Birk Sproxton. " 'Malcolm's Katie': Images and Songs." *Canadian Literature*, no. 65 (Summer 1975): 55–64.

JANE CROOKS [pseud.]. *See* Jean Devanny

DYMPHNA CUSACK (1904–) Australia
General Works
Baker, Catherine A.W. "Dymphna Cusak: A Biographical Note." *Armidale and District Historical Society Journal and Proceedings* 15 (1971–1972): 77–79.

D

CHARLOTTE DACRE. *See* Rose Matilda

ALICE DALGLIESH (1893–) U.S.
General Works
"You Meet Such Interesting People." *Publishers Weekly* (March 21, 1960): 37–38.

ELIZABETH DALY (1878–1967) U.S.
General Works
Waldron, Ann. "The Golden Years of Elizabeth Daly." *Armchair Detective* 7 (1973): 25–28.

KATHLEEN DALZIEL. *See* Kath Walker

MARY DANBY (1941?–) Great Britain
General Works
"Newsmakers." *Newsweek* (April 16, 1973): 51.

MARCIA DAVENPORT, née Gluck (1903–) U.S.
General Works
"Reticent Autobiographer." *Time* (December 8, 1967): 119.
Whitbread, J. "Remarkable Marcia Davenport." *Good Housekeeping* (April 1960): 26.

ELIZABETH GOULD DAVIS (1910?–1974) U.S.
General Works
Lerman, R. "In Memoriam." *Ms.* (December 1974): 74–75.

JULIA DAVIS (1904–) U.S.
General Works
"Julia Davis." *Negro History Bulletin* 25 (April 1962): 168.

REBECCA HARDING DAVIS (1831–1910) U.S.
Bibliography

Eppard, P.B. "Rebecca Harding Davis: A Misattribution." *Papers of the Bibliographical Society of America* 69 (1975): 265–67.
General Works
Austin, James C. "Success and Failure of Rebecca Harding Davis." *Midcontinent American Studies Journal* 3 (1962): 44–49.
Grayburn, William Frazer. "The Major Fiction of Rebecca Harding Davis." *Dissertation Abstracts* 26 (1965): 2211 (Penn. State).

MARY DAVYS (fl. 1750s) Great Britain
General Works
Stefanson, Donald H. "The Works of Mary Davys: A Critical Edition (Vol. 1 and 2)." *Dissertation Abstracts International* 32 (1972): 5203A (Iowa).

SARAH MORGAN DAWSON (fl. 1860s) U.S.
General Works
Williams, Ora G. "Muskets and Magnolias: Four Civil War Diaries by Louisiana Girls." *Louisiana Studies* 4 (Fall 1965): 187–99.

MARGARET DELAND, née Margaretta Wade Campbell (1857–1945) U.S.
Individual Works
John Ward, Preacher (1888)
Kantor, J. R. K. "*The Damnation of Theron Ware* and *John Ward, Preacher*." *Serif* 3 (March 1966): 16–21.

MARY DELANY (1700–1788) Great Britain
General Works
Lyons, N.J.L. "William Shenstone, Mary Graves and Mrs. Delany." *Notes and Queries* 19 (October 1972): 379–80.

Marie Louise de la Ramée. *See* Ouida

Jean Devanny [pseud. Jane Crooks] (fl. 1920s–1940s)
General Works
Store, Ronald E., and Richard Anderson. "Jean Devanny: A Biographical and Bibliographical Note." *Australian Academic and Research Libraries* (1969): 66–72.

Nicolette Devas, née MacNamara (1911–) Great Britain
General Works
"Bohemian Girl." *Time* (April 7, 1967): 98.

Monica Dickens (1915–) Great Britain
General Works
Hamblen, Abigail. "An Another Dickens Come to Judgment." *Cresset* 33 (January 1970): 12–15.
"Where Are They Now?" *Newsweek* (December 27, 1965): 9.

Emily Dickinson (1830–1886) U.S.
Bibliography
Buckingham, Willis J. "1880–1968 Addenda to the Buckingham Bibliography." *Emily Dickinson Bulletin* 26 (1974): 103–28.
Freis, Susan. "Emily Dickinson: A Checklist of Criticism, 1930–1966." *Papers of the Bibliographical Society of America* 61 (1967): 359–85.
Ledwell, Sister Marguerite. "Some Historical Criticism of Dickinson's Poetry." *Studies in American Literature* 8 (1972): 1–14.
Morey, Frederick L. "Emily Dickinson Treasures in the Library of Congress." *Emily Dickinson Bulletin* 22 (1972): 125–27.
Morey, Frederick L. "Major Emily Dickinson Collections." *Emily Dickinson Bulletin* 2 (1968): 1–2.
Morey, Frederick L. "Minor Emily Dickinson Collections." *Emily Dickinson Bulletin* 4 (1968): 2–9.
Smidt, Aagot K. "Emily Dickinson." *Vinduet* 15 (Fall 1961): 220–23.
White, William. "Emily Dickinsoniana: An Annotated Checklist of Books about the Poet." *Bulletin of Bibliography* 26 (October–December 1969): 100–105.
White, William. "Emily Dickinson's 'An Amazing Sense': Addendum to Buckingham." *Papers of the Bibliographical Society of America* 68 (1974): 66–67.
White, William. "Emily Dickinson's *Poems: Third Series:* A Bibliographical Note." *Serif* 9 (Summer 1972): 37–41.

General Works
Adams, Richard P. "Dickinson Concrete." *Emerson Society Quarterly* 44 (1966): 31–35.
Agrawal, Ishwar Nath. "Emily Dickinson: A Study of Diction." *Literary Criterion* 5 (1962): 95–100.
Agrawal, Ishwar Nath. "Emily Dickinson and the Living Word." *Literary Criterion* 6 (1965): 52–55.
Anderson, John Q. "Emily Dickinson's Butterflies and Tigers." *Emerson Society Quarterly* 47 (1967): 43–48.
Anderson, John Q. "The Funeral Procession in Dickinson's Poetry." *Emerson Society Quarterly* 44 (1966): 8–12.
Anderson, Paul W. "The Metaphysical Mirth of Emily Dickinson." *Georgia Review* 20 (Spring 1966): 72–83.
Ando, Midori. "A View of Nature in Emily Dickinson's Poems." *Gakuen* 280 (April 1963): 63–76.
Anselmo, Sister Peter Marie. "Renunciation in the Poems and Letters of Emily Dickinson." *Dissertation Abstracts* 26 (1965): 2178 (Notre Dame).
Anthony, Mother Mary. "Emily Dickinson's Scriptural Echoes." *Massachusetts Review* 2 (Spring 1961): 557–61.
Arp, Thomas Roscoe. "Dramatic Poses in the Poetry of Emily Dickinson." *Dissertation Abstracts* 23 (1962): 2130–31 (Stanford).
Avery, Christine. "Science, Technology, and Emily Dickinson." *British Association for American Studies Bulletin* 9 (1964): 47–55.
Baldi, Sergio. "The Poetry of Emily Dickinson." *Sewanee Review* 68 (July 1960): 438–49.
Ball, Kenneth R. "Emily Dickinson and the Beautiful." *Southern Humanities Review* 7 (Summer 1973): 287–94.
Ballanger, Martha. "The Metaphysical Echo." *English Studies in Africa* 8 (March 1965): 71–80.
Banzer, Judith. " 'Compound Manner': Emily Dickinson and the Metaphysical Poets." *American Literature* 32 (January 1961): 417–33.
Bickman, Martin Elliott. "Voyages of the Mind's Return: A Jungian Study of Poe, Emerson, Whitman, and Dickinson." *Dissertation Abstracts International* 36 (1975): 266A (Penn.).
Birdsall, Virginia Ogden. "Emily Dickinson's

Intruder in the Soul." *American Literature* 37 (March 1965): 54–64.

Bolin, Donald W. "Emily Dickinson and the Particular Object." *Forum* 3 (Fall 1962): 28–31.

Bouraoui, H. A. " 'Leaning against the Sun': Emily Dickinson, the Poet as Seer." *Research Studies* 37 (1969): 208–17.

Bridgman, Richard. "Emily Dickinson: A Winter Poet in a Spring Land." *Moderna Sprak* 56 (1962): 1–8.

Burns, Graham. "Emily Dickinson's Creative Passivity." *Critical Review* 16 (1973): 73–90.

Cambon, Glauco. "On Translating Dickinson." *Chelsea Review* 7 (May 1960): 77–87.

Cambon, Glauco. "Violence and Abstraction in Emily Dickinson." *Sewanee Review* 68 (July 1960): 450–64.

Cameron, Kenneth Walter. "Emily Dickinson and Hesperian Depression." *American Transcendental Quarterly* 14 (1972): 184–85.

Cameron, Sharon. "Emily Dickinson's Poetry: A Study of Tone." *Dissertation Abstracts International* 34 (1973): 307A (Brandeis).

Capps, Jack Lee. "Emily Dickinson's Reading, 1836–1886: A Study of the Sources of Her Poetry." *Dissertation Abstracts* 24 (1963): 1611–12 (Penn.).

Carter, Charles W. " 'In Sumptuous Solitude': A Study of Method and Design in the Love Poems of Emily Dickinson." *Dissertation Abstracts International* 33 (1973): 4402A (North Carolina).

Cate, Hollis L. "Emily Dickinson and 'The Prisoner of Chillon.' " *American Notes and Queries* 6 (September 1967): 6–7.

Chaliff, Cynthia. "Emily Dickinson Against the World: An Interpretation of the Poet's Life and Work." *Dissertation Abstracts* 28 (1967): 1070A (N.Y.U.).

Chaliff, Cynthia. "The Psychology of Economics in Emily Dickinson." *Literature and Psychology* 18 (1968): 93–100.

Chrysostom, Sister Mary. " 'Pang Is Good': The Gamut of Joy in Emily Dickinson's Poems." *Wisconsin Studies in Literature* 3 (1966): 24–36.

Clemons, W. "Real Emily." *Newsweek* (January 6, 1975): 59.

Cody, John. "Emily Dickinson and Nature's Dining Room." *Michigan Quarterly Review* 7 (Fall 1968): 249–54.

Cody, John. "Emily Dickinson's Vesuvian Face." *American Imago* 24 (Fall 1967): 161–80.

Cody, John. "Metamorphosis of a Malady: Summary of a Psychoanalytic Study of Emily Dickinson." *Hartford Studies in Literature* 2 (1970): 113–32.

Coleman, Earle C. "Emily Dickinson." *Princeton University Library Chronicle* 25 (Spring 1964): 230–31.

Coursen, Herbert R., Jr. "Nature's Center." *College English* 24 (March 1963): 467–69.

Cunningham, J. V. "Sorting Out: The Case of Dickinson." *Southern Review* (U.S.) 5 (1969): 436–56.

Curtis, Jared R. "Edward Taylor and Emily Dickinson: Voices and Visions." *Susquehanna University Studies* 7 (June 1964): 159–67.

Daghlian, Carlos. "Emily Dickinson in the Brazilian Classroom." *Emily Dickinson Bulletin* 24 (1973): 227–30.

Dailey, Mary Ann. "The Locomotive as Visualized by Walt Whitman and Emily Dickinson." *Lit* 6 (Spring 1965): 23–25.

Das, Sarbeswar. "Emily Dickinson's Letters to Her 'Master.' " *Calcutta Review* 2 (January–March 1971): 353–63.

Davidson, Frank. " 'This Consciousness': Emerson and Dickinson." *Emerson Society Quarterly* 44 (1966): 2–7.

Davis, William F. "The Art of Peace: The Moral Vision of Emily Dickinson." *Dissertation Abstracts* 29 (1968): 896A (Yale).

D'Avanzo, Mario L. "Emily Dickinson's and Emerson's Presentiment." *Emerson Society Quarterly* 58 (1970): 157–59.

D'Avanzo, Mario L. " 'Unto the White Creator': The Snow of Dickinson and Emerson." *New England Quarterly* 45 (June 1972): 278–80.

DeJong, Mary Cynthia. "Structure in the Poetry of Ralph Waldo Emerson, Emily Dickinson and Robert Frost." *Dissertation Abstracts* 29 (1968): 867A (Michigan).

Di Salvo, Leta Perry. "The Arrested Syllable: A Study of the Death Poetry of Emily Dickinson." *Dissertation Abstracts* 27 (1966): 1816A (Denver).

Donaldson, Scott. "Minding Emily Dickinson's Business." *New England Quarterly* 41 (December 1968): 574–82.

Drew, David P. "Emily Brontë and Emily Dickinson as Mystic Poets." *Brontë Society Transactions* 15

(1968): 227–32.

Elliott, Gary D. "The Solitary Dissenter: A Study of Emily Dickinson's Concept of God." *Emily Dickinson Bulletin* 21 (1972): 32–48.

Emblen, D. L. "A Comment on Structural Patterns in the Poetry of Emily Dickinson." *American Literature* 37 (March 1965): 64–65.

England, Martha Winburn. "Emily Dickinson and Isaac Watts: Puritan Hymnodist." *Bulletin of the New York Public Library* 69 (February 1965): 83–116.

Fasel, Ida. " 'Called Back': A Note on Emily Dickinson." *Iowa English Yearbook* 8 (Fall 1963): 73.

Fasel, Ida. "Emily Dickinson's Walden." *Iowa English Yearbook* 7 (Fall 1962): 22–28.

Feit, Joanne, " 'Another Way to See': Dickinson and Her English Romantic Precursors." *Dissertation Abstracts International* 35 (1975): 4514A (Yale).

Finkelstein, Miriam R. Banker. "Emily Dickinson and the Practice of Poetry." *Dissertation Abstracts International* 32 (1971): 2683A (S.U.N.Y., Stony Brook).

Fles, Robert A. "Round the Steep Air: Visual and Kinesthetic Imagery in the Poetry of Emily Dickinson." *Dissertation Abstracts International* 33 (1972): 7210A–11A (Michigan State).

Flick, Robert Gene. "Emily Dickinson: Mystic and Skeptic." *Dissertation Abstracts* 29 (1967): 227A (Florida).

Folsom, L. Edwin. " 'The Souls that Snow': Winter in the Poetry of Emily Dickinson." *American Literature* 47 (November 1975): 361–76.

Ford, Thomas Wellborn. "Emily Dickinson and Death." *Midwest Quarterly* 4 (Autumn 1962): 33–44.

Ford, Thomas Wellborn. "Emily Dickinson and the Civil War." *University of Kansas City Review* 31 (1965): 199–203.

Frank, Bernhard. "The Wiles of Words: Ambiguity in Emily Dickinson's Poetry." *Dissertation Abstracts* 27 (1966): 1784A (Pittsburgh).

Franklin, R.W. "Two Emily Dickinson Manuscripts." *Papers of the Bibliographical Society of America* 69 (1975): 114–15.

Franklin, Ralph W. "Early Editing of the Poetry of Emily Dickinson." *Dissertation Abstracts* 26 (1965): 3335 (Northwestern).

Fraser, G.S. "Muffled Poetry." *New Statesman* (October 13, 1961): 520–21.

Freeman, Margaret H. "Emily Dickinson's Prosody: A Study in Metrics." *Dissertation Abstracts International* 33 (1972): 2915A (Massachusetts).

Funato, Hideo. "On Emily Dickinson." *Kamereon* 5 (August 1962): 38–49.

Garrison, J. M. "Emily Dickinson: From Ballerina to Gymnast." *English Literary History* 42 (Spring 1975): 107–24.

Garrow, A. Scott. "Alcoholic Beverage Imagery in the Poems of Emily Dickinson." *Markham Review* 2 (September 1969): 12–16.

Gelpi, Albert Joseph. "The Business of Circumference: The Mind and Art of Emily Dickinson." *Dissertation Abstracts* 22 (1962): 137 (Harvard).

Gimmestad, Nancy C. "Lamps and Lenses: Emily Dickinson and Her Adolescent Audience." *Dissertation Abstracts International* 33 (1973): 6310A (Michigan).

Goffin, Robert. "Emily Dickinson." *New Hungarian Quarterly* 5 (Autumn 1964): 181–86.

Goudie, Andrea Kay. "The Earth Has Many Keys: A Study of Emily Dickinson's Responses to Nature." *Dissertation Abstracts* 30 (1969): 1134A (Indiana).

Greene, Elsa. "Emily Dickinson Was a Poetess." *College English* 34 (October 1972): 63–70.

Greene, Elsa. "The Splintered Crown: A Study of Eve and Emily Dickinson." *Dissertation Abstracts* 31 (1969): 387A (Minnesota).

Griffith, Clark. "Emily and 'Him': A Modern Approach to Emily Dickinson's Love Poetry." *Iowa English Yearbook* 6 (Fall 1961): 13–22.

Griffith, Clark. "Emily Dickinson's Love Poetry." *University of Kansas City Review* 27 (1960): 93–100.

Grolnick, Simon A. "Emily and the Psychobiographer." *Literature and Psychology* 23 (1973): 68–81.

Grover, D.C. "Garland's Emily Dickinson: A Case of Mistaken Identity." *American Literature* 46 (May 1974): 219–20.

Hagenbuchze, Rolland. "Precision and Indeterminacy in the Poetry of Emily Dickinson." *Emerson Society Quarterly* n.s. 20 (1974): 33–56.

Hall, Sister Mary Louise. "The Relation of Love and Death in the Poetry of Emily Dickinson." *Dissertation Abstracts International* 32 (1971): 1512A (Loyola, Chicago).

Higgins, David James Monroe. "Portrait of Emily Dickinson: The Poet and Her Prose." *Dissertation*

Abstracts 22 (1961): 246–47 (Columbia).

Higgins, David James Monroe. "Twenty-five Poems by Emily Dickinson: Unpublished Variant Versions." *American Literature* 38 (March 1966): 1–21.

Hijiya, James A. "The Rascal Emily Dickinson." *Emily Dickinson Bulletin* 24 (1973): 224–26.

Holmes, Theodore. "The Voice of a Poet: The Art of Emily Dickinson." *Dalhousie Review* 48 (Winter 1968–1969): 551–55.

Howard, Richard. "A Consideration of the Writings of Emily Dickinson." *Prose* 6 (1973): 67–97.

Howard, Ursula Elisabeth. "The Mystical Trends in the Poetry of Emily Dickinson and Annette von Droste-Hülshoff." *Dissertation Abstracts International* 35 (1975): 4525A (Illinois).

Hughes, James Michos. "The Dialectic of Death in Poe, Dickinson, Emerson and Whitman" *Dissertation Abstracts* 31 (1969): 1280A (Penn.).

Hungville, Maurice. "Creation and Salvation: A Study of the Pain Images in the Major Themes." *Emily Dickinson Bulletin* 24 (1973): 231–33.

Iwayama, Tajiro. "Process of Transition of Emily Dickinson's Idea: From Death to Immortality." *Studies in the Humanities* 64 (March 1963): 1–26.

Jennings, Elizabeth. "Emily Dickinson and Poetry of the Inner Life." *Review of English Literature* 3 (April 1962): 78–87.

Jones, Betty H. " 'Experience Is the Angled Road': Patterns of Spiritual Experience in the Poetry of Emily Dickinson." *Dissertation Abstracts International* 33 (1973): 5681A–82A (Bryn Mawr).

Jones, Rowena Revis. "Emily Dickinson's 'Flood Subject': Immortality." *Dissertation Abstracts* 21 (1960): 1554–55 (Northwestern).

Kahn, Salamatullah. "The Love Poetry of Emily Dickinson." *Literary Criterion* 6 (1965): 37–51.

Kappel, Lawrence. "Emily Dickinson and the Private Vision." *Dissertation Abstracts International* 33 (1973): 4348A (Indiana).

Kaufman, J.S. "Emily Dickinson and the Involvement of Retreat." *Tulane Studies in English* 21 (1974): 77–90.

Kher, Inder Nath. "The Landscape of Absence: Emily Dickinson's Poetry." *Dissertation Abstracts* 30 (1970): 224A (Alberta).

Kintgen, Eugene R. "Nonrecoverable Deletion and Compression in Poetry." *Foreign Language* 9 (1972): 98–104.

Kohn, John S. Van E. "Giving Emily Dickinson to the World." *Princeton University Library Chronicle* 31 (Autumn 1969): 47–54.

Kriesberg, Ruth M. "The Poetry of Emily Dickinson." *Dissertation Abstracts* 27 (1967): 3872A–73A (N.Y.U.).

Lair, Robert L. "Emily Dickinson's Fracture of Grammar." *Dissertation Abstracts* 27 (1967): 3052A–53A (Ohio State).

Lambert, Robert Graham, Jr. "The Prose of a Poet: A Critical Study of Emily Dickinson's Letters." *Dissertation Abstracts* 29 (1968): 1228A (Pittsburgh).

Larkin, Philip. "Big Victims: Emily Dickinson and Walter de la Mare." *New Statesman* (March 13, 1970): 367–68.

Laverty, Carroll D. "Structural Patterns in Emily Dickinson's Poetry." *Emerson Society Quarterly* 44 (1966): 12–17.

Lawrence, Robert R. "The Mind Alone, Part II." *Emily Dickinson Bulletin* 22 (1972): 107–24.

Leyda, Jay, and George Monteiro. "Refutation of 'Fugitive' Poems." *Emily Dickinson Bulletin* 24 (1973): 207–9.

Lindberg, Brita. "Emily Dickinson's Punctuation." *Studia Neophilologica* 37 (1965): 327–59.

Lindberg, Brita. "The Theme of Death in Emily Dickinson's Poetry." *Studia Neophilologica* 34 (1962): 269–81.

Long, E. Hudson. "Tom Sawyer's 'Pitchiola.' " *Twainian* 20 (September–October 1961): 4.

Luisi, David. "Some Aspects of Emily Dickinson's Food and Liquor Poems." *English Studies* 52 (1971): 32–40.

Lynen, John F. "Three Uses of the Present: The Historian's, the Critic's, and Emily Dickinson's." *College English* 28 (November 1966): 126–36.

Lyons, Eleanor. "A Psychiatric Look at Emily Dickinson." *Hartford Studies in Literature* 4 (1972): 174–79.

Mabbott, Thomas O. " 'Boanerges' a Horse?" *American Notes and Queries* 2 (December 1963): 57.

Manierre, William R. "Emily Dickinson: Visions and Revisions." *Texas Studies in Literature and Language* 5 (Spring 1963): 5–16.

Mann, John S. "The Leashed Serpent: A Study of Emily Dickinson's Poetry." *Dissertation Abstracts International* 33 (1972): 1735A (Penn.).

Marcus, Mordecai. "Walt Whitman and Emily Dickinson." *Personalist* 43 (Autumn 1962): 497–514.

McCarthy, Paul. "An Approach to Emily Dickinson's Poetry." *Emerson Society Quarterly* 44 (1966): 22–31.

McElderry, Bruce Robert, Jr. "Emily Dickinson: Viable Transcendentalist." *Emerson Society Quarterly* 44 (1966): 17–21.

McIntosh, Margaret. "Emily Dickinson's Poems about Pain: A Study of Interrelated Moral, Theological, and Linguistic Freedoms." *Dissertation Abstracts* 27 (1967): 166A (Harvard).

Merideth, Robert. "Emily Dickinson and the Acquisitive Society." *New England Quarterly* 37 (December 1964): 435–52.

Miller, James E., Jr. "Emily Dickinson: The Thunder's Tongue." *Minnesota Review* 2 (Spring 1962): 289–304.

Miller, James E., Jr. "Emily Dickinson's Bright Orthography." *Hudson Review* 14 (Summer 1961): 301–6.

Moldenhauer, Joseph J. "Emily Dickinson's Ambiguity: Notes on Technique." *Emerson Society Quarterly* 44 (1966): 35–44.

Molson, Francis Joseph. "The 'Forms' of God: A Study of Emily Dickinson's Search for and Test of God." *Dissertation Abstracts* 26 (1965): 5415–16 (Notre Dame).

Monteiro, George. "Emily Dickinson and Brazil." *Notes and Queries* 9 (August 1962): 312–13.

Monteiro, George. "Emily Dickinson's Brazilian Poems." *Inter-American Review of Bibliography* 22 (October–December 1972): 404–10.

Monteiro, George. "The One and Many Emily Dickinsons." *American Literary Realism* 7 (1974): 137–42.

Morey, Frederick L. "The Austin Dickinson–Mabel Todd Relationship." *Higginson Journal of Poetry* 3 (1973): 67–76.

Morey, Frederick L. "Emily Dickinson's Literary History." *Dissertation Abstracts International* 33 (1972): 320A (Howard).

Morey, Frederick L. "Evaluation of Japanese Dickinsonian Scholarship." *Emily Dickinson Bulletin* 21 (1972): 57–77.

Morey, Frederick L. "The Four Fundamental Archetypes in Mythology as Exemplified in Emily Dickinson's Poems." *Emily Dickinson Bulletin* 24 (1973): 195–206.

Morey, Frederick L. "From Reading to Publishing Emily Dickinson: The Pre-Natal History of the *Emily Dickinson Bulletin*." *Emily Dickinson Bulletin* 22 (1972): 128–30.

Morey, Frederick L. "Placing Dickinson in a School." *Markham Review* 1 (May 1969): 18–20.

Morey, Frederick L. "The Poetry Levels of Emily Dickinson." *Markham Review* 2 (October 1970): 74–78.

Morey, Frederick L. "Reader's Edition: History and Suggestions." *Emily Dickinson Bulletin* 23 (1973): 144–55.

Morey, Frederick L. "Reference Books of the 1970's Shore Up Emily Dickinson's Reputation." *Emily Dickinson Bulletin* 23 (1973): 172–83.

Mudge, Jean McC. "Emily Dickinson and the Image of Home." *Dissertation Abstracts International* 34 (1973): 3420A (Yale).

Mulqueen, James E. "Is Emerson's Work Central to the Poetry of Emily Dickinson?" *Emily Dickinson Bulletin* 24 (1973): 211–20.

Newman, Charles. "Candor Is the Only Wile." *TriQuarterly* 7 (Fall 1966): 39–64.

Nims, Irene D. "Tone in the Poetry of Emily Dickinson: A Linguistic Analysis with Pedagogical Reflections." *Dissertation Abstracts International* 32 (1972): 4594A (Indiana).

Noda, Hisashi. "Emily Dickinson and Transcendentalism." *Kyushu American Literature* 11 (1968): 44–58.

Noda, Hisashi. "Emily Dickinson's Poetry: An Essay on the Symbols of 'Death.' " *Kyushu American Literature* 6 (1963): 23–29.

Noda, Hisashi. "Notes on Emily Dickinson." *Kyushu American Literature* 5 (1962): 63–70.

Noverr, Douglas A. "Emily Dickinson and the Art of Despair." *Emily Dickinson Bulletin* 23 (1973): 161–67.

O'Brien, Anthony. "Emily Dickinson: The World, the Body, and the Reflective Life." *Melbourne Critical Review* 9 (1966): 69–80.

Olpin, Larry Roy. "The Comic Spirit of Emily Dickinson." *Dissertation Abstracts International* 32 (1971): 394A (Massachusetts).

O'Shea, Dennis J. "Dickinson's Search for Metaphors: A Study of Selected Images." *Dissertation Abstracts International* 33 (1973): 5740A (Oregon).

Packard, J.K. "The Christ Figure in Dickinson's Poetry." *Renascence* 22 (Autumn 1969): 26–33.

Parsons, Thornton H. "The Indefatigable Casuist." *University Review* (Kansas) 30 (1963): 19–25.

Patterson, Rebecca. "The Cardinal Points Symbolism of Emily Dickinson." *Midwest Quarterly* 14 (Summer 1973): 293–317; 15 (Autumn 1973): 31–48.

Patterson, Rebecca. "The Dating of Emily Dickinson's Letters to the Bowles Family, 1858–1862." *Emily Dickinson Bulletin* 21 (1972): 1–28.

Patterson, Rebecca. "Emily Dickinson's Debt to Gunderode." *Midwest Quarterly* 9 (Summer 1967): 331–54.

Patterson, Rebecca. "Emily Dickinson's 'Double' Time: Masculine Identification." *American Imago* 28 (Winter 1971): 330–62.

Patterson, Rebecca. "Emily Dickinson's Geography: Latin America." *Papers on Language and Literature* 5 (1969): 441–57.

Patterson, Rebecca. "Emily Dickinson's Jewel Imagery." *American Literature* 42 (January 1971): 495–520.

Patterson, Rebecca. "Emily Dickinson's Palette." *Midwest Quarterly* 5 (Summer 1964): 271–91; 6 (Autumn 1964): 97–117.

Perrine, Laurence. "All of Emily Dickinson." *Southwest Review* 46 (Spring 1961): 178–79.

Perrine, Laurence. "Dickinson Distorted." *College English* 36 (October 1974): 212–13.

Phelan, Joan D. "Puritan Tradition and Emily Dickinson's Poetic Practice." *Dissertation Abstracts International* 33 (1973): 5136A (Bryn Mawr).

Phillips, Emma J. "The Mystical World View of Emily Dickinson." *Dissertation Abstracts* 28 (1967): 2259A (Indiana).

Pollak, Vivian R. "Emily Dickinson's Early Poems and Letters." *Dissertation Abstracts* 31 (1969): 366A (Brandeis).

Pollak, Vivian R. "Emily Dickinson's Valentines." *American Quarterly* 26 (March 1974): 60–78.

Pollak, Vivian R. " 'That Fine Prosperity': Economic Metaphors in Emily Dickinson's Poetry." *Modern Language Quarterly* 34 (June 1973): 161–79.

Porter, David. "The Crucial Experience in Dickinson's Poetry." *Emerson Society Quarterly,* n.s. 20 (1974): 280–90.

Porter, David Thomas. "The Art of Emily Dickinson's Early Poetry." *Dissertation Abstracts* 25 (1964): 1921–22 (Rochester).

Porter, David Thomas. "Emily Dickinson: The Formative Years." *Massachusetts Review* 6 (Summer 1965): 559–69.

Porter, David Thomas. "Emily Dickinson: The Po-

etics of Doubt." *Emerson Society Quarterly* 60 (1970): 86–93.

Rabe, Olive H. "Emily Dickinson as a Mystic." *Colorado Quarterly* 14 (Winter 1966): 280–88.

Reed, Evelyn C. "Emily Dickinson's Treasury of Images: The Book of Revelation." *Emily Dickinson Bulletin* 23 (1973): 156–60.

Richmond, Lee John. "Success in Circuit: The Poetic Craft of Emily Dickinson." *Dissertation Abstracts International* 31 (1970): 6069A (Syracuse).

Rogers, B. J. "The Truth Told Slant: Emily Dickinson's Poetic Mode." *Texas Studies in Literature and Language* 14 (Summer 1972): 329–36.

Rosenbaum, S.P. "Emily Dickinson and the Machine." *Studies in Bibliography* 18 (1965): 207–27.

Rothenberg, Albert. "The Flesh-and-Blood Face on the Commemorative Stamp." *Saturday Review* (September 11, 1971): 33–38.

Sandeen, Ernest. "Delight Deterred by Retrospect: Emily Dickinson's Late Summer Poems." *New England Quarterly* 40 (December 1967): 483–500.

Scott, Winfield T. "Errand from My Heart." *Horizon* (New York) 3 (July 1961): 100–105.

Searles, Jo C. "The Art of Dickinson's 'Household Thought.' " *Concerning Poetry* 6 (1973): 46–51.

Sewall, Richard B. "The Lyman Letters: New Light on Emily Dickinson and Her Family." *Massachusetts Review* 6 (Autumn 1965): 693–780.

Sexton, Carol. "The Relation of Emily Dickinson to God." *Aspects* 2 (January 1965): 30–43.

Shapiro, Karl. "Emily Dickinson and Katherine Anne Porter." *Poetry* 98 (April 1961): 2–3.

Sherwood, William Robert. "Circumference and Circumstance: Stages in the Mind and Art of Emily Dickinson." *Dissertation Abstracts* 26 (1965): 2193 (Columbia).

Simon, Myron. " 'Self' in Whitman and Dickinson." *College English Association Critic* 30 (December 1967): 8.

Sletto, Arle Duane. "Emily Dickinson's Poetry: The Fascicles." *Dissertation Abstracts International* 35 (1975): 3719A (New Mexico).

Srinath, C.N. "The Poetry of Emily Dickinson: Some First Impressions." *Literary Criterion* 9 (1969): 19–28.

St. Armand, Barton L. "In the American Manner: An Inquiry into the Aesthetics of Emily Dickinson and Edgar Allan Poe." *Dissertation Abstracts* 30 (1969): 294A (Brown).

Stamm, Edith Perry. "Emily Dickinson: Poetry and Punctuation." *Saturday Review* (March 30, 1963): 26.

Stein, William Bysshe. "Emily Dickinson's Parodic Masks." *University Review* (Kansas) 36 (1969): 49–55.

Stephenson, William E. "Emily Dickinson and Watts's Songs for Children." *English Language Notes* 3 (June 1966): 278–81.

"Symposium on Emily Dickinson's Poetry." *Emerson Society Quarterly* 44 (1966): 2–44.

Talbot, Norman. "The Child, the Actress and Miss Emily Dickinson." *Southern Review* (U.S.) 8 (1972): 102–24.

Terris, Virginia R. "Emily Dickinson and the Genteel Critics." *Dissertation Abstracts International* 34 (1973): 1257A–58A (N.Y.U.).

Thomas, Owen, Jr. "Father and Daughter: Edward and Emily Dickinson." *American Literature* 40 (January 1969): 510–23.

Thomas, Owen Paul, Jr. "The Very Press of Imagery: A Reading of Emily Dickinson." *Dissertation Abstracts* 20 (1960): 119 (California, Los Angeles).

Thundyil, Zacharias. "Circumstance, Circumference and Center: Immanence and Transcendence in Emily Dickinson's Poems of Extreme Situations." *Hartford Studies in Literature* 3 (1972): 73–92.

Todd, John Emerson. "Emily Dickinson's Use of the Persona." *Dissertation Abstracts* 26 (1965): 3309–10 (Wisconsin).

Todd, John Emerson. "The Persona in Emily Dickinson's Love Poems." *Michigan Academician* 1 (Winter 1969): 197–207.

Todd, R. "Are You Too Deeply Occupied to Say If My Verse Is Alive?" *Atlantic Monthly* (January 1975): 74.

Waggoner, Hyatt H. "Emily Dickinson: The Transcendent Self." *Criticism* 7 (1965): 297–334.

Ward, Theodora. "The Finest Secret: Emotional Currents in the Life of Emily Dickinson after 1865." *Harvard Library Bulletin* 8 (1960): 82–106.

Waugh, D. "Nature Is Harmony." *Garden Journal* 21 (December 1971): 172–74.

Weisbuch, Robert A. "Compound Vision: Emily Dickinson's Poetic Strategies and Patterns." *Dissertation Abstracts International* 33 (1973): 3680A (Yale).

Wells, Anna Mary. "Was Emily Dickinson Psychotic?" *American Imago* 19 (Winter 1962): 309–21.

Wheatcroft, John Stewart. "Emily Dickinson and the Orthodox Tradition." *Dissertation Abstracts* 21 (1960): 1186 (Rutgers).

Wheatcroft, John Stewart. "Emily Dickinson's Poetry and Jonathan Edwards on the Will." *Bucknell Review* 10 (December 1961): 102–27.

White, James E., Jr. "Emily Dickinson: Metaphysician and Miniaturist." *College English Association Critic* 29 (March 1967): 17–18.

White, William. "Dickinson and Dover Publications." *American Notes and Queries* 11 (September 1972): 7.

White, William. "Emily on the Stage: Characterization of Emily Dickinson in the American Theater." *American Book Collector* 19 (November 1968): 13–16.

White, William. "Nostalgia Revisited: The Emily Dickinson Industry." *American Book Collector* 20 (November 1969): 27–28.

Wilner, Eleanor. "The Poetics of Emily Dickinson." *English Literary History* 38 (March 1971): 126–54.

Wilson, Suzanne M. "Emily Dickinson and Twentieth Century Poetry of Sensibility." *American Literature* 36 (November 1964): 349–58.

Wilson, Suzanne M. "Structural Patterns in the Poetry of Emily Dickinson." *American Literature* 35 (March 1963): 53–59.

Wycherley, H. Alan. "Emily Dickinson's Greatest Poems." *College English Association Critic* 35 (November 1972): 28.

Wylder, Edith Perry. "The Voice of the Poet: Selected Poems of Emily Dickinson with an Introduction to the Rhetorical Punctuation of the Manuscripts." *Dissertation Abstracts* 28 (1967): 4194A (New Mexico).

Yamamoto, Shuji. "Emily Dickinson: Person and Poetry." *Kyushu American Literature* 3 (1960): 15–20.

Yetman, Michael G. "Emily Dickinson and the English Romantic Tradition." *Texas Studies in Literature and Language* 15 (Spring 1973): 129–47.

Individual Works

As by the Dead We Love to Sit (1859)

Henry, Nat. "Dickinson's *As by the Dead We Love to Sit*." *Explicator* 31 (January 1973): Item 35.

Lair, Robert L. "Dickinson's *As by the Dead We Love to Sit.*" *Explicator* 25 (March 1967): Item 58.

Perrine, Laurence. "Dickinson's *As by the Dead We Love to Sit.*" *Explicator* 33 (February 1975): Item 49.

As Watchers Hang Upon the East (1859)

Catto, Brenda Ann. "Dickinson's *As Watchers Hang Upon the East.*" *Explicator* 33 (March 1975): Item 55.

Aurora Is the Effort (1865)

Newell, Kenneth B. "Dickinson's *Aurora Is the Effort.*" *Explicator* 20 (September 1961): Item 5.

A Bird Came Down the Walk (1862)

Metzger, Charles R. "Emily Dickinson's Sly Bird." *Emerson Society Quarterly* 44 (1966): 21–22.

The Bustle in a House (1866)

Jordan, Raymond J. "Dickinson's *The Bustle in a House.*" *Explicator* 22 (February 1963): Item 49.

The Butterfly Obtains (c. 1859)

Houghton, Donald E. "Dickinson's *The Butterfly Obtains.*" *Explicator* 27 (September 1968): Item 5.

A Clamor in the Treetops (1895)

Gullans, Charles, and John Espey. "Emily Dickinson: Two Uncollected Poems." *American Literature* 44 (May 1972): 306–7.

A Clock Stopped (1861)

Bolin, Donald W. "Dickinson's *A Clock Stopped.*" *Explicator* 22 (December 1963): Item 27.

Rossky, William. "Dickinson's *A Clock Stopped.*" *Explicator* 22 (September 1963): Item 3.

Sheffler, R.A. "Emily Dickinson's *A Clock Stopped.*" *Massachusetts Studies in English* 1 (1967): 52–54.

The Crickets Sang (1867)

Tugwell, Simon. "Dickinson's *The Crickets Sang.*" *Explicator* 23 (February 1965): Item 46.

Death Is a Dialogue Between (1864)

Adair, Virginia H. "Dickinson's *Death Is a Dialogue Between.*" *Explicator* 27 (March 1969): Item 52.

Richmond, Lee J. "Dickinson's *Death Is a Dialogue Between.*" *Emily Dickinson Bulletin* 23 (1973): 171.

Elysium Is As Far As To (1882)

Whicher, Stephen. "Dickinson's *Elysium Is As Far As To.*" *Explicator* 19 (April 1961): Item 45.

"Faith" Is a Fine Invention (1866)

Witherington, Paul. "Dickinson's *'Faith' Is a Fine Invention.*" *Explicator* 26 (April 1968): Item 65.

The Feet of People Walking Home (1858)

Pebworth, T.L., and J.C. Summers. "Dickinson's *The Feet of People Walking Home.*" *Explicator* 27

(May 1969): Item 76.

The First Day's Night Had Come (1862)

Rooke, Constance. "*The First Day's Night Had Come*: An Explication of J.410." *Emily Dickinson Bulletin* 24 (1973): 221–23.

Further in Summer than the Birds (1866)

Burnshaw, Stanley. "The Three Revolutions in Modern Poetry." *Sewanee Review* 70 (Summer 1962): 427–28.

Lind, Sidney E. "Emily Dickinson's *Further in Summer than the Birds* and Nathaniel Hawthorne's 'The Old Manse.' " *American Literature* 39 (May 1967): 163–69.

I Asked No Other Thing (1862)

Lavin, J. A. "Emily Dickinson and Brazil." *Notes and Queries* 7 (July 1960): 270–71.

I Cautious, Scanned My Little Life (1860)

Elliott, Gary D. "A Note on Dickinson's *I Cautious, Scanned My Little Life.*" *Markham Review* 2 (October 1970): 78–79.

I Dreaded That First Robin, So (1862)

Pommer, Henry F. "Emily Dickinson's *I Dreaded That First Robin, So.*" *Re: Arts and Letters* 6 (Spring 1972): 29–47.

I Felt a Funeral in My Brain (1861)

McCall, Dan. "*I Felt a Funeral in My Brain* and 'The Hollow of the Three Hills.' " *New England Quarterly* 42 (September 1969): 432–35.

Monteiro, George. "Traditional Ideas in Dickinson's *I Felt a Funeral in My Brain.*" *Modern Language Notes* 75 (December 1960): 656–63.

I Had Not Minded Walls (1862)

Merideth, Robert. "Dickinson's *I Had Not Minded Walls.*" *Explicator* 23 (November 1964): Item 25.

I Heard a Fly Buzz When I Died (1862)

Beck, Ronald. "Dickinson's *I Heard a Fly Buzz When I Died.*" *Explicator* 26 (December 1967): Item 31.

Connelly, James T. "Dickinson's *I Heard a Fly Buzz When I Died.*" *Explicator* 25 (December 1966): Item 34.

Cunningham, Donald H. "Emily Dickinson's *I Heard a Fly Buzz When I Died.*" *American Notes and Queries* 6 (May 1968): 150–51.

Hogue, Caroline. "Dickinson's *I Heard a Fly Buzz When I Died.*" *Explicator* 20 (November 1961): Item 26.

Hollahan, Eugene. "Dickinson's *I Heard a Fly Buzz When I Died.*" *Explicator* 25 (September 1966): Item 6.

I Like to See It Lap the Miles (1862)

Lowrey, Robert E. " 'Boanerges': An Encomium for Edward Dickinson." *Arizona Quarterly* 26 (Spring 1970): 54–58.

Mabbott, Thomas O. " 'Boanerges' a Horse?" *American Notes and Queries* 2 (December 1963): 57.

McNally, James. "Perspectives in Movement—A Poem by Emily Dickinson." *College English Association Critic* 26 (November 1963): 9–10.

I Never Lost As Much But Twice (1858)

Lackey, Allen D. "Dickinson's *I Never Lost As Much But Twice*." *Explicator* 34 (November 1975): Item 18.

Rapin, Rene. "Dickinson's *I Never Lost As Much But Twice*." *Explicator* 31 (March 1973): Item 52.

I Never Saw a Moor (1865)

Herget, William. "Dickinson's *I Never Saw a Moor*." *Explicator* 30 (March 1972): Item 55.

I Started Early—Took My Dog (1862)

Carlson, Eric W. "Dickinson's *I Started Early—Took My Dog*." *Explicator* 20 (May 1962): Item 72.

Lensing, George S. "Dickinson's *I Started Early—Took My Dog*." *Explicator* 31 (December 1972): Item 30.

I Taste a Liquor Never Brewed (1860)

Cohen, H. "Dickinson's *I Taste a Liquor Never Brewed*." *Explicator* 33 (January 1975): Item 41.

Davis, Lloyd M. "Dickinson's *I Taste a Liquor Never Brewed*." *Explicator* 23 (March 1965): Item 53.

Dorinson, Zahava Karl. "*I Taste a Liquor Never Brewed*: A Problem in Editing." *American Literature* 35 (November 1963): 363–65.

Eby, Cecil D., Jr. "*I Taste a Liquor Never Brewed*: A Variant Reading." *American Literature* 36 (January 1965): 514–18.

Garrow, A. Scott. "A Note on Manzanilla." *American Literature* 35 (November 1963): 366.

Hauser, Charles J., Jr. "Dickinson's *I Taste a Liquor Never Brewed*." *Explicator* 31 (September 1972): Item 2.

Malbone, Richard. "Dickinson's *I Taste a Liquor Never Brewed*." *Explicator* 26 (October 1967): Item 14.

I Years Had Been from Home (1862)

Axelrod, Steven. "Terror in the Everyday: Emily Dickinson's *I Years Had Been from Home*." *Concerning Poetry* 6 (1973): 53–56.

If God Upon the Seventh Day Did Rest From His Labors (1895)

Gullans, Charles, and John Espey. "Emily Dickinson: Two Uncollected Poems." *American Literature* 44 (May 1972): 306–7.

If You Were Coming in the Fall (1862)

Niikura, Toshikazu. "Emily Dickinson's *If You Were Coming in the Fall*." *Meiji Gakuen Ronso* 73 (November 1962): 139–50.

Richmond, Lee J. "Emily Dickinson's *If You Were Coming in the Fall*: An Explication." *English Journal* 59 (September 1970): 771–73.

I'm Nobody! Who Are You? (1861)

Backus, Joseph M. "Two No-Name Poems." *Names* 15 (1967): 1–7.

It Dropped So Low—In My Regard (1863)

Hill, Archibald A. "Figurative Structure and Meaning: Two Poems by Emily Dickinson." *Texas Studies in Literature and Language* 16 (Spring 1974): 195–209.

I've Seen a Dying Eye (1862)

D'Avanzo, Mario L. "Emily Dickinson's Dying Eye." *Renascence* 19 (Winter 1967): 110–11.

The Lamp Burns Sure Within (1861)

Lewis, S. "Dickinson's *The Lamp Burns Sure Within* and 'The Poets Light but Lamps.' " *Explicator* 28 (September 1969): Item 4.

A Mien to Move a Queen (1861)

Miller, F. De Wolfe. "Emily Dickinson: Self-Portrait in the Third Person." *New England Quarterly* 46 (March 1973): 119–24.

My Life Closed Twice Before Its Close (1896)

Faber, M.D. "Psychoanalytic Remarks on a Poem by Emily Dickinson." *Psychology Review* 56 (1969): 247–64.

My Life Had Stood—A Loaded Gun (1863)

Perrine, Laurence. "Dickinson's *My Life Had Stood—A Loaded Gun*." *Explicator* 21 (November 1962): Item 21.

Wylder, Edith. "The Speaker of Emily Dickinson's *My Life Had Stood—A Loaded Gun*." *Bulletin of the Rocky Mountain Modern Language Association* 23 (1969): 3–8.

No Brigadier Throughout the Year (1883)

Forde, Sister Victoria Marie. "Dickinson's *No Brigadier Throughout the Year*." *Explicator* 27 (February 1969): Item 41.

No Rack Can Torture Me (1862)

Omoto, Tsuyoshi. "Emily Dickinson's Poem *No Rack Can Torture Me*." *Hiroshima Studies in English Language and Literature* 9 (1963): 45–50.

Not with a Club the Heart Is Broken (1874)

Marcus, Mordecai. "Dickinson's *Not with a Club the Heart Is Broken*." *Explicator* 20 (March 1962):

Item 54.

Of Bronze and Blaze (1861)

Hiatt, David. "Dickinson's *Of Bronze and Blaze.*" *Explicator* 21 (September 1962): Item 6.

On This Wondrous Sea (1853)

Monteiro, George. "Dickinson's *On This Wondrous Sea.*" *Explicator* 33 (May 1975): Item 74.

One Day Is There of the Series (1864)

Adair, Virginia H. "Dickinson's *One Day Is There of the Series.*" *American Notes and Queries* 5 (November 1966): 35.

Williams, Paul O. "Dickinson's *One Day Is There of the Series.*" *Explicator* 23 (December 1964): Item 28.

One Dignity Delays for All (1859)

Essig, Erhardt H. "Dickinson's *One Dignity Delays for All.*" *Explicator* 23 (October 1964): Item 16.

Michel, Pierre. "The Last Stanza of Emily Dickinson's *One Dignity Delays for All.*" *English Studies* 50 (1969): 98–100.

Our Journey Had Advanced (1862)

Gillespie, Robert. "A Circumference of Emily Dickinson." *New England Quarterly* 46 (June 1973): 250–71.

The Poets Light but Lamps (1864)

Lewis, S. "Dickinson's 'The Lamp Burns Sure Within' and *The Poets Light but Lamps.*" *Explicator* 28 (September 1969): Item 4.

Portraits Are to Daily Faces (1860)

Tugwell, Simon. "Notes on Two Poems by Emily Dickinson." *Notes and Queries* 13 (September 1966): 342–43.

Praise It—'Tis Dead (1876)

Mullican, J.S. "Dickinson's *Praise It—'Tis Dead.*" *Explicator* 27 (April 1969): Item 62.

Presentiment (1863)

Hirsch, David H. "Emily Dickinson's 'Presentiment.'" *American Notes and Queries* 1 (November 1962): 36–37.

Perrine, Laurence. "Emily Dickinson's *Presentiment* Again." *American Notes and Queries* 3 (April 1965): 119–20.

The Reticent Volcano Keeps (1896)

D'Avanzo, Mario L. "Dickinson's *The Reticent Volcano* and Emerson." *American Transcendental Quarterly* 14 (1972): 11–13.

Reverse Cannot Befall (1862)

Anderson, Charles R. "Dickinson's *Reverse Cannot Befall.*" *Explicator* 18 (May 1960): Item 46.

The Robin Is the One (1864)

Perrine, Laurence. "Dickinson's *The Robin Is the One.*" *Explicator* 33 (December 1974): Item 33.

The Soul Selects Her Own Society (1862)

Faris, Paul. "Dickinson's *The Soul Selects Her Own Society.*" *Explicator* 25 (April 1967): Item 65.

Hill, Archibald A. "Figurative Structure and Meaning: Two Poems by Emily Dickinson." *Texas Studies in Literature and Language* 16 (Spring 1974): 195–209.

Rubin, Larry. "Dickinson's *The Soul Selects Her Own Society.*" *Explicator* 30 (April 1972): Item 67.

Tugwell, Simon. "Dickinson's *The Soul Selects Her Own Society.*" *Explicator* 27 (January 1969): Item 37.

Witherington, Paul. "The Neighborhood Humor of Dickinson's *The Soul Selects Her Own Society.*" *Concerning Poetry* 2 (1969): 5–9.

A Spider Sewed at Night (1869)

Nist, John. "Two American Poets and a Spider." *Walt Whitman Birthplace Bulletin* 4 (January 1961): 8–11.

Summer Has Two Beginnings (1877)

Walz, Laurence. "Dickinson's *Summer Has Two Beginnings.*" *Explicator* 33 (October 1974): Item 16.

Superfluous Were the Sun (1865)

Lindberg, Brita. "Further Notes on a Poem by Emily Dickinson." *Notes and Queries* 15 (May 1968): 179–80.

Tugwell, Simon. "Notes on Two Poems by Emily Dickinson." *Notes and Queries* 13 (September 1966): 342–43.

Tell All the Truth but Tell It Slant (1868)

Gross, John J. "Tell All the Truth But—" *Ball State University Forum* 10 (Winter 1969–1970): 71–77.

There Are Two Ripenings (1862)

Perrine, Laurence. "Dickinson's *There Are Two Ripenings.*" *Explicator* 31 (April 1973): Item 65.

There Came a Wind Like a Bugle (n.d.)

D'Avanzo, Mario L. "*Came a Wind Like a Bugle*: Dickinson's Poetic Apocalypse." *Renascence* 17 (Fall 1964): 29–31.

There's a Certain Slant of Light (1861)

Eulert, Donald. "Emily Dickinson's 'Certain Slant of Light.'" *American Transcendental Quarterly* 14 (1972): 164–66.

Monteiro, George. "Dickinson's *There's a Certain Slant of Light.*" *Explicator* 31 (October 1972): Item 13.

These Are the Days When Birds Come Back (1859)

Berner, Robert L. "Dickinson's *These Are the Days When Birds Come Back.*" *Explicator* 30 (May 1972): Item 78.

The Thought Beneath So Slight a Film (1860)

Perrine, Laurence. "Sea and Surging Boom." *College English Association Critic* 30 (November 1967): 9.

White, James E., Jr. "Emily Dickinson: Metaphysician and Miniaturist." *College English Association Critic* 29 (March 1967): 17–18.

The Tint I Cannot Take Is Best (1862)

Fitzgerald, E. "Dickinson's *The Tint I Cannot Take Is Best.*" *Explicator* 28 (November 1969): Item 29.

'Twas Like a Maelstrom (1862)

Fodaski, Martha. "Dickinson's *'Twas Like a Maelstrom.*" *Explicator* 19 (January 1961): Item 24.

Two Butterflies Went Out at Noon (1862)

Asals, Frederick, Jr. "Dickinson's *Two Butterflies Went Out at Noon.*" *Emerson Society Quarterly* 63 (1971): 29–31.

Matchett, William H. "Dickinson's Revision of *Two Butterflies Went Out at Noon.*" *Publications of the Modern Language Association* 77 (1962): 436–41.

Perrine, Laurence. "The Importance of Tone in the Interpretation of Literature." *College English* 24 (February 1963): 389–95.

Water Makes Many Beds (1877)

Mullican, James S. "Dickinson's *Water Makes Many Beds.*" *Explicator* 27 (November 1968): Item 23.

We Should Not Mind So Small a Flower (1859)

Newell, Kenneth B. "Dickinson's *We Should Not Mind So Small a Flower.*" *Explicator* 19 (April 1961): Item 65.

What Soft Cherubic Creatures (1862)

Harvey, Nancy L. "Dickinson's *What Soft Cherubic Creatures.*" *Explicator* 28 (October 1969): Item 17.

Purdy, Dwight H. "Dickinson's *What Soft Cherubic Creatures.*" *Explicator* 33 (April 1975): Item 67.

Where Ships of Purple Gently Toss (1861)

Perrine, Laurence. "The Nature of Proof in the Interpretation of Poetry." *English Journal* 51 (September 1962): 393–98.

Wild Night—Wild Nights (1861)

Connelly, James T. "Dickinson's *Wild Nights.*" *Explicator* 25 (January 1967): Item 44.

Ditsky, John. "The Wildness of Dickinson's *Wild Nights.*" *Lakehead University Review* 4 (1971): 50–56.

Faris, Paul. "Eroticism in Emily Dickinson's *Wild Nights.*" *New England Quarterly* 40 (June 1967): 269–74.

Wegelin, Christof. "Dickinson's *Wild Nights.*" *Explicator* 26 (November 1967): Item 25.

The Wind Drew Off (1863)

Doyle, Connie M. "Emily Dickinson's *The Wind Drew Off.*" *English Language Notes* 12 (March 1975): 182–84.

Would You Like Summer? Taste of Ours (1863)

Adkins, Carla. "Emily Dickinson's *Would You Like Summer? Taste of Ours*: A Note on the Composition Date." *English Language Notes* 7 (September 1969): 53–55.

JOAN DIDION (1934–) U.S.
General Works
Stineback, David C. "On the Limits of Fiction." *Midwest Quarterly* 14 (Summer 1973): 339–48.
Individual Works
Play It As It Lays (1970)

Geherin, David. "Nothingness and Beyond: Joan Didion's *Play It As It Lays.*" *Critique* 16 (1974): 64–78.

Schorer, Mark. "Novels and Nothingness." *American Scholar* 40 (Winter 1970–1971): 168–74.

ANNIE DILLARD (1945–) U.S.
General Works
"Name Dropping." *Living Wilderness* 39 (Spring 1975): 4.
Individual Works
Pilgrim at Tinker Creek (1974)

Baker, J.F. "Story Behind the Book: *Pilgrim at Tinker Creek.*" *Publishers Weekly* (March 18, 1974): 28.

Wymard, Eleanor B. "A New Existential Voice." *Commonweal* (October 24, 1975): 495–96.

"Young, Successful, and First." *Saturday Evening Post* (October 1974): 51.

ISAK DINESEN [pseud. of Karen Blixen] (1885–1962) Denmark
General Works
Green, Howard. "Isak Dinesen." *Hudson Review* 17 (Winter 1964–1965): 517–30.

Hannah, Donald. "In Memoriam Karen Blixen: Some Aspects of Her Attitude to Life." *Sewanee Review* 71 (Autumn 1963): 585–604.

Langbaum, Robert. "Ehrengard and Isak Dinesen." *American Scholar* 32 (Autumn 1963): 639–56.

Thurman, Judith. "Isak Dinesen/Karen Blixen: A Very Personal Memoir." *Ms.* (September 1973): 72.

Whissen, T.R. "Bow of the Lord: Isak Dinesen's Portrait of the Artist." *Scandinavian Studies* 46 (Winter 1974): 47–58.

Individual Works

Echoes (1957)

Grossman, Ann. "Sacramental Imagery." *Contemporary Literature* 4 (Autumn 1963): 321–26.

The Monkey (1934)

Phillips, Robert S. "Dinesen's 'Monkey' and Mc-Cullers' 'Ballad': A Study in Literary Affinity." *Studies in Short Fiction* 1 (Spring 1964): 184–90.

Out of Africa (1938)

Heiskanen-Makela, Sirkka. "Isak Dinesen's *Out of Africa*: Regressum ad Originem." *Neuphilologische Mitteilungen* 75 (1974): 453–71.

DORIS MILES DISNEY (1907–) U.S.

General Works

Mercier, J.F. "Doris Miles Disney and Isabella Taylor." *Publishers Weekly* (August 13, 1973): 24–25.

ROSEMARY DOBSON (1920–) Australia

General Works

Burrows, J.F. "Rosemary Dobson's Sense of the Past." *Southerly* 30 (1970): 163–76.

Heales, Robyn S. "Rosemary Dobson: The Influence of Art." *Australian Literary Studies* 6 (1974): 249–58.

Hope, A.D. "Rosemary Dobson—A Portrait in a Mirror." *Quadrant* 16 (1972): 10–14.

McAuley, James. "The Poetry of Rosemary Dobson." *Australian Literary Studies* 6 (1973): 3–10.

MARY ABIGAIL DODGE [pseud. Gail Hamilton] (1833–1896) U.S.

General Works

"Lion's Side of the Lion Question." *North American Review* 258 (Winter 1973): 69–74.

Pulsifer, Janice Goldsmith. "Gail Hamilton, 1833–1896." *Essex Institute Historical Collections* 104 (1968): 165–216.

HILDA DOOLITTLE [pseud. H.D.] (1886–1961) U.S.

Bibliography

Bryer, Jackson R., and R. Roblyer. "H.D.: A Preliminary Checklist." *Contemporary Literature* 10 (Autumn 1969): 632–75.

General Works

Bryer, Jackson R. "H.D.: A Note on Her Critical Reputation." *Contemporary Literature* 10 (Autumn 1969): 627–31.

Dembo, L.S. "Norman Holmes Pearson on H.D.: An Interview." *Contemporary Literature* 10 (Autumn 1969): 435–46.

Duncan, Robert. "Two Chapters from H.D." *Tri-Quarterly* 12 (Spring 1968): 67–98.

Engel, Bernard. "Poems That Matter and Dilutions." *Contemporary Literature* 10 (Autumn 1969): 507–22.

Friedman, Susan S. "Mythology, Psychoanalysis, and the Occult in the Late Poetry of H.D." *Dissertation Abstracts International* 34 (1974): 6638A (Wisconsin).

Gibbons, Kathryn Gibbs. "The Art of H.D." *Mississippi Quarterly* 15 (Fall 1962): 152–60.

Greenwood, E.B. "H.D. and the Problem of Escapism." *Essays in Criticism* 21 (October 1971): 365–76.

Gregory, H. "Speaking of Books." *New York Times Book Review* (October 22, 1961): 2.

Holland, Joyce Marie. "H.D.: The Shape of a Career." *Dissertation Abstracts International* 35 (1975): 7906A–7A (Brown).

Holland, Norman N. "H.D. and the 'Blameless Physician.'" *Contemporary Literature* 10 (Autumn 1969): 474–506.

Jacobsen, Josephine. "H.D. in Greece and Egypt." *Poetry* 100 (June 1962): 187–90.

Levertov, Denise. "H.D.: An Appreciation." *Poetry* 100 (June 1962): 182–86.

Pondrom, Cyrena N. "Selected Letters from H.D. to F. S. Flint: A Commentary on the Imagist Period." *Contemporary Literature* 10 (Autumn 1969): 557–86.

Riddle, Joseph N. "H.D. and the Poetics of 'Spiritual Realism.'" *Contemporary Literature* 10 (Autumn 1969): 447–73.

"Talk with the Author." *Newsweek* (May 2, 1960): 92–93.

Weatherhead, A. Kingsley. "Style in H.D.'s Novels." *Contemporary Literature* 10 (Autumn 1969): 537–56.

Individual Works

Helen in Egypt (1961)

Robinson, Janice S. "H.D.'s *Helen in Egypt*: A Recollection." *Dissertation Abstracts International*

35 (1974): 1122A (California, Santa Cruz).

Wagner, Linda Welshimer. "*Helen in Egypt*: A Culmination." *Contemporary Literature* 10 (Autumn 1969): 523–36.

SARAH ANNE DORSEY (1829–1879) U.S.
General Works
Anderson, John Q. "Louisiana and Mississippi Lore in the Fiction of Sarah Anne Dorsey (1829–1970)." *Louisiana Studies* 11 (Fall 1972): 230–39.

Burd, Van Akin. "A Louisiana Estimate of an 'American Rousseau': Sarah Anne Dorsey on Henry David Thoreau." *Louisiana History* 5 (Summer 1964): 296–309.

OLIVE CUSTANCE DOUGLAS (1879–1944) Great Britain
Bibliography
Hawkey, Nancy J. "Olive Custance Douglas: Introduction to a Bibliography." *English Literature in Transition* 15 (1972): 49–56.

MARGARET DRABBLE (1939–) Great Britain
General Works
Apter, T.E. "Margaret Drabble: The Glamour of Seriousness." *Human World* 12 (August 1973): 18–28.

Beards, Virginia K. "Margaret Drabble: Novels of a Cautious Feminist." *Critique* 15 (1973): 35–47.

Bonfond, François. "Margaret Drabble: How to Express Subjective Truth through Fiction." *Revue des Langues Vivantes* 40 (1974): 41–55.

Hardin, Nancy S. "An Interview with Margaret Drabble." *Contemporary Literature* 14 (Summer 1973): 273–95.

Libby, M.V. "Fate and Feminism in the Novels of Margaret Drabble." *Contemporary Literature* 16 (Spring 1975): 175–92.

Poland, N. "Margaret Drabble: There Must Be a Lot of People Like Me." *Midwest Quarterly* 16 (Spring 1975): 255–67.

Rose, Ellen Cronan. "Margaret Drabble: Surviving the Future." *Critique* 15 (1973): 5–21.

Trevor, William. "A Life in Limbo." *New Statesman* (May 23, 1969): 738.
Individual Works
The Millstone (1965)
Hardin, Nancy S. "Drabble's *The Millstone*: A Fable for Our Times." *Critique* 15 (1973): 22–34.

Wikborg, Eleanor. "A Comparison of Margaret Drabble's *The Millstone* with its *Vecko-Rebyn* Adaptation, *Barnett Du Gav Mig* (The Child You Gave Me)." *Moderna Sprak* 65 (1971): 305–11.

Realms of Gold (1975)
Oates, Joyce Carol. "*Realms of Gold*." *Saturday Review* (November 15, 1975): 20–22.

HENRIETTA DRAKE-BROCKMAN (1901–) Australia
General Works
Barnes, John. "Henrietta Drake-Brockman." *Westerly*, no. 2 (1967): 71.

Durack, Mary. "Henrietta as I Knew Her." *Overland*, no. 39 (1967): 46–47.

Ewers, John K. "Henrietta and the Fellowship of Australian Writers." *Westerly*, no. 2 (1967): 75–78.

Hasluck, Alexandra. "Henrietta Drake-Brockman." *Meanjin Quarterly* 27 (1968): 233–37.
Individual Works
Voyage to Disaster (1963)
Hasluck, Alexandra. "Henrietta as Historian." *Westerly*, no. 2 (1967): 72–74.

ROSALYN DREXLER (fl. 1960s–1970s) U.S.
General Works
Goulianos, J. "Women and the Avant-Garde Theater: Interview." *Massachusetts Review* 13 (Winter–Spring 1972): 264–67.

MARY DUCLAUX (1857–1944) Great Britain
Bibliography
Holmes, Ruth Van Zuyle. "Mary Duclaux (1857–1944): Primary and Secondary Checklists." *English Literature in Transition* 10 (1967): 27–46.

HELEN SELINA SHERIDAN LADY DUFFERIN [pseud. Impulsia Gushington] (1807–1867) Great Britain
General Works
McGurk, J. N. "Lady Dufferin Wrote Ballads of the Poor." *Irish Digest* 82 (February 1965): 41–44.

ALICE DUNBAR-NELSON, née Moore (1875–) U.S.
General Works
Williams, Ruby Ora. "An In-Depth Portrait of Alice Dunbar-Nelson." *Dissertation Abstracts International* 35 (1975): 7278A (California, Irvine).

JANE DUNCAN, née Cameron (1910–) Scotland
General Works
Hart, Francis R. "Jane Duncan's Friends and the

Reachfar Story." *Studies in Scottish Literature* 6 (January 1969): 156–74.

SARA JEANNETTE DUNCAN, Mrs. Everard Cotes (1862–1922) Canada
General Works
Burness, J. "Sara Jeannette Duncan—A Neglected Canadian Author." *Ontario Library Review* 45 (August 1962): 205–6.
Cloutier, Pierre. "First Exile." *Canadian Literature*, no. 59 (Winter 1974): 30–37.
Ross, M.E. "Sara Jeannette Duncan: Personal Glimpses." *Canadian Literature*, no. 27 (Winter 1966): 15–19.
Smith, Marion. "Period Pieces." *Canadian Literature*, no. 10 (Autumn 1961): 72–77.
Individual Works
The Imperialist (1904)
Bailey, Alfred G. "The Historical Setting of Sara Duncan's *The Imperialist*." *Journal of Canadian Fiction* 2 (1973): 205–10.
Gerson, Carole. "Duncan's Web." *Canadian Literature*, no. 63 (Winter 1975): 73–80.

ABIGAIL S. DUNIWAY (1835–1915) U.S.
General Works
Richey, Elinor. "The Unsinkable Abigail." *American Heritage* 26 (February 1975): 72.

MARY CHAVELITA DUNNE. *See* George Egerton

MARY DURACK (1913–) Australia
General Works
King, A. "Our Mythical Ancestors." *Westerly*, no. 1 (1960): 35–36.
Richardson, B. E. "The Image of the Outsider in the Writing of Mary Durack." *Westerly*, no. 4 (1971): 53–54.

MARILYN DURHAM (1930–) U.S.
General Works
Duffy, M. "Women's Lib Western." *Time* (August 7, 1972): 73.
Durham, Michael. "The 'Cat Dancing' Lady Cures the Middle-Age Blahs." *Life* (December 8, 1972): 89.
"Marilyn Durham: The Lady Who Loves Libraries." *American Libraries* 4 (January 1973): 26–28.
Norwood, M.G. "I Was Forty, so I Wrote a Best Seller: Interview." *Vogue* (October 1972): 162.
Individual Works
The Man Who Loved Cat Dancing (1972)
Bannon, B.A. "Story behind the Book: *The Man Who Loved Cat Dancing* (1972)." *Publishers Weekly* (July 31, 1972): 60–61.

MARGARET VAN HORN DWIGHT (fl. 1810–1819) U.S.
General Works
Holmes, J. Welfred. "Three Uncommon Records of the Commonplace." *College Language Association Journal* 9 (March 1966): 215–24.

E

Lady Elizabeth Eastlake (1809–1893) Great Britain

General Works

Robertson, D. A., Jr. "Queen Victoria's Lady Novelists: The Lady Who Reviewed *Jane Eyre*." *Gazette of the Grolier Club* (February 12, 1970): 2–10.

Mary Baker Eddy (1821–1910) U.S.
General Works

Parker, Gail. "Mary Baker Eddy and Sentimental Womanhood." *New England Quarterly* 43 (March 1970): 3–18.

Sowd, David. "The Dusky Genius of Mary Baker Eddy." *Ball State University Forum* 14 (Summer 1973): 38–43.

Emily Eden (1797–1869) India (Born in Great Britain)

General Works

Hannay, Prudence. "Emily Eden as a Letter Writer." *History Today* 21 (July 1971): 491–501.

Maria Edgeworth (1768–1849) Ireland (Born in Great Britain)

Bibliography

Colvin, Christina Edgeworth. "Maria Edgeworth's Literary Manuscripts in the Bodleian Library." *Bodleian Library Review* 8 (April 1970): 196–201.

General Works

Altieri, Joanne. "Style and Purpose in Maria Edgeworth's Fiction." *Nineteenth Century Fiction* 23 (December 1968): 265–78.

Buckley, Mary. "Attitudes to Nationality in Four Nineteenth-Century Novelists: 1. Maria Edgeworth." *Journal of Cork Historical and Archaeological Society* 78 (1973): 27–34.

Butler, Marilyn, and Christina Edgeworth Colvin.

"A Revised Date of Birth for Maria Edgeworth." *Notes and Queries* 18 (September 1971): 339–40.

Butler, Ruth F. "Maria Edgeworth." *Times Literary Supplement* (February 4, 1972): 129.

Colvin, Christina Edgeworth. "Maria Edgeworth." *Times Literary Supplement* (September 29, 1972): 1157.

Colvin, Christina Edgeworth. "Maria Edgeworth's Tours in Ireland, Part I." *Studia Neophilologica* 42 (1970): 319–29. Part II, 43 (1971): 252–56; Part III, 43 (1971): 474–83.

Colvin, Christina Edgeworth. "Two Unpublished Mss. by Maria Edgeworth." *Review of English Literature* 8 (October 1967): 53–61.

Colvin, Christina Edgeworth. "A Visit to Abbotsford." *Review of English Literature* 5 (January 1964): 56–65.

Craig, Charles R. "Maria Edgeworth and the Common-Sense School." *Dissertation Abstracts International* 32 (1971): 913A (Nebraska).

Eisenstadt, Elizabeth. "A Study of Maria Edgeworth's Fiction." *Dissertation Abstracts International* 35 (1975): 2217A (Washington).

Evans, Lord. "Maria Edgeworth: A Bicentenary Lecture." *Essay by Divers Hands* 35 (1969): 40–64.

Gladstone, Joan. "Maria Edgeworth's Tales and Novels: Variant Binding of the Second Collected Edition." *Book Collector* 22 (Spring 1973): 92.

Kennedy, Eileen. "Genesis of a Fiction: The Edgeworth–Turgenev Relationship." *English Language Notes* 6 (June 1969): 271–73.

McWhorter, Oleta Elizabeth. "Maria Edgeworth's Art of Prose Fiction." *Dissertation Abstracts* 26 (1965): 1024 (Arkansas).

Murray, Patrick. "The Irish Novels of Maria Edgeworth." *Irish Quarterly Review* 59 (Autumn

1970): 267–78.

Murray, Patrick. "Maria Edgeworth and Her Father: The Literary Partnership." *Eire* 6 (1971): 39–50.

Newcomer, James. "Maria Edgeworth and the Critics." *College English* 26 (December 1964): 214–18.

Pritchett, V.S. "Across the Irish Sea." *New Statesman* (August 18, 1972): 227.

Rudolf, Jo-Ellen S. "The Novels That Taught the Ladies: A Study of Popular Fiction Written by Women, 1702–1834." *Dissertation Abstracts International* 33 (1972): 1695A (California, San Diego).

Welsh, Alexander. "Maria Edgeworth and More Dickens." *Yale Review* 62 (Winter 1972): 281–87.

Individual Works

Belinda (1801)

Maxwell, J. C. "Jane Austen and *Belinda*." *Notes and Queries* 21 (May 1974): 175–76.

Castle Rackrent (1800)

Edwards, Duane. "The Narrator of *Castle Rackrent*." *South Atlantic Quarterly* 71 (Winter 1972): 124–29.

Newcomer, James. "*Castle Rackrent*: Its Structure and Its Irony." *Criticism* 8 (1966): 170–79.

Newcomer, James. "The Disingenuous Thady Quirk." *Studies in Short Fiction* 2 (Fall 1964): 44–50.

Ross, A.S.C. "Estonian Quotation in *Castle Rackrent*." *Notes and Queries* 22 (January 1975): 26.

Solomon, Stanley J. "Ironic Perspective in Maria Edgeworth's *Castle Rackrent*." *Journal of Narrative Technique* 2 (1972): 68–73.

Unthank, Tessa B. "Little But Good." *Michigan Quarterly Review* 11 (Spring 1972): 119–21.

Helen (1834)

Butler, Marilyn. "The Uniqueness of Cynthia Kirkpatrick: Elizabeth Gaskell's *Wives and Daughters* and Maria Edgeworth's *Helen*." *Review of English Studies* 23 (August 1972): 278–90.

Mademoiselle Panache (1795)

Moler, Kenneth L. "*Sense and Sensibility* and Its Sources." *Review of English Studies* 17 (November 1966): 413–19.

Ormond (1817)

Jeffares, A. Norman. "Maria Edgeworth's *Ormond*." *English* 18 (Autumn 1969): 85–90.

The Parent's Assistant (1796–1801)

Pollard, M. "The First Irish Edition of Maria Edgeworth's *Parent's Assistant*." *Irish Book* 1 (1962): 85–88.

Pollard, M. "Maria Edgeworth's *The Parent's Assistant*: The First Edition." *Book Collector* 20 (Autumn 1971): 347–51.

Renier, Anne. "Maria Edgeworth's *The Parent's Assistant*, 1796, First Edition: An Unrecorded Copy of Part II, Vol. II." *Book Collector* 21 (Spring 1972): 127–28.

Schiller, Justin G. "Maria Edgeworth's *The Parent's Assistant*, 1796, First Edition: Part I." *Book Collector* 23 (Summer 1974): 258–59.

AMELIA ANN BLANFORD EDWARDS (1831–1892) Great Britain

General Works

Crownover, D. "Amelia Edwards and the New Aswan Dam." *Expedition* 4 (Spring 1962): 24–27.

Grosskurth, Phyllis. "Amelia Edwards: A Redoubtable Victorian Female." *Review of English Literature* 6 (January 1965): 80–92.

GEORGE EGERTON [pseud. of Mary Chavelita Dunne] (1859–1945) Australia

General Works

Harris, Wendell V. "Egerton: Forgotten Realist." *Victorian Newsletter* 33 (Spring 1968): 31–35.

ANNE ELDER (fl. 1960s–1970s) Australia

General Works

Steele, Peter. "Two Southern Poets." *Poetry Australia* 8 (1972): 56–60.

GEORGE ELIOT [pseud. of Mary Ann Evans] (1819–1880) Great Britain

Bibliography

Geibel, James W. "An Annotated Bibliography of British Criticism of George Eliot, 1858–1900." *Dissertation Abstracts* 30 (1970): 4450A (Ohio State).

Haight, Gordon S. "The George Eliot and George Henry Lewes Collection." *Yale University Library Gazette* 35 (1961): 170–71.

Hutchison, B. "George Eliot, 1819–1880." *Book Collecting and Library Monthly* 3 (July 1968): 17.

Marshall, William H. "A Selective Bibliography of Writings about George Eliot to 1965." *Bulletin of Bibliography* 25 (May–August 1967): 70–72; 25 (September–December 1967): 88–93.

General Works

Adam, Ian. "Character and Destiny in George Eliot's Fiction." *Nineteenth Century Fiction* 20 (September 1965): 127–43.

Adams, Kathleen. "George Eliot Week." *Times Literary Supplement* (September 26, 1968): 1090.

Allott, Miriam. "George Eliot in the 1860's." *Victorian Studies* 5 (December 1961): 93–108.

Althaus, Donald C. "The Love Triangle as a Structural Principle in the Novels of George Eliot." *Dissertation Abstracts International* 32 (1971): 2631A (Ohio).

Anderson, Roland Frank. "Formative Influences on George Eliot, with Special Reference to George Henry Lewes." *Dissertation Abstracts* 25 (1964): 1205–6 (Toronto).

Auerbach, Nina J. "Reality as Vision in the Novels of Jane Austen and George Eliot." *Dissertation Abstracts International* 31 (1971): 4701A–2A (Columbia).

Baker, William. "George Eliot's Projected Napoleonic War Novel: An Unnoted Reading List." *Nineteenth Century Fiction* 29 (March 1975): 453–60.

Baker, William. "John Walter Cross to Herbert Spencer, December 23, 1880: An Unpublished Letter concerning George Eliot's Death." *English Language Notes* 13 (September 1975): 39–40.

Barolini, Helen. "George Eliot as Mary Ann Cross." *South Atlantic Quarterly* 71 (Summer 1972): 292–306.

Barton, Robert E. "Saving Religion: A Comparison of Matthew Arnold and George Eliot." *Dissertation Abstracts International* 34 (1974): 4240A–41A (Washington).

Bedient, Calvin Bernard. "The Fate of the Self: Self and Society in the Novels of George Eliot, D. H. Lawrence, and E. M. Forster." *Dissertation Abstracts* 25 (1964): 1187 (Washington).

Bell, Brenda Joyce Harrison. "The Figure of the Child in the Novels of George Eliot." *Dissertation Abstracts International* 35 (1975): 6701A (South Carolina).

Bell, Srilekha. "George Eliot: A Study in the Intellectual Development of Her Novels." *Dissertation Abstracts* 32 (1972): 6918A–19A (Wisconsin).

Bell, Vereen M. "Character and Point of View in Representative Victorian Novels." *Dissertation Abstracts* 20 (1960): 3740–41 (Duke).

Bennett, Joan. "Unpublished George Eliot Letters." *Times Literary Supplement* (May 16, 1968): 507–8.

Benson, James D. "The Moral-Aesthetic Problem in George Eliot's Fiction." *Dissertation Abstracts* 31 (1970): 1789A–90A (Toronto).

Benson, James D. "Sympathetic Criticism: George Eliot's Response to Contemporary Reviewing." *Nineteenth Century Fiction* 29 (March 1975): 428–40.

Benvenuto, Richard. "At the Crossroads: The Life and Thought of George Eliot." *Studies in the Novel* 2 (Fall 1970): 355–61.

Billingsley, Bruce Adler. " 'Take Her Up Tenderly': A Study of the Fallen Woman in the Nineteenth-Century English Novel." *Dissertation Abstracts* 23 (1962): 1681–82 (Texas).

Bolstad, R. Montelle. "The Myth of Sensibility in George Eliot." *Recovering Literature* 1 (1972): 26–39.

Bonaparte, Felicia. "George Eliot: Tragedy in a Minor Key." *Dissertation Abstracts* 31 (1970): 2374A (N.Y.U.).

Bradley, Anthony G. "Pastoral in the Novels of George Eliot." *Dissertation Abstracts International* 33 (1973): 4334A (S.U.N.Y., Buffalo).

Burns, John Sandidge. "The Wider Life: A Study of the Writings of George Eliot." *Dissertation Abstracts* 25 (1964): 1903–4 (Rice).

Carlisle, Janice M. "The Moral Imagination: Dickens, Thackeray, and George Eliot." *Dissertation Abstracts International* 34 (1974): 6630A (Cornell).

Carroll, David. "An Image of Disenchantment in the Novels of George Eliot." *Review of English Studies* 11 (February 1960): 29–41.

Casson, Allan Perham. "The Early Novels of George Eliot." *Dissertation Abstracts* 21 (1960): 120 (Harvard).

Cate, Hollis L. "The Initial Publication of George Eliot's Novels in America." *Ball State University Forum* 10 (Spring 1969): 65–69.

Cate, Hollis L. "The Literary Reception of George Eliot's Novels in America (1858–1882)." *Dissertation Abstracts* 23 (1963): 3885–86 (Georgia).

Chandler, Jagdish. "Religious and Moral Ideas in the Novels of George Eliot." *Dissertation Abstracts* 24 (1964): 2905 (Wisconsin).

Clark, Robert N. "The Idealist, the Missionary, and the Overreacher in the Novels of George Eliot." *Dissertation Abstracts* 30 (1971): 3903A (Florida).

Collins, Rowland Lee. "The Present Past: The Origin and Exposition of Theme in the Prose Fiction of George Eliot." *Dissertation Abstracts* 22 (1962): 3657 (Stanford).

Combs, John R. "George Eliot's Mind and the Clerical Characters in Her Fiction." *Dissertation Abstracts* 29 (1968): 563A (Texas).

Conway, Richard H. "The Difficulty of Being a Woman: A Study of George Eliot's Heroines." *Dissertation Abstracts International* 34 (1973): 722A (Denver).

Cunningham, Valentine. "George Eliot, Julian Fane and Heine." *Notes and Queries* 18 (July 1971): 252–54.

Daiches, David. "The Return of George Eliot." *Nation* (June 9, 1962): 518–19.

Davis, Norma J. "Pictorialism in George Eliot's Art." *Dissertation Abstracts International* 33 (1973): 5673A (Northwestern).

Decavalcante, Frank. "Sexual Politics in Four Victorian Novels." *Dissertation Abstracts International* 35 (1974): 1618A (Kent State).

Deegan, Thomas F. "George Eliot's Historical Thought and Her Novels of the Historical Imagination." *Dissertation Abstracts International* 31 (1971): 3500A (Northwestern).

Deegan, Robert H. "George Eliot's Novels of the Historical Imagination." *Clio* 1 (1972): 21–33.

DeMeritt, William. "George Eliot as a Tragic Novelist: Her Theory and Practice." *Dissertation Abstracts International* 31 (1971): 4114A–15A (Rutgers).

Deneau, Daniel P. "The River and the Web in the Works of George Eliot." *Research Studies* 35 (1967): 155–66.

Diamond, Naomi June. "Vision and the Role of the Past in the Novels of George Eliot." *Dissertation Abstracts* 20 (1960): 2782–83 (Washington).

Dignon, Hugh Alexander. "Love and Courtship in the Novels of George Eliot, Thomas Hardy, and D. H. Lawrence: A Comparative Study." *Dissertation Abstracts International* 35 (1975): 4425A (N.Y.U.).

Doyle, Sister Mary Ellen. "Distance and Narrative Technique in the Novels of George Eliot." *Dissertation Abstracts* 29 (1969): 3094A–95A (Notre Dame).

Duncan, Charles Freeman. "Time-Levels and Value-Structures in George Eliot's Novels." *Dissertation Abstracts* 26 (1965): 1039 (Emory).

Dunham, Robert H. "Wordsworthian Themes and Attitudes in George Eliot's Novels." *Dissertation Abstracts International* 32 (1972): 5734A (Stanford).

Dylla, Sandra Marie. "Jane Austen and George Eliot: The Influence of Their Social Worlds on Their Women Characters." *Dissertation Abstracts International* 35 (1975): 899A (Wisconsin, Milwaukee).

Edwards, M. "George Eliot and Negative Form." *Critical Quarterly* 17 (Summer 1975): 171–79.

Eisner, Greta, "George Eliot: The Problem Novels." *Dissertation Abstracts International* 35 (1975): 7253A (California, Irvine).

Elsbree, Langdon. "The Breaking Chain: A Study of the Dance in the Novels of Jane Austen, George Eliot, Thomas Hardy, and D. H. Lawrence." *Dissertation Abstracts* 24 (1963): 2476 (Claremont).

Engel, Mary T.J. "The Literary Reputation of George Eliot in Germany 1857–1970." *Dissertation Abstracts International* 34 (1974): 7702A–3A (Detroit).

Ermarth, Elizabeth. "Incarnations: George Eliot's Conception of 'Undeviating Law.'" *Nineteenth Century Fiction* 29 (December 1974): 273–86.

Euwena, Ben. "Denial and Affirmation in Victorian Thought." *Journal of General Education* 21 (October 1969): 201–13.

Evans, C.F.H., and A.C. Wood. "George Eliot's Maternal Ancestry." *Notes and Queries* 19 (November 1972): 409–16.

Feeney, Mary E. "Women in the Major Fiction of George Eliot." *Dissertation Abstracts International* 35 (1974): 446A (Massachusetts).

Feltes, N.N. "George Eliot and the Unified Sensibility." *Publications of the Modern Language Association* 79 (1964): 130–36.

Feltes, N.N. "George Eliot's 'Pier-Glass': The Development of a Metaphor." *Modern Philology* 67 (August 1969): 69–71.

Feltes, N.N. "Phrenology: From Lewes to George Eliot." *Studies in Literary Imagination* 1 (April 1968): 13–22.

Freemen, J. "George Eliot's Great Poetry." *Cambridge Quarterly* 5 (1970): 25–40.

Friedberg, Joan B. "Tragedy in George Eliot and Thomas Hardy." *Dissertation Abstracts International* 33 (1972): 1141A (Pittsburgh).

Fuermann, Warren Bryan. "The Novels of George

Eliot: A Critical Commentary." *Dissertation Abstracts International* 35 (1975): 7254A (Illinois).

Fulmer, Constance M. "Contrasting Pairs of Heroines in George Eliot's Fiction." *Studies in the Novel* 6 (Fall 1974): 288–94.

Fulmer, Constance M. "She Being Dead Yet Speaketh: A Study of George Eliot's Moral Aesthetic." *Dissertation Abstracts* 31 (1970): 2875A (Vanderbilt).

Furniss, John N. "George Eliot and the Protestant Work Ethic." *Dissertation Abstracts International* 34 (1974): 4199A (Duke).

Gelley, Alexander. "Symbolic Setting in the Novel: Studies in Goethe, Stendhal and George Eliot." *Dissertation Abstracts* 26 (1965): 2210–11 (Yale).

Godwin, G. "George Eliot." *New York Times Book Review* (September 7, 1975): 27–28.

Godwin, G. "Would We Have Heard of Marian Evans?" *Ms.* (September 1974): 72–75.

Goldsberry, Dennis M. "George Eliot's Use of the Tragic Mode." *Dissertation Abstracts International* 34 (1973): 273A–74A (North Carolina).

Greene, Philip Leon. "Henry James and George Eliot." *Dissertation Abstracts* 24 (1964): 4188–89 (N.Y.U.).

Haight, Gordon S. "George Eliot and John Blackwood." *Blackwood's* 306 (1969): 385–400.

Haight, Gordon S. "A New George Eliot Letter." *Times Literary Supplement* (February 12, 1971): 187.

Haight, Gordon S. "A New George Eliot Letter." *Yale University Library Gazette* 46 (1971): 24–28.

Haight, Gordon S. "New George Eliot Letters to John Blackwood." *Times Literary Supplement* (March 10, 1972): 281–82.

Haight, Gordon S. "Original Mss Bound In." *Times Literary Supplement* (March 15, 1974): 264.

Haight, Gordon S. "Unpublished George Eliot Letters." *Times Literary Supplement* (May 30, 1968): 553.

Hall, Roland. "Some Antedatings from George Eliot and Other Nineteenth-Century Authors." *Notes and Queries* 15 (November 1968): 410–12.

Harris, Mason D., Jr. "George Eliot and the Problems of Agnosticism: A Study of Philosophical Psychology." *Dissertation Abstracts International* 32 (1971): 1513A (S.U.N.Y., Buffalo).

Harris, Stephen Le Roy. "The Mask of Morality: A Study of the Unconscious Hypocrite in Representative Novels of Jane Austen, Charles Dickens, and

George Eliot." *Dissertation Abstracts* 25 (1965): 4699 (Cornell).

Harvey, W.J. "Ideas in George Eliot." *Modern* (1969): 294–323.

Harvey, W.J. "Ideas in George Eliot." *Modern Language Quarterly* 27 (March 1966): 86–92.

Hennelly, Mark M. "Sibyl in the Gloom: A Study of Guilt in the Life and Novels of George Eliot." *Dissertation Abstracts International* 32 (1971): 920A (St. Louis).

Hester, Waverly Erwin. "George Eliot's Messengers." *Studies in English Literature, 1500–1900* 7 (Autumn 1967): 679–90.

Hester, Waverly Erwin. "George Eliot's Technique as a Novelist." *Dissertation Abstracts* 22 (1962): 2396–97 (North Carolina).

Higdon, David L. "George Eliot and the Art of the Epigraph." *Nineteenth Century Fiction* 25 (September 1970): 127–51.

Higdon, David L. "The Sovereign Fragments: A Study of George Eliot's Epigraphs." *Dissertation Abstracts* 30 (1969): 725A (Kansas).

Hirschberg, Edgar W. "George Eliot and Her Husband." *English Journal* 56 (May 1967): 809–17.

Hoffman, Bruce H. "The Credibility of George Eliot's Major Characters: A Study of Character, Moral Patterns and the Nature of Society in Her Novels." *Dissertation Abstracts International* 31 (1971): 4718A (S.U.N.Y., Buffalo).

Horowitz, Lenore Wisney. "Present, Past, and Future: The Vision of Society in George Eliot's Novels." *Dissertation Abstracts International* 32 (1972): 4567A (Cornell).

Hudson, Stewart M. "George Henry Lewes' Evolutionism in the Fiction of George Eliot." *Dissertation Abstracts International* 31 (1971): 6059A (Southern California).

Hurley, Edward T. "Death and Immortality: George Eliot's Solution." *Nineteenth Century Fiction* 24 (September 1969): 222–27.

Hurley, Edward T. "The Family as an Instrument for Theme and Structure in the Fiction of George Eliot." *Dissertation Abstracts* 28 (1967): 677A (Michigan).

Hurley, Edward T. "Piero di Cosimo: An Alternate Analogy for George Eliot's Realism." *Victorian Newsletter* 31 (Spring 1967): 54–56.

Jackson, Arlene M. "Ideals and Realities in Victorian England: A Study of the Idealistic Quest Theme in the Novels of George Eliot and Thomas Hardy."

Dissertation Abstracts 29 (1968): 872A (Michigan).

James, Glenn J. "Walter Scott and George Eliot: A Common Tradition." *Dissertation Abstracts International* 34 (1974): 4207A (Emory).

John, Joseph. "Pan-Humanism in the Novels of George Eliot." *Dissertation Abstracts International* 36 (1975): 316A (Marquette).

Kakar, H. S. "George Eliot's Treatment of Pain and Suffering." *Literary Half-Yearly* 6 (July 1965): 40–45.

Katona, Anna. "The Changing Image of George Eliot." *Hungarian Studies in English* 2 (1965): 47–59.

Kearney, John P. "George Eliot's Treatment of Time." *Dissertation Abstracts* 29 (1968): 4491A (Wisconsin).

Kenda, Margaret E.M. "Poetic Justice in the Novels of George Eliot and William Makepeace Thackeray." *Dissertation Abstracts International* 32 (1972): 5232A–33A (Iowa).

Kermode, Frank. "Lawrence and the Apocalyptic Types." *Critical Quarterly* 10 (Spring–Summer 1968): 14–38.

Kilcullen, Elizabeth A. "George Eliot's Treatment of Marriage." *Dissertation Abstracts* 30 (1970): 5447A–48A (Toronto).

Knoepflmacher, U.C. "George Eliot, Feuerbach, and the Question of Criticism." *Victorian Studies* 7 (March 1964): 306–9.

Knoepflmacher, U.C. "Mr. Haight's George Eliot: 'Wahrheit und Dichtung.'" *Victorian Studies* 3 (June 1960): 422–30.

Knoepflmacher, U.C. "Of Time, Rivers, and Tragedy: George Eliot and Matthew Arnold." *Victorian Newsletter* 33 (Spring 1968): 1–5.

Knoepflmacher, U.C. "The Victorian Novel of Religious Humanism: A Study of George Eliot, Walter Pater, and Samuel Butler." *Dissertation Abstracts* 22 (1962): 2794–95 (Princeton).

Kraft, Stephanie B. "Women and Society in the Novels of George Eliot and Edith Wharton." *Dissertation Abstracts International* 34 (1973): 2632A (Rochester).

Kumar, Anita S. "Recurring Patterns of Behavior in the Women Characters of George Eliot." *Triveni* 40 (1971): 21–26.

Laing, Robert Cutter, Jr. "Humor in George Eliot's Novels." *Dissertation Abstracts* 22 (1962): 3666 (Pittsburgh).

Ledger, Marshall A. "George Eliot and Nathaniel Hawthorne." *Notes and Queries* 11 (June 1964): 225–26.

Ledlie, Olive. "George Eliot's Narrative Technique in the Dramatic Delineation of Her Mentors." *Dissertation Abstracts International* 35 (1974): 2229A–30A (Rice).

Lee, Robin. "Irony and Attitude in George Eliot and D.H. Lawrence." *English Studies in Africa* 16 (March 1973): 15–21.

Lerner, Laurence. "The Cool Gaze and the Warm Heart." *Listener* (September 29, 1960): 518–19.

Levenson, Shirley Frank. "The Artist and the Woman in George Eliot's Novels." *Dissertation Abstracts International* 35 (1975): 2849A–50A (Brandeis).

Levine, George. "Determinism and Responsibility in the Works of George Eliot." *Publications of the Modern Language Association* 77 (1962): 268–79.

Levine, George. "Determinism in the Novels of George Eliot." *Dissertation Abstracts* 20 (1960): 4112 (Minnesota).

Liebman, Sheldon. "The Counterpoint of Characters in George Eliot's Novels." *Revue des Langues Vivantes* 34 (1968): 9–23.

Linehan, Katherine B. "George Eliot's Use of Comedy and Satire." *Dissertation Abstracts International* 34 (1974): 5919A (Stanford).

MacAndrew, E., and S. Gorsky. "Why Do They Faint and Die? The Birth of the Delicate Heroine." *Journal of Popular Culture* 8 (Spring 1975): 735–45.

Mahar, Margaret Anne. "The Shape of a History: Eliot, Hardy and Lawrence." *Dissertation Abstracts International* 35 (1975): 3734A (Yale).

Marotta, Kenny R. "The Literary Relationship of George Eliot and Harriet Beecher Stowe," *Dissertation Abstracts International* 35 (1974): 3751A (Johns Hopkins).

Marquand, David. "The Invisible Power." *New Society* (September 11, 1969): 403.

Martin, Bruce K. "Standards of Behavior in George Eliot's Novels." *Dissertation Abstracts* 28 (1968): 3191A (Cincinnati).

Masters, Donald C. "George Eliot and the Evangelicals." *Dalhousie Review* 41 (Winter 1961–1962): 505–12.

McMahon, Catherine Rose. "George Eliot and the Feminist Movement in Nineteenth-Century England." *Dissertation Abstracts* 22 (1962): 3649–50

(Stanford).

Merton, Stephen. "George Eliot and William Hale White." *Victorian Newsletter* 25 (Spring 1964): 13–15.

Miller, J. H. "Narrative and History." *English Literary History* 41 (Fall 1974): 455–73.

Nadel, Ira Bruce. "The Alternate Vision: Renunciation in the Novels of George Eliot and Thomas Hardy." *Dissertation Abstracts* 31 (1970): 2929A (Cornell).

Newton, K.M. "George Eliot, George Henry Lewes, and Darwinism." *Durham University Journal* 66 (June 1974): 278–93.

Newton, K. M. "The Role of the Narrator in George Eliot's Novels." *Journal of Narrative Technique* 3 (1973): 97–107.

Norman, Liane. "The Novel as Moral Experiment: George Eliot's Novels." *Dissertation Abstracts* 28 (1968): 2257A (Brandeis).

North, Douglas M. "Inheritance in the Novels of Jane Austen, Charles Dickens, and George Eliot." *Dissertation Abstracts International* 31 (1971): 5419A (Virginia).

Palko, Albert J. "Latter-Day Saints: George Eliot's New Saint Theresa in Image and Symbol." *Dissertation Abstracts International* 34 (1974): 4277A (Notre Dame).

Paris, Bernard J. "George Eliot and the Higher Criticism." *Anglia* 84 (1966): 59–73.

Paris, Bernard J. "George Eliot, Science Fiction, and Fantasy." *Extrapolation* 5 (1964): 26–30.

Paris, Bernard J. "George Eliot's Religion of Humanity." *English Literary History* 29 (December 1962): 418–43.

Peck, Susan C. "George Eliot's Development as a Psychological Novelist." *Dissertation Abstracts International* 32 (1972): 6997A (Wisconsin).

Peterson, Virgil Allison. "Moral Growth in the Heroines of George Eliot." *Dissertation Abstracts* 21 (1960): 119 (California, Los Angeles).

Pinney, Thomas. "The Authority of the Past in George Eliot's Novels." *Nineteenth Century Fiction* 21 (September 1966): 131–48.

Pinney, Thomas. "George Eliot's Reading of Wordsworth: The Record." *Victorian Newsletter* 24 (Fall 1963): 20–22.

Pinney, Thomas. "More Leaves from George Eliot's Notebook." *Huntington Library Quarterly* 29 (August 1966): 353–76.

Pinney, Thomas. "Wordsworth's Influence on

George Eliot." *Dissertation Abstracts* 21 (1960): 124 (Yale).

Price, Theodore. "The Ugly Duckling: Recurrent Themes in George Eliot." *Dissertation Abstracts International* 35 (1975): 2854A (Rutgers).

Pritchett, V.S. "Great Horse-faced Bluestocking." *New Statesman* (October 11, 1968): 463–64.

Pritchett, V. S. "The Pains of Others." *New Statesman* (November 12, 1965): 737–38.

Reisen, Diana Mary Cohart. "Pilgrims of Mortality: The Quest for Identity in the Novels of George Eliot." *Dissertation Abstracts International* 35 (1975): 6730A (Columbia).

Reishman, John V. "Six Moral Fables: A Study of the Redemptive Vision in George Eliot's Short Fiction." *Dissertation Abstracts International* 32 (1972): 4577A (Virginia).

Ringler, Ellin J. "The Problem of Evil: A Correlative Study in the Novels of Nathaniel Hawthorne and George Eliot." *Dissertation Abstracts* 28 (1968): 5068A (Illinois).

Roazen, Deborah H. "George Eliot and Wordsworth: 'The Natural History of German Life' and Peasant Psychology." *Research Studies* 41 (1973): 166–78.

Rogal, Samuel J. "Hymns in George Eliot's Fiction." *Nineteenth Century Fiction* 29 (September 1974): 173–84.

Rounds, Stephen R. "George Eliot's Progressive Alienation from English Life." *Dissertation Abstracts International* 31 (1971): 6567A (Indiana).

Rust, James Davies. "George Eliot's Periodical Contribution." *Dissertation Abstracts* 27 (1966): 186A (Yale).

Sale, William M., Jr. "George Eliot's Moral Dilemma." *Cornell Library Journal* 4 (1968): 1–12.

Sambrook, A. J. "The Natural Historian of Our Social Classes." *English* 14 (Summer 1962): 130–34.

Sealy, R. J. "Brunetière, Montégut—and George Eliot." *Modern Language Review* 66 (January 1971): 66–75.

Secor, Cynthia A. "The Poems of George Eliot: A Critical Edition with Introduction and Notes." *Dissertation Abstracts* 30 (1970): 5457A–58A (Cornell).

Shumaker, Ronald C. "The Rhetoric of George Eliot's Fiction." *Dissertation Abstracts International* 35 (1974): 2299A (Pittsburgh).

Siff, David H. "The Choir Invisible: The Relation of

George Eliot's Poetry and Fiction." *Dissertation Abstracts* 30 (1969): 293A–94A (N.Y.U.).

Simon, Irene. "George Eliot and Hendrik Conscience." *Revue des Langues Vivantes* 26 (1960): 386–89.

Skye, June. "George Eliot and St. Peter's." *Notes and Queries* 19 (July 1972): 263–64.

Smally, Barbara M. "The Pattern of Illusion: A Correlative Study in the Novels of Flaubert and George Eliot." *Dissertation Abstracts* 30 (1969): 340A–41A (Illinois).

Smith, Corless Ann. "George Eliot and the Romantic Enterprise." *Dissertation Abstracts International* 36 (1975): 286A–87A (Missouri).

Smith, David J. "The Arrested Heart: Familial Love and Psychic Conflict in Five Mid-Victorian Novels." *Dissertation Abstracts* 27 (1966): 1839A (Washington).

Spivey, Ted R. "George Eliot: Victorian Romantic and Modern Realist." *Studies in Literary Imagination* 1 (October 1968): 5–21.

Steele, Karen Beth. "Social Change in George Eliot's Fiction." *Dissertation Abstracts International* 35 (1975): 7329A (Brown).

Sukenick, Lynn. "Sense and Sensibility in Women's Fiction: Studies in the Novels of George Eliot, Virginia Woolf, Anais Nin and Doris Lessing." *Dissertation Abstracts International* 35 (1975): 4563A (C.U.N.Y.).

Sullivan, William J. "George Eliot and the Fine Arts." *Dissertation Abstracts International* 31 (1971): 4736A (Wisconsin).

Swann, Brian. "George Eliot and Realism: The Development of a Concept of Symbolic Form." *Dissertation Abstracts International* 31 (1971): 6635A–36A (Princeton).

Szanto, Alison A. "Between Liberalism and Democracy: George Eliot's Novels and the Structure of Mid-Victorian Social Reality." *Dissertation Abstracts International* 34 (1974): 4220A (California, San Diego).

Szirotny, June S. "The Religious Background of George Eliot's Novels." *Dissertation Abstracts* 27 (1967): 2547A (Stanford).

Templin, Charlotte H. "The Treatment of Community in the Novels of George Eliot." *Dissertation Abstracts International* 33 (1973): 5753A (Indiana).

Templin, Laurence H. "George Eliot: A Study of the Omniscient Point of View in Her Fiction."

Dissertation Abstracts 25 (1964): 2967–68 (Indiana).

Tesler, Rita Weinberg. "George Eliot and the Inner Self." *Dissertation Abstracts International* 35 (1975): 2229A (N.Y.U.).

Thomson, Patricia. "The Three Georges (Sand, Eliot, Lewes)." *Nineteenth Century Fiction* 18 (September 1963): 137–50.

Thuente, David R. "Channels of Feeling: George Eliot's Search for the Natural Bases of Religion." *Dissertation Abstracts International* 34 (1974): 5207A–8A (Kentucky).

Tomlinson, T.B. "Literature and History—The Novel." *Melbourne Critical Review* 4 (1961): 93–101.

Tucker, Houston Clay. "George Eliot's Ideal Self: A Study of Subjective Influences on Her Prose Fiction." *Dissertation Abstracts* 21 (1961): 2723 (Vanderbilt).

Turner, William H. "George Eliot's Narrative Technique." *Dissertation Abstracts* 31 (1970): 1818A (Toronto).

Tye, J.R. "George Eliot's Unascribed Mottoes." *Nineteenth Century Fiction* 22 (December 1967): 235–49.

Unger, William E., Jr. "Implied Authors and Created Readers in Thackeray, Trollope, Charlotte Brontë, and George Eliot." *Dissertation Abstracts International* 35 (1974): 2956A–57A (Ohio State).

Waddington, Patrick. "Turgenev and George Eliot: A Literary Friendship." *Modern Language Review* 66 (October 1971): 751–59.

Wade, Rosalind. "George Eliot: Journalist (Mary Ann Evans 1819–1880)." *Contemporary Review* 215 (1969): 88–92.

Wade, Rosalind. "George Eliot and Her Poetry." *Contemporary Review* 204 (1963): 38–42.

Watson, Kathleen. "George Eliot and Mrs. Oliphant: A Comparison in Social Attitudes." *Essays in Criticism* 19 (October 1969): 410–19.

Wheatley, James Holbrook. "George Eliot and the Art of Thought: Studies in the Early Novels." *Dissertation Abstracts* 21 (1960): 120 (Harvard).

Whitlock, Roger D. "Charles Dickens and George Eliot: Moral Art in the 'Age of Equipoise.'" *Dissertation Abstracts International* 35 (1974): 484A (Washington).

Williams, Raymond. "The Knowable Community in George Eliot's Novels." *Novel* 2 (Spring 1969):

255–68.

Wilson, Jack H. "Eggleston's Indebtedness to George Eliot in *Roxy*." *American Literature* 42 (March 1970): 38–49.

Wilson, Jack H. "George Eliot in America, Her Vogue and Influence, 1858–1900." *Dissertation Abstracts* 27 (1966): 190A (North Carolina).

Wilson, Lillian. "George Eliot and the Victorian Ideal." *Dissertation Abstracts* 29 (1968): 3114A (Ohio).

Witemeyer, Hugh. "George Eliot, Naumann, and the Nazarenes." *Victorian Studies* 18 (December 1974): 145–58.

Wolff, Michael. "The Uses of Context: Aspects of the 1860's." *Victorian Studies* 9, Supplement (1965): 47–63.

Woodcock, John A. "The Moral Dimension of Beauty in George Eliot's Heroines." *Dissertation Abstracts International* 32 (1972): 4639A (S.U.N.Y., Stony Brook).

Zak, Michele W. "Feminism and the New Novel." *Dissertation Abstracts International* 34 (1974): 5215A (Ohio State).

Zimmerman, Bonnie S. " 'Appetite for Submission': The Female Role in the Novels of George Eliot." *Dissertation Abstracts International* 35 (1974): 1639A (S.U.N.Y., Buffalo).

Individual Works

Adam Bede (1859)

Adam, I. W. "Restoration through Feeling in George Eliot's Fiction: A New Look at Hetty Sorrel." *Victorian Newsletter* 22 (Fall 1962): 9–12.

Adam, Ian. "Structure of Realisms in *Adam Bede*." *Nineteenth Century Fiction* 30 (September 1975): 127–49.

Anderson, Roland F. "George Eliot Provoked: John Blackwood and Chapter Seventeen of *Adam Bede*." *Modern Philology* 71 (August 1973): 39–47.

Beeton, D.R. "Aspects of *Adam Bede*." *English Studies in Africa* 14 (March 1971): 13–36.

Beyers, Brian. "*Adam Bede*: Society in Flux." *Unisa English Studies* 11 (September 1973): 25–29.

Buchen, Irving H. "Arthur Donnithorne and *Zeluco*: Characterization via Literary Allusion in *Adam Bede*." *Victorian Newsletter* 23 (Spring 1963): 18–19.

Burton, Thomas G. "Hetty Sorrel, the Forlorn Maiden." *Victorian Newsletter* 30 (Fall 1966): 24–26.

Cartwright, Jerome D. "Authorial Commentary in the Novels of George Eliot as Primarily Exemplified in *Adam Bede, The Mill on the Floss*, and *Middlemarch*." *Dissertation Abstracts* 30 (1970): 5402A (Wisconsin).

Casson, Allan. "*The Scarlet Letter* and *Adam Bede*." *Victorian Newsletter* 20 (Fall 1961): 18–19.

Colby, Robert A. "Miss Evans, Miss Mulock and Hetty Sorrel." *English Language Notes* 2 (March 1965): 206–11.

Edwards, Michael. "A Reading of *Adam Bede*." *Critical Quarterly* 14 (Autumn 1972): 205–18.

Griffith, Philip M. "Symbols of the Arm and Handclasp in George Eliot's *Adam Bede*." *South Central Bulletin* 33 (1973): 200–202.

Herbert, Christopher. "Preachers and the Schemes of Nature in *Adam Bede*." *Nineteenth Century Fiction* 29 (March 1975): 412–27.

Higdon, David L. "The Iconographic Backgrounds of *Adam Bede*, Chapter 15." *Nineteenth Century Fiction* 27 (September 1972): 155–70.

Higdon, David L. "*Sortes Biblicae* in *Adam Bede*." *Papers on Language and Literature* 9 (1973): 396–405.

Jones, W. Gareth. "George Eliot's *Adam Bede* and Tolstoy's Conception of *Anna Karenina*." *Modern Language Review* 61 (July 1966): 473–81.

Knoepflmacher, U.C. "The Post-Romatic Imagination: *Adam Bede*, Wordsworth and Milton." *English Literary History* 34 (December 1967): 518–40.

Martin, B. K. "Rescue and Marriage in *Adam Bede*." *Studies in English Literature, 1500–1900* 12 (Autumn 1972): 745–63.

Ryals, Clyde De L. "The Thorn Imagery in *Adam Bede*." *Victorian Newsletter* 22 (Fall 1962): 12–13.

Selig, Robert L. "The Red Haired Lady Orator: Parallel Passages in *The Bostonians* and *Adam Bede*." *Nineteenth Century Fiction* 16 (September 1961): 164–69.

Squires, Michael. "*Adam Bede* and the *Locus Amoenus*." *Studies in English Literature, 1500–1900* 13 (Autumn 1973): 670–76.

Ten Harmsel, Henrietta. "From Animal to Christ in *Adam Bede*." *Christianity and Literature* 20 (Spring 1971): 17–24.

Watson, Kathleen. "Dinah Morris and Mrs. Evans: A Comparative Study of Methodist Diction." *Review of English Studies* 22 (August 1971): 282–94.

Wiesenfarth, Joseph. "*Adam Bede* and Myth." *Papers on Language and Literature* 8 (1972): 39–52.

Daniel Deronda (1876)

Alley, Henry M. "*Middlemarch* and *Daniel Deronda*, Heroes of Erudition and Experience." *Dissertation Abstracts International* 32 (1972): 4552A (Cornell).

Baker, William. "George Eliot's Readings in Nineteenth-Century Jewish Historians: A Note on the Background of *Daniel Deronda*." *Victorian Studies* 15 (June 1972): 463–73.

Beeton, D.R. "George Eliot's Greatest and Poorest Novel: An Appraisal of *Daniel Deronda*." *English Studies in Africa* 8 (September 1965): 8–27.

Carroll, D.R. "*Mansfield Park, Daniel Deronda* and Ordination." *Modern Philology* 62 (February 1965): 217–26.

Fisch, Harold. "*Daniel Deronda* or Gwendolen Harleth?" *Nineteenth Century Fiction* 19 (March 1965): 345–56.

Fricke, Douglas C. "Art and Artists in *Daniel Deronda*." *Studies in the Novel* 5 (Summer 1973): 220–28.

Handley, Graham. "A Missing Month in *Daniel Deronda*." *Times Literary Supplement* (February 3, 1961): 73.

Handley, Graham. "A Note on *Daniel Deronda*." *Notes and Queries* 7 (April 1960): 147–48.

Hester, Waverly Erwin. "George Eliot's Use of Historical Events in *Daniel Deronda*." *English Language Notes* 4 (December 1966): 115–18.

Higdon, David Leon. "Eliot's *Daniel Deronda*." *Explicator* 31 (November 1972): Item 15.

Holland, John G. "George Eliot's *Daniel Deronda* with Particular Consideration of the Jewish Elements." *Dissertation Abstracts International* 33 (1972): 1727A–28A (North Carolina).

Kearney, John P. "Time and Beauty in *Daniel Deronda*: 'Was She Beautiful or not Beautiful?' " *Nineteenth Century Fiction* 26 (December 1971): 286–306.

Knoepflmacher, Ulrich Camillus. "*Daniel Deronda* and William Shakespeare." *Victorian Newsletter* 19 (Spring 1961): 27–28.

Kriefall, Luther H. "A Victorian Apocalypse: A Study of George Eliot's *Daniel Deronda* and Its Relation to David F. Strauss' *Das Leben Jesu*." *Dissertation Abstracts* 28 (1967): 234A (Michigan).

Lainoff, Seymour. "James and Eliot: The Two Gwendolens." *Victorian Newsletter* 21 (Spring 1962): 23–24.

Leavis, F.R. "George Eliot's Zionist Novel." *Commentary* 30 (October 1960): 317–25.

Lerner, Laurence. "The Education of Gwendolen Harleth." *Critical Quarterly* 7 (Winter 1965): 355–64.

Levenson, Shirley Frank. "The Use of Music in *Daniel Deronda*." *Nineteenth Century Fiction* 24 (December 1969): 317–34.

Levine, George. "Isabel, Gwendolen, and Dorothea." *English Literary History* 30 (September 1963): 244–57.

Lund, Mary G. "George Eliot and the Jewish Question." *Discourse* 13 (Summer 1970): 390–97.

Mason, Kenneth M., Jr. "George Eliot and the Question of Tragic Redemption: A Study of Imaginative Sympathy in *The Mill on the Floss* and *Daniel Deronda*." *Dissertation Abstracts International* 33 (1973): 5735A (Cornell).

Preyer, Robert. "Beyond the Literal Imagination: Vision and Unreality in *Daniel Deronda*." *Victorian Studies* 4 (September 1960): 33–54.

Robinson, Carole. "The Severe Angel: A Study of *Daniel Deronda*." *English Literary History* 31 (September 1964): 278–300.

Sedgley, Anne. "*Daniel Deronda*." *Critical Review* 13 (1970): 3–19.

Steinhoff, William R. "The Metaphorical Texture of *Daniel Deronda*." *Books Abroad* 35 (Summer 1961): 220–24.

Sudrann, Jean. "*Daniel Deronda* and the Landscape of Exile." *English Literary History* 37 (September 1970): 433–55.

Sullivan, William J. "The Allusion to Jenny Lind in *Daniel Deronda*." *Nineteenth Century Fiction* 29 (September 1974): 211–14.

Swann, Brian. "Eyes in the Mirror: Imagery and Symbolism in *Daniel Deronda*." *Nineteenth Century Fiction* 23 (March 1969): 434–45.

Swann, Brian. "George Eliot and the Play: Symbol and Metaphor of the Drama in *Daniel Deronda*." *Dalhousie Review* 52 (Summer 1972): 191–202.

Swann, Brian. "George Eliot's Ecumenical Jew: Or, The Novel as Outdoor Temple." *Novel* 8 (Fall 1974): 39–50.

Wiesenfarth, Joseph. "The Medea in *Daniel Deronda*." *Neueren Sprachen* 22 (1973): 103–8.

Wing, George. "The Motto to Chapter 21 of *Daniel Deronda*: A Key to All George Eliot's Mythologies?" *Dalhousie Review* 54 (Spring 1974): 16–32.

Wolfe, Thomas P., II. "The Inward Vocation: An Essay on George Eliot's *Daniel Deronda.*" *Dissertation Abstracts International* 34 (1974): 6610A–11A (Rutgers).

Felix Holt the Radical (1866)

Bamber, Linda. "Self-Defeating Politics in George Eliot's *Felix Holt.*" *Victorian Studies* 18 (June 1975): 419–35.

Carroll, David R. *"Felix Holt*: Society as Protagonist." *Nineteenth Century Fiction* 17 (December 1962): 237–52.

Craig, David. "Fiction and the Rising Industrial Classes." *Essays in Criticism* 17 (January 1967): 64–73.

Horowitz, Lenore Wisney. "George Eliot's Vision of Society in *Felix Holt the Radical.*" *Texas Studies in Literature and Language* 17 (Spring 1975): 175–91.

Myers, W.F.T. "Politics and Personality in *Felix Holt.*" *Renaissance and Modern Studies* 10 (1966): 5–33.

Thomson, Fred C. *"Felix Holt* as Classic Tragedy." *Nineteenth Century Fiction* 16 (June 1961): 47–58.

Thomson, Fred C. "The Legal Plot in *Felix Holt.*" *Studies in English Literature, 1500–1900* 7 (Autumn 1967): 691–704.

The Lifted Veil (1878)

Hurley, Edward. *"The Lifted Veil*: George Eliot as Anti-Intellectual." *Studies in Short Fiction* 5 (Spring 1968): 257–62.

Rubinstein, Elliott L. "A Forgotten Tale by George Eliot." *Nineteenth Century Fiction* 17 (September 1962): 175–83.

Middlemarch: A Study of Provincial Life (1871–1872)

Adam, Ian. "A Huxley Echo in *Middlemarch.*" *Notes and Queries* 11 (June 1964): 227.

Alley, Henry M. *"Middlemarch* and *Daniel Deronda,* Heroes of Erudition and Experience." *Dissertation Abstracts International* 32 (1972): 4552A (Cornell).

Bedient, Calvin. *"Middlemarch*: Touching Down." *Hudson Review* 22 (Spring 1969): 70–84.

Blumberg, Edwina J. "Tolstoy and the English Novel: A Note on *Middlemarch* and *Anna Karenina.*" *Slavic Review* 30 (1971): 561–69.

Bush, Gertrude E.B. *"Middlemarch* and the Tradition of the English Provincial Novel." *Dissertation*

Abstracts International 35 (1974): 3672A (Wisconsin).

Byrd, Scott. "The Fractured Crystal in *Middlemarch* and *The Golden Bowl.*" *Modern Fiction Studies* 18 (Winter 1972–1973): 551–54.

Cartwright, Jerome D. "Authorial Commentary in the Novels of George Eliot as Primarily Exemplified in *Adam Bede, The Mill on the Floss,* and *Middlemarch.*" *Dissertation Abstracts* 30 (1970): 5402A (Wisconsin).

Coles, R. "Irony in the Mind's Life." *Virginia Quarterly Review* 49 (Autumn 1974): 526–52.

Collins, T. J. *"Middlemarch* and Moral Stupidity." *Melbourne Critical Review* 10 (1967): 88–98.

Curry, Martha. *"Middlemarch*: Unity and Diversity." *Barat Review* 5 (1970): 83.

Damm, Robert F. "Sainthood and Dorothea Brooke." *Victorian Newsletter* 35 (Spring 1969): 18–22.

Degroot, Elizabeth M. *"Middlemarch* and Dorothea Brooke: The Saints Go Marching Out." *Christianity and Literature* 22 (Fall 1972): 13–18.

Deneau, Daniel P. "Eliot's Casaubon and Mythology." *American Notes and Queries* 6 (April 1968): 125–27.

Di Pasquale, Pasquale. "The Imagery and Structure of *Middlemarch.*" *English Studies* 52 (1971): 425–35.

Duerksen, Roland A. "Shelley in *Middlemarch.*" *Keats-Shelley Journal* 14 (1965): 23–31.

Duncan-Jones, E. E. "Hazlitt's Mistake." *Times Literary Supplement* (January 27, 1966): 68.

Durr, Volker O. "The World and Its Protagonists: Goethe's *Wilhelm Meister* and George Eliot's *Middlemarch.*" *Dissertation Abstracts International* 34 (1973): 724A (Princeton).

Edwards, Lee R. "Women, Energy and *Middlemarch.*" *Massachusetts Review* 13 (Winter–Spring 1972): 223–38.

Ferguson, Suzanne C. "Mme. Lauré and Operative Irony in *Middlemarch*: A Structural Analogy." *Studies in English Literature, 1500–1900* 3 (Autumn 1963): 509–16.

Fernando, Lloyd. "George Eliot, Feminism and Dorothea Brooke." *Review of English Literature* 4 (January 1963): 76–90.

Fernando, Lloyd. "Special Pleading and Art in *Middlemarch*: The Relations between the Sexes." *Modern Language Review* 67 (January 1972): 44–49.

Fleissner, Robert F. *"Middlemarch* and Idealism:

Newman, Naumann, Goethe." *Greyfriar* 14 (1973): 21–26.

French, A.L. "A Note on *Middlemarch*." *Nineteenth Century Fiction* 26 (December 1971): 339–47.

Gillespie, Harold R., Jr. "George Eliot's Tertius Lydgate and Charles Kingsley's Tom Thurnall." *Notes and Queries* 11 (June 1964): 226–27.

Goldfarb, Russell M. "Caleb Garth of *Middlemarch*." *Victorian Newsletter* 26 (Fall 1964): 14–19.

Green, Mildred S. "Isolation and Integrity: Madame de La Fayette's Princesse de Clèves and George Eliot's Dorothea Brooke." *Revue de Littérature Comparée* 44 (1970): 145–54.

Greenberg, Robert A. "The Heritage of Will Ladislaw." *Nineteenth Century Fiction* 15 (March 1961): 355–58.

Greenberg, Robert A. "Plexuses and Ganglia: Scientific Allusion in *Middlemarch*." *Nineteenth Century Fiction* 30 (June 1975): 33–52.

Griffin, Robert P. "Image and Intent: Some Observations on Style in *Middlemarch*." *Ball State University Forum* 10 (Summer 1969): 60–63.

Hagan, John. "*Middlemarch*: Narrative Unity in the Story of Dorothea Brooke." *Nineteenth Century Fiction* 16 (June 1961): 17–31.

Hall, Margaret M. "Modes of Narrative Irony: A Reading of *Middlemarch* and *Madame Bovary*." *Dissertation Abstracts International* 32 (1972): 4564A (Virginia).

Halperin, John W. "The Language of Meditation: Four Studies in Nineteenth Century Fiction." *Dissertation Abstracts International* 32 (1972): 6976A–77A (Johns Hopkins).

Hastings, Robert. "Dorothea Brooke: The Struggle for Existence in *Middlemarch*." *Thoth* 4 (1963): 61–66.

Heywood, C. "A Source for *Middlemarch*: Miss Braddon's *The Doctor's Wife* and *Madame Bovary*." *Revue de Littérature Comparée* 44 (1970): 184–94.

Hoggart, Richard. "A Victorian Masterpeice." *Listener* (March 8, 1962): 407–8.

Hollahan, E. "The Concept of 'Crisis' in *Middlemarch*." *Nineteenth Century Fiction* 28 (March 1974): 450–57.

Hornback, Bert G. "The Moral Imagination of George Eliot." *Papers on Language and Literature* 8 (1972): 380–94.

Hornback, Bert G. "The Organization of *Middlemarch*." *Papers on Language and Literature*, 2

(1966): 169–75.

Hulme, Hilda. "*Middlemarch* as Science-Fiction: Notes on Language and Imagery." *Novel* 2 (Fall 1968): 36–45.

Isaacs, Neil D. "*Middlemarch*: Crescendo of Obligatory Drama." *Nineteenth Century Fiction* 18 (June 1963): 21–34.

Jackson, Arlene M. "Dorothea Brooke of Middlemarch: Idealism and Victorian Reality." *Cithara* 12 (1973): 91–102.

Katz, Judith N. "Rooms of Their Own: Forms and Images of Liberation in Five Novels." *Dissertation Abstracts International* 34 (1973): 1283A (Penn. State).

Kenney, Edwin J., Jr. "George Eliot's Presence in *Middlemarch*." *Dissertation Abstracts* 29 (1968): 570A (Cornell).

Knoepflmacher, U.C. "*Middlemarch*: An Avuncular View." *Nineteenth Century Fiction* 30 (June 1975): 53–81.

Lee, Robin. "*Middlemarch*—A Hundred Years Later." *Standpunte* 27 (1973): 16–20.

Levine, George. "Isabel, Gwendolen, and Dorothea." *English Literary History* 30 (September 1963): 244–57.

Luecke, Sister Jane Marie. "Ladislaw and the *Middlemarch* Vision." *Nineteenth Century Fiction* 19 (June 1964): 55–64.

Lyons, Richard S. "The Method of *Middlemarch*." *Nineteenth Century Fiction* 21 (June 1966): 35–47.

Lyons, Richard S. "A Study of *Middlemarch*." *Dissertation Abstracts* 21 (1961): 2276–77 (Princeton).

Mason, Michael Y. "*Middlemarch* and History." *Nineteenth Century Fiction* 15 (March 1961): 417–31.

Mason, Michael Y. "*Middlemarch* and Science: Problems of Life and Mind." *Review of English Studies* 23 (May 1972): 151–69.

McCarthy, Patrick J. "Lydgate: The New Young Surgeon of *Middlemarch*." *Studies in English Literature, 1500–1900* 10 (Autumn 1970): 805–16.

McMaster, Juliet. "*Middlemarch* Centennial Conference." *Victorian Studies* 16 (September 1972): 387–89.

Meyer, S. P. "*Middlemarch*." *Times Literary Supplement* (January 25, 1968): 93.

Nash, Deanna C. "The Web as an Organic Metaphor in *The Marble Faun, Middlemarch: A Study of Provincial Life*, and *The Golden Bowl*: The Growth of Contextualism as an Aesthetic Theory in the Nineteenth Century." *Dissertation Abstracts International* 31 (1971): 4131A (North Carolina).

Newton, K.M. "Historical Prototypes in *Middlemarch.*" *English Studies* 56 (1975): 403–8.

Pinney, Thomas. "Another Note on the Forgotten Past of Will Ladislaw." *Nineteenth Century Fiction* 17 (June 1962): 69–73.

Pratt, John Clark. "A *Middlemarch* Miscellany: An Edition with Introduction and Notes of George Eliot's 1868–1871 Notebook." *Dissertation Abstracts* 26 (1966): 6050 (Princeton).

Riemer, A.P. "Ariadne and Cleopatra: The Treatment of Dorothea in *Middlemarch.*" *Southern Review* (Australia) 2 (1966): 50–58.

Robbins, Larry M. "*Mill* and *Middlemarch*: The Progress of Public Opinion." *Victorian Newsletter* 31 (Spring 1967): 37–39.

Scott, James F. "George Eliot, Positivism, and the Social Vision of *Middlemarch.*" *Victorian Studies* 16 (September 1972): 59–76.

Swann, Brian. "*Middlemarch*: Realism and Symbolic Form." *English Literary History* 39 (June 1972): 279–308.

Swann, Brian. "*Middlemarch* and Myth." *Nineteenth Century Fiction* 28 (September 1973): 210–14.

Szirotny, J. S. "A Classical Reference in *Hard Times* and in *Middlemarch.*" *Notes and Queries* 15 (November 1968): 421–22.

Tomlinson, T.B. "*Middlemarch* and Modern Society." *Melbourne Critical Review* 6 (1963): 44–55.

Troost, Betty Todd. "English Wit: George Eliot in *Scenes of Clerical Life* and *Middlemarch.*" *Mankato State College Studies* 3 (December 1968): 19–26.

Warner, Frances Claire. "Toward *Middlemarch*: The Heroine's Search for Guidance as Motif in the Earlier Novels of George Eliot." *Dissertation Abstracts International* 35 (1975): 4462A (Illinois).

Willey, Frederick. "Appearance and Reality in *Middlemarch.*" *Southern Review* (U.S.) 5 (1969): 419–35.

The Mill on the Floss (1860)

Auerbach, N. "Power of Hunger: Demonism and Maggie Tulliver." *Nineteenth Century Fiction* 30 (September 1975): 150–71.

Bellringer, A.W. "Education in *The Mill on the Floss.*" *Review of English Literature* 7 (July 1966): 52–61.

Brown, Keith. "The Ending of *The Mill on the Floss.*" *Notes and Queries* 11 (June 1964): 226.

Cartwright, Jerome D. "Authorial Commentary in the Novels of George Eliot as Primarily Exemplified in *Adam Bede*, *The Mill on the Floss*, and *Middlemarch.*" *Dissertation Abstracts* 30 (1970): 5402A (Wisconsin).

Casson, Allan. "*The Mill on the Floss* and Keller's *Romeo und Julia auf dem Dorfe.*" *Modern Language Notes* 75 (January 1960): 20–22.

Ermarth, Elizabeth. "Maggie Tulliver's Long Suicide." *Studies in English Literature, 1500–1900* 14 (Autumn 1974): 587–601.

Goldfarb, Russell M. "Robert P. Warren's Tollivers and George Eliot's Tullivers." *University Review* (Kansas) 36 (1970): 275–79.

Hagan, John. "A Reinterpretation of *The Mill on the Floss.*" *Publications of the Modern Language Association* 87 (1972): 53–63.

Higdon, David L. "Failure of Design in *The Mill on the Floss.*" *Journal of Narrative Technique* 3 (1973): 183–92.

Lee, R.H. "The Unity of *The Mill on the Floss.*" *English Studies in Africa* 7 (March 1964): 34–53.

Levine, George. "Intelligence as Deception: *The Mill on the Floss.*" *Publications of the Modern Language Association* 80 (1965): 402–9.

Makurath, Paul A., Jr. "The Symbolism of the Flood in Eliot's *Mill on the Floss.*" *Studies in the Novel* 7 (Summer 1975): 298–330.

Mason, Kenneth M., Jr. "George Eliot and the Question of Tragic Redemption: A Study of Imaginative Sympathy in *The Mill on the Floss* and *Daniel Deronda.*" *Dissertation Abstracts International* 33 (1973): 5735A (Cornell).

Moldstad, David. "*The Mill on the Floss* and *Antigone.*" *Publications of the Modern Language Association* 85 (1970): 527–31.

Osgerby, J.R. "Eliot's *Mill on the Floss.*" *Use of English* 17 (Autumn 1965): 18–24.

Paris, Bernard J. "The Inner Conflicts of Maggie Tulliver: A Horneyan Analysis." *Centennial Review of Arts and Sciences* 13 (1969): 166–99.

Putzell, Sara M. " 'An Antagonism of Valid Claims': Dynamics of *The Mill on the Floss.*" *Studies in the Novel* 7 (Summer 1975): 227–44.

Robbins, Larry M. "*Mill* and *Middlemarch*: The Progress of Public Opinion." *Victorian Newsletter* 31 (Spring 1967): 37–39.

Roberts, Lynne T. "Perfect Pyramids: *The Mill on the Floss.*" *Texas Studies in Literature and Language* 13 (Spring 1971): 111–24.

Siefert, Susan Elizabeth. "The Dilemma of the Talented Woman: A Study in Nineteenth Century Fiction." *Dissertation Abstracts International* 36 (1975): 285A–86A (Marquette).

Smith, David J. "The Arrested Heart: Familial Love and Psychic Conflict in Five Mid-Victorian Novels." *Dissertation Abstracts* 27 (1966): 1839A (Washington).

Smith, David J. "Incest Patterns in Two Victorian Novels." *Literature and Psychology* 15 (1965): 135–62.

Smith, Grover. "A Source for Hopkins' 'Spring and Fall' in *The Mill on the Floss*." *English Language Notes* 1 (September 1963): 43–46.

Speck, Paul S. "Self and Self-Sacrifice in *The Mill on the Floss*." *Innisfree* 1 (1974): 21–28.

Steig, Michael. "Anality in *The Mill on the Floss*." *Novel* 5 (Fall 1971): 42–53.

Sullivan, William J. "Music and Musical Allusion in *The Mill on the Floss*." *Criticism* 16 (1974): 232–46.

Mr. Gilfil's Love-Story (1857)

Knoepflmacher, U. C. "George Eliot's Anti-Romantic Romance: *Mr. Gilfil's Love-Story*." *Victorian Newsletter* 31 (Spring 1967): 11–15.

Question and Answer (1836)

Stang, Maurice. "The German Original of a George Eliot Poem." *Notes and Queries* 21 (January 1974): 15.

Romola (1863)

Bullen, J.B. "George Eliot's *Romala* as a Positivist Allegory." *Review of English Studies* 26 (November 1975): 425–35.

Dahl, Curtis. "When the Deity Returns: *The Marble Faun* and *Romola*." *Papers on Language and Literature* 5 (1969): 82–99.

Delaura, David J. "*Romola* and the Origin of the Paterian View of Life." *Nineteenth Century Fiction* 21 (December 1966): 225–33.

Hill, D.L. "Pater's Debt to *Romala*." *Nineteenth Century Fiction* 22 (March 1968): 361–77.

Perry, Jill. " 'Esse Videtur' in *Romola*." *Notes and Queries* 17 (January 1970): 19.

Peterson, Virgil A. "*Romola*: A Victorian Quest for Values." *West Virginia University Bulletin: Philological Papers* 16 (November 1967): 49–62.

Poston, Lawrence, III. "*Romola* and Thomas Trollope's *Filippo Strozzi*." *Victorian Newsletter* 25 (Spring 1964): 20–22.

Poston, Lawrence, III. "Setting and Theme in *Romola*." *Nineteenth Century Fiction* 20 (March 1966): 355–66.

Robinson, Carole. "*Romola*: A Reading of the Novel." *Victorian Studies* 6 (September 1962): 29–42.

Santangelo, Gennaro A. "The Background of George Eliot's *Romola*." *Dissertation Abstracts* 24 (1963): 2485–86 (North Carolina).

Santangelo, Gennaro A. "Villari's *Life and Times of Savonarola*: A Source for George Eliot's *Romola*." *Anglia* 90 (1972): 118–31.

Sullivan, William J. "Piero di Cosimo and the Higher Primitivism in *Romola*." *Nineteenth Century Fiction* 26 (March 1972): 390–405.

Sullivan, William J. "The Sketch of the Three Masks in *Romola*." *Victorian Newsletter* 41 (Spring 1972): 9–13.

Tuman, Myron C. "*Frederick the Great, Romola, The Ring and the Book* and the Mid-Victorian Crisis in Historicism," *Dissertation Abstracts International* 34 (1974): 7251A (Tulane).

Wilson, Jack H. "Howells' Use of George Eliot's *Romola* in *April Hopes*." *Publications of the Modern Language Association* 84 (1969): 1620–27.

Scenes of Clerical Life (1857)

Deneau, Daniel P. "Imagery in the *Scenes of Clerical Life*." *Victorian Newsletter* 28 (Fall 1965): 18–22.

Grossman, Richard H. "Drama and Background in George Eliot's *Scenes of Clerical Life*." *Dissertation Abstracts International* 33 (1973): 5679A (California, San Diego).

Higdon, David Leon. "*Scenes of Clerical Life*: Idea through Image." *Victorian Newsletter* 33 (Spring 1968): 56–58.

Laski, Marghanita. "Some Words from George Eliot's *Scenes of Clerical Life*." *Notes and Queries* 9 (August 1962): 304–5.

Nicholl, Catherine C. "*Scenes of Clerical Life*: George Eliot's Apprenticeship." *Dissertation Abstracts International* 32 (1971): 1523A (Minnesota).

Troost, Betty Todd. "English Wit: George Eliot in *Scenes of Clerical Life* and *Middlemarch*." *Mankato State College Studies* 3 (December 1968): 19–26.

Silas Marner, or the Weaver of Raveloe (1861)

Higdon, David Leon. "Sortilege in George Eliot's *Silas Marner*." *Papers on Language and Literature* 10 (1974): 51–57.

Martin, Bruce K. "Similarity within Dissimilarity: The Dual Structure of *Silas Marner*." *Texas Studies in Literature and Language* 14 (Fall 1972): 479–89.

Milner, Ian. "Structure and Quality in *Silas Marner.*" *Studies in English Literature, 1500–1900* 6 (Autumn 1966): 717–29.

Quick, Jonathan R. "A Critical Edition of George Eliot's *Silas Marner.*" *Dissertation Abstracts* 29 (1969): 3980A (Yale).

Quick, Jonathan R. "*Silas Marner* as Romance: The Example of Hawthorne." *Nineteenth Century Fiction* 29 (December 1974): 287–98.

Thomson, Fred C. "The Theme of Alienation in *Silas Marner.*" *Nineteenth Century Fiction* 20 (June 1965): 69–84.

Wiesenfarth, Joseph. "Demythologizing *Silas Marner.*" *English Literary History* 37 (June 1970): 226–45.

ELIZABETH F. ELLET (1818–1877) U.S.
General Works

Reece, James B. "A Reexamination of a Poe Date: Mrs. Ellet's Letters." *American Literature* 42 (May 1970): 157–64.

ELIZABETH I (1533–1603) Great Britain
General Works

Bradner, L. "The Xenophon Translation Attributed to Elizabeth I." *Journal of the Warburg and Courtauld Institutes* 27 (1964): 324–26.

Phillips, James E. "Elizabeth I as a Latin Poet: An Epigram on Paul Melissus." *Renaissance News* 16 (1963): 289–98.

SARAH BARNWELL ELLIOTT (1848–1928) U.S.
General Works

MacKenzie, Clara C. "Sarah Barnwell Elliott: A Biography." *Dissertation Abstracts International* 32 (1971): 3259A (Case Western Reserve).

Maness, Dinford Gray. "The Novels of Sarah Barnwell Elliott." *Dissertation Abstracts International* 35 (1975): 890A (South Carolina).

ELIZABETH ELSTOB (1683–1756) Great Britain
General Works

Collins, Sarah H. "Elizabeth Elstob: A Biography." *Dissertation Abstracts International* 31 (1971): 5356A (Indiana).

FLORENCE FARR EMERY (1860–1917) Great Britain

General Works

Drummond, Ann. "Florence Farr Emery." *Discourse* 4 (Spring 1961): 97–100.

ALIDA CHANLER EMMET (1873?–) U.S.
General Works

"Grandes Dames Who Grace America." *Life* (January 26, 1968): 44.

MARGARET ANNIE ENGLAND, née Hill [pseud. Eric Harrison] (d. 1959) Great Britain
General Works

Haden, A. J. "The Identity of 'Eric Harrison.'" *Notes and Queries* 7 (April 1960): 149.

LOULA GRACE ERDMAN (1910?–) U.S.
General Works

Sewell, Ernestine. "An Interview with Loula Grace Erdman." *Southwestern American Literature* 2 (1972): 33–41.

HELEN EUSTIS (1916–) U.S.
Individual Works
The Fool Killer (1954)

Burns, Stuart L. "St. Petersburg Re-Visited: Helen Eustis and Mark Twain." *Western American Literature* 5 (Summer 1970): 99–112.

ABBIE HOUSTON EVANS (1835–1909) U.S.
General Works

Silver, Philip. "Miss Evans' Expanding Universe." *Approach*, no. 46 (Winter 1963): 5–10.

AUGUSTA JANE EVANS, Mrs. Wilson (1835–1909) U.S.
General Works

Bargard, Robert. "Amelia Barr, Augusta Evans Wilson and the Sentimental Novel." *Marab* 1 (Winter 1965–1966): 13–25.

MARI EVANS (fl. 1960s–1970s) U.S.
General Works

Sedlack, Robert P. "Mari Evans: Consciousness and Craft." *College Language Association Journal* 15 (June 1972): 465–76.

MARY ANN EVANS. *See* George Eliot

F

Cecily Isabel Fairfield. *See* Dame Rebecca West

Eliza Ware Farrar, née Rotch (1791–1870) U.S.
General Works
Schlesinger, E.B. "Two Early Harvard Wives: Eliza Farrar and Eliza Follen." *New England Quarterly* 38 (June 1965): 147–67.

Daisy Fellowes, née Decazes (d. 1962) Great Britain
General Works
Pope-Hennessey, J. "Daisy Fellowes." *Vogue* (March 1964): 148.

Mary McNeil Fenollosa (1865–1954) U.S.
General Works
Delaney, Caldwell. "Mary McNeil Fenollosa, an Alabama Woman of Letters." *Alabama Review* 16 (July 1963): 163–73.

Edna Ferber (1887–1968) U.S.
General Works
Plante, Patricia R. "Mark Twain, Edna Ferber and the Mississippi." *Mark Twain Journal* 13 (Winter 1965–1966): 8–10.

Edna Fergusson (1888–1964) U.S.
Individual Works
Dancing Gods (1931)
Powell, Laurence C. "Edna Fergusson and *Dancing Gods.*" *Westways* 63 (March 1971): 13–17.

Fanny Fern [pseud.]. *See* Sara Payson Willis

Susan Edmonstone Ferrier (1782–1854)
General Works
Lochhead, Marion. "Susan Ferrier." *Blackwood's* 305

(1969): 122–33.
Rudolf, Jo-Ellen S. "The Novels That Taught the Ladies: A Study of Popular Fiction Written by Women, 1702–1834." *Dissertation Abstracts International* 33 (1972): 1695A (California, San Diego).
Valdes, Helen Joyce. "Style in the Novels of Susan Ferrier." *Dissertation Abstracts* 22 (1961): 1982 (Texas).
Individual Works
Marriage (1818)
Bushnell, Nelson S. "Susan Ferrier's *Marriage* as Novel of Manners." *Studies in Scottish Literature* 5 (April 1968): 216–28.

Sara Bard Field (1882–) U.S.
General Works
Fry, A. "Along the Suffrage Trail." *American West* 6 (January 1969): 16–25.

Annie Adams Fields (1834–1915) U.S.
General Works
Rotundo, B. "148 Charles Street." *American Heritage* 22 (February 1971): 10–15.

Anne Finch, Countess of Winchilsea (1661–1720) Great Britain
General Works
Sena, John F. "Melancholy in Anne Finch and Elizabeth Carter: The Ambivalence of an Idea." *Yearbook of English Studies* 1 (1971): 108–19.

Dorothy Canfield Fisher (1879–1958) U.S.
General Works
Lovering, Joseph P. "Dorothy Canfield Fisher." *Vermont History* 29 (October 1961): 234–38.

ZELDA SAYRE FITZGERALD (1899?–1948) U.S.
General Works
Bensky, L.M. "Zelda Fitzgerald." *New York Times Book Review* (August 13, 1967): 32.
Bruccoli, Matthew J., et al. "Scott and Zelda: An Excerpt from a Pictorial Autobiography." *American Heritage* 25 (October 1974): 4–13.
"The Catalogue of Zelda Fitzgerald's Paintings." *Fitzgerald-Hemingway Annual* (1972): 35–37.
Cooper, Arthur. "Brief for Zelda." *Newsweek* (July 12, 1971): 84.
"The Far Side of Zelda Fitzgerald." *Esquire* (December 1964): 158–59.
Going, William T. "Two Alabama Writers: Zelda Sayre Fitzgerald and Sara Haardt Menchen." *Alabama Review* 23 (January 1970): 3–29.
McLendon, W. "Scott and Zelda: Interview." *Ladies' Home Journal* (November 1974): 58.
Milford, Nancy. "The Golden Dreams of Zelda Fitzgerald." *Harper's* (January 1969): 46–53.
Milford, Nancy. "What the Woman Lived." *New York Times Book Review* (December 16, 1973): 1–2.
"Not So Tender Was the Night." *Time* (June 15, 1970): 99.
"Scandalabra Program." *Fitzgerald-Hemingway Annual* (1972): 97–98.
Tomkins, C. "Living Well Is the Best Revenge." *New Yorker* (July 28, 1962): 31–32.
Zimmerman, R. D. "Beautiful and Damned." *Newsweek* (June 15, 1970): 102.

JULIA A. FLETCHER (1858–1938) U.S.
Individual Works
Little Drops of Water (1895)
Loomis, C. Grant. "*Little Drops of Water*." *Western Folklore* 25 (January 1964): 39.

MARY FLETCHER, Lady Richardson (b. 1802) Scotland
Individual Works
Concealment (1837)
Scheele, Dorothy R. "The Authorship of *Concealment* (1837)." *Notes and Queries* 17 (October 1970): 382–83.

MRS. MARMADUKE FLOYD (d. 1960s) U.S.
General Works
O'Hara, Constance. "Mrs. Marmaduke Floyd: A Triumphant Life." *Georgia Historical Quarterly* 52

(September 1968): 293–304.

ELIZA LEE CABOT FOLLEN (1787–1860) U.S. (Born in Germany)
General Works
Schlesinger, E. B. "Two Early Harvard Wives: Eliza Farrar and Eliza Follen." *New England Quarterly* 38 (June 1965): 147–67.

MARY HALLOCK FOOTE (1847–1938) U.S.
Bibliography
Etulain, Richard W. "Mary Hallock Foote (1847–1938)." *American Literary Realism* 5 (1972): 145–50.
General Works
Etulain, Richard W. "The New Western Novel." *Idaho Yesterdays* 15 (Winter 1972): 12–17.
Schopf, Bill. "The Image of the West in *The Century*, 1881–1889." *The Possible Sack* 3 (March 1972): 8–13.

JANET FRAME, née Clutha (1924–) Australia
General Works
Delbaere-Garant, J. "Daphne's Metamorphoses in Janet Frame's Early Novels." *Ariel* 6 (1975): 23–37.
Evans, Patrick. "Alienation and the Imagery of Death: The Novels of Janet Frame." *Meanjin Quarterly* 32 (1973): 294–303.
Rhodes, H. Winston. "Preludes and Parables: A Reading of Janet Frame's Novels." *Landfall* 26 (June 1972): 135–46.
Robertson, Robert T. "Bird, Hawk, Bogie: Janet Frame 1952–1962." *Studies in the Novel* 4 (Summer 1972): 186–99.

MARIANNE FRANCES (1790–1832) Great Britain
General Works
Menagh, Diana. "An Edition of the Letters of Marianne Frances (1790–1832) to Hester Lynch Piozzi (1741–1821), 1808–1810." *Dissertation Abstracts International* 35 (1975): 2223A (C.U.N.Y.).

PAMELA FRANKAU (1908–1967) Great Britain
General Works
Frankau, Pamela. "The Creative Self of the Catholic Writer." *Catholic World* (February 1962): 291–95.
Nichols, L. "Miss Frankau." *New York Times Book*

Review (November 12, 1961): 8.

STELLA MILES FRANKLIN (1879–1954) Australia
General Works
Sutherland, A. Bruce. "Stella Miles Franklin's American Years." *Meanjin Quarterly* 24 (1965): 439–54.

LADY ANTONIA FRASER, née Pakenham (1932?–) Great Britain
General Works
Baker, A.T. "Begone You Rogues." *Time* (November 5, 1973): 109.
Boston, R. "Elizabeth of the Writing Pakenhams." *New York Times Book Review* (March 1, 1970): 6.
"Daughter of Debate." *Time* (October 17, 1969): 110.
Steele, Richard, and John Barnes. "Hell Hath No Fury." *Newsweek* (August 11, 1975): 39–40.
Strolley, R.B. "Lively Lady Was a Secret Scholar." *Life* (February 20, 1970): 43–44.

MARY CRAWFORD FRASER (d. 1922) Japan
General Works
Barr, Pat. "Mary Crawford Fraser: The Diplomatist's Wife." *Cornhill Magazine*, no. 1068 (Summer 1971): 464–72.

MARY E. WILKINS FREEMAN (1852–1930) U.S.
Bibliography
Blanck, Jacob. "BAL Addenda." *Papers of the Bibliographical Society of America* 55 (1961): 152–53.
O'Connor, Robert B. "BAL Addenda M. E. W. Freeman—Entry No. 6380." *Papers of the Bibliographical Society of America* 61 (1967): 127.
Westbrook, Perry D. "Mary E. Wilkins Freeman (1852–1930):" *American Literary Realism* 2 (1969): 139–42.
General Works
Diomedi, Claudette A. "Mary Wilkins Freeman and the Romance-Novel Tradition." *Dissertation Abstracts* 31 (1971): 4155A–56A (Maryland).
Parker, Jeraldine. " 'Uneasy Survivors': Five Women Writers, 1896–1923." *Dissertation Abstracts International* 34 (1973): 1927A (Utah).
Quina, James H., Jr. "Character Types in the Fiction of Mary Wilkins Freeman." *Colby Library Quarterly* 9 (June 1971): 432–39.
Toth, Susan A. "Defiant Light: A Positive View of Mary Wilkins Freeman." *New England Quarterly*

46 (March 1973): 82–93.
Toth, Susan A. "More than Local-Color: A Reappraisal of Rose Terry Cooke, Mary Wilkins Freeman and Alice Brown." *Dissertation Abstracts* 30 (1969): 3004A (Minnesota).
Wood, Ann Douglas. "The Literature of Impoverishment: The Women Local Colorists in America 1865–1914." *Women's Studies* 1 (1972): 3–40.
Individual Works
A New England Nun (1891)
Hirsch, David H. "Subdued Meaning in *A New England Nun*." *Studies in Short Fiction* 2 (Winter 1965): 124–36.
The Revolt of Mother (1903)
Gallagher, Edward J. "Freeman's *The Revolt of Mother*." *Explicator* 27 (March 1969): Item 48.
The Three Old Sisters and the Old Beau (1900)
Toth, Susan Allen. "Mary Wilkins Freeman's Parable of Wasted Life." *American Literature* 42 (January 1971): 564–67.

ALICE FRENCH [pseud. Octave Thanet] (1850–1934) U.S.
General Works
Bush, Robert. "The Literary Paternalism of Octave Thanet." *Newberry Library Bulletin* 6 (November 1962): 24–28.
McQuin, Susan C. "Alice French's View of Women." *Books at Iowa*, no. 20 (1974): 34–42.

BETTY FRIEDAN (1921–) U.S.
General Works
Friedan, Betty. "Visit with Pope Paul." *McCall's* (February 1974): 72.
Kurtz, Paul. "Humanism and Feminism, New Directions: Interview." *Humanist* 34 (May 1974): 10–13.
Tornabene, L. "Liberation of Betty Friedan." *McCall's* (May 1971): 84.
"Who's She? Women Activists in U.S. History." *Senior Scholastic* (November 9, 1970): 14.
Wilkes, P. "Mother Superior to Women's Lib." *New York Times Magazine* (November 29, 1970): 27–29.

MARGARET FULLER, Marchioness Ossoli (1810–1850): U.S.
General Works
Allen, Margaret V. "The Political and Social Criti-

cism of Margaret Fuller." *South Atlantic Quarterly* 72 (Autumn 1973): 560–73.

Allen, Margaret V. "This Impassioned Yankee: Margaret Fuller's Writing Revisited." *Southwest Review* 58 (Spring 1973): 162–71.

Barolini, Helen. "A Study in Contrast: Effie in Venice and the Roman Spring of Margaret Fuller." *American Review* 28 (Winter 1968–1969): . 461–76.

Berger, Patrick F. "Margaret Fuller: Critical Realist as Seen in Her Works." *Dissertation Abstracts International* 34 (1974): 5157A (St. Louis).

Brown, John. "Margaret Fuller." *Palestra* 1 (1962): 178–87.

Carter, Ray Cecil. "Margaret Fuller and the Two Sages." *Colby Library Quarterly* 6 (March 1963): 198–201.

Durning, Russell E. "Margaret Fuller, Citizen of the World: An Intermediary between European and American Literature." *Dissertation Abstracts* 26 (1965): 3949 (North Carolina).

Durning, Russell E. "Margaret Fuller's Translation of Goethe's *Prometheus.*" *Jahrbuch für Amerikastudien* 12 (1967): 240–45.

Ehrlich, Heyward. "The Origin of Lowell's *Miss Fooler.*" *American Literature* 37 (January 1966): 473–75.

Golemba, Henry L. "The Balanced View in Margaret Fuller's Literary Criticism." *Dissertation Abstracts* 32 (1971): 2641A (Washington).

Guerin, Sister Kathleen Deirdre. "Margaret Fuller d'Ossoli: Modern American Humanist." *Dissertation Abstracts International* 35 (1975): 3713A (Minnesota).

Hopkins, Vivian C. "Margaret Fuller: American Nationalist Critic." *Emerson Society Quarterly* 55 (1969): 24–41.

Hopkins, Vivian C. "Margaret Fuller: Pioneer Women's Liberationist." *American Transcendental Quarterly* 18 (1973): 29–35.

Kearns, Francis E. "Margaret Fuller and the Abolition Movement." *Journal of the History of Ideas* 25 (1964): 120–27.

Kearns, Francis E. "Margaret Fuller as Model for Hester Prynne." *Jahrbuch für Amerikastudien* 10 (1965): 191–97.

Kearns, Francis E. "Margaret Fuller's Social Criticism." *Dissertation Abstracts* 22 (1962): 3646 (North Carolina).

McGavran, Margaret R. "Mary and Margaret: The Triumph of Woman." *Dissertation Abstracts International* 34 (1973): 1248A (Cornell).

Myerson, Joel. "Caroline Dall's Reminiscences of Margaret Fuller." *Harvard Library Bulletin* 22 (1974): 414–28.

Myerson, Joel. "A Margaret Fuller Addition to Thoreau's Library." *Thoreau Society Bulletin* 123 (Spring 1973): 3.

Shapiro, Fred C. "Lost Women: The Transcending Margaret Fuller." *Ms.* (November 1972): 36–39.

Strauch, Carl F. "Atred's Swift Repulsions: Emerson, Margaret Fuller and Others." *Studies in Romanticism* 7 (Winter 1968): 65–103.

Warders, Donald F. " 'The Progress of the Hour and the Day': A Critical Study of *The Dial* (1840–1844)." *Dissertation Abstracts International* 34 (1974): 7790A–91A (Kansas).

Individual Works

Lines . . . on the Death of C.C.E. (1836)

Cameron, Kenneth W. "Margaret Fuller's Poem on the Death of Charles Chauncy Emerson." *Emerson Society Quarterly* 18 (1960): 49–50.

Woman in the Nineteenth Century (1845)

Urbanski, Marie M. O. "Margaret Fuller's *Woman in the Nineteenth Century.*" *Dissertation Abstracts International* 35 (1974): 1636A (Kentucky).

G

PEGGY GADDIS, née Dern (1895–1966) U.S.
General Works
Nichols, L. "Madam Nurse." *New York Times Book Review* (July 17, 1966): 8.

FRANCES GAITHER (1889–1955) U.S.
General Works
Simms, L. Moody, Jr. "Frances Gaither: A Sketch." *Notes on Mississippi Writers* 3 (Fall 1970): 73–78.

ZONA GALE (1874–1938) U.S.
General Works
Forman, Henry James. "Zona Gale: A Touch of Greatness." *Wisconsin Magazine of History* 46 (Autumn 1962): 32–37.
Simonson, Harold P. "Zona Gale (1874–1938)." *American Literary Realism*, no. 3 (Summer 1968): 14–17.
Individual Works
Mr. Torrence's Metrical Art (1905)
Monteiro, George. "Zona Gale and Ridgely Torrence." *American Literary Realism* 3 (1970): 77–79.

MAVIS GALLANT (1922–) Canada
General Works
Stevens, Peter. "Perils of Compassion." *Canadian Literature*, no. 56 (Spring 1973): 61–70.

MENNA GALLIE, née Humphreys (1920–) U.S.
General Works
Stephens, Raymond. "The Novelist and Community: Menna Gallie." *Anglo-Welsh Review* 14 (1964–1965): 52–63.

ISABELLA GARDNER (1915–) U.S.
General Works
English, Maurice. "Isabella Gardner: A Rhetoric of Passion." *Tri-Quarterly* 7 (Fall 1966): 145–49.
Logan, John. "The Poetry of Isabella Gardner." *Sewanee Review* 70 (Spring 1962): 250–53.
Sutton, D. "Queen Bee of Boston." *Times Literary Supplement* (March 21, 1975): 302.

NATALIE BARNEY GARLAND (1876–1972) U.S.
General Works
Wickes, G., ed. "Natalie Barney Garland." *Paris Review* 16 (Spring 1975): 84–134.

JEAN GARRIGUE (1914–1972) U.S.
General Works
Lieberman, Laurence. "New Poetry: The Muse of History." *Yale Review* 63 (October 1973): 113–36.

BARBARA GARSON (1941?–) U.S.
Individual Works
Macbird! (1967)
Gilman, Richard. "*Macbird!* and Its Audience." *New American Review* 1 (1967): 123–24.
"Much Ado About Mac." *Newsweek* (February 27, 1967): 99.

ELIZABETH CLEGHORN GASKELL, née Stevenson (1810–1865) Great Britain
Bibliography
Davis, Marjorie Taylor. "An Annotated Bibliography of Criticism on Elizabeth Cleghorn Gaskell, 1848–1973." *Dissertation Abstracts International* 35 (1975): 4424A (Mississippi).
General Works
Allott, Miriam. "Elizabeth Gaskell." *British Book News*, no. 124 (1960): 7–46.
Axe, Kathryn J. "Elizabeth Cleghorn Gaskell: A

Critical Evaluation of Her Novels." *Dissertation Abstracts International* 35 (1974): 1034A–35A (Kansas).

Axton, W.F. "Mrs. Gaskell in Apotheosis." *Modern Language Quarterly* 28 (June 1967): 240–47.

Barry, James D. "Elizabeth Cleghorn Gaskell and Charles Kingsley." *Victorian Fiction* 27 (1969): 245–76.

Boyle, Patricia M. "Elizabeth C. Gaskell: Her Development and Achievement." *Dissertation Abstracts International* 31 (1972): 5352A (Penn.).

Brill, Barbara. "Getting to Know Elizabeth Gaskell." *Library Review* 20 (1965): 227–33.

Carnall, Geoffrey. "Dickens, Mrs. Gaskell, and the Preston Strike." *Victorian Studies* 8 (September 1964): 31–48.

Carwell, Virginia Alice. "Serialization and the Fiction of Mrs. Gaskell." *Dissertation Abstracts* 26 (1965): 3328 (Northwestern).

Chapple, J. A. V. "Gaskell Letters." *Times Literary Supplement* (August 25, 1966): 770.

Chapple, John A.V. "The Letters of Mrs. Gaskell the Novelist." *Manuscripts* 16 (Winter 1964): 3–5.

Ehrenpreis, Anne H. "Elizabeth Gaskell and Nathaniel Hawthorne." *Nathaniel Hawthorne Journal* (1973): 89–119.

Ellis J. B. "Mrs. Gaskell on the Continent." *Notes and Queries* 14 (October 1967): 372–73.

Franko, Patricia. "The Emergence of Harmony: Development in the Novels of Mrs. Gaskell." *Dissertation Abstracts International* 34 (1973): 769A (Temple).

Gill, Stephen. "A Manuscript of Branwell Brontë, with Letters of Mrs. Gaskell." *Brontë Society Transactions* 15 (1970): 408–11.

Gross, John. "Early-Victorian Writer with Charm." *Listener* (March 11, 1965): 361–63.

Johnson, C.A. "Russian Gaskelliana." *Review of English Literature* 7 (July 1966): 39–51.

"A Letter from Mrs. Gaskell (to the Rev. R. S. Oldham of Glasgow, 1 June 1857)." *Brontë Society Transactions* 14 (1965): 50.

Lucas, J. "Mrs. Gaskell Reconsidered." *Victorian Studies* 11 (June 1968): 528–33.

Lutyens, Mary. "Mrs. Gaskell and Effie." *Times Literary Supplement* (March 23, 1967): 243.

Mantovani, Juanita M. "The Feminine World View of Elizabeth Cleghorn Gaskell." *Dissertation Abstracts International* 35 (1974): 1053A (Southern California).

McVeagh, J. "Notes on Mrs. Gaskell's Narrative Technique." *Essays in Criticism* 18 (October 1968): 461–70.

Murray, Philip. "Fantasia on a Theme by Mrs. Gaskell." *Poetry* 120 (July 1972): 228–29.

Nickel, M.A. "The Dating of a Mrs. Gaskell Letter." *Notes and Queries* 22 (March 1975): 113.

Nickel, Marjorie A. "The Reconciliation of Opposites in the Work of Elizabeth Gaskell." *Dissertation Abstracts International* 35 (1974): 2288A (Notre Dame).

Oram, Eanne. "Brief for Miss Branwell." *Brontë Society Transactions* 14 (1964): 28–38.

Pollard, Arthur H. "The Novels of Mrs. Gaskell." *Bulletin of the John Rylands Library* 43 (March 1961): 403–25.

Rotner, Arnold H. "Mrs. Gaskell's Art." *Dissertation Abstracts* 29 (1968): 272A (Colorado).

Sawdey, Barbara Christiane Meihofer. "Between Two Worlds: A Study of the Heroine in the Novels of Elizabeth Gaskell." *Dissertation Abstracts International* 35 (1975): 2855A (Illinois).

Schneewind, Jerome B. "Moral Problems and Moral Philosophy in the Victorian Period." *Victorian Studies* 9, Supplement (1965): 29–46.

Schwartz, Stephen L. "Elizabeth Gaskell: The Novelist as Artist." *Dissertation Abstracts International* 32 (1971): 3269A (Rochester).

Willens, Susan P. "The Novels of Elizabeth Gaskell: The Comic Vision." *Dissertation Abstracts International* 33 (1973): 6889A (Catholic U.).

Individual Works

Cranford (1853)

Dodsworth, Martin. "Women without Men in *Cranford*." *Essays in Criticism* 13 (April 1963): 132–45.

Edwards, Tudor. "Portrait of Knutsford: The *Cranford* of Mrs. Gaskell." *Country Life* 138 (1965): 1274–75.

Tarratt, Margaret. "*Cranford* and 'the Strict Code of Gentility.'" *Essays in Criticism* 18 (April 1968): 152–63.

Wolfe, Patricia A. "Structure and Movement in *Cranford*." *Nineteenth Century Fiction* 23 (September 1968): 161–76.

Wright, Edgar. "Mrs. Gaskell and the World of *Cranford*." *Review of English Literature* 6 (January 1965): 68–79.

Five Humorous Epistles (1865)

Sharps, J.G. "Articles by Mrs. Gaskell in *The Pall*

Mall Gazette (1865)." *Notes and Queries* 12 (August 1965): 301–2.

Life of Charlotte Brontë (1857)

Easson, Angus. "Two Suppressed Opinions in Mrs. Gaskell's *Life of Charlotte Brontë.*" *Brontë Society Transactions* 16 (1974): 281–83.

Pollard, Arthur, and Albert H. Preston. "Mrs. Gaskell's *Life of Charlotte Brontë* with an Appendix on Some New Gaskell Letters." *Bulletin of the John Rylands Library* 47 (March 1965): 453–88.

Sharps, John Geoffrey. "Charlotte Brontë and the Mysterious 'Miss H': A Detail in Mrs. Gaskell's *Life.*" *English* 14 (Autumn 1963): 236.

Mary Barton (1848)

Handley, Graham. "Mrs. Gaskell's Reading: Some Notes on Echoes and Epigraphs in *Mary Barton.*" *Durham University Journal* 59 (June 1967): 131–38.

Kay, Brian, and James Knowles. "Where *Jane Eyre* and *Mary Barton* Were Born." *Brontë Society Transactions* 15 (1967): 145–48.

Smith, David. "*Mary Barton* and *Hard Times*: Their Social Insights." *Mosaic* 5 (1972): 97–112.

Sucksmith, H.P. "Mrs. Gaskell's *Mary Barton* and William Mudford's *The Iron Shroud.*" *Nineteenth Century Fiction* 29 (March 1975): 460–63.

Wheeler, Michael D. "The Writer as Reader in *Mary Barton.*" *Durham University Journal* 67 (March 1974): 92–102.

North and South (1855)

Chapple, J.A.V. "*North and South*: A Reassessment." *Essays in Criticism* 17 (October 1967): 461–72; 18 (October 1968): 461–70.

Collins, Dorothy W. "The Composition of Mrs. Gaskell's *North and South.*" *Bulletin of the John Rylands Library* 54 (Autumn 1971): 67–93.

The Old Nurse's Story (1852)

Allott, Miriam. "Mrs. Gaskell's *The Old Nurse's Story*: A Link between *Wuthering Heights* and *The Turn of the Screw.*" *Notes and Queries* 8 (March 1961): 101–2.

Ruth (1853)

Page, Norman. "*Ruth* and *Hard Times*: A Dickens Source." *Notes and Queries* 18 (November 1971): 413.

Sylvia's Lovers (1863)

Handley, Graham. "The Chronology of *Sylvia's Lovers.*" *Notes and Queries* 12 (August 1965): 302–3.

McVeagh, John. "The Making of *Sylvia's Lovers.*"

Modern Language Review 65 (April 1970): 272–93.

Wives and Daughters (1865)

Butler, Marilyn. "The Uniqueness of Cynthia Kirkpatrick: Elizabeth Gaskell's *Wives and Daughters* and Maria Edgeworth's *Helen.*" *Review of English Studies* 23 (August 1972): 278–90.

Easson, Angus. "*Wives and Daughters.*" *Times Literary Supplement* (June 14, 1974): 641.

MARY GAUNT (fl. 1900s) Great Britain
General Works

Miller, C. "Between Two Worlds: The Educated African in Three Novels by Mary Gaunt." *College Language Association Journal* 18 (June 1975): 521–31.

JEAN CRAIGHEAD GEORGE (1919–) U.S.
General Works

"Gee, What a Big Best-Seller Jean George Has: Interview." *Writer's Digest* 54 (March 1974): 9–11.

ANNE GILCHRIST (1828–1885) Great Britain
General Works

Frelazzo, Paul J. "Anne Gilchrist, Critic of Walt Whitman." *South Dakota Review* 10 (Winter 1972–1973): 63–79.

KATYA GILDEN (fl. 1960s) U.S.
General Works

"Literary Duet." *Life* (February 5, 1965): 45–46.

CAROLINE HOWARD GILMAN (1794–1888) U.S.
General Works

Howe, D.W. "Massachusetts Yankee in Senator Calhoun's Court: Samuel Gilman in South Carolina." *New England Quarterly* 44 (June 1971): 197–220.

DAME MARY GILMORE, née Cameron (1865–1962) Australia

General Works

Balkin, Mary. "Mary and William Gilmore: A Family Note." *Australian Literary Studies* 5 (1972): 430–31.

Cato, Nancy. "Woman and Poet." *Overland*, no. 26 (1963): 28–29.

Fitzgerald, Robert D. "Mary Gilmore: Poet and

Great Australian." *Meanjin Quarterly* 19 (1960): 341–56.

Foster, J.M. "Mary Gilmore: A Memoir." *Australian Literary Studies* 5 1972): 414–16.

Heseltine, H.P. "C. Hartley Grattan in Australia: Some Correspondence, 1937–1938." *Meanjin Quarterly* 29 (1970): 356–64.

Mackaness, George. "Dame Mary Gilmore and Henry Lawson." *Southerly* 24 (1964): 42–43.

Mares, F.H. "Dame Mary Gilmore." *Southerly* 25 (1965): 234–45.

Neilson, John Shaw. "Shaw Neilson and Mary Gilmore." *Australian Literary Studies* 5 (1972): 431–32.

Robertson, Constance. "Mary Gilmore." *Southerly* 25 (1965): 247–50.

"Some Mary Gilmore Letters." *Australian Literary Studies* 5 (1972): 417–30.

Tolchard, Clifford. "Mary Gilmore: Crusader and Poet." *Walkabout* 34 (1967): 12–15.

Webster, Owen. "Frank Dalby Davison." *Overland*, no. 44 (1969): 35–37.

Wilde, W.H. "Mary Gilmore—The Hidden Years." *Meanjin Quarterly* 32 (1973): 425–32.

NIKKI GIOVANNI (1943–) U.S.
General Works
Palmer, R. Roderick. "The Poetry of Three Revolutionists: Don L. Lee, Sonia Sanchez and Nikki Giovanni." *College Language Association Journal* 15 (September 1971): 25–36.

CARY GLASGOW (1863–1911) U.S.
Individual Works
A Successful Failure (1883)
Duke, Maurice. "The First Novel by a Glasgow: Cary's *A Successful Failure*." *Ellen Glasgow Newsletter* 1 (1974): 7–9.

ELLEN GLASGOW (1874–1945) U.S.
Bibliography
MacDonald, Edgar E. "Ellen Glasgow: An Essay in Bibliography." *Resources for American Literary Studies* 2 (1972): 131–56.
General Works
Adams, J. Donald. "Speaking of Books." *New York Times Book Review* (June 16, 1963): 2.

Allsup, Judith L. "Feminism in the Novels of Ellen Glasgow." *Dissertation Abstracts International* 35 (1974): 1083A (Southern Illinois).

Bates, Rudolph D. "Changing Views: A Study of Ellen Glasgow's Fluctuating Social Philosophy." *Dissertation Abstracts* 30 (1969): 311A (South Carolina).

Becker, Allen W. "Ellen Glasgow and the Southern Literary Tradition." *Modern Fiction Studies* 5 (Winter 1959–1960): 295–303.

Beckham, Beverly S. "The Satire of Ellen Glasgow." *Dissertation Abstracts International* 33 (1973): 5163A (Georgia).

Bressler, Maybelle J. "A Critical Study of the Published Novels of Ellen Glasgow." *Dissertation Abstracts* 26 (1965): 2745 (Nebraska).

Colvert, James B. "Agent and Author: Ellen Glasgow's Letters to Paul Revere Reynolds." *Studies in Bibliography* 14 (1961): 177–96.

Curlee, Joan. "Ellen Glasgow's South." *Ball State Teachers College Forum* 2 (Winter 1961–1962): 53–59.

Day, Douglas. "Ellen Glasgow's Letters to the Saxtons." *American Literature* 35 (May 1963): 230–36.

Dillard, R.H.W. "Pragmatic Realism: A Biography of Ellen Glasgow's Novels." *Dissertation Abstracts* 26 (1966): 6019A (Virginia).

Duke, Maurice. "Cabell's and Glasgow's Richmond: The Intellectual Background of the City." *Mississippi Quarterly* 27 (Fall 1974): 375–91.

Dunn, Norma E. "Ellen Glasgow's Search for Truth." *Dissertation Abstracts* 29 (1969): 2257A (Penn.).

Eaton, C. "Breaking a Path for the Liberation of Women in the South." *Georgia Review* 28 (Summer 1974): 196–98.

Edwards, Herbert W. "A Study of Values in Selected Published Prose of Ellen Glasgow." *Dissertation Abstracts* 22 (1961): 258 (N.Y.U.).

Gatlin, Judith T. "Ellen Glasgow's Artistry." *Dissertation Abstracts* 30 (1969): 720A–21A (Iowa).

Heald, William F. "Ellen Glasgow and the Grotesque." *Mississippi Quarterly* 18 (Winter 1964–1965): 7–11.

Heinemann, K.A. "Ellen Glasgow: The Death of the Chivalrous Tradition." *Forum* 4 (Fall 1966): 37–41.

Hewitt, Rosalie. "Aristocracy and the Modern American Novel of Manners: Edith Wharton, F. Scott Fitzgerald, Ellen Glasgow, and James Gould Cozzens." *Dissertation Abstracts* 31 (1970): 4163A (Purdue).

Holman, Hugh. "April in Queensborough: Ellen Glasgow's Comedies of Manners." *Sewanee Review* 82 (Spring 1974): 263–83.

Hughes, Nina E. "Ellen Glasgow and the 'Literature of Place.' " *Dissertation Abstracts International* 32 (1971): 2692A–93A (Columbia).

Kish, Dorothy. " 'An Immortal Part, in This Place': Setting in Ellen Glasgow's Novels." *Dissertation Abstracts International* 31 (1970): 2387A–88A (Pittsburgh).

MacDonald, Edgar E. "Biographical Notes on Ellen Glasgow." *Resources for American Literary Studies* 3 (1973): 249–53.

MacDonald, Edgar E. "Glasgow, Cabell, and Richmond." *Mississippi Quarterly* 27 (Fall 1974): 393–413.

MacDonald, Edgar E. "The Glasgow–Cabell Entente." *American Literature* 41 (March 1969): 76–91.

McCollum, Nancy Minter. "Glasgow's and Cabell's Comedies of Virginia." *Georgia Review* 18 (Summer 1964): 236–41.

Parker, Jeraldine. " 'Uneasy Survivors': Five Women Writers, 1896–1923." *Dissertation Abstracts International* 34 (1973): 1927A (Utah).

Peck, Ellen M. McK. "Exploring the Feminine: A Study of Janet Lewis, Ellen Glasgow, Anais Nin and Virginia Woolf." *Dissertation Abstracts International* 35 (1974): 3761A (Stanford).

Raper, Julius R., Jr. "Ellen Glasgow and Darwinism, 1873–1906." *Dissertation Abstracts* 27 (1967): 2541A–42A (Northwestern).

Richards, Marion Kazmann. "The Development of Ellen Glasgow as a Novelist." *Dissertation Abstracts* 22 (1962): 2797–98 (Columbia).

Rouse, Blair. "Ellen Glasgow: Manners and Art." *Cabellian* 4 (1972): 96–98.

Rouse, Blair. "Ellen Glasgow: The Novelist in America." *Cabellian* 4 (1971): 25–35.

Santas, Joan Foster. "Ellen Glasgow's American Dream." *Dissertation Abstracts* 24 (1963): 2040–41 (Cornell).

Scura, Dorothy. "Glasgow and the Southern Renaissance: The Conference at Charlottesville." *Mississippi Quarterly* 27 (Fall 1974): 415–34.

Scura, Dorothy M. "One West Main." *Ellen Glasgow Newsletter* 1 (1974): 3–6.

Sharma, O.P. "Feminist Image in the Novels of Ellen Glasgow: The Early Phase." *Research Bulletin* 60 (1968): 1–20.

Steele, O.L., Jr. "Gertrude Stein and Ellen Glasgow: Memoir of a Meeting." *American Literature* 33 (March 1961): 76–77.

White, James Edward, Jr. "Symbols in the Novels of Ellen Glasgow." *Dissertation Abstracts* 25 (1964): 2991 (Boston).

Individual Works

Barren Ground (1925)

Marshall, G.O., Jr. "Hardy's *Tess* and Ellen Glasgow's *Barren Ground*." *Texas Studies in Literature and Language* 1 (Winter 1960): 517–21.

Murr, Judy Smith. "History in *Barren Ground* and *Vein of Iron*: Theory, Structure and Symbol." *Southern Literary Journal* 8 (Fall 1975): 39–54.

Beyond Defeat (c. 1942)

Gore, Luther Y. "Ellen Glasgow's *Beyond Defeat*, a Critical Edition: Volume One, Editor's Introduction; Volume Two, the Text of *Beyond Defeat*." *Dissertation Abstracts* 26 (1965): 2751 (Virginia).

Life and Gabriella (1916)

Kristiansen, Marianne. "Work and Love, or How the Fittest Survive: A Study of Ellen Glasgow's *Life and Gabriella*." *Language and Literature* 2 (1973): 105–25.

Literary Realism or Nominalism (1962)

Gore, Luther Y. " 'Literary Realism or Nominalism' by Ellen Glasgow: An Unpublished Essay." *American Literature* 34 (March 1962): 72–79.

The Miller of Old Church (1911)

Steele, Oliver L., Jr. "Early Impressions of Ellen Glasgow's *The Miller of Old Church*." *Library* 16 (March 1961): 50–52.

The Past (1920)

Dillard, R.H.W. "The Writer's Best Solace: Textual Revisions in Ellen Glasgow's *The Past*." *Studies in Bibliography* 19 (1966): 245–50.

The Professional Instinct (1962)

Kelly, William W. "*The Professional Instinct*: An Unpublished Short Story by Ellen Glasgow." *Western Humanities Review* 16 (Autumn 1962): 301–17.

The Sheltered Life (1932)

Hudspeth, Robert. "Point of View in Ellen Glasgow's *The Sheltered Life*." *Thoth* 4 (1963): 83–87.

McDowell, Frederick P.W. "Theme and Artistry in Ellen Glasgow's *The Sheltered Life*." *Texas Studies in Literature and Language* 1 (Winter 1960): 502–16.

Raper, J.R., Jr. "Glasgow's Psychology of Deceptions and *The Sheltered Life.*" *Southern Literary Journal* 8 (Fall 1975): 27–38.

They Stooped to Folly (1929)

Murphy, John J. "Marriage and Desire in Ellen Glasgow's *They Stooped to Folly.*" *Descant* 10 (1965): 35–40.

Vein of Iron (1935)

Murr, Judy Smith. "History in *Barren Ground* and *Vein of Iron*: Theory, Structure and Symbol." *Southern Literary Journal* 8 (Fall 1975): 39–54.

Virginia (1913)

Patterson, D.W. "Ellen Glasgow's Plan for a Social History of Virginia." *Modern Fiction Studies* 5 (Winter 1959–1960): 353–60.

Steele, O.L., Jr. "Ellen Glasgow, Social History, and the 'Virginia Edition,'" *Modern Fiction Studies* 7 (Summer 1961): 173–76.

Steele, Oliver, Jr. Ellen Glasgow's *Virginia*: Preliminary Notes." *Studies in Bibliography* 27 (1974): 265–89.

The Voice of the People (1900)

Godshalk, William L. "Addendum to Kelly: Ellen Glasgow's *The Voice of the People.*" *Papers of the Bibliographical Society of America* 67 (1973): 68–69.

The Wheel of Life (1906)

Steele, O.L., Jr. "Evidence of Plate Damage as Applied to the First Impressions of Ellen Glasgow's *The Wheel of Life* (1906)." *Studies in Bibliography* 16 (1963): 223–31.

The Woman Within (1954)

"From *The Woman Within.*" *Aphra* 5 (Spring 1974): 54–72.

SUSAN GLASPELL (1882–1948) U.S.
Bibliography

Bach, Gerhard P. "Susan Glaspell: Supplementary Notes." *American Literary Realism* 5 (1972): 71–73.

Waterman, Arthur E. "Susan Glaspell (1882–1948)." *American Literary Realism* 4 (1971): 183–91.

General Works

Waterman, Arthur E. "Susan Glaspell and the Provincetown." *Modern Drama* 7 (September 1964): 174–84.

CAROLINE GLYN (1947–) Great Britain
General Works

Huston, P. "Caroline Glyn, Britain's Teen-Age

Novelist." *Life* (May 13, 1966): 59–60.

GAIL GODWIN (1937–) U.S.
Individual Works

A Sorrowful Woman (1971)

Gardiner, Judith K. " 'A Sorrowful Woman': Gail Godwin's Feminist Parable." *Studies in Short Fiction* 12 (Summer 1975): 286–90.

PATRICIA GOEDICKE, née McKenna (1921–) U.S.
General Works

Gerber, Philip L., and Robert J. Gemmett. "Myth of the Self: A Conversation with Patricia Goedicke." *Southern Humanities Review* 5 (Fall 1971) 319–32.

NADINE GORDIMER (1923–) South Africa
General Works

Abrahams, Lionel. "Nadine Gordimer: The Transparent Ego." *English Studies in Africa* 3 (September 1960): 146–51.

Gullason, Thomas A. "The Short Story: An Underrated Art." *Studies in Short Fiction* 2 (Fall 1964): 28–30.

Laredo, Ursula. "The Novels of Nadine Gordimer." *Journal of Commonwealth Literature* 8 (June 1973): 42–53.

Margarey, Kevin. "Cutting the Jewel: Facets of Art in Nadine Gordimer's Short Stories." *Southern Review* (U.S.) 10 (1974): 3–25.

McGuinness, Frank. "The Novels of Nadine Gordimer." *London Magazine* 5 (June 1965): 97–102.

Woodward, Anthony. "Nadine Gordimer." *Theoria* 26 (1961): 1–12.

CAROLINE GORDON (1895–) U.S.
General Works

Bradford, M.E. "Quest for a Hero." *National Review* (August 18, 1972): 906–7.

Brown, Ashley. "The Achievement of Caroline Gordon." *Southern Humanities Review* 2 (Summer 1968): 279–90.

Brown, Ashley. "Caroline Gordon's Short Fiction." *Sewanee Review* 81 (Spring 1973): 365–70.

Brown, Jerry Elizah. "The Rhetoric of Form: A Study of the Novels of Caroline Gordon." *Dissertation Abstracts International* 35 (1975): 7898A–99A (Vanderbilt).

Chappell, Charles M. "The Hero Figure and the Problem of Unity in the Novels of Caroline

Gordon." *Dissertation Abstracts International* 34 (1973): 2615A (Emory).

Fletcher, Marie. "The Fate of Woman in the Changing South: A Persistent Theme in the Fiction of Caroline Gordon." *Mississippi Quarterly* 21 (Winter 1967–1968): 17–28.

Gordon, Caroline. "Always Summer." *Southern Review* (U.S.) 7 (1971): 430–46.

O'Connor, Mary. "On Caroline Gordon." *Southern Review* (U.S.) 7 (1971): 463–66.

Rocks, James E. "The Mind and Art of Caroline Gordon." *Dissertation Abstracts* 27 (1966): 1835A (Duke).

Rocks, James E. "The Mind and Art of Caroline Gordon." *Mississippi Quarterly* 21 (Winter 1967–1968): 1–16.

Rocks, James E. "The Short Fiction of Caroline Gordon." *Tulane Studies in English* 18 (1970): 115–35.

Squires, Radcliffe. "The Underground Stream: A Note on Caroline Gordon's Fiction." *Southern Review* (U.S.) 7 (1971): 467–79.

Stanford, Donald E. "Caroline Gordon: From *Penhally* to *A Narrow Heart*." *Southern Review* (U.S.) 7 (1971): xv–xx.

Stanford, Donald E. "The Fiction of Caroline Gordon." *Southern Review* (U.S.) 8 (1972): 458.

Individual Works

The Captive (1945)

Baum, Catherine B., and Floyd C. Watkins. "Caroline Gordon and *The Captive*: An Interview." *Southern Review* (U.S.) 7 (1971): 447–62.

Rubin, Larry. "Christian Allegory in Caroline Gordon's *The Captive*." *Studies in Short Fiction* 5 (Spring 1968): 283–89.

The Glory of Hera (1929)

Baker, Howard. "The Stratagems of Caroline Gordon, or, the Art of the Novel and the Novelty of Myth." *Southern Review* (U.S.) 9 (1973): 523–49.

Lewis, Janet. "*The Glory of Hera*." *Sewanee Review* 81 (Winter 1973): 185–94.

Green Centuries (1941)

Landess, Thomas H. "The Function of Ritual in Caroline Gordon's *Green Centuries*." *Southern Review* (U.S.) 7 (1971): 495–508.

The Malefactors (1956)

Cheney, Brainard. "Caroline Gordon's Ontological Quest." *Renascence* 16 (Fall 1963): 3–12.

Cheney, Brainard. "Caroline Gordon's *The Malefac-*

tors." *Sewanee Review* 79 (Summer 1971): 360–72.

None Shall Look Back (1937)

Brown, Ashley. "*None Shall Look Back*: The Novel as History." *Southern Review* (U.S.) 7 (1971): 480–94.

Penhally (1931)

Stanford, Donald E. "Caroline Gordon: From *Penhally* to *A Narrow Heart*." *Southern Review* (U.S.) 7 (1971): xv–xx.

The Strange Children (1951)

Rocks, James E. "The Christian Myth as Salvation: Caroline Gordon's *The Strange Children*." *Tulane Studies in English* 16 (1968): 149–60.

Smith, Patrick J. "Typology and Peripety in Four Catholic Novels." *Dissertation Abstracts* 28 (1967): 2265A (California, Davis).

MARY GORDON (fl. 1850–1900) Great Britain
Bibliography

Wilson, F.A.C. "Checklist of Writings by Mary Gordon." *Victorian Poetry* 9 (Spring–Summer 1971): 257.

General Works

Wilson, F.A.C. "Swinburne in Love: Some Novels by Mary Gordon." *Texas Studies in Literature and Language* 11 (Winter 1970): 1415–26.

Wilson, F.A.C. "Swinburne's Prose Heroines and Mary's Femmes Fatales." *Victorian Poetry* 9 (Spring–Summer 1971): 249–57.

PHYLLIS GOTLIEB, née Bloom (1926–) Canada
Individual Works

Ordinary, Moving (1969)

Barbour, Douglas. "Phyllis Gotlieb's Children of the Future: *Sunburst* and *Ordinary, Moving*." *Journal of Canadian Fiction* 3 (1974): 72–76.

Sunburst (1969)

Barbour, Douglas. "Phyllis Gotlieb's Children of the Future: *Sunburst* and *Ordinary, Moving*." *Journal of Canadian Fiction* 3 (1974): 72–76.

ELIZABETH GOUDGE (1900–) Great Britain
General Works

Duffy, M. "On the Road to Manderley." *Time* (April 12, 1971): 96.

ALICE WALWORTH GRAHAM (1905–) U.S.
General Works

Simms, L. Moody, Jr. "Alice Walworth Graham: Popular Novelist." *Notes on Mississippi Writers* 6 (Winter 1974): 63–68.

SARAH GRAND [pseud. of Frances Elizabeth M'Fall, née Clarke] (1862–1943) Great Britain
Individual Works
The Heavenly Twins (1893)
Rowlette, Robert. "Mark Twain, Sarah Grand and *The Heavenly Twins*." *Mark Twain Journal* 16 (Summer 1972): 17–18.
Weintraub, Stanley. "G.B.S. Borrows from Sarah Grand: *The Heavenly Twins* and *You Never Can Tell*." *Modern Drama* 14 (December 1971): 288–97.

SHIRLEY ANN GRAU (1929–) U.S.
Bibliography
Grissom, Margaret S. "Shirley Ann Grau: A Checklist." *Bulletin of Bibliography* 28 (July–September 1971): 76–78.
General Works
Berland, Alwyn. "The Fiction of Shirley Ann Grau." *Critique* 6 (1963): 78–84.
Donohue, H.E.F. "Shirley Ann Grau." *Publishers Weekly* (December 3, 1973): 10–13.
Keith, Don L. "New Orleans Note." *Delta Review* 2 (1967): 11.
Keith, Don L. "A Visit with Shirley Ann Grau." *Contempora* 2 (1972): 10–14.
Pearson, A. "Shirley Ann Grau: Nature Is the Vision." *Critique* 17 (1975): 47–58.
Individual Works
The House on Coliseum Street (1961)
Hicks, Granville. "Filled with Sawdust and Sadness." *Saturday Review* (June 16, 1961): 20.
The Keepers of the House (1964)
Coles, Robert. "Mood and Revelation in the South." *New Republic* (April 18, 1964): 17–19.
Going, William T. "Alabama Geography in Shirley Ann Grau's *The Keepers of the House*." *Alabama Review* 20 (January 1967): 62–68.

JOANNE GREENBERG (1932–) U.S.
Individual Works
I Never Promised You a Rose Garden (1973)
Rubin, Stephen E. "Conversations with the Author of *I Never Promised You a Rose Garden*." *Psychoanalytic Review* 59 (Summer 1972): 201–15.

GERMAINE GREER (1939–) Great Britain
General Works
Bonfante, J. "Germaine Greer." *Life* (May 7, 1971): 30–32.
"Sex and the Super-Groupie." *Time* (April 12, 1971): 75.
Individual Works
The Female Eunuch (1971)
Korengold, R. "The Female Eunuch." *Newsweek* (March 22, 1971): 48.

CORDIA GREER-PETRIE (d. 1964) U.S.
Individual Works
Angeline at the Seelbach (1922)
Houchens, Mariam S. "Cordia Greer-Petrie and *Angeline at the Seelbach*." *Southern Folklore Quarterly* 29 (1965): 164–68.

LADY ISABELLA AUGUSTA GREGORY (1852–1932) Great Britain
General Works
Ayling, Ronald. "Charwoman of the Abbey." *Shaw Review* 4 (September 1961): 7–15.
Ayling, Ronald. "That Laurelled Head: A Literary Portrait of Lady Gregory." *English Studies in Africa* 4 (September 1961): 162–73.
Coxhead, Elizabeth. "J. M. Synge and Lady Gregory." *British Book News*, no. 149 (1962): 1–35.
Edwards, A.C. "The Lady Gregory Letters to Sean O'Casey." *Modern Drama* 8 (May 1965): 95–111.
Grigson, Geoffrey. "Synge." *New Statesman* (October 19, 1962): 528–29.
"Lady Gregory, the Abbey, Yeats, Moore, Synge." *Times Literary Supplement* (July 16, 1970): 761–62.
Leslie, Sir Shane. "Ireland's Boadicea." *National Review* (November 18, 1961): 344–45.
McHugh, Robert. "Sean O'Casey and Lady Gregory." *James Joyce Quarterly* 8 (Fall 1970): 119–23.
Mullet, Olive G. "The Way with Women and Words: Lady Gregory's Destructive, Celtic Folklore Woman." *Dissertation Abstracts International* 34 (1973): 3351A (Wisconsin).
Murphy, Daniel Joseph. "Lady Gregory Letters to G. B. Shaw." *Modern Drama* 10 (February 1968): 331–45.
Murphy, Daniel Joseph. "Letters from Lady Gregory: A Record of Her Friendship with T.J. Kiernan." *Bulletin of the New York Public Library*

71 (December 1967): 621–61; 72 (January 1968): 19–63; 72 (February 1968): 123–31.

Murphy, Daniel Joseph. "The Letters of Lady Gregory to John Quinn." *Dissertation Abstracts* 22 (1962): 3204 (Columbia).

O'Malley, G., and D.T. Torchiana, eds. "John Butler Yeats to Lady Gregory: New Letters." *Massachusetts Review* 5 (Spring 1964): 269–77.

Ramaswamy, S. "Two Faces of Cathleen." *Indian Journal of English Studies* 10 (1969): 40–46.

Smythe, Colin. "Collecting Yeats and Publishing Lady Gregory." *Private Library* 4 (Spring 1971): 4–24.

Tanner, William E. "A Study of Lady Gregory's Translations of Molière." *Dissertation Abstracts International* 33 (1972): 734A (Tulsa).

Torchiana, Donald T., and Glenn O'Malley, eds. "Some New Letters from W. B. Yeats to Lady Gregory." *Review of English Literature* 4 (July 1963): 9–47.

Individual Works
The Rising of the Moon (1909)

Murphy, Daniel J. "Yeats and Lady Gregory: A Unique Dramatic Collaboration." *Modern Drama* 7 (December 1964): 322–28.

The Shoelace (1929)

Saddlemeyer, Ann, ed. "*The Shoelace.*" *Malahat Review* 16 (October 1970): 20–30.

The Workhouse Ward (1909)

Henchy, Patrick. "The Origins of *The Workhouse Ward.*" *Irish Book* 1 (1960): 21–22.

SARAH LAWRENCE GRIFFIN (fl. 1840s) U.S.
Individual Works
The Family Companion (1841–1843)

Rees, Robert A., and Marjorie Griffin. "Index to *The Family Companion* (1841–1843)." *Studies in Bibliography* 25 (1972): 205–12.

ELIZABETH GRYMESTON (1563–1601/4) Great Britain
Individual Works
Miscelanea (1609)

Krueger, Robert. "Manuscript Evidence for Dates of Two *Short-Title Catalogue* Books: George Wilkins' *Three Miseries of Babary* (1606) and the Third Edition of Elizabeth Grymeston's *Miscelanea.*" *Library* 16 (June 1961): 141–42.

LADY CHARLOTTE ELIZABETH GUEST (1812–1895) Wales
General Works

Fraser, Maxwell. "Lady Llanover and Lady Charlotte Guest." *Anglo-Welsh Review* 13 (1963): 36–43.

Gray, J. M. "Source and Symbol in *Geraint and Enid*: Tennyson's Doorm and Limours." *Victorian Poetry* 4 (Spring 1966): 131–32.

LOUISE IMOGEN GUINEY (1861–1920) U.S.
General Works

Cohen, E. H. "Jewett to Guiney: An Earlier Letter." *Colby Library Quarterly* 9 (December 1970): 231–32.

Lucey, William L. "Louise I. Guiney on American Woman Poets." *Boston Public Library Quarterly* 12 (April 1960): 110–15.

IMPULSIA GUSHINGTON [pseud.]. *See* Helen Selina Sheridan Lady Dufferin

H

H.D. [pseud.]. *See* Hilda Doolittle

HELEN E. HAINES (1872–1961) U.S.
Bibliography
Sive, M. R. "Helen E. Haines: An Annotated Bibliography." *Journal of Library History* 5 (April 1970): 146–64.

SARAH JOSEPHA HALE, née Buell (1788–1879) U.S.
Individual Works
The Genius of Oblivion (1823)
Dahl, Curtis. "Mound-Builders, Mormons and William Cullen Bryant." *New England Quarterly* 34 (June 1961): 178–90.
Ferguson, C. W. "Sarah Josepha Hale." *PTA Magazine* 60 (January 1966): 10–12.

SHARLOT MABRIDTH HALL (1870–1943) U.S.
General Works
Weston, J. J. "Sharlot Hall: Arizona's Pioneer Lady of Literature." *Journal of the West* 4 (October 1965): 539–52.

BETSY HAMILTON [pseud. of Idora McClellan Plowman Moore] (1843–1929) U.S.
General Works
Williams, Benjamin B. " 'Betsy Hamilton': Alabama Local Colorist." *Alabama Historical Quarterly* 26 (Summer 1964): 235–39.

EDITH HAMILTON (1867–1963) U.S. (Born in Germany)
Bibliography
Parker, Franklin, and Joyce Bronough. "Edith Hamilton at 94: A Partial Bibliography." *Bulletin of Bibliography* 23 (May–August 1962): 184–88.
General Works

White, John. "The Hamilton Way." *Georgia Review* 24 (Summer 1970): 132–57.

GAIL HAMILTON [pseud.]. *See* Mary Abigail Dodge

LUCY BARBARA HAMMOND, née Bradby (1873–1961) Great Britain
Individual Works
The Village Labourer, 1760–1832 (1911)
Fraser, John. "Theories and Practices: The Hammonds' *The Village Labourer.*" *Review of English Literature* 8 (April 1967): 24–37.

MARY HANES (1946?–) U.S.
Individual Works
Lovechild (1972)
Seligmann, J. A. "Raisin in the Sun." *Newsweek* (August 28, 1972): 83.

LORRAINE HANSBERRY (1930–1965) U.S.
General Works
Baldwin, James. "Sweet Lorraine." *Esquire* (November 1969): 139–40.
Farrison, W. Edward. "Lorraine Hansberry's Last Dramas." *College Language Association Journal* 16 (December 1972): 188–97.
Gill, Glenda. "Techniques of Teaching Lorraine Hansberry: Liberation from Boredom." *Negro American Literature Forum* 8 (1974): 226–28.
Hansberry, Lorraine. " 'Me Tink Me Hear Sounds in de Night.' " *Theatre Arts* 45 (October 1961): 9–11.
Hansberry, Lorraine. "My Name Is Lorraine Hansberry: I Am a Writer." *Esquire* (November 1969): 139–41.
Isaacs, H.R. "Five Writers and Their African Ancestors." *Phylon* 21 (1960): 329–36.

99

Willis, Robert J. "Anger and the Contemporary Black Theatre." *Negro American Literature Forum* 8 (1974): 213–15.

Individual Works
A Raisin in the Sun (1959)

Brown, Lloyd W. "Lorraine Hansberry as Ironist: A Reappraisal of *A Raisin in the Sun.*" *Journal of Black Studies* 4 (March 1974): 237–47.

Hays, Peter L. "*Raisin in the Sun* and *Juno and the Paycock.*" *Phylon* 33 (1972): 175–76.

ELIZABETH HARDWICK (1916–) U.S.
General Works

Durant, D.N. "London Visit, 1591." *History Today* 24 (July 1974): 497–503.

Hardwick, Elizabeth. "Scene from an Autobiography." *Prose* 4 (1972): 51–63.

Rahv, Philip. "The Editor Interviews Elizabeth Hardwick." *Modern Occasions* 2 (Spring 1972): 159–67.

CORRA HARRIS (1869–1935) U.S.
General Works

Edwards, C.H. "The Early Literary Criticism of Corra Harris." *Georgia Review* 17 (Winter 1963): 449–55.

Simms, L. Moody, Jr. "Corra Harris on the Declining Influence of Thomas Nelson Page." *Mississippi Quarterly* 28 (Fall 1975): 505–10.

Simms, L. Moody, Jr. "Corra Harris on Southern and Northern Fiction." *Mississippi Quarterly* 27 (Fall 1974): 475–81.

Talmadge, John E. "Corra Harris Goes to War." *Georgia Review* 18 (Summer 1964): 150–56.

ERIC HARRISON [pseud.]. *See* Margaret Annie England

ELIZABETH HARROWER (1928–) Australia
General Works

Burns, Robert. "The Underdog-Outsider: The Achievement of Mather's Trap." *Meanjin Quarterly* 29 (1970): 95–105.

Geering, R. G. "Elizabeth Harrower's Novels: A Survey." *Southerly* 30 (1970): 131–47.

"The Novels of Elizabeth Harrower." *Australian Letters* 4 (1962): 16–18.

JULIA CATHERINE HART (1796–1867) Canada
General Works

Bennett, C. L. "An Unpublished Manuscript of the First Canadian Novelist." *Dalhousie Review* 43 (Autumn 1963): 317–32.

GWEN HARWOOD (fl. 1960s) Australia
General Works

Douglas, Dennis. "Gwen Harwood: The Poet as Doppelganger." *Quadrant* 13 (1969): 15–19.

Douglas, Dennis. "A Prodigious Dilemma: Gwen Harwood's Professor Eisenbart and the Vices of the Intellect." *Australian Literary Studies* 6 (1973): 77–82.

Hope, A.D. "Gwen Harwood and the Professors." *Australian Literary Studies* 5 (1972): 227–32.

JOAN HASLIP (fl. 1970s) U.S.
General Works

Mercier, J. F. "Joan Haslip." *Publishers Weekly* (June 26, 1972): 28–29.

MARY HAYS (1760–1843) Great Britain
General Works

Luria, Gina M. "Mary Hays: A Critical Biography." *Dissertation Abstracts International* 33 (1972): 2898A (N.Y.U.).

Pollin, Burton R. "Mary Hays on Women's Rights in the *Monthly Magazine.*" *Etudes Anglaises* 23 (1970): 271–82.

ELIZA HAYWOOD, née Fowler (1693?–1756) Great Britain
General Works

Elwood, John R. "The Stage Career of Eliza Haywood." *Theatre Survey* 5 (November 1964): 107–16.

Erickson, James Paul. "The Novels of Eliza Haywood." *Dissertation Abstracts* 22 (1962): 2792 (Minnesota).

Heinemann, Marcia. "Eliza Haywood's Career in the Theatre." *Notes and Queries* 20 (January 1973): 9–13.

Kent, John P. "Crébillon fils, Mrs. Eliza Haywood and *Les Heureux Orphelins*: A Problem of Authorship." *Romance Notes* 11 (Winter 1969): 326–32.

Rudolf, Jo-Ellen S. "The Novels That Taught the Ladies: A Study of Popular Fiction Written by Women, 1702–1834." *Dissertation Abstracts International* 33 (1972): 1695A (California, San Diego).

Individual Works
The History of Miss Betsy Thoughtless (1751)

Elwood, John Robert. "A Critical Edition of Eliza Haywood's *The History of Miss Betsy Thoughtless*: Text of the First Edition in Four Volumes." *Dissertation Abstracts* 24 (1963): 2462 (Illinois).

Erickson, James P. "*Evelina* and *Betsy Thoughtless*." *Texas Studies in Literature and Language* 6 (Spring 1964): 96–103.

CAROLINE HAZARD (1856–1945) U.S.
General Works

Burt, C.R. "Addendum to Baird and Greenwood: Hazard." *Papers of the Bibliographical Society of America* 68 (1974): 74–75.

SHIRLEY HAZZARD (1931–) Australia
General Works

Colmer, John. "Patterns and Preoccupations of Love: The Novels of Shirley Hazzard." *Meanjin Quarterly* 29 (1970): 461–67.

ALOISE BUCKLEY HEATH (1918–1967) U.S.
General Works

Buckley, W.F., Jr., and P.L. Buckley. "Aloise B. Heath, RIP." *National Review* (February 7, 1967): 140–44.

Dubois, L.C. "First Family of Conservatism." *New York Times Magazine* (August 9, 1970): 10–11.

ERNEST HELFENSTEIN [pseud.]. *See* Elizabeth Oakes Smith

LILLIAN HELLMAN (1905–) U.S.
Bibliography

Triesch, Manfred. "Lillian Hellman: A Selective Bibliography." *American Book Collector* 14 (Summer 1964): 57.

General Works

Adler, Jacob H. "Professor Moody's Miss Hellman." *Southern Literary Journal* 5 (Spring 1973): 131–40.

Angermeier, Brother Carrol. "Moral and Social Protest in the Plays of Lillian Hellman." *Dissertation Abstracts International* 32 (1972): 3986A (Texas).

Brockington, John. "A Critical Analysis of the Plays of Lillian Hellman." *Dissertation Abstracts* 23 (1962): 211 (Yale).

Ephron, Nora. "Lillian Hellman: Walking, Cooking, Writing, Talking." *New York Times Book Review* (September 23, 1973): 2.

Goldstein, M. "Body and Soul on Broadway." *Modern Drama* 7 (February 1965): 411–21.

Grant, A. "Lively Lady." *Newsweek* (June 30, 1969): 89–90.

Haller, C. David. "Concept of Moral Failure in the Eight Original Plays of Lillian Hellman." *Dissertation Abstracts* 28 (1967): 4303A (Tulane).

Hellman, Lillian. "Theatre Pictures." *Esquire* (August 1973): 64.

Hellman, Lillian. "Turtle." *Esquire* (June 1973): 146.

Johnson, Annette B. "A Study of Recurrent Character Types in the Plays of Lillian Hellman." *Dissertation Abstracts International* 31 (1971): 6614A (Massachusetts).

Keller, Alvin Joseph. "Form and Content in the Plays of Lillian Hellman." *Dissertation Abstracts* 26 (1966): 6715 (Stanford).

Larimer, Cynthia D.M. "A Study of Female Characters in the Eight Plays of Lillian Hellman. *Dissertation Abstracts International* 31 (1971): 5410A (Purdue).

Phillips, John, and Anne Hollander. "Lillian Hellman: An Interview—The Art of the Theater, I." *Paris Review* 6 (Winter–Spring 1965): 65–95.

Triesch, Manfred. "The Lillian Hellman Collection." *Library Chronicle* (Texas) 8 (Spring 1965): 17–20.

Whitesides, Glenn E. "Lillian Hellman: A Biography and Critical Study." *Dissertation Abstracts* 29 (1969): 2287A (Florida State).

Individual Works
Another Part of the Forest (1946)

Triesch, Manfred. "Hellman's *Another Part of the Forest*." *Explicator* 24 (October 1965): Item 20.

The Autumn Garden (1951)

Felheim, Marvin. "*The Autumn Garden*: Mechanics and Dialectics." *Modern Drama* 3 (September 1960): 191–95.

The Children's Hour (1934)

Armato, Philip M. "Good and Evil in Lillian Hellman's *The Children's Hour*." *Educational Theatre Journal* 25 (December 1973): 443–47.

The Little Foxes (1939)

Eatman, James. "The Image of American Destiny: *The Little Foxes*." *Players* 48 (December–January 1973): 70–73.

Pentimento (1973)

Duffy, M. "Half-Told Tales." *Time* (October 1, 1973): 114.

Toys in the Attic (1960)
Adler, Jacob H. "Miss Hellman's Two Sisters." *Educational Theatre Journal* 15 (May 1963): 112–17.

MARTHA HENNISART. *See* Emma Lathen

JOSEPHINE FREY HERBST (1897–1969) U.S.
General Works
Gourlie, John MacLeod. "The Evolution of Form in the Works of Josephine Herbst." *Dissertation Abstracts* 35 (1975): 2205A (N.Y.U.).
Kempthorne, Dion Q. "Josephine Herbst: A Critical Introduction." *Dissertation Abstracts International* 34 (1974): 6645A (Wisconsin).

DOROTHY HEWETT (1923–) Australia
Individual Works
Bonbons and Roses for Dolby (1970s)
Luke, Margot. "Insight and Outrage: Dorothy Hewett's New Play." *Westerly*, no. 4 (1971): 38–40.
The Chapel Perilous (1970s)
Whitehead, Jean. "Ordeal of Freedom." *Westerly*, no. 4 (1971): 41–44.

ELEANOR ALICE BURFORD HIBBERT [pseud. Victoria Holt, Jean Plaidy] (1906–) Great Britain
General Works
Duffy, M. "On the Road to Manderley." *Time* (April 12, 1971): 96.
Nichols, L. "Add Gothics." *New York Times Book Review* (January 8, 1967): 8.

JANET GERTRUDE HIGGINS. *See* Nettie Palmer

PATRICIA HIGHSMITH (1921–) U.S.
General Works
"The Talented Miss Patricia Highsmith." *Times Literary Supplement* (September 24, 1971): 1147–48.

SUSAN HILL (1942–) Great Britain
General Works
"Susan Hill's Aldeburgh." *Listener* (July 12, 1973): 54–56.

SUSIE E. HINTON (1948?–) U.S.
General Works
"Face to Face with a Teen-Age Novelist." *Seventeen* (October 1967): 133.

LAURA ZAMETKIN HOBSON (1900–) U.S.
General Works
"Where Are They Now?" *Newsweek* (September 2, 1963): 12.

ALICE ALBRIGHT HOGE (1941?–) U.S.
General Works
"Replating the Front Page." *Newsweek* (October 14, 1968): 58.

CECELIA HOLLAND [pseud. Roberta Stone Pryor] (1943–) U.S.
General Works
Cocks, J. "Nom de Plume." *Time* (August 17, 1970): 66.
Junker, H. "Historical Chick." *Newsweek* (February 10, 1969): 88A.
Nichols, L. "First Novelist." *New York Times Book Review* (January 9, 1966): 8.

SAXE HOLM [pseud.]. *See* Helen Hunt Jackson

CONSTANCE HOLME (1881–1955) Great Britain
General Works
Brown, Alan L. "Constance Holme (1881–1955)." *Serif* 1 (April 1964): 21–24.

MARJORIE HOLMES (1910–) U.S.
General Works
Jablonski, J.M. "Marjorie Holmes Has to Talk to Somebody." *Writer's Digest* 54 (December 1974): 18–24.

VICTORIA HOLT [pseud.]. *See* Eleanor Alice Burford Hibbert

ABIGAIL ADAMS HOMANS (1879?–) U.S.
General Works
"Memoirs of a Spry Matriarch." *Life* (October 28, 1966): 61–62.
Nichols, L. "Ladies of Boston." *New York Times Book Review* (January 22, 1967): 8.

PAULINE HOPKINS (1859–1930) U.S.
General Works
Shockley, Ann Allen. "Pauline Elizabeth Hopkins: A Biographical Excursion into Obscurity." *Phylon* 33 (1972): 22–26.

JULIA WARD HOWE (1819–1910) U.S.
General Works
Gale, R.L. "Four Letters to Francis Marion Crawford: From Theodore Roosevelt, Clyde Fitch, Julia Ward Howe, Henry James." *Literary Review* 3 (Spring 1960): 438–43.

FANNIE HURST (1889–1968) U.S.
General Works
"Where Are They Now?" *Newsweek* (September 2, 1963): 12.

ZORA NEALE HURSTON (1903–1960) U.S.
General Works
Blake, E.L. "Zora Neale Hurston (1903–1960)." *Negro History Bulletin* 29 (April 1966): 149–50.
Hurst, Fannie. "Zora Hurston: A Personality Sketch." *Yale University Library Gazette* 35 (1960): 17–22.
Jordan, June. Notes toward a Balancing of Love and Hatred: On Richard Wright and Zora Neale Hurston." *Black World* 23 (August 1974): 4–8.
Kilson, Marion. "The Transformation of Eatonville's Ethnographer." *Phylon* 33 (1972): 112–19.
Rayson, A.L. "Novels of Zora Neale Hurston." *Studies in Black Literature* 5 (Winter 1974): 1–10.
Southerland, Ellease. "Zora Neale Hurston: The Novelist-Anthropologist's Life/Works." *Black World* 23 (August 1974): 20–30.
Walker, Alice. "In Search of Zora Neale Hurston." *Ms.* (March 1975): 74–79.
Individual Works
Dust Tracks on a Road (1942)
Rayson, Ann L. "*Dust Tracks on a Road*: Zora Neale Hurston and the Form of Black Autobiography." *Negro American Literature Forum* 7 (1973): 39–45.
Their Eyes Were Watching God (1937)
Giles, James R. "The Significance of Time in Zora Neale Hurston's *Their Eyes Were Watching God*." *Negro American Literature Forum* 6 (1972): 52.
Walker, J. "Zora Neale Hurston's *Their Eyes Were Watching God*: Black Novel of Sexism." *Modern Fiction Studies* 20 (Winter 1974–1975): 519–27.
Washington, Mary H. "The Black Woman's Search for Identity: Zora Neale Hurston's Work." *Black World* 21 (August 1972): 68–75.

MAUDE HUTCHINS (1889?–) U.S.
General Works
Ippolito, Donna. " 'Why, What's the Matter, Adam?' " *Oyez Review* (Roosevelt University) 9 (Spring 1975): 17–23.

ANNE HUTCHINSON, née Marbury (1591–1643) U.S.
General Works
Goldman, Maureen. "American Women and the Puritan Heritage: Anne Hutchinson to Harriet Beecher Stowe." *Dissertation Abstracts International* 35 (1975): 1503A–4A (Boston).
Koehler, Lyle. "The Case of the American Jezebels: Anne Hutchinson and Female Agitation during the Years of Antinomian Turmoil, 1636–1640." *William and Mary Quarterly* 31 (January 1974): 55–78.
Newcomb, Wellington. "Anne Hutchinson versus Massachusetts." *American Heritage* 25 (June 1974): 12–15.

ROBIN HYDE [pseud. of Iris Wilkinson] (1906–) New Zealand
General Works
Partridge, Colin J. "Wheel of Words: The Poetic Development of Robin Hyde." *Journal of Commonwealth Literature* 5 (July 1968): 92–104.

I

ELIZABETH INCHBALD, née Simpson (1753–1821)
Great Britain
Individual Works
Lovers' Vows (1798)
De Beer, E.S. "*Lovers' Vows:* The Dangerous Insignificance of the Butler." *Notes and Queries* 9 (November 1962): 421–22.

Fryxell, Donald R. "*Lovers' Vows* in *Mansfield Park.*" *Midwest Review* (Spring 1961): 75–78.
Kirkham, M. "Theatricals in *Mansfield Park* and Frederick in *Lovers' Vows.*" *Notes and Queries* 22 (September 1975): 388–89.

RALPH IRON [pseud.]. *See* Olive Schreiner

J

HELEN HUNT JACKSON [pseud. Saxe Holm] (1830–1885) U.S.

Bibliography

Byers, John R., Jr. "Helen Hunt Jackson." *American Literary Realism* 2 (1969): 143–48.

Byers, John R., Jr., and Elizabeth S. Byers. "Helen Hunt Jackson (1830–1885): A Critical Bibliography of Secondary Comment." *American Literary Realism* 6 (1973): 196–242.

General Works

McConnell, Virginia. "H.H., Colorado and the Indian Problem." *Journal of the West* 12 (April 1973): 272–80.

Individual Works

A Century of Dishonor (1881)

Turner, F.W., III. "Century after *A Century of Dishonor*: American Conscience and Consciousness." *Massachusetts Review* 16 (Autumn 1975): 715–31.

SHIRLEY JACKSON (1919–1965) U.S.

Bibliography

Phillips, Robert S. "Shirley Jackson: A Checklist." *Papers of the Bibliographical Society of America* 56 (1962): 110–13.

Phillips, Robert S. "Shirley Jackson: A Chronology and a Supplementary Checklist." *Papers of the Bibliographical Society of America* 60 (1966): 203–13.

General Works

Hyman, S.E. "Shirley Jackson, 1919–1965." *Saturday Evening Post* (December 18, 1965): 63.

Miller, Raymond R., Jr. "Shirley Jackson's Fiction: An Introduction." *Dissertation Abstracts International* 35 (1974): 3000A (Delaware).

Nichols, L. "Demonologist." *New York Times Book Review* (October 7, 1962): 8.

Parks, John G. "The Possibility of Evil: The Fiction of Shirley Jackson." *Dissertation Abstracts International* 35 (1974): 1667A (New Mexico).

Phillips, Robert S. "Tribute to Excellence: Five Syracuse Authors." *Syracuse Alumni News* 44 (Spring 1963): 19.

"School of One." *Newsweek* (August 23, 1965): 83B.

Individual Works

The Lottery (1949)

Nebeker, Helen E. "*The Lottery*: Symbolic Tour de Force." *American Literature* 46 (March 1974): 100–107.

We Have Always Lived in the Castle (1962)

Woodruff, Stuart C. "The Real Horror Elsewhere: Shirley Jackson's Last Novel." *Southwest Review* 52 (Spring 1967): 152–62.

The Witch (1949)

Kelly, Robert L. "Jackson's *The Witch*: A Satanic Gem." *English Journal* 60 (December 1971): 1204–8.

JANE JACOBS (1916–) U.S.

General Works

Marty, L. S. "Inefficiency Expert." *Newsweek* (June 2, 1969): 63.

Mead, M. "Where American Women Are Now." *Vogue* (May 1969): 180.

RONA JAFFE (1932?–) U.S.

General Works

Ebert, A. "Fears of the Famous." *Good Housekeeping* (May 1973): 107.

Walters, R., Jr. "Career Girl." *New York Times Book Review* (September 4, 1960): 8.

ANNA JAMESON, née Murphy (1794–1860) Canada (Born in Ireland)

General Works

Agelasto, C.P. "Days of Industry: Anna Jameson, 1794–1860." *Library Review* 23 (1971): 22–24.

Thomas, Clara. "Anna Jameson and Nineteenth Century Taste." *Humanities Association Bulletin* 17 (Spring 1966): 53–61.

Thomas, Clara. "Journeys to Freedom." *Canadian Literature*, no. 51 (Winter 1972): 11–19.

PATRICIA ANN JELLICOE (1927–) Great Britain
General Works

"Ann Jellicoe, Interviewed by Robert Rubens." *Transatlantic Review* 12 (Spring 1963): 27–34.

ELIZABETH JOAN JENNINGS (1926–) Great Britain
General Works

Ghose, Zulfikar. "Impetus for Poetry." *Umbrella* 11 (Summer 1962): 171–77.

Harrison, Janet E. "The Quiet Pursuit: Poetry of Elizabeth Jennings." *Dissertation Abstracts* 29 (1968): 1227A (Ohio).

Levi, Peter. "The Poetry of Elizabeth Jennings." *Month* (December 1967): 332–34.

SARAH ORNE JEWETT (1849–1909) U.S.
Bibliography

Bowditch, Mrs. Ernest. "The Jewett Library." *Colby Library Quarterly* 5 (December 1961): 357–64.

Cary, Richard. "Sarah Orne Jewett (1849–1909)." *American Literary Realism* 1 (1967): 61–66.

Cary, Richard. "Some Bibliographic Ghosts of Sarah Orne Jewett." *Colby Library Quarterly* 8 (September 1968): 139–45.

Cary, Richard. "The Uncollected Short Stories of Sarah Orne Jewett." *Colby Library Quarterly* 9 (December 1971): 385–408.

Eichelberger, Clayton L. "Sarah Orne Jewett (1849–1909): A Critical Bibliography of Secondary Comment." *American Literary Realism* 2 (1969): 189–262.

Frost, John E. "Sarah Orne Jewett Bibliography: 1949–1963." *Colby Library Quarterly* 6 (June 1964): 405–17.

Green, David Bonnell. "The Sarah Orne Jewett Canon: Additions and a Correction." *Papers of the Bibliographical Society of America* 55 (1961): 141–42.

General Works

Blanc, M.T. "Madame Blanc's *Le Roman de la Femme-Medicin.*" *Colby Library Quarterly* 7 (September 1967): 488–503.

Boggio-Sola, Jean. "The Poetic Realism of Sarah Orne Jewett." *Colby Library Quarterly* 7 (June 1965): 74–78.

Cary, Richard. "Jewett and the Gilman Women." *Colby Library Quarterly* 5 (March 1960): 94–103.

Cary, Richard. "Jewett on Writing Short Stories." *Colby Library Quarterly* 6 (June 1964): 425–40.

Cary, Richard. "Jewett's Literary Canons." *Colby Library Quarterly* 7 (June 1965): 82–87.

Cary, Richard. "Miss Jewett and Madame Blanc." *Colby Library Quarterly* 7 (September 1967): 467–88.

Cary, Richard. "The Other Face of Jewett's Coin." *American Literary Realism* 2 (1969): 263–70.

Cary, Richard. "The Rise, Decline, and Rise of Sarah Orne Jewett." *Colby Library Quarterly* 9 (December 1972): 650–63.

Cary, Richard. "The Sculptor and the Spinster: Jewett's Influence on Cather." *Colby Library Quarterly* 10 (September 1973): 168–78.

Cary, Richard. "Violet Paget to Sarah Orne Jewett." *Colby Library Quarterly* 9 (December 1970): 235–43.

Cary, Richard. "Whittier Letters to Sarah Orne Jewett." *Emerson Society Quarterly* 50 (1968): 11–22.

Cary, Richard. " 'Yours Always Lovingly': Sarah Orne Jewett to John Greenleaf Whittier." *Essex Institute Historical Collections* 107 (1971): 412–50.

Chase, Mary Ellen. "Five Literary Portraits." *Massachusetts Review* 3 (Spring 1962): 511–16.

Chase, Mary Ellen. "Sarah Orne Jewett as a Social Historian." *Prairie Schooner* 36 (Fall 1962): 231–37.

Cohen, E. H. "Jewett to Guiney: An Earlier Letter." *Colby Library Quarterly* 9 (December 1970): 231–32.

Coyle, Lee. "Sarah Orne Jewett and Irish Roger." *Colby Library Quarterly* 6 (June 1964): 441–43.

Eakin, Paul John. "Sarah Orne Jewett and the Meaning of Country Life." *American Literature* 38 (January 1967): 508–31.

Fultz, Mary C. "The Narrative Art of Sarah Orne Jewett." *Dissertation Abstracts* 29 (1968): 3135A–36A (Virginia).

Green, David Bonnell. "The World of Dunnet Landing." *New England Quarterly* 34 (December 1961): 514–17.

Hollis, C. Carroll. "Letters of Sarah Orne Jewett to

Anne Laurens Dawes." *Colby Library Quarterly* 8 (September 1968): 97–138.

Magowan, Robin. "Fromentin and Jewett: Pastoral Narrative in the Nineteenth Century." *Comparative Literature* 16 (1964): 331–37.

McAlpin, Sister Sara. "Enlightening the Commonplace: The Art of Sarah Orne Jewett, Willa Cather and Ruth Suckow." *Dissertation Abstracts International* 32 (1971): 2061A (Penn.).

McGuire, Mary Agnes. "Sarah Orne Jewett." *Dissertation Abstracts* 25 (1965): 7275 (Columbia).

Noyes, Sylvia G. "Mrs. Almira Todd, Herbalist-Conjurer." *Colby Library Quarterly* 9 (December 1972): 643–49.

Pool, Eugene H. "The Child in Sarah Orne Jewett." *Colby Library Quarterly* 7 (September 1967): 503–9.

Rhode, Robert D. "Sarah Orne Jewett and the Palpable Present Intimate." *Colby Library Quarterly* 8 (September 1968): 146–55.

St. Armand, Barton L. "Jewett and Marin: The Inner Vision." *Colby Library Quarterly* 9 (December 1972): 632–43.

Toth, Susan Allen. "Sarah Orne Jewett and Friends: A Community of Interest." *Studies in Short Fiction* 9 (Summer 1972): 233–42.

Toth, Susan Allen. "The Value of Age in the Fiction of Sarah Orne Jewett." *Studies in Short Fiction* 8 (Summer 1971): 433–41.

VanDerBeets, R., and J.K. Bowen. "Miss Jewett, Mrs. Turner and the Chautauqua Circle." *Colby Library Quarterly* 9 (December 1970): 233–34.

Willoughby, John. "Sarah Orne Jewett and Her Shelter Island." *Confrontation* 8 (Spring 1974): 72–86.

Wood, Ann Douglas. "The Literature of Impoverishment: The Women Local Colorists in America 1865–1914." *Women's Studies* 1 (1972): 3–40.

Individual Works
The Country of the Pointed Firs (1896)

Fike, Francis. "An Interpretation of *Pointed Firs*." *New England Quarterly* 34 (December 1961): 478–91.

Magowan, Robin. "The Outer Island Sequence in *Pointed Firs*." *Colby Library Quarterly* 6 (June 1964): 418–24.

Magowan, Robin. "Pastoral and the Art of Landscape in *The Country of the Pointed Firs*." *New England Quarterly* 36 (June 1963): 229–40.

Stouck, David. "*The Country of the Pointed Firs:* A Pastoral of Innocence." *Colby Library Quarterly* 9 (December 1970): 213–20.

Vella, Michael W. "Sarah Orne Jewett: A Reading of *The Country of the Pointed Firs*." *Emerson Society Quarterly* 19 (1973): 275–82.

Voelker, P.D. "*The Country of the Pointed Firs:* A Novel by Saran [sic] Orne Jewett." *Colby Library Quarterly* 9 (June 1971): 201–13.

The Courting of Sister Wisby (1887)

Humma, John B. "The Art and Meaning of Sarah Orne Jewett's *The Courting of Sister Wisby*." *Studies in Short Fiction* 10 (Winter 1973): 85–91.

Deephaven (1877)

Horn, Robert L. "The Power of Jewett's *Deephaven*." *Colby Library Quarterly* 9 (December 1972): 617–31.

The Tory Lover (1901)

Parsons, Helen V. "*The Tory Lover*, Oliver Wiswell and Richard Carvel." *Colby Library Quarterly* 9 (December 1970): 220–31.

A White Heron (1886)

Jobes, Katharine T. "From Stowe's Eagle Island to Jewett's 'A White Heron.'" *Colby Library Quarterly* 10 (December 1974): 515–21.

GERALDINE ENDSOR JEWSBURY (1812–1880): Great Britain

General Works
Fahnestock, Jeanne R. "Geraldine Jewsbury: The Power of the Publisher's Reader." *Nineteenth Century Fiction* 28 (December 1973): 253–72.

DIANE JOHNSON (1934–) U.S.
General Works
Ryan, Marjorie. "The Novels of Diane Johnson." *Critique* 16 (1974): 53–63.

PAMELA HANSFORD JOHNSON, Baroness Snow [pseud. Nap Lombard] (1912–) Great Britain
General Works
Janeway, E. "Important to Me." *New York Times Book Review* (September 14, 1975): 18.

"People Are Talking About. . . ." *Vogue* (March 1961): 141.

Individual Works
Night and Silence Who Is Here? (1963)

Webster, Harvey Curtis. "Farce and Faith." *Kenyon Review* 25 (1963): 747–51.

PAULINE JOHNSON (1862–1913) Canada
General Works

Shrive, Norman. "What Happened to Pauline Johnson?" *Canadian Literature*, no. 13 (Summer 1962): 25–38.

MARY JOHNSTON (1870–1936) U.S.
General Works

Hartley, Gayle M. "The Novels of Mary Johnston: A Critical Study." *Dissertation Abstracts International* 32 (1972): 6929A (South Carolina).

ERICA JONG (1942–) U.S.
General Works

Francke, L. "Mother Confessor." *Newsweek* (December 16, 1974): 65–66.

Jong, Erica. "Writing a First Novel." *Twentieth Century Literature* 20 (October 1974): 262–69.

"Loves of Isadora." *Time* (February 3, 1975): 69–70.

Peer, E. "Lusty Lady with Talent, Too." *Newsweek* (May 5, 1975): 71.

Peer, E. "Sex and the Woman Writer." *Newsweek* (May 5, 1975): 70–72.

"People." *Time* (January 20, 1975): 44–45.

Showalter, Elaine, and Carol Smith. "Interview with Erica Jong." *Columbia Forum*, n.s. 44 (Winter 1975): 12–17.

JUNE JORDAN (1936–) U.S.
General Works

Bragg, P. "June Jordan." *Publishers Weekly* (February 21, 1972): 60–61.

JULIANA OF NORWICH (c. 1343–c. 1443) Great Britain
General Works

Reynolds, Anna Maria. "Juliana of Norwich." *Month* (January 1960): 133–44.

Stone, Robert Karl. "Middle English Prose Style: Margery Kempe and Juliana Norwich." *Dissertation Abstracts* 24 (1963): 288–9 (Illinois).

SUSANNA JULIUSBERGER (1957?–) U.S.
Individual Works

Beginnings (1974)

Mercier, J. F. "Story behind the Book: *Beginnings*." *Publishers Weekly* (November 4, 1974): 61.

K

PAULINE KAEL (1919–) U.S.
General Works
"Critic as Superstar." *Newsweek* (December 24, 1973): 97.
Lerman, L. "The Influentials." *Vogue* (September 1973): 284–85.

JOAN KAHN (1914?–) U.S.
General Works
Nichols, L. "Mystery Lady." *New York Times Book Review* (April 28, 1968): 20.

KATHY KAHN (1945–) U.S.
General Works
Orth, M. "Stubborn People." *Newsweek* (September 24, 1973): 116.

BEL KAUFMAN (fl. 1960s) U.S.
Individual Works
Up the Down Staircase (1965)
Romano, Josefina. "The Novel into Film: *Up the Down Staircase.*" *Diliman Review* 14 (January 1966): 27–39.

THERESA KAY [pseud.]. *See* Theresa de Kerpely

SHEILA KAYE-SMITH (1887–1956) Great Britain
Bibliography
Doyle, Paul A. "Sheila Kaye-Smith: An Annotated Bibliography of Writings about Her." *English Literature in Transition* 15 (1972): 189–98.

DORIS H. KEARNS (1943?–) U.S.
General Works
Michener, C., et al. "Spoils of London." *Newsweek* (August 4, 1975): 67–68.

"200 Faces for the Future." *Time* (July 15, 1974): 53.

ELIZABETH HOBBS KECKLEY (1824–1907) U.S.
Individual Works
Behind the Scenes (1868)
Wefer, M. "Another Assassination, Another Widow, Another Embattled Book." *American Heritage* 18 (August 1967): 79–88.

HELEN KELLER (1880–1968) U.S.
General Works
Chambliss, Amy. "The Friendship of Helen Keller and Mark Twain." *Georgia Review* 24 (Fall 1970): 305–10.

FANNY KEMBLE (1809–1893) Great Britain
General Works
"Fanny Kemble in New York." *Columbia Library Columns* 11 (1961): 13–17.
Melchiori, Barbara. "Fanny Kemble in Rome, with Some Unpublished Letters." *English Miscellany* 20 (1969): 269–89.
Myers, Andrew B. "Miss Kemble's Keys." *Columbia Library Columns* 11 (1961): 3–12.
Individual Works
Journal of a Residence on a Georgian Plantation (1863)
Ashby, Clifford. "Fanny Kemble's 'Vulgar' Journal." *Pennsylvania Magazine of History and Biography* 98 (1974): 58–66.
Scott, John A. "On the Authenticity of Fanny Kemble's *Journal of a Residence on a Plantation in Georgia 1838–1839.*" *Journal of Negro History* 46 (October 1961): 233–49.

MARGERY KEMPE (c.1373–c.1440) Great Britain
General Works
Stone, Robert Karl. "Middle English Prose Style:
Margery Kempe and Juliana Norwich." *Disserta-
tion Abstracts* 24 (1963): 2889 (Illinois).

ADRIENNE LITA KENNEDY (1931–) U.S.
General Works
Tener, R.L. "Theatre of Identity: Adrienne Ken-
nedy's Portrait of the Black Woman." *Studies in
Black Literature* 6 (Summer 1975): 1–5.

THERESA DE KERPELY [pseud. Theresa Kay] (1898–)
U.S.
General Works
Jenkins, Donald. "The Novels of Theresa de Ker-
pely." *Critique* 13 (1971): 48–58.

JEAN COLLINS KERR (1923–) U.S.
General Works
"As the Mop Flops." *Newsweek* (December 5,
1960): 106.
"Children Run Longer Than Plays." *Time* (April
14, 1961): 82–86.
Davis, J. "She Never Does the Dishes." *Ladies' Home
Journal* (June 1964): 64–65.
Gehman, R. "Jean Kerr." *Theatre Arts* 45 (March
1961): 14–16.

GRACE ELIZABETH KING (1851–1932) U.S.
Bibliography
Bush, Robert. "Grace King (1851–1932)." *American
Literary Realism* 8 (1975): 43–52.
General Works
Bush, Robert. "Charles Gayarré and Grace King."
Southern Literary Journal 7 (Fall 1974): 100–131.
Bush, Robert. "Grace King and Mark Twain."
American Literature 44 (March 1972): 31–51.
Fletcher, Marie. "Grace Elizabeth King: Her Delin-
eation of the Southern Heroine." *Louisiana Studies*
5 (Spring 1966): 50–60.
Frisby, James R., Jr. "New Orleans Writers and the
Negro: George Washington Cable, Grace King,
Ruth McEnery Stuart, Kate Chopin, and Lafcadio
Hearn, 1870–1900." *Dissertation Abstracts Interna-
tional* 33 (1972): 2890A (Emory).
Simpson, Claude M., Jr. "Grace King: The Histo-
rian as Apologist." *Southern Literary Journal* 6
(Spring 1974): 130–38.
Slayton, Gail Cathy. "Grace Elizabeth King: Her

Life and Works." *Dissertation Abstracts International* 35 (1975): 5428A (Penn.).

ELIZABETH CLEMENTINE KINNEY, née Dodge (1810–
1889) U.S.
General Works
Upjohn, E.M. "Minor Poet Meets Hiram Powers."
Art Bulletin 42 (March 1960): 63–66.

CAROLINE KIRKLAND [pseud. Mrs. Mary Clavers]
(1801–1864) U.S.
General Works
Mabbott, Thomas O. "Mrs. Kirkland's Essay on
Fiction." *Bulletin of the New York Public Library*
64 (July 1960): 395–97.
Riordan, Daniel G. "The Concept of Simplicity in
the Works of Mrs. Caroline M. Kirkland." *Disser-
tation Abstracts International* 34 (1974): 5926A–
27A (North Carolina).
Stronks, James B. "Author Rejects Publisher: Car-
oline Kirkland and *The Gift*." *Bulletin of the New
York Public Library* 64 (October 1960): 548–50.
Individual Works
A New Home—Who'll Follow? (1839)
McCloskey, John C. "Jacksonian Democracy in Mrs.
Kirkland's *A New Home—Who'll Follow?*" *Michi-
gan History* 45 (December 1961): 347–52.

CAROLYN KIZER (1925–) U.S.
General Works
Chappell, Fred. " 'I'm in the Racket': Carolyn
Kizer's Poetry." *St. Andrew's Review* 1 (Fall-
Winter 1971): 13–16.
Howard, Richard. "Carolyn Kizer." *Tri-Quarterly* 7
(Fall 1966): 109–17.

SARAH KEMBLE KNIGHT (1666–1727) U.S.
General Works
Stephens, Robert O. "The Odyssey of Sarah Kemble
Knight." *College Language Association Journal* 7
(March 1964): 247–55.
Thorpe, Peter. "Sarah Kemble Knight and the Pica-
resque Tradition." *College Language Association
Journal* 10 (December 1966): 114–21.
Individual Works
The Journal of Madam Knight (1825)
Margolis, Alan. "The Editing and Publication of *The
Journal of Madam Knight*." *Papers of the Bibli-
ographical Society of America* 58 (1964): 25–32.

SUSANNE KNOWLES (1912–) Great Britain
General Works
Clapp, Susannah. "Susanne Knowles Praised." *Listener* (June 29, 1972): 866–67.

MAXINE KUMIN, née Winokur (1925–) U.S.
General Works
Ciardi, John. "The Art of Maxine Kumin." *Saturday Review* (March 25, 1972): 12.

L

JOYCE A. LADNER (1943?–) U.S.
General Works
"Black New Grey Matter." *Esquire* (January 1973): 132.

LADY CAROLINE LAMB (1785–1828) Great Britain
General Works
Doherty, Francis. "An Unpublished Letter of Lady Caroline Lamb to Clare." *Notes and Queries* 14 (August 1967): 297–99.
Fremantle, A. "Lady Caroline Lamb." *New York Times Book Review* (February 18, 1973): 6.
Hoge, James O., Jr. "Lady Caroline Lamb on Byron and Her Own Wasted Life: Two New Letters." *Notes and Queries* 21 (September 1974): 331–33.

MARY ANN LAMB (1764–1847) Great Britain
Bibliography
Braendel, Doris. "The Lamb Collection at the Rosenbach Foundation: A Checklist." *Wordsworth Circle* 2 (Summer 1971): 80–91.
General Works
Braekman, W. "Two Hitherto Unpublished Letters of Charles and Mary Lamb to the Morgans." *English Studies* 44 (1963): 108–18.
Skeat, T.C. "Letters of Charles and Mary Lamb and Coleridge." *British Museum Quarterly* 26 (September 1962): 17–21.

SUSANNE LANGER (1895–) U.S.
General Works
Barry, Jackson G. "Form or Formula: Comic Structure in Northrop Frye and Susanne Langer." *Educational Theatre Journal* 16 (December 1964): 333–40.
Bertocci, Angelo. "Susanne Langer, or the Symbol Abstracted." *Philological Quarterly* 48 (April 1969): 261–77.
Richards, Chris. "The Aesthetic Theories of Roger Fry, Clive Bell, and Susanne Langer: Some Comparisons." *Virginia Woolf Quarterly* 1 (Spring 1973): 22–31.

ANNA MARGARETTA LARPENT (fl. 1773–1786) Great Britain
General Works
Conolly, L.W. "Anna Margaretta Larpent, the Duchess of Queensberry and Gay's *Polly* in 1777." *Philological Quarterly* 50 (October 1972): 955–57.
Conolly, L.W. "The Censor's Wife at the Theater: The Diary of Anna Margaretta Larpent, 1790–1800." *Huntington Library Quarterly* 35 (November 1971): 49–64.

NELLA LARSEN (1893–1963) U.S.
Individual Works
Passing (1929)
Youman, Mary Mabel. "Nella Larsen's *Passing*: A Study in Irony." *College Language Association Journal* 18 (December 1974): 235–41.
Quicksand (1928)
Thornton, Hortense. "Sexism as Quagmire: Nella Larsen's *Quicksand*." *College Language Association Journal* 16 (March 1973): 285–301.

EMMA LATHEN [pseud. of Mary J. Latis and Martha Hennisart] (fl. 1970s)
General Works
Bakerman, Jane S. "Women and Wall Street: Portraits of Women in Novels by Emma Lathen." *Armchair Detective* 8 (1974): 36–41.

MARGERY LATIMER (1899–1931) U.S.
General Works

McCarthy, D.P. "Just Americans: A Note on Jean Toomer's Marriage to Margery Latimer." *College Language Association Journal* 17 (June 1974): 474–79.

MARY J. LATIS. *See* Emma Lathen

MARGARET LAURENCE (1926–) Canada
General Works

Callaghan, Barry. "The Writings of Margaret Laurence." *Tamarack Review* 36 (Summer 1965): 45–51.

Djwa, Sandra. "False Gods and the True Covenant: Thematic Continuity between Margaret Laurence and Sinclair Ross." *Journal of Canadian Fiction* 1 (1972): 43–50.

Forman, Denyse, and Uma Parameswaran. "Echoes and Refrains in the Canadian Novels of Margaret Laurence." *Centennial Review* 16 (1972): 233–53.

Githae-Mugo, Micere M. "Visions of Africa in the Fiction of Chinua Achebe, Margaret Laurence, Elspeth Huxley and Ngugi wa Thiongo." *Dissertation Abstracts International* 34 (1974): 5968A–69A (New Brunswick).

Gom, Leona M. "Margaret Laurence and the First Person." *Dalhousie Review* 55 (Summer 1975): 236–51.

Laurence, Margaret. "Ten Years' Sentences." *Canadian Literature*, no. 41 (Summer 1969): 10–16.

Pesando, Frank. "In a Nameless Land: The Use of Apocalyptic Mythology in the Writings of Margaret Laurence." *Journal of Canadian Fiction* 2 (1973): 53–58.

Read, S. E. "The Maze of Life: The Work of Margaret Laurence." *Canadian Literature*, no. 27 (Winter 1966): 5–14.

Swayze, Walter E. "The Odyssey of Margaret Laurence." *English Quarterly* 3 (Fall 1970): 7–17.

Thomas, Clara. "A Conversation about Literature: An Interview with Margaret Laurence and Irving Layton." *Journal of Canadian Fiction* 1 (1972): 65–69.

Thomas, Clara. "The Novels of Margaret Laurence." *Studies in the Novel* 4 (Summer 1972): 154–64.

Thomas, Clara. "Proud Lineage: Willa Cather and Margaret Laurence." *Canadian Review of American Studies* 2 (Spring 1971): 3–12.

Thomas, Clara. "The Short Stories of Margaret Laurence." *World Literature Written in English* 11 (1972): 25–33.

MARY LAVIN (1912–) Great Britain
Bibliography

Doyle, Paul A. "Mary Lavin: A Checklist." *Papers of the Bibliographical Society of America* 63 (1969): 317–21.

General Works

Martin, Augustine. "A Skeleton Key to the Stories of Mary Lavin." *Studies* (Ireland) 52 (Winter 1963): 393–406.

Murray, Thomas J. "Mary Lavin's World: Lovers and Strangers." *Eire* 7 (1972): 122–31.

EMILY LAWLESS (1845–1913) Ireland
General Works

Linn, William J. "The Life and Works of the Hon. Emily Lawless, First Novelist of the Irish Literary Revival." *Dissertation Abstracts* 32 (1972): 4007A (N.Y.U.).

FRIEDA VON RICHTHOFEN LAWRENCE (1879–1956) U.S. (Born in Germany)
Bibliography

Hoffman, Lois. "A Catalogue of the Frieda Lawrence Manuscripts in German at the University of Texas." *Library Chronicle of the University of Texas*, n.s. 6 (December 1973): 86–105.

General Works

Arnold, Armir. "Three Unknown Letters from Frieda Lawrence to Bertrand Russell." *D. H. Lawrence Review* 2 (1969): 157–61.

Green, Martin. "The Other Lawrence." *Commonweal* (December 4, 1964): 346–48.

Morrill, Claire. "Three Women of Taos: Frieda Lawrence, Mabel Luhan, and Dorothy Brett." *South Dakota Review* 2 (Spring 1965): 3–22.

Sale, R. "Who Is Frieda Lawrence?" *Sewanee Review* 75 (Spring 1967): 355–58.

HELEN LAWRENSON (fl. 1930s) U.S.
General Works

"Backstage with *Esquire*." *Esquire* (March 1973): 16.

EMMA LAZARUS (1849–1887) U.S.
General Works

Goldstein, A.A. "Americans Not Everybody Knows." *PTA Magazine* 60 (April 1966): 10–12.

Halliday, E.M. "I Lift My Lamp Beside the Golden Door." *American Heritage* 17 (February 1966): 97.

Lyons, Joseph. "In Two Divided Streams." *Midstream* 7 (Autumn 1961): 78–85.

Monk, Samuel H. "The Golden Door." *Times Literary Supplement* (August 14, 1969): 979.

Postal, B. "Sonnet of Liberty." *Coronet* (May 1960): 82.

HARPER LEE (1926–) U.S.
General Works

McDonald, W.U., Jr. "Harper Lee's College Writings." *American Notes and Queries* 6 (May 1968): 132.

VERNON LEE [pseud.]. *See* Violet Paget

JULIA LEGRAND (fl. 1860s) U.S.
General Works

Williams, Ora G. "Muskets and Magnolias: Four Civil War Diaries by Louisiana Girls." *Louisiana Studies* 4 (Fall 1965): 187–99.

URSULA K. LE GUIN (1929–) U.S.
General Works

Barbour, Douglas. "Wholeness and Balance in the Hainish Novels of Ursula K. Le Guin." *Science Fiction Studies* 1 (Spring 1974): 164–73.

Scholes, Robert. "The Good Witch of the West." *Hollins Critic* 11 (April 1974): 1–12.
Individual Works
The Left Hand of Darkness (1969)

Ketterer, David. "*The Left Hand of Darkness*: Ursula K. Le Guin's Archetypal 'Winter-Journey.'" *Riverside Quarterly* 5 (April 1973): 288–97.

A Wizard of Earthsea (1968)

Barbour, Douglas. "On Ursula Le Guin's *A Wizard of Earthsea*." *Riverside Quarterly* 6 (April 1974): 119–23.

ROSAMOND LEHMANN (1904–) Great Britain
General Works

Gindin, James. "Rosamond Lehmann: A Revaluation." *Contemporary Literature* 15 (Spring 1974): 203–11.

Kaplan, Sydney Janet. "The Feminine Consciousness in the Novels of Five Twentieth Century British Women." *Dissertation Abstracts International* 32 (1971): 4615A (California, Los Angeles).

Lehmann, John, and Phillip Fry. "An Interview in Austin with John Lehmann." *Studies in the Novel* 3 (Spring 1971): 80–96.

Thornton, Laurence. "Rosamond Lehmann, Henry James and the Temporal Matrix of Fiction." *Virginia Woolf Quarterly* 1 (Spring 1973): 66–75.
Individual Works
The Echoing Grove (1953)

Coopman, Tony. "Symbolism in Rosamond Lehmann's *The Echoing Grove*." *Revue des Langues Vivantes* 40 (1974): 116–21.

Nest of Tigers (1968)

Holroyd, Michael. "A Delightful but Deleterious Trio." *Book World* (September 23, 1968): 5.

CHARLOTTE RAMSAY LENNOX (1720–1804) Great Britain
Bibliography

Isles, Duncan. "The Lennox Collection." *Harvard Library Bulletin* 18 (1970): 317–44; 19 (1971): 36–60, 165–86, 416–35.
General Works

Isles, Duncan. "Johnson and Charlotte Lennox." *New Rambler*, no. 103 (1967): 34–48.
Individual Works
The Female Quixote; or, The Adventures of Arabella (1752)

Hayes, Elizabeth Gentry. "Charlotte Ramsay Lennox: *The Female Quixote; or, The Adventures of Arabella*. Edited with an Introduction and Notes, Two Volumes in One." *Dissertation Abstracts* 25 (1964): 2489 (Stanford).

Kauvar, Elaine M. "Jane Austen and *The Female Quixote*." *Studies in the Novel* 2 (Summer 1970): 211–21.

The Sister (1769)

Eddy, Donald O. "John Hawkesworth: Book Reviewer in *Gentleman's Magazine*." *Philological Quarterly* 43 (April 1964): 223–38.

ELIZABETH ANNE LENOIR (1755?–1841) Great Britain
General Works

Sherbo, Arthur. "Anecdotes by Mrs. Lenoir." *Durham University Journal* 57 (June 1965): 166–69.

LOIS LENSKI (1893–1974) U.S.

General Works

Wilson, George P. "Lois Lenski's Use of Regional Speech." *North Carolina Folklore* 9 (December 1961): 1–3.

ELIZA LESLIE (1787–1858) U.S.
Individual Works
The Daughters of Dr. Byles (1842)
Byers, John R., Jr. "*The House of the Seven Gables* and *The Daughters of Dr. Byles*: A Probable Source." *Publications of the Modern Language Association* 89 (1974): 174–77.

DORIS LESSING (1919–) Great Britain
Bibliography
Burkom, Selma R. "A Doris Lessing Checklist." *Criticism* 11 (1968): 69–81.
Krouse, Agate N. "A Doris Lessing Checklist." *Contemporary Literature* 14 (Autumn 1973): 590–97.

General Works
Alcorn, Noeline E. "Vision and Nightmare: A Study of Doris Lessing's Novels." *Dissertation Abstracts International* 32 (1971): 1500A (California, Irvine).
Bergonzi, Bernard. "In Pursuit of Doris Lessing." *New York Review of Books* (February 11, 1965): 12.
Brooks, Ellen W. "Fragmentation and Integration: A Study of Doris Lessing's Fiction." *Dissertation Abstracts International* 32 (1972): 3989A–90A (N.Y.U.).
Burkom, Selma R. " 'Only Connect': Form and Content in the Works of Doris Lessing." *Criticism* 11 (1968): 51–68.
Burkom, Selma R. "A Reconciliation of Opposites: A Study of the Works of Doris Lessing." *Dissertation Abstracts International* 31 (1971): 5390A (Minnesota).
Carey, Father Alfred Augustine. "Doris Lessing: The Search for Reality: A Study of the Major Themes in Her Novels." *Dissertation Abstracts* 26 (1965): 3297 (Wisconsin).
Corner, M. "Arnold, Lessing, and the Preface of 1835." *Journal of English and Germanic Philology* 72 (April 1973): 223–25.
De Courtivron, Isabelle. "Androgyny, Misogyny, and Madness: Three Essays on Women in Literature." *Dissertation Abstracts International* 34 (1974): 5905A–6A (Brown).

De Mott, Benjamin. "Toward a More Human World." *Saturday Review* (March 13, 1971): 86–87.
"The Fog of War." *Times Literary Supplement* (April 27, 1962): 280.
Foote, T. "Portrait of a Lady." *Time* (May 2, 1973): 99.
Gindin, James. "Lessing Criticism." *Contemporary Literature* 14 (Autumn 1973): 586–89.
Grant, Velma Fudge. "The Quest for Wholeness in the Novels by Doris Lessing." *Dissertation Abstracts International* 35 (1975): 901A (Rutgers).
Halliday, Patricia A. Y. "The Pursuit of Wholeness in the Work of Doris Lessing: Dualities, Multiplicities, and the Resolution of Patterns in Illumination." *Dissertation Abstracts International* 34 (1973): 2626A–27A (Minnesota).
Hardin, Nancy S. "Doris Lessing and the Sufi Way." *Contemporary Literature* 14 (Autumn 1973): 565–81.
Hove, David A. "Lessing's Heroines and Their Literary Models." *Dissertation Abstracts International* 35 (1974): 404A (Iowa).
Howe, Florence. "A Conversation with Doris Lessing (1966)." *Contemporary Literature* 14 (Autumn 1973): 418–36.
Howe, Florence. "Doris Lessing's Free Women." *Nation* (January 11, 1965): 34–37.
Howe, Florence. "A Talk with Doris Lessing." *Nation* (March 6, 1967): 311–13.
Kaplan, Sydney J. "The Limits of Consciousness in the Novels of Doris Lessing." *Contemporary Literature* 14 (Autumn 1973): 536–49.
Kaplan, Sydney Janet. "The Feminine Consciousness in the Novels of Five Twentieth Century British Women." *Dissertation Abstracts International* 32 (1971): 4615A (California, Los Angeles).
Karl, Frederick R. "Doris Lessing in the Sixties: The New Anatomy of Melancholy." *Contemporary Literature* 13 (Winter 1972): 15–33.
Krouse, Agate. "The Feminism of Doris Lessing." *Dissertation Abstracts International* 34 (1973): 322A (Wisconsin).
Manning, Margaret. "Doris Lessing's Belief in Survival." *Atlantic Monthly* (June 1973): 116–18.
Marchino, Lois. "Papers on Doris Lessing: An Introductory Comment." *World Literature Written in English* 12 (1973): 148–49.
Marchino, Lois A. "The Search for Self in the Novels

of Doris Lessing." *Studies in the Novel* 4 (Summer 1972): 252–61.

Markow, Alice B. "The Pathology of Feminine Failure in the Fiction of Doris Lessing." *Critique* 16 (1974): 88–100.

McDowell, Frederick P.W. "The Fiction of Doris Lessing: An Interim View." *Arizona Quarterly* 21 (Winter 1965): 315–45.

Naumer, Mary Ann S. "The City and the Veld: A Study of the Fiction of Doris Lessing." *Dissertation Abstracts International* 34 (1974): 5984A–85A (Oregon).

Oates, Joyce Carol. "A Visit with Doris Lessing." *Southern Review* (U.S.) 9 (1973): 873–82.

O'Fallon, Kathleen. "Quest for a New Vision." *World Literature Written in English* 12 (1973): 180–89.

Pratt, Annis. "Introduction [to a Special Issue on Doris Lessing]." *Contemporary Literature* 14 (Autumn 1973): 413–17.

Raskin, Jonah. "Doris Lessing at Stony Brook: An Interview." *New American Review* 8 (1970): 166–79.

Ryf, Robert S. "Beyond Ideology: Doris Lessing's Mature Vision." *Modern Fiction Studies* 21 (Summer 1975): 193–202.

Schlueter, Paul G. "A Study of the Major Novels of Doris Lessing." *Dissertation Abstracts* 29 (1969): 3619A–20A (Southern Illinois).

Scholl, Diane G. "*The Novels of Doris Lessing*, by Paul Schlueter." *Christianity and Literature* 23 (Spring 1974): 39–45.

Seligman, Dee. "The Sufi Quest." *World Literature Written in English* 12 (1973): 190–206.

Spacks, Patricia M. "Free Women." *Hudson Review* 24 (Winter 1972): 559–73.

Spilka, M. "Lessing and Lawrence: The Battle of the Sexes." *Contemporary Literature* 16 (Spring 1975): 218–40.

Sukenick, Lynn. "Feeling and Reason in Doris Lessing's Fiction." *Contemporary Literature* 14 (Autumn 1973): 515–35.

Sukenick, Lynn. "Sense and Sensibility in Women's Fiction: Studies in the Novels of George Eliot, Virginia Woolf, Anais Nin and Doris Lessing." *Dissertation Abstracts International* 35 (1975): 4563A (C.U.N.Y.).

Taubman, Robert. "Free Women." *New Statesman* (April 20, 1962): 569.

Taubman, Robert. "Near Zero." *New Statesman* (November 8, 1963): 653–54.

"Witness as Prophet." *Time* (July 25, 1969): 75.

Individual Works

The Antheap (1953)

Graves, Nora C. "Doris Lessing's Two Antheaps." *Notes on Contemporary Literature* 2 (May 1972): 6–8.

Briefing for a Descent into Hell (1971)

Bolling, Douglass. "Structure and Theme in *Briefing for a Descent into Hell*." *Contemporary Literature* 14 (Autumn 1973): 550–64.

Kildahl, Karen Ann. "The Political and Apocalyptical Novels of Doris Lessing: A Critical Study of *Children of Violence, The Golden Notebook*, Briefing for a Descent into Hell." *Dissertation Abstracts International* 35 (1975): 4528A (Washington).

Richey, Clarence W. "Professor Watkins' 'Sleep of Necessity': A Note on the Parallel between Doris Lessing's *Briefing for a Descent into Hell* and the G. I. Gurdjieff–P.D. Ouspensky System of Esoteric Psychology." *Notes on Contemporary Literature* 2 (March 1972): 9–11.

Children of Violence (1952)

Kildahl, Karen Ann. "The Political and Apocalyptical Novels of Doris Lessing: A Critical Study of *Children of Violence, The Golden Notebook, Briefing for a Descent into Hell*." *Dissertation Abstracts International* 35 (1975): 4528A (Washington).

Owen, Roger. "A Good Man Is Hard to Find." *Commentary* 39 (April 1965): 79–82.

Porter, Nancy. "Silenced History: *Children of Violence* and *The Golden Notebook*." *World Literature Written in English* 12 (1973): 161–79.

Rose, Ellen C. "Doris Lessing's *Children of Violence* as a Bildungsroman: An Eriksonian Analysis." *Dissertation Abstracts International* 35 (1974): 3006A–7A (Massachusetts).

Smith, Diane E. S. "A Thematic Study of Doris Lessing's *Children of Violence*." *Dissertation Abstracts International* 32 (1971): 1530A (Loyola).

The Four-Gated City (1969)

Barnouw, Dagmar. "Disorderly Company: From *The Golden Notebook* to *The Four-Gated City*." *Contemporary Literature* 14 (Autumn 1973): 491–514.

The Golden Notebook (1962)

Barnouw, Dagmar. "Disorderly Company: From

The Golden Notebook to The Four-Gated City." Contemporary Literature 14 (Autumn 1973): 491–514.

Brooks, Ellen W. "The Image of Woman in Lessing's The Golden Notebook." Critique 15 (1973): 101–9.

Carey, John L. "Art and Reality in The Golden Notebook." Contemporary Literature 14 (Autumn 1973): 437–56.

Craig, Joanne. "The Golden Notebook: The Novelist as Heroine." University of Windsor Review 10 (1974): 55–66.

Hinz, Evelyn J., and John J. Teunissen. "The Pietà as Icon in The Golden Notebook." Contemporary Literature 14 (Autumn 1973): 457–70.

Hynes, Joseph. "The Construction of The Golden Notebook." Iowa Review 4 (Summer 1973): 100–113.

Joyner, Nancy. "The Underside of the Butterfly: Lessing's Debt to Woolf." Journal of Narrative Technique 4 (1974): 204–11.

Kildahl, Karen Ann. "The Political and Apocalyptical Novels of Doris Lessing: A Critical Study of Children of Violence, The Golden Notebook, Briefing for a Descent into Hell." Dissertation Abstracts International 35 (1975): 4528A (Washington).

Lessing, Doris. "On The Golden Notebook." Partisan Review 40 (1973): 14–30.

Libby, Marion V. "Sex and the New Woman in The Golden Notebook." Iowa Review 5 (Fall 1974): 106–20.

Lightfoot, Marjorie J. "Breakthrough in The Golden Notebook." Studies in the Novel 7 (Summer 1975): 277–84.

Morgan, Ellen. "Alienation of the Woman Writer in The Golden Notebook." Contemporary Literature 14 (Autumn 1973): 471–80.

Mulkeen, Anne M. "Twentieth Century Realism: The Grid Structure of The Golden Notebook." Studies in the Novel 4 (Summer 1972): 262–74.

Mutti, Giuliana. "Female Roles and the Function of Art in The Golden Notebook." Massachusetts Studies in English 3 (1972): 78–83.

Porter, Dennis. "Realism and Failure in The Golden Notebook." Modern Language Quarterly 35 (March 1974): 56–65.

Porter, Nancy. "Silenced History: Children of Violence and The Golden Notebook." World Literature Written in English 12 (1973): 161–79.

Pratt, Annis. "The Contrary Structure of Doris Lessing's The Golden Notebook." World Literature Written in English 12 (1973): 150–60.

Spencer, Sharon. "'Femininity' and the Woman Writer: Doris Lessing's The Golden Notebook and the Diary of Anaïs Nin." Women's Studies 1 (1973): 247–57.

The Grass Is Singing (1950)

Zak, Michele W. "The Grass Is Singing: A Little Novel about the Emotions." Contemporary Literature 14 (Autumn 1973): 481–90.

The Summer Before the Dark (1973)

Lefcowitz, B. F. "Dream and Action in Lessing's The Summer Before the Dark." Critique 17 (1975): 107–20.

Widmann, R.L. "Lessing's The Summer Before the Dark." Contemporary Literature 14 (Autumn 1973): 582–85.

ADA LEVERSON (1865–1936) Great Britain
General Works
Burkhart, Charles. "Ada Leverson and Oscar Wilde." English Literature in Transition 13 (1970): 193–200.

Pritchett, V. S. "The Knightsbridge Kennels." New Statesman (August 31, 1962): 257–58.

Wyndham, Violet. "Ada Leverson." Cornhill Magazine, no. 1036 (Spring 1963): 147–63.

DENISE LEVERTOV (1923–) U.S. (Born in Great Britain)

General Works
Baker, A.T. "Poetry Today" Low Profile, Flatted Voire." Time (July 13, 1971): 61.

Bowering, George. "Denise Levertov." Antigonish Review 7 (Autumn 1971): 77–78.

Crunk. "The Work of Denise Levertov." Sixties, no. 9 (Spring 1967): 48–65.

Duddy, Thomas A. "To Celebrate: A Reading of Denise Levertov." Criticism 10 (1968): 138–52.

Gitzen, Julian. "From Reverence to Attention: The Poetry of Denise Levertov." Midwest Quarterly 16 (Spring 1975): 328–41.

Howard, Richard. "Denise Levertov." Tri-Quarterly 7 (Fall 1966): 133–44.

Nelson, Rudolph L. "Edge of the Transcendent: The Poetry of Levertov and Duncan." Southwest Review 54 (Spring 1969): 188–202.

"Origins of a Poem: An Interview." Michigan Quarterly Review 7 (Fall 1968): 232–38.

Reid, Ian. "Everyman's Land: Ian Reid Interviews

Denise Levertov." *Southern Review* (Australia) 5 (1972): 231–36.

Sutton, Walter. "A Conversation with Denise Levertov." *Minnesota Review* 5 (Spring 1965): 322–38.

Wagner, Linda W. "The Significance of Sound." *Laurel Review* 6 (1966): 3–12.

Wosk, Julie Helen. "Prophecies for America: Social Criticism in the Recent Poetry of Bly, Levertov, Corso, and Ginsburg." *Dissertation Abstracts International* 35 (1975): 6169A (Wisconsin).

Younkins, Ronald. "Denise Levertov and the Hasidic Tradition." *Descant* 19 (1974): 40–48.

Individual Works

The Five Day Rain (1958)

Morrow, Patrick. "Denise Levertov's *The Five Day Rain*." *Notes on Contemporary Literature* 2 (January 1972): 4–6.

One A.M. (1958)

Hopkins, Mary Frances. "Linguistic Analysis as a Tool for the Oral Interpreter." *Speech Teacher* 18 (1969): 200–203.

The Poet in the World (1973)

Carruth, Hayden. "Levertov." *Hudson Review* 27 (Autumn 1974): 475–80.

Six Variations (1958)

Kyle, Carol A. "Every Step an Arrival: *Six Variations* and the Musical Structure of Denise Levertov's Poetry." *Centennial Review* 17 (1973): 281–96.

The Sorrow Dance (1967)

Hunt, Jean M. "The New Grief-Language of Denise Levertov: *The Sorrow Dance*." *University Review* (Kansas) 35 (1968): 149–53.

The Stonecarver's Poem (1962)

Pryse, Marjorie. " 'The Stonecarver's Poem'—A Linguistic Interpretation." *Language and Style* 7 (1974): 62–71.

JANET LEWIS (1899–) U.S.
General Works

Davie, Donald. "The Historical Narratives of Janet Lewis." *Southern Review* (U.S.) 2 (1966): 40–60.

Hofheins, Roger, and Dan Tooker. "A Conversation with Janet Lewis." *Southern Review* (U.S.) 10 (1974): 329–41.

Inglis, Fred. "The Novels of Janet Lewis." *Critique* 7 (1964–1965): 47–64.

Killoh, Ellen. "Patriarchal Women: A Study of Three Novels by Janet Lewis." *Southern Review* (U.S.) 10 (1974): 342–64.

Peck, Ellen M. McK. "Exploring the Feminine: A Study of Janet Lewis, Ellen Glasgow, Anais Nin and Virginia Woolf." *Dissertation Abstracts International* 35 (1974): 3761A (Stanford).

LYN LIFSHIN (fl. 1970s) U.S.
General Works

Evans, James. "Lyn Lifshin." *Windless Orchard*, no. 10 (Summer 1972): 55–62.

ANNE MORROW LINDBERGH (1906–) U.S.
General Works

Baker, A.T. "So Well Remembered." *Time* (March 11, 1974): K11.

Bevington, H. "Bring Me a Unicorn." *New York Times Book Review* (February 27, 1972): 3.

Kazin, A. "Hour of Gold, Hour of Lead." *New York Times Book Review* (March 4, 1973): 1.

"Lindbergh Nightmare." *Time* (February 5, 1973): 35.

Morrow, L. "Colonel's Lady." *Time* (March 27, 1972): 1–2.

Ross, W. S. "Charles and Anne Morrow Lindbergh: America's Most Remarkable Parents." *Ladies' Home Journal* (January 1968): 43–46.

Stafford, J. "Anne Morrow Lindbergh's Ordeal." *McCall's* (March 1973): 80–81.

DOROTHY LIVESAY (1909–) Canada
General Works

Gibbs, Jean. "Dorothy Livesay and the Transcendentalist Tradition." *Humanities Association Bulletin* 21 (Spring 1970): 24–39.

Leland, Doris. "Dorothy Livesay: Poet of Nature." *Dalhousie Review* 51 (Autumn 1971): 404–12.

Lever, B. "Interview with Dorothy Livesay." *Canadian Forum* 55 (September 1975): 45–52.

Livesay, Dorothy. "Song and Dance." *Canadian Literature*, no. 41 (Summer 1969): 40–48.

Mitchell, Beverley. " 'How Silence Sings' in the Poetry of Dorothy Livesay." *Dalhousie Review* 54 (Autumn 1974): 510–28.

O'Donnell, Kathleen. "Dorothy Livesay and Simone Routier: A Parallel Study." *Humanities Association Bulletin* 23 (Fall 1972): 28–37.

Skelton, Robin. "Livesay's Two Seasons." *Canadian Literature*, no. 58 (Autumn 1973): 77–82.

Stevens, Peter. "Dorothy Livesay: The Love Poetry." *Canadian Literature*, no. 47 (Winter 1971): 26–43.

Stevens, Peter. "Out of the Silence and Across the Distance: The Poetry of Dorothy Livesay." *Queen's Quarterly* 78 (1971): 579–91.

Zimmerman, Susan. "Livesay's Houses." *Canadian Literature*, no. 61 (Summer 1974): 32–45.

Individual Works

A Winnipeg Childhood (1974)

Harrison, R.T. "Taking the Prairies Seriously: Dorothy Livesay's *A Winnipeg Childhood*; Laurence Ricou's *Vertical Man/Horizontal World*; Donald Stephens' *Writers of the Prairies*." *World Literature Written in English* 13 (1974): 266–74.

FRANCES LOUISE LOCKRIDGE, née Davis (1896?–1963) U.S.

General Works

Nichols, L. "The Norths." *New York Times Book Review* (July 15, 1962): 8.

NORAH LOFTS (1904–) Great Britain

General Works

Paul, Barbara. "Norah Lofts and the Problem of Historical Form." *University Review* (Kansas) 36 (1970): 226–30.

NAP LOMBARD [pseud.]. *See* Pamela Hansford Johnson

ELIZABETH HARMAN LONGFORD, née Pakenham (1906–) Great Britain

General Works

Boston, R. "Elizabeth of the Writing Pakenhams." *New York Times Book Review* (March 1, 1970): 6.

ANITA LOOS (1893–) U.S.

General Works

Clemons, W. "Loos Talk." *Newsweek* (August 12, 1974): 77.

Drake, Robert, Jr. "Retrospect: Gentlemen, Blondes and Brunettes." *National Review* (March 26, 1963): 245–46.

Loos, Anita. "My First Trip." *McCall's* (May 1967): 142.

Loos, Anita. "Vachel, Mae and I." *Saturday Review* (August 26, 1961): 5–6.

KATIE SCOFIELD LOUCHHEIM (1903–) U.S.

General Works

Ehrlich, H. "State Department's Poetic Powerhouse." *Look* (October 17, 1967): 118.

"Kiss of the Muse." *Newsweek* (October 17, 1966): 32.

"With Pen and Dream." *Time* (October 14, 1966): 38.

AMY LOWELL (1874–1925) U.S.

General Works

Anderson, Norman A. "Corrections to Amy Lowell's Reading of Keats' Marginalia." *Keats-Shelley Journal* 23 (1974): 25–31.

Bedford, W.C. "Musical Apprentice: Amy Lowell to Carl Engel." *Music Quarterly* 58 (October 1972): 519–42.

Healey, Clare. "Amy Lowell Visits London." *New England Quarterly* 46 (September 1973): 439–53.

Healey, Claire. "Some Imagist Essays: Amy Lowell." *New England Quarterly* 43 (March 1970): 134–38.

Hirsch, John C. "John Gould Fletcher and Amy Lowell: New Evidence of Their Relationship." *Harvard Library Bulletin* 22 (1974): 72–75.

Kenner, Hugh. "Mao or Presumption." *Shenandoah* 21 (1970): 84–93.

Self, Robert T. "The Correspondence of Amy Lowell and Barrett Wendell, 1915–1919." *New England Quarterly* 47 (March 1974): 65–86.

Widdemer, Margaret. "The Legend of Amy Lowell." *Texas Quarterly* 6 (Summer 1963): 193–200.

Individual Works

Patterns (1916)

Overmyer, Janet. "Which Broken Pattern?—A Note on Amy Lowell's 'Patterns.'" *Notes on Contemporary Literature* 1 (September 1971): 14–15.

MOLLY LOWELL (1882?–) U.S.

General Works

Nichols, L. "Ladies of Boston." *New York Times Book Review* (January 22, 1967): 8.

MINA LOY (fl. 1920s) Great Britain

General Works

Kouidis, Virginia M. "The Cerebral Forager: An Introduction to the Poetry of Mina Loy." *Dissertation Abstracts International* 33 (1973): 6918A (Iowa).

Morse, Samuel French. "The Rediscovery of Mina Loy and the Avant-Garde." *Wisconsin Studies in Contemporary Literature* 2 (Spring–Summer 1961): 12–19.

Victoria Lucas [pseud.]. *See* Sylvia Plath

Clare Boothe Luce (1903–) U.S.
General Works
Lawrenson, Helen. "The Woman." *Esquire* (August 1974): 75–82.

Mabel Dodge Luhan (1879–1962) U.S.
General Works
Gallup, Donald. "The Mabel Dodge Luhan Papers." *Yale University Library Gazette* 37 (1963): 97–105.
Morrill, Claire. "Three Women of Taos: Frieda Lawrence, Mabel Luhan, and Dorothy Brett." *South Dakota Review* 2 (Spring 1965): 3–22.

M

DAME ROSE MACAULAY (1881–1958) Great Britain
Bibliography
Gerger, H.E., and E.S. Lauterback. "Bibliography News and Notes." *English Literature in Transition* 5 (1962): 35–50.
General Works
Babbington-Smith, Constance, ed. "Letters to a Friend." *American Scholar* 31 (Spring 1962): 259–73.
Bensen, Alice R. "The Ironic Aesthete and the Sponsoring of Causes: A Rhetorical Quandary in Novelistic Technique." *English Literature in Transition* 9 (1966): 39–43.
Chase, Mary Ellen. "Five Literary Portraits." *Massachusetts Review* 3 (Spring 1962): 511–16.
Kuehn, Robert Earl. "The Pleasure of Rose Macaulay: An Introduction to Her Novels." *Dissertation Abstracts* 24 (1962): 2136–37 (Wisconsin).
"Not for Burning." *Time* (March 16, 1962): 88.
Swinnerton, Frank. "Rose Macaulay." *Kenyon Review* 29 (1967): 591–608.
Individual Works
Going Abroad (1934)
Bensen, Alice R. "The Skeptical Balance: A Study of Rose Macaulay's *Going Abroad*." *Papers of the Michigan Academy of Science, Arts and Letters* 48 (1963): 675–83.

SELINA MACAULAY (fl. 1820s–1830s) Great Britain
General Works
Zall, Paul M. "Selina Macaulay's Diary." *Bulletin of the New York Public Library* 66 (September 1962): 440–43.

CYNTHIA MACDONALD (fl. 1960s–1970s) U.S.
Individual Works
Amputations (1972)
Widmann, R.L. "The Poetry of Cynthia MacDonald." *Concerning Poetry* 7 (1974): 19–26.

KATHERINE SHERWOOD MACDOWELL [pseud. Sherwood Bonner] (1849–1883) U.S.
General Works
Frank, William L., ed. "Sherwood Bonner's Diary for the Year 1869." *Notes on Mississippi Writers* 3 (Winter 1971): 111–30; 4 (Spring 1971): 22–40; 4 (Fall 1971): 64–83.
Moore, Rayburn S. "Sherwood Bonner's Contributions to *Lippincott's Magazine* and *Harper's New Monthly*." *Mississippi Quarterly* 17 (Fall 1964): 226–30.
Pierle, Robert C. "Sherwood Who? A Study in the Vagaries of Literary Evaluation." *Notes on Mississippi Writers* 1 (Spring 1968): 18–22.
Polhemus, G.W. "The Correct Spelling of Sherwood Bonner's Name." *Notes and Queries* 7 (July 1960): 265.

GWENDOLYN MACEWEN (1941–) Canada
General Works
Atwood, Margaret. "MacEwen's Muse." *Canadian Literature*, no. 45 (Summer 1970): 24–32.
Individual Works
Julian the Magician (1963)
Gose, E.B., Jr. "They Shall Have Arcana." *Canadian Literature*, no. 21 (Summer 1964): 36–45.

HELEN MACINNES (1907–) Great Britain
General Works
Baker, J.F. "Helen MacInnes." *Publishers Weekly* (June 17, 1974): 10.
"Queen of the Spies." *Time* (March 18, 1966): 114.

MARY MACKAY. *See* Marie Corelli

DOROTHEA MACKELLAR (fl. 1940s) Australia
Individual Works
My Country (1945)
Bladen, Peter. "My Country." *Expression* 7 (1967): 13–15.
Hankel, Valmai. "Notes on the Publication of Dorothea Mackellar's Poem, *My Country.*" *South Australiana* 8 (1968): 11–16.

MARY DE LA RIVIÈRE MANLEY (1663–1724) Great Britain
General Works
Bennett, Gilbert. "Conventions of the Stage Villain." *Anglo-Welsh Review* 14 (1964): 92–102.
Snyder, Henry L. "New Light on Mrs. Manley?" *Philological Quarterly* 52 (October 1973): 767–70.
Winton, Calhoun. "Steele, Mrs. Manley, and John Lacy." *Philological Quarterly* 42 (April 1963): 272–75.

OLIVIA MANNING (1916?–) Great Britain
General Works
Emerson, Sally. "Olivia Manning." *Books and Bookmen* 17 (November 1971): 30–31.
Parkhill-Rathbone, James. "Olivia Manning's Dilemmas." *Books and Bookmen* 16 (August 1971): 22–23.

KATHERINE MANSFIELD [pseud. of Kathleen Mansfield Murry, née Beauchamp] (1888–1923) Great Britain (Born in New Zealand)
Bibliography
Bardas, Mary L. "The State of Scholarship on Katherine Mansfield, 1950–1970." *World Literature Written in English* 11 (1972): 77–93.
General Works
Baldeshwiler, Eileen. "Katherine Mansfield's Theory of Fiction." *Studies in Short Fiction* 7 (Summer 1970): 421–32.
Beachcroft, T.O. "Katherine Mansfield's Encounter with Theocritus." *English* 23 (Spring 1974): 13–19.
Brett, Dorothy, and John Manchester. "Reminiscence of Katherine." *Adam*, no. 370–375 (1973): 84–92.
Brophy, Brigid. "Katherine Mansfield." *London Magazine* 2 (December 1962): 41–47.
Brophy, Brigid. "Katherine Mansfield's Self-Depic-

tion." *Michigan Quarterly Review* 5 (Spring 1966): 89–93.
Busch, Frieda. "Katherine Mansfield and Literary Impressionism in France and Germany." *Arcadia* 5 (March 1970): 58–76.
Dickinson, John W. "Katherine Mansfield and S. S. Koteliansky: Some Unpublished Letters." *Revue de Littérature Comparée* 45 (1971): 79–99.
Gordan, John D. "Letters to an Editor: Georgia Poetry 1912–1922: An Exhibition from the Berg Collection." *Bulletin of the New York Public Library* 71 (May 1967): 284.
Grindea, Miron. "Only One K.M.? Notes and Footnotes to a Biography." *Adam*, no. 370–375 (1973): 2–18.
Hughes, Derek. "Katherine Mansfield and the Short Story." *Literary Criterion* 10 (1973): 22–32.
Iversen, Anders. "Life and Letters: Katherine Mansfield Drawing on Kathleen Beauchamp." *English Studies* 52 (1971): 44–54.
Justus, James H. "Katherine Mansfield: The Triumph of Egoism." *Mosaic* 6 (1973): 13–22.
King, Russell S. "Katherine Mansfield as an Expatriate Writer." *Journal of Commonwealth Literature* 8 (June 1973): 97–109.
Kleine, Don W. "An Eden for Insiders: Katherine Mansfield's New Zealand." *College English* 27 (December 1965): 201–9.
Kluth, Kathe. "The Contemporary English Short Story." *Philologica Pragensia* 5 (1962): 84–95.
Kurylo, Charanne C. "Chekhov and Katherine Mansfield: A Study in Literary Influence." *Dissertation Abstracts International* 35 (1974): 3748A (North Carolina).
Litvinov, Ivy. "How I Never Met K.M." *Adam*, no. 370–375 (1973): 94–95.
Mansfield, Katherine. "Fifteen Letters from K.M. to Virginia Woolf." *Adam*, no. 370–375 (1973): 19–24.
Mansfield, Katherine. "Katherine Mansfield's Juvenilia." *Adam*, no. 370–375 (1973): 42–44.
Mansfield, Katherine. "Letters to Bertrand Russell." *Adam*, no. 370–375 (1973): 37–41.
Mansfield, Katherine. "Letters to Richard Murry." *Adam*, no. 370–375 (1973): 25–36.
Mansfield, Katherine. "Other Unpublished Manuscripts of Katherine Mansfield." *Adam*, no. 370–375 (1973): 45–72.
Mansfield, Katherine. "Six Unknown Poems." *Adam*, no. 370–375 (1973): 72–74.

Mantz, Ruth. "In Consequence: Katherine and Kot." *Adam*, no. 370–375 (1973): 95–107.

Mantz, Ruth. "K.M.—Fifty Years After." *Adam*, no. 370–375 (1973): 117–27.

McIntosh, A.D. "The New Zealand Background of K.M." *Adam*, no. 370–375 (1973): 76–83.

Morse, Lucille M. "Juxtaposition in the Short Stories of Katherine Mansfield." *Dissertation Abstracts International* 33 (1972): 760A–61A (Oklahoma State).

Mortelier, Christiane. "The Genesis and Development of the Katherine Mansfield Legend in France." *Journal of the Australasian Universities Language and Literature Association* 34 (November 1970): 252–63.

Napier, James J., and Philip Waldron. "Two Letters on Katherine Mansfield." *Modern Fiction Studies* 19 (Winter 1973–1974): 573–77.

Renshaw, Jeanne. "The Beauchamp Family." *Adam*, no. 370–375 (1973): 74–75.

Schwinn, Liesel. "Katherine Mansfield." *Hochland* 53 (1961): 333–42.

Scott, M. "The Extant Manuscripts of Katherine Mansfield." *Etudes Anglaises* 26 (1973): 413–19.

Sutherland, Ronald. "Katherine Mansfield: Plagiarist, Disciple, or Ardent Admirer?" *Critique* 5 (1962–1963): 58–76.

Walker, Nancy. "Faint Praise." *Hartford Studies in Literature* 4 (1972): 251–58.

Walt, James. "Conrad and Katherine Mansfield." *Conradiana* 4 (1972): 41–52.

Wright, Celeste Turner. "Katherine Mansfield's Dog Image." *Literature and Psychology* 10 (1960): 80–81.

Individual Works

Bliss (1920)

Nebeker, Helen E. "The Pear Tree: Sexual Implication in Katherine Mansfield's *Bliss*." *Modern Fiction Studies* 18 (Winter 1972–1973): 545–51.

The Fly (1922)

Bateson, F.W., and I. Shahevitch. "Katherine Mansfield's *The Fly*: A Critical Exercise." *Essays in Criticism* 12 (January 1962): 39–53.

Bell, Pauline P. "Mansfield's *The Fly*." *Explicator* 19 (December 1960): Item 20.

Boyle, Ted E. "The Death of the Boss: Another Look at Katherine Mansfield's *The Fly*." *Modern Fiction Studies* 11 (Summer 1965): 183–85.

"Critical Forum: Katherine Mansfield's *The Fly*." *Essays in Criticism* 12 (July 1962): 335–51.

Hagopian, John V. "Capturing Mansfield's *Fly*." *Modern Fiction Studies* 9 (Winter 1963–1964): 385–90.

Michel-Michot, Paulette. "Katherine Mansfield's *The Fly*: *An Attempt to Capture the Boss*." *Studies in Short Fiction* 11 (Winter 1974): 85–92.

Rea, J. "Mansfield's *The Fly*." *Explicator* 23 (May 1965): Item 68.

Thomas, J. D. "Symbolism and Parallelism in *The Fly*." *College English* 22 (January 1961): 256–62. (Reply by Clinton W. Oleson, 22 (May 1961): 585–86; by Mr. Thomas, p. 586.)

The Garden Party (1922)

Davis, Robert Murray. "The Unity of *The Garden Party*." *Studies in Short Fiction* 2 (Fall 1964): 61–65.

Iversen, Anders. "A Reading of Katherine Mansfield's *The Garden Party*." *Orbis Litterarum* 23 (1968): 5–34.

Kleine, D.W. "*The Garden Party*: A Portrait of the Artist." *Criticism* 5 (1963): 360–71.

Robinson, Fred C. "Mansfield's *The Garden Party*." *Explicator* 24 (April 1966): Item 66.

Journal (1927)

Waldron, Philip. "Katherine Mansfield's *Journal*." *Twentieth Century Literature* 20 (January 1974): 11–18.

The Man Without a Temperament (1920)

Kleine, Don W. "Katherine Mansfield and the Prisoner of Love." *Critique* 3 (1960): 20–33.

Marriage à la Mode (1921)

Kleine, Don W. "The Chekhovian Source of *Marriage à la Mode*." *Philological Quarterly* 42 (April 1963): 284–88.

Miss Brill (1920)

Gargano, James W. "Mansfield's *Miss Brill*." *Explicator* 19 (November 1960): Item 10.

Hull, Robert L. "Alienation in *Miss Brill*." *Studies in Short Fiction* 5 (Fall 1967): 74–77.

Madden, David. "Katherine Mansfield's *Miss Brill*." *University Review* (Kansas) 31 (1964): 89–92.

Thorpe, Peter. "Teaching *Miss Brill*." *College English* 23 (May 1962): 661–63.

Voice of the Air (ms)

Waldron, Philip. "A Katherine Mansfield Poem Printed Incomplete." *Notes and Queries* 21 (October 1974): 365–66.

ADRIENNE MARCUS (1935–) U.S.

Individual Works

The Moon Is a Marrying Eye (1972)

Moore, Rosalie. "Aspects of Flying." *Works* 4 (Summer 1973): 105–7.

DUCHESS OF MARLBOROUGH (fl. 1700–1710) Great Britain

General Works

Morrison, Lois G. "Eustace Budgell and the Duchess of Marlborough." *Notes and Queries* 20 (June 1973): 212–13.

Snyder, Henry L. "Daniel Defoe, the Duchess of Marlborough and the *Advice to the Electors of Great Britain*." *Huntington Library Quarterly* 29 (November 1965): 53–62.

EMMA MARTIN MARSHALL (1830–1899) U.S.

General Works

Smith, C.N. "Emma Marshall and Longfellow: Some Additions to Hilen's *Letters*." *Journal of American Studies* 8 (April 1974): 81–90.

LENORE GUINZBURG MARSHALL (1897–1971) U.S.

General Works

"Lenore Marshall." *Saturday Review* (October 9, 1971): 29.

PAULE MARSHALL (1929–) U.S.

General Works

Kapai, Seela. "Dominant Themes and Techniques in Paule Marshall's Fiction." *College Language Association Journal* 16 (September 1972): 49–59.

Individual Works

Brown Girl, Brownstones (1959)

Miller, Adam David. "Review of *Brown Girl, Brownstones*." *Black Scholar* 3 (1972): 56–58.

The Chosen Place, the Timeless People (1969)

Nazareth, Peter. "Paule Marshall's Timeless People." *New Letters* 40 (Autumn 1973): 116–31.

Stoelting, Winifred L. "Time Past and Time Present: The Search for Viable Links in *The Chosen Place, the Timeless People*." *College Language Association Journal* 16 (September 1972): 60–71.

CATHERINE MARTIN (1848–1937) Australia

General Works

Byrnes, John V. "Catherine Martin and the Critics." *Australian Letters* 3 (1961): 15–24.

VIOLET FLORENCE MARTIN [pseud. Martin Ross] (1862–1915) Ireland

General Works

Flanagan, Thomas. "The Big House of Ross-Drishane." *Kenyon Review* 28 (1966): 54–78.

Individual Works

The Real Charlotte (1894)

Pritchett, V. S. "Anglo-Irish Attitudes." *New Statesman* (March 9, 1973): 343.

HARRIET MARTINEAU (1802–1876) Great Britain

General Works

Dentler, Robert A. "The American Studies of Harriet Martineau." *Midcontinent American Studies Journal* 3 (1962): 3–12.

"Severe to the Point of Injustice: Two Letters by Harriet Martineau Purchased." *Brontë Society Transactions* 16 (1973): 199–202.

Vann, J. Don. "An Unpublished Harriet Martineau Letter." *English Language Notes* 2 (December 1964): 109–11.

Individual Works

Oliver Weld (1851)

Lever, Sir Tresham. "Harriet Martineau and Her Novel *Oliver Weld*." *Brontë Society Transactions* 16 (1974): 270–73.

SUSAN MASSIE (fl. 1970s) U.S.

Individual Works

Journey (1975)

Jefferson, M. "Blood Scourge." *Newsweek* (May 26, 1975): 75.

Stoler, P. "Blood Will Tell." *Time* (May 19, 1975): 75–76.

ROSE MATILDA [pseud. of Charlotte Dacre] (1722–1831) Great Britain

Individual Works

George the Fourth (1822)

Erdman, David U. "Byron's Mock Review of Rose Matilda's Epic on the Prince Regent—A New Attribute." *Keats-Shelley Journal* 19 (1970): 101–17.

Pollin, Burton R. "Byron, Poe and Miss Matilda." *Names* 16 (1968): 390–414.

BERNADETTE MAYER (1945–) U.S.

General Works

Alpert, Barry. "Bernadette Mayer: An Interview." *World* (April 1974): 76–84.

JOYCE MAYNARD (1953?–) U.S.
General Works
Baumgold, J. "Happy Birthday, Joyce Maynard, Happy Birthday to You." *Esquire* (March 1974): 82–84.
"Joyce Maynard, at 18, a Doubleday Author." *Publishers Weekly* (June 5, 1972): 122.
Maynard, J. "American Woman Writer." *Vogue* (June 1973): 102.

MARY McCARTHY (1912–) U.S.
General Works
Aaron, Daniel. "The Thirties—Now and Then." *American Scholar* 35 (Summer 1966): 490–94.
Aldridge, John W. "Egalitarian Snobs." *Saturday Review* (May 8, 1971): 21–24.
Barry, Joseph. "Letter from Abroad." *McCall's* (June 1966): 40.
Bower, Robert O. "The Writer at the University." *Inland* 3 (Winter 1960): 21–27.
Brower, Brock. "Mary McCarthyism." *Esquire* (July 1962): 62.
Chamberlain, John. "The Conservative Miss McCarthy." *National Review* (October 22, 1963): 353–55.
"Contrary Mary—Vassar '33." *Newsweek* (September 2, 1963): 80–83.
Cook, Bruce. "Mary McCarthy: One of Ours?" *Catholic World* (April 1964): 34–42.
De Mott, Benjamin. "Poets, Presidents and Preceptors." *Harper's* (October 1963): 98.
Duffy, M. "Tale of Two Cultures." *Time* (May 31, 1971): 88.
Enright, D.J. "Contrary Wise." *New Statesman* (July 27, 1962): 115–16.
Fallows, J. "Mary McCarthy: The Blinders She Wears." *Washington Monthly* (May 1974): 5–17.
Gottfried, Alex, and Sue Davidson. "Utopia's Children: An Interpretation of Three Political Novels." *Western Political Quarterly* 15 (March 1962): 17–32.
Grumbach, Doris. "The Subject Objected." *New York Times Book Review* (June 11, 1967): 6.
Hardwick, Elizabeth. "The New Books." *Harper's* (January 1962): 91–93.
"Lady with a Switchblade." *Life* (September 20, 1963): 61–62.
Mailer, Norman. "The Mary McCarthy Case." *New York Review of Books* (October 17, 1963): 1–3.
Niebuhr, Elisabeth. "The Art of Fiction." *Paris Review* 3 (Winter–Spring 1962): 59–94.
Rahv, Philip. "The Editor Interviews Mary McCarthy." *Modern Occasions* 1 (Fall 1970): 14–25.
Revel, Jean-François. "Miss McCarthy Explains." *New York Times Book Review* (May 16, 1971): 2.
Ross, P. "Underpinning of Birds of America: An Interview." *Harper's Bazaar* (June 1971): 92–93.
Schlueter, Paul. "The Amoralist: Mary McCarthy." *Motive* 25 (December 1964): 46–50.
Taylor, G.O. "Cast a Cold I: Mary McCarthy on Vietnam." *Journal of American Studies* 9 (April 1975): 103–14.
"Tea at the War Crimes Museum." *Time* (May 24, 1968): 80.
Tyler, R.L. "The I.W.W. and the West." *American Quarterly* 12 (Summer 1960): 175–87.
Individual Works
The Group (1963)
Abrahams, William. "After the Daisy Chain." *Partisan Review* 31 (1964): 107–10.
Mathewson, Ruth. "The Vassar Joke." *Columbia University Forum* 6 (Fall 1963): 10–16.
McCarthy, Mary. "Letter to a Translator—About *The Group*." *Encounter* 23 (November 1964): 69.
Ohmann, Carol B. and Richard M. "Class Notes from Vassar." *Commonweal* (September 27, 1963): 12–15.
Soule, George. "Must a Novelist Be an Artist?" *Carleton Miscellany* 5 (Spring 1964): 92–98.
The Unspoiled Reaction (1946)
Gillen, Francis. "The Failure of Ritual in *The Unspoiled Reaction*." *Renascence* 24 (Spring 1972): 155–58.
Kreutz, Irving. "Mary McCarthy's *The Unspoiled Reaction*: Pejorative as Satire." *Descant* 13 (1968): 32–48.

NELLIE LETITIA McCLUNG, née Mooney (1873–1951)
Canada
General Works
"Nellie McClung." *Americas* 26 (November 1974): S–22.

CARSON McCULLERS (1917–1967) U.S.
Bibliography
Dorsey, J.E. "Carson McCullers and Flannery O'Connor: A Checklist of Graduate Research." *Bulletin of Bibliography* 32 (October–December 1975): 162–67.

Phillips, Robert S. "Carson McCullers: 1956–1964: A Selected Checklist." *Bulletin of Bibliography* 24 (September–December 1964): 113–16.

Stanley, William T. "Carson McCullers: 1965–1969: A Selected Checklist." *Bulletin of Bibliography* 27 (October–December 1970): 91–93.

General Works

Albee, Edward. "Carson McCullers—The Case of the Curious Magician." *Harper's Bazaar* (January 1963): 98–99.

Armes, Nancy Ruth. "The Feeder: A Study of the Fiction of Eudora Welty and Carson McCullers." *Dissertation Abstracts International* 35 (1975): 2817A (Illinois).

Bauerly, Donna M. "Patterns of Imagery in Carson McCullers' Major Fiction." *Dissertation Abstracts International* 34 (1973): 2606A (Marquette).

Buchen, I. H. "Divine Collusion: The Art of Carson McCullers." *Dalhousie Review* 54 (Autumn 1974): 529–41.

Buchen, Irving H. "Carson McCullers: A Case of Convergence." *Bucknell Review* 21 (Spring 1973): 15–28.

Carlton, Ann R. "Patterns in Carson McCullers' Portrayal of Adolescence." *Dissertation Abstracts International* 33 (1972): 302A (Ball State).

Carney, Christina F. "A Study of Themes and Techniques in Carson McCullers' Prose Fiction." *Dissertation Abstracts International* 34 (1973): 307A–8A (Columbia).

Carr, Virginia S. "Carson McCullers and the Search for Meaning." *Dissertation Abstracts International* 33 (1972): 2924A–25A (Florida State).

Clark, Charlene Kerne. "Carson McCullers and the Tradition of Romance." *Dissertation Abstracts International* 35 (1975): 5391A (Louisiana State).

Clark, Charlene Kerne. "Pathos with a Chuckle: The Tragicomic Vision in the Novels of Carson McCullers." *Studies in American Humor* 1 (January 1975): 161–66.

Clemons, W. "Prodigious Tomboy." *Newsweek* (July 7, 1975): 57–58.

Dodd, Wayne D. "The Development of Theme through Symbol in the Novels of Carson McCullers." *Georgia Review* 17 (Summer 1963): 206–13.

Evans, Oliver. "The Achievement of Carson McCullers." *English Journal* 51 (May 1962): 301–8.

Evans, Oliver. "The Case of Carson McCullers." *Georgia Review* 18 (Spring 1964): 40–45.

Evans, Oliver. "Pad in Brooklyn Heights." *Nation* (July 13, 1964): 15–16.

Everett, Howard Dean. "Love and Alienation: The Sad, Dark Vision of Carson McCullers." *Dissertation Abstracts International* 35 (1975): 3711A–12A (New Mexico).

Finger, Larry L. "Elements of the Grotesque in Selected Works of Welty, Capote, McCullers, and O'Connor." *Dissertation Abstracts International* 33 (1972): 1721A–22A (George Peabody College for Teachers).

Folk, Barbara N. "The Sad Sweet Music of Carson McCullers." *Georgia Review* 16 (Summer 1962): 202–9.

Hamilton, Alice. "Loneliness and Alienation: The Work of Carson McCullers." *Dalhousie Review* 50 (Summer 1970): 215–29.

Hassan, Ihab H. "Carson McCullers: The Alchemy of Love and Aesthetics of Pain." *Modern Fiction Studies* 5 (Winter 1959–1960): 311–26.

Hassan, Ihab H. "Laughter in the Dark: The New Voice in American Fiction." *American Scholar* 33 (Autumn 1964): 638.

Hendrick, George. "Almost Everyone Wants to Be the Lover: The Fiction of Carson McCullers." *Books Abroad* 42 (Summer 1968): 389–91.

Hughes, Catharine. "A World of Outcasts." *Commonweal* (October 13, 1961): 73–75.

Hunt, Tann H. "Humor in the Novels of Carson McCullers." *Dissertation Abstracts International* 34 (1973): 775A (Florida State).

Joyce, Edward T. "Race and Sex: Opposition and Identity in the Fiction of Carson McCullers." *Dissertation Abstracts International* 34 (1973): 3403A–4A (S.U.N.Y., Stony Brook).

Lubbers, Klaus. "The Necessary Order: A Study of Theme and Structure in Carson McCullers' Fiction." *Jahrbuch für Amerikastudien* 8 (1963): 187–204.

Maddocks, M. "Little Precious." *Time* (July 21, 1975): 63–64.

McGill, R. "Carson McCullers: 1917–1967." *Saturday Review* (October 21, 1967): 31.

McGill, Ralph. "Growing Up in Georgia." *New York Times Book Review* (April 12, 1964): 18.

Montgomery, Marion. "The Sense of Violation: Notes Toward a Definition of 'Southern' Fiction." *Georgia Review* 19 (Fall 1965): 278–87.

Moore, Jack B. "Carson McCullers: The Heart Is a Timeless Hunter." *Twentieth Century Literature*

11 (July 1965): 76–81.

Pachmuss, Temira. "Dostoevsky, D.H. Lawrence, and Carson McCullers: Influences and Confluences." *Germano-Slavica* 4 (1974): 59–68.

Phillips, R. "Lonely Hunter." *New York Times Book Review* (August 24, 1975): 7.

Presley, Delma E. "Carson McCullers and the South." *Georgia Review* 28 (Spring 1974): 19–32.

Presley, Delma E. "Carson McCullers' Descent to Earth." *Descant* 17 (1972): 54–50.

Presley, Delma E. "The Man Who Married Carson McCullers." *Issue* 2 (1973): 13–16.

Rechnitz, Robert M. "The Failure of Love: The Grotesque in Two Novels by Carson McCullers." *Georgia Review* 22 (Winter 1968): 454–63.

Individual Works

The Ballad of the Sad Café (1951)

Broughton, Panthea Reid. "Rejection of the Feminine in Carson McCullers: *The Ballad of the Sad Café*." *Twentieth Century Literature* 20 (January 1974): 34–43.

Gaillard, Dawson F. "The Presence of the Narrator in Carson McCullers' *The Ballad of the Sad Café*." *Mississippi Quarterly* 25 (Fall 1972): 419–27.

Griffith, Albert J. "Carson McCullers' Myth of the Sad Café." *Georgia Review* 21 (Spring 1967): 46–56.

McNally, John. "The Introspective Narrator in *The Ballad of the Sad Café*." *South Atlantic Bulletin* 38 (1973): 40–44.

Millichap, Joseph R. "Carson McCullers' Literary Ballad." *Georgia Review* 27 (Fall 1973): 329–39.

Phillips, Robert S. "Dinesen's 'Monkey' and McCullers' 'Ballad': A Study in Literary Affinity." *Studies in Short Fiction* 1 (Spring 1964): 184–90.

Phillips, Robert S. "Painful Love: Carson McCullers' Parable." *Southwest Review* 51 (Winter 1966): 80–86.

Townley, Janice. "McCullers' *The Ballad of the Sad Café*." *Explicator* 29 (November 1970): Item 27.

Clock Without Hands (1961)

Emerson, Donald. "The Ambiguities of *Clock Without Hands*." *Wisconsin Studies in Contemporary Literature* 3 (Autumn 1962): 15–28.

Hicks, Granville. "The Subtle Corruption." *Saturday Review* (September 23, 1961): 14.

Parker, Dorothy. "*Clock Without Hands* Belongs in Yesterday's Tower of Ivory." *Esquire* (December 1961): 72–73.

Correspondence (1942)

Edmonds, Dale. "*Correspondence*: A Forgotten Carson McCullers Short Story." *Studies in Short Fiction* 9 (Winter 1972): 89–92.

A Domestic Dilemma (1955)

Grinnell, James W. "Delving *A Domestic Dilemma*." *Studies in Short Fiction* 9 (Summer 1972): 270–71.

Perrine, Laurence. "Restoring *A Domestic Dilemma*." *Studies in Short Fiction* 11 (Winter 1974): 101–4.

The Heart Is a Lonely Hunter (1940)

Evans, Oliver. "The Case of the Silent Singer: A Revaluation of *The Heart Is a Lonely Hunter*." *Georgia Review* 19 (Summer 1965): 188–203.

Fremont-Smith, Eliot. "The Heart Stands Out." *New York Times Book Review* (September 30, 1967): 47.

Madden, David. "The Paradox of the Need for Privacy and the Need for Understanding in Carson McCullers' *The Heart Is a Lonely Hunter*." *Literature and Psychology* 17 (1967): 128–40.

Mizuta, Juichiro. "Carson McCullers' *The Heart Is a Lonely Hunter*." *Rikkyo Review* 22 (1961): 79–95.

The Member of the Wedding (1946)

Desmond, F.B. "Doing Her Own Thing: Carson McCullers' Dramatization of *Member of the Wedding*." *South Atlantic Bulletin* 40 (1975): 47–52.

Phillips, Robert S. "The Gothic Architecture of *The Member of the Wedding*." *Renascence* 16 (Winter 1964): 59–72.

The Mortgaged Heart (1971)

Madden, David. "Transfixed Among the Self-Inflicted Ruins: Carson McCullers' *The Mortgaged Heart*." *Southern Literary Journal* 5 (Fall 1972): 137–62.

PHYLLIS McGINLEY (1905–) U.S.

General Works

"Conversation between Phyllis McGinley and Donald McDonald." *Critic* 18 (June–July 1960): 7.

Deedy, John. "The Poet Laureate of Suburbia." *U.S. Catholic and Jubilee* 34 (December 1969): 22–27.

Hasley, Louis. "The Poetry of Phyllis McGinley." *Catholic World* (August 1970): 211–15.

"Lady in Larchmont." *Newsweek* (September 26, 1960): 120–21.

McGinley, Phyllis. "The Light Side of the Moon." *American Scholar* 34 (Autumn 1965): 555–68.

"People." *Time* (March 31, 1975): 55.

Richart, Bette. "The Light Touch." *Commonweal* (December 9, 1960): 277–79.

JANET MCNEILL (1907–) Ireland
General Works
Foster, John Wilson. "Zoo Stories: The Novels of Janet McNeill." *Eire* 9 (1974): 104–14.

SARA HAARDT MENCHEN (d. 1935) U.S.
General Works
Going, William T. "Two Alabama Writers: Zelda Sayre Fitzgerald and Sara Haardt Menchen." *Alabama Review* 23 (January 1970): 3–29.

LOUISE MERIWETHER (fl. 1970s) U.S.
Individual Works
Daddy Was a Number Runner (1970)
Giovanni, Nikki. "Review of *Daddy Was a Number Runner*." *Black World* 19 (July 1970): 85–86.
King, Helen. "Review of *Daddy Was a Number Runner*." *Black World* 19 (May 1970): 51–52.
Marshall, Paule. "Review of *Daddy Was a Number Runner*." *New York Times Book Review* (June 28, 1970): 31.

GRACE METALIOUS, née de Repentiany (1924–1964) U.S.
Individual Works
Peyton Place (1956)
Friedrich, Otto. "Farewell to Peyton Place." *Esquire* (December 1971): 160.
Miller, M. "Tragedy of Grace Metalious and Peyton Place." *Ladies' Home Journal* (June 1965): 58–59.

CHARLOTTE MARY MEW (1869–1928) Great Britain
General Works
Bishop, Jimmy D. "Ascent into Nothingness: The Poetry of Charlotte Mew." *Dissertation Abstracts* 29 (1969): 3126A (Louisiana State).
Boll, T.E.M. "The Mystery of Charlotte Mew and May Sinclair: An Inquiry." *Bulletin of the New York Public Library* 74 (September 1970): 445–53.
Davidow, Mary C. "The Charlotte Mew–May Sinclair Relationship: A Reply." *Bulletin of the New York Public Library* 75 (April 1971): 295–300.
Davidow, Mary Celine. "Charlotte Mew: Biography and Criticism." *Dissertation Abstracts* 24 (1963): 1613–14 (Brown).

ALICE MEYNELL (1847–1922) Great Britain
General Works
Bluen, Herbert. "The Poetry of Alice Meynell."

Aryan Path 37 (May 1966): 226–29.
Medford, Elizabeth R. "Alice Meynell." *Dissertation Abstracts* 29 (1968): 572A (Texas).

FRANCES ELIZABETH M'FALL. *See* Sarah Grand

MARGARET MIELKE (fl. 1960s–1970s) U.S.
General Works
Dixon, Richard M. "Alaskan Men of Letters: Margaret Mielke." *Alaska Review* 1 (Winter 1965): 46–50.

EMMA BELL MILES (1880–1919) U.S.
General Works
Rowell, Adelaide. "Emma Bell Miles, Artist, Author and Poet of the Tennessee Mountains." *Tennessee Historical Quarterly* 25 (Spring 1966): 77–89.

JOSEPHINE MILES (1911–) U.S.
General Works
Mooney, Stephen. "Josephine Miles: Successive Views." *Voyages* 2 (Fall 1968): 21–24.

MARGARET ELLIS STURM MILLAR (1915–) U.S.
General Works
"Margaret and Kenneth Millar." *Publishers Weekly* (November 28, 1960): 30–31.
Sokolov, R.A. "Art of Murder." *Newsweek* (March 22, 1971): 101–2.

EDNA ST. VINCENT MILLAY [pseud. Nancy Boyd] (1892–1950) U.S.
Bibliography
Brenni, Vito J., and John E. James. "Edna St. Vincent Millay: Selected Criticism." *Bulletin of Bibliography* 23 (May–August 1962): 177–78.
Patton, J.J. "A Comprehensive Bibliography of Criticism of Edna St. Vincent Millay." *Serif* 5 (September 1968): 10–32.
General Works
Cheney, Martha A. "Millay in the Village." *Dissertation Abstracts International* 34 (1974): 6631A (Florida State).
Dell, Floyd. "My Friend Edna St. Vincent Millay." *Mark Twain Journal* 12 (Spring 1964): 1–3.
Gassman, Janet. "Edna St. Vincent Millay: Nobody's Own." *Colby Library Quarterly* 9 (June 1971): 297–310.
Minot, Walter S. "Edna St. Vincent Millay: A Critical Revaluation." *Dissertation Abstracts Inter-*

national 31 (1971): 4173A (Nebraska).

Minot, W.S. "Millay's Ungrafted Tree: The Problem of the Artist as Woman." *New England Quarterly* 48 (June 1975): 260–68.

Orel, Harold. "Tarnished Arrows: The Last Phase of Edna St. Vincent Millay." *Kansas Magazine* (1960): 73–78.

Patton, John Joseph. "Edna St. Vincent Millay as a Verse Dramatist." *Dissertation Abstracts* 23 (1963): 4363 (Colorado).

Patton, John Joseph. "An Unpublished Hardy Letter to Millay." *Colby Library Quarterly* 5 (June 1961): 284–85.

Tanner, Louise. "Best Years of Their Lives." *Coronet* (March 1960): 76–79.

Westbrook, P.D. "Edna St. Vincent Millay at Steepletop." *Conservationist* 29 (December 1974): 16–19.

Zeschin, R. "Ladies of the Libretto." *Opera News* (March 18, 1972): 26–29.

Individual Works

Aria da Capo (1921)

McKee, Mary J. "Millay's *Aria da Capo*: Form and Meaning." *Modern Drama* 9 (September 1966): 165–69.

Distressing Dialogues (1924)

Brittin, Norman A. "Edna St. Vincent Millay's Nancy Boyd Stories." *Ball State University Forum* 10 (Spring 1969): 31–36.

Patton, John J. "Satiric Fiction in Millay's *Distressing Dialogues*." *Modern Language Studies* 2 (1972): 63–67.

The Lyric Year (1912)

Tanselle, G. Thomas. "*The Lyric Year*: A Bibliographical Study." *Papers of the Bibliographical Society of America* 56 (1962): 454–71.

Recuerdo (1940)

Tanselle, G. Thomas. "Millay, Dell and *Recuerdo*." *Colby Library Quarterly* 6 (March 1963): 202–5.

VASSAR MILLER (1924–) U.S.
General Works

Fowler, Helen. "Energy versus Excitement." *Approach*, no. 44 (Summer 1962): 40–42.

Owen, Guy. "Vassar Miller: A Southern Metaphysical." *Southern Literary Journal* 3 (Fall 1970): 83–88.

Individual Works

My Bones Being Wiser (1963)

Fowler, Albert. "Possessed by the Holy Spirit: The

Poetry of Thomas Merton and Vassar Miller." *Approach*, no. 51 (Spring 1964): 33–42.

KATE MILLETT (1934?–) U.S.
General Works

Edmiston, S. "Day in the Life of Kate Millett: Interview." *Mademoiselle* (February 1971): 138–39.

Fallows, J. "Making It with Mailer, Millett, and Capote." *Washington Monthly* (June 1974): 57–61.

Harris, J.H. "D. H. Lawrence and Kate Millett." *Massachusetts Review* 15 (Summer 1974): 522–29.

"Liberation of Kate Millett." *Time* (August 31, 1970): 18–19.

"Loose Upper Lib." *Time* (July 1, 1974): 64.

Seligson, M. "Kate Millett." *New York Times Book Review* (September 6, 1970): 8.

Wrenn, M.C. "Furious Young Philosopher Who Got It Down on Paper." *Life* (September 4, 1970): 22.

HOPE MIRRLEES (fl. 1910–1920s) Great Britain
General Works

Henig, Suzanne. "Queen of Lud: Hope Mirrlees." *Virginia Woolf Quarterly* 1 (Fall 1972): 8–22.

Individual Works

Paris (1919)

Bailey, Bruce. "A Note on *The Waste Land* and Hope Mirrlees' *Paris*." *T. S. Eliot Newsletter* 1 (Fall 1974): 3–4.

MARGARET MITCHELL (1900–1949) U.S.
General Works

Cole, Lois Dwight. "The Story Begins at a Bridge Luncheon in Atlanta." *New York Times Book Review* (June 25, 1961): 7.

Draper, John W. "A Letter from Margaret Mitchell." *West Virginia University Bulletin: Philological Papers* 17 (June 1970): 81–83.

Edwards, Augusta D. "My Most Unforgettable Character." *Reader's Digest* (March 1962): 117–21.

Farr, Fini. "Margaret Mitchell of Atlanta: The Author of *Gone With the Wind*." *McCall's* (July 1965): 85–87.

Grover, Robert L. "Margaret Mitchell, the Lady from Atlanta." *Georgia Historical Quarterly* 52 (March 1968): 53–69.

Jones, Marian Elder, ed. "Me and My Book." *Geor-*

gia Review 16 (Summer 1962): 180–87.
Individual Works
Gone With the Wind (1936)

Cordell, A. "Strange Story behind *Gone With the Wind.*" *Coronet* (February 1961): 98–104.

Gaillard, Dawson. "*Gone With the Wind* as Bildungsroman or Why Did Rhett Butler Really Leave Scarlett O'Hara." *Georgia Review* 28 (Spring 1974): 9–18.

Gutwilling, Robert. "In History There's Never Been Anything Like It." *New York Times Book Review* (June 25, 1961): 6.

Knebel, Fletcher. "Scarlett O'Hara's Millions." *Look* (December 3, 1963): 39.

Matthews, J.W. "The Civil War of 1936: *Gone With the Wind* and *Absalom, Absalom!*" *Georgia Review* 21 (Winter 1967): 462–69.

Stern, Jerome. "*Gone With the Wind*: The South as America." *Southern Humanities Review* 6 (Winter 1972): 5–12.

Watkins, Floyd C. "*Gone With the Wind* as Vulgar Literature." *Southern Literary Journal* 2 (Spring 1970): 86–103.

SUSAN L. MITCHELL (1866–1926) Ireland
Individual Works
The Irish Council Bill 1907

Skelton, Robin. "Susan L. Mitchell: An Unrecorded Item." *Irish Book* 1 (1962): 104.

JESSICA MITFORD (1917–) U.S.
General Works

Gardner, P. "Jessica Mitford." *Publishers Weekly* (October 1, 1973): 32–33.

Jensen, P. "Uh-oh: The Interview This Month Is with Jessica Mitford." *Writer's Digest* 54 (August 1974): 16–20.

Mitford, J. "My Short and Happy Life as a Distinguished Professor." *Atlantic Monthly* (October 1974): 90–92.

"Queen of Muckrakers." *Time* (July 20, 1970): 52.

MARY RUSSELL MITFORD (1787–1855) Great Britain
General Works

Duncan-Jones, Katherine. "Miss Mitford and *Adonais.*" *Review of English Studies* 22 (May 1971): 170–72.

Jones, S. "B. R. Haydon on Some Contemporaries: A New Letter." *Review of English Studies* 26 (May 1975): 183–89.

Lauterbach, Charles E. "Let the Printer Do It." *Notes and Queries* 10 (January 1963): 17–18.

Lewis, Jenny. "Mary Russell Mitford Letters." *British Museum Quarterly* 29 (Winter 1964–1965): 6–10.

Rausch, Sister M. Sheila. "Mary Russell Mitford and Regional Realism." *Dissertation Abstracts* 29 (1968): 907A–8A (Minnesota).

Raymond, Meredith B. "A Report on the Published and Unpublished Letters of Elizabeth Barrett Browning to Mary Russell Mitford." *Browning Institute Studies* 1 (1973): 37–62.
Individual Works
Our Village (1824–1832)

Owen, J.C. "Utopia in Little: Mary Russell Mitford and *Our Village.*" *Studies in Short Fiction* 5 (Spring 1968): 245–56.

NANCY MITFORD, née Rodd (1904–1973) Great Britain
General Works
Mitford, Nancy. "Self-Portrait." *Esquire* (August 1962): 104.

HARRIET MONROE (1860–1936) U.S.
Bibliography

Bond, Judith. "The Harriet Monroe Manuscript Collection of the University of Chicago Library." *Manuscripts* 13 (Spring 1961): 34–44.
General Works

Lowe, R.L. "Edwin Arlington Robinson to Harriet Monroe: Some Unpublished Letters." *Modern Philology* 60 (August 1962): 31–40.

Williams, Ellen. "Harriet Monroe." *Antigonish Review* 7 (Summer 1971): 77–82.

Zabel, M.D. "H.M.: In Memory." *Poetry* 97 (January 1961): 241–54.

ELIZABETH MONTAGU, née Robinson (1720–1800) Great Britain
General Works

Boulton, James T. "Mrs. Elizabeth Montagu (1720–1800)." *Burke Newsletter* 3 (Winter–Spring 1961–1962): 96–98.

Ewert, Leonore H. "Elizabeth Montagu to Elizabeth Carter: Literary Gossip and Critical Opinions from the Pen of the Queen of the Blues." *Dissertation Abstracts* 29 (1968): 566A–67A (Claremont).

Ross, Ian. "A Bluestocking over the Border: Mrs. Montagu's Aesthetic Adventures in Scotland."

Huntington Library Quarterly 28 (May 1965): 213–33.

LADY MARY WORTLEY MONTAGU (1689–1762)
Great Britain
General Works
Corrigan, Beatrice. "Three Englishwomen in Italy." *Queen's Quarterly* 79 (1972): 147–58.
Franke, Wolfgang. "Elizabeth Lady Craven on Lady Mary Wortley Montagu: Some Eighteenth-Century Hints on the Authorship of the Five Spurious Letters." *Notes and Queries* 20 (November 1973): 417–20.
Grundy, Isobel. "A Moon of Literature: Verse by Lady Mary Wortley Montagu." *New Rambler*, no. 112 (1972): 6–22.
Grundy, Isobel. "Some Unpublished Early Verse of Henry Fielding." *New Rambler*, no. 107 (1969): 2–18.
Halsband, Robert. "Lady Mary Wortley Montagu: Her Place in the Eighteenth Century." *History Today* 16 (February 1966): 94–102.
Halsband, Robert. "Lady Mary Wortley Montagu and Eighteenth Century Fiction." *Philological Quarterly* 45 (January 1966): 145–56.
Halsband, Robert. "Lady Mary Wortley Montagu as Letter Writer." *Publications of the Modern Language Association* 80 (1965): 155–63.
Halsband, Robert. "A 'New' Lady Mary Letter." *Philological Quarterly* 44 (April 1965): 180–84.
Knipps, Charles C. "Types of Orientalism in Eighteenth Century English Literature." *Dissertation Abstracts International* 35 (1974): 2944A–45A (California, Berkeley).
Pritchett, V.S. "Nature's Lady." *New Statesman* (January 21, 1966): 90–91.
"Simplicity." *Johnsonian Newsletter* 27 (1967): 2.
Individual Works
Epistle from Mrs. Y—— to Her Husband (1724)
Grundy, Isobel. "Ovid and Eighteenth-Century Divorce: An Unpublished Poem by Lady Mary Wortley Montagu." *Review of English Studies* 23 (November 1972): 417–28.

LUCY MAUD MONTGOMERY (1874–1942) Canada
General Works
Frazer, F.M. "Scarcely an End." *Canadian Literature*, no. 63 (Winter 1975): 89–92.

SUSANNA MOODIE, née Strickland (1803–1885) Can-
ada (Born in Great Britain)
General Works
Ballstadt, Carl. "Susanna Moodie and the English Sketch." *Canadian Literature*, no. 51 (Winter 1972): 32–38.
Gairdner, William D. "Traill and Moodie: Two Realities." *Journal of Canadian Fiction* 1 (1972): 35–42.
Purdy, A.W. "Atwood's Moodie." *Canadian Literature*, no. 47 (Winter 1971): 80–83.
Stouck, David. "Secrets of the Prison-House: Mrs. Moodie and the Canadian Imagination." *Dalhousie Review* 54 (Summer 1974): 463–72.
Thomas, Clara. "Journeys to Freedom." *Canadian Literature*, no. 51 (Winter 1972): 11–19.

IDORA McCLELLAN PLOWMAN MOORE. *See* Betsy Hamilton

JULIA A. MOORE (1847–1920) U.S.
General Works
Michaelson, L. W. "The Worst American Novel." *North Dakota Quarterly* 32 (1964): 101–3.

MARIANNE MOORE (1887–1972) U.S.
Bibliography
Abbott, Craig S. "Marianne Moore: A Descriptive Bibliography." *Dissertation Abstracts International* 34 (1974): 5951A–52A (Texas).
General Works
Brumbaugh, Thomas B. "In Pursuit of Miss Moore." *Mississippi Quarterly* 15 (Spring 1962): 74–80.
Cannell, Kathleen. "Marianne Moore." *Informations et Documents* (May 1, 1961): 28–33.
Cecilia, Sister Mary. "The Poetry of Marianne Moore." *Thought* 38 (1963): 354–74.
Durso, J. "Marianne Moore, Baseball Fan." *Saturday Review* (July 12, 1969): 51–52.
Edsal, Constance H. "Values and the Poems of Marianne Moore." *English Journal* 58 (April 1969): 516–18.
Engel, Bernard F. "A Democratic Vista of Religion." *Georgia Review* 20 (Spring 1966): 84–89.
Engel, Bernard F. "Marianne Moore and 'Objectivism.' " *Papers of the Michigan Academy of Letters, Arts and Sciences* 48 (1963): 657–64.
Foss, L. "Miss Moore." *Christian Century* (May 8, 1968): 611.
Glatstein, Jacob. "The Poetry of Marianne Moore." *Prairie Schooner* 47 (Summer 1973): 133–41.

Guillory, Daniel L. "Hart Crane, Marianne Moore and the Brooklyn Bridge." *Ball State University Forum* 15 (Summer 1974): 48–49.

Hadas, Pamela G. "Efforts of Affection: The Poetry of Marianne Moore." *Dissertation Abstracts International* 34 (1973): 2561A (Washington).

Hall, Donald. "The Art of Poetry IV." *Paris Review* 7 (Summer–Fall 1961): 41–66.

Hartsock, Mildred E. "Marianne Moore: 'A Salvo of Barks.' " Bucknell Review 11 (December 1962): 14–37.

Hoffman, Daniel. "Two Ladies of Legend." *Reporter* (December 28, 1967): 41–43.

Howard, J. "Leading Lady of U.S. Verse." *Life* (January 13, 1967): 37–38.

"Interview with Marianne Moore." *McCall's* (December 1965): 74.

Kennedy, X.J. "Marianne Moore," *Minnesota Review* 2 (Spring 1962): 369–76.

Kenner, Hugh. "Experience of the Eye: Marianne Moore's Tradition." *Southern Review* (U.S.) 1 (1965): 754–69.

Kenner, Hugh. "Meditation and Enactment." *Poetry* 102 (May 1963): 109–15.

Kindley, Jeffrey B. "Efforts of Affection: The Poetry of Marianne Moore." *Dissertation Abstracts International* 34 (1974): 7758A–59A (Columbia).

"Literary Portraits: 1 Marianne Moore." *Library Chronicle of the University of Texas*, n.s. 1 (March 1970): 30–31.

"Marianne Moore's Brooklyn." *Look* (May 7, 1963): 54.

McCord, Howard. "Marianne Moore's Chinese Tadpoles." *American Notes and Queries* 3 (September 1964): 5–6.

"Miss Moore in Manhattan." *New Yorker* (January 29, 1966): 24–26.

Moore, Marianne. "Marianne Moore: A Self-Portrait." *Esquire* (July 1962): 99.

Moore, Marianne. "Ten Answers: Letter from an October Afternoon." *Harper's* (November 1964): 91–98.

Moore, Marianne. "The Ways Our Poets Have Taken in 15 Years Since the War." *New York Herald Tribune Book Review* (April 3, 1960): 1.

Moore, Marianne. "When I Was Sixteen." *Good Housekeeping* (October 1968): 99–100.

Parkin, Rebecca P. "Some Characteristics of Marianne Moore's Humor." *College English* 27 (February 1966): 403–8.

Plimpton, George. "The World Series with Marianne Moore: Letter from an October Afternoon." *Harper's* (October 1964): 50–58.

"The Poet as Patron." *Wilson Library Bulletin* 36 (January 1962): 365–71.

Replogle, Justin. "Marianne Moore and the Art of Intonation." *Contemporary Literature* 12 (Winter 1971): 1–17.

Schulman, Grace, ed. "Conversation with Marianne Moore." *Quarterly Review of Literature* 16 (1969): 154–71.

Shankar, D.A. "The Poetry of Marianne Moore." *Literary Criterion* 5 (1962): 141–47.

Smith, William Jay. "A Place for the Genuine." *New Republic* (February 24, 1968): 34–36.

Tomlinson, Charles. "Marianne Moore: Her Poetry and Her Critics." *Agenda* 6 (Autumn–Winter 1968): 137–42.

Vonalt, Larry P. "Marianne Moore's Medicines." *Sewanee Review* 78 (Autumn 1970): 669–78.

Warlow, Francis W. "Marianne Moore: Unfalsifying Sun and Solid Gilded Star." *Dissertation Abstracts* 20 (1960): 2814 (Penn.).

Wasserstrom, William. "Marianne Moore, *The Dial*, and Kenneth Burke." *Western Humanities Review* 17 (Summer 1963): 249–62.

Weatherhead, A.K. "Two Kinds of Vision in Marianne Moore." *English Literary History* 31 (December 1964): 482–96.

Weatherhead, A. Kingsley. "Imagination and Fancy: Marianne Moore." *Texas Studies in Literature and Language* 6 (Summer 1964): 188–99.

Individual Works

Apparition of Splendor (1952)

Parkin, Rebecca P. "Certain Difficulties in Reading Marianne Moore: Exemplified in Her *Apparition of Splendor*." *Publications of the Modern Language Association* 81 (1966): 167–72.

Dream (1965)

Going, William T. "Marianne Moore's *Dream*: Academic By-path to Xanadu." *Papers on Language and Literature* 5, Supplement (1969): 145–53.

The Fish (1935)

Renick, Sue. "Moore's *The Fish*." *Explicator* 21 (September 1962): Item 7.

In Distrust of Merits (1944)

Fowler, Albert. "That I May Yet Recover." *Fellowship* (March 1966): 5–6.

In Lieu of the Lyre (1966)

Seymour-Smith, Martin. "*In Lieu of the Lyre*."

Spectator (May 10, 1968): 634–35.
The Jerboa (1935)
Joost, Nicholas. "The Pertinence of Marianne Moore's Notes to *The Jerboa*." *Delta Epsilon Sigma Bulletin* 7 (May 1962): 1–30.
The Monkeys (1935)
Miller, Lois. "I Went to the Animal Fair: An Analysis of Marianne Moore's *The Monkeys*." *English Journal* 52 (January 1963): 66–67.
Spenser's Ireland (1967)
O'Sullivan, Maurice J., Jr. "Native Genius for Disunion: Marianne Moore's *Spenser's Ireland*." *Concerning Poetry* 7 (1974): 42–47.
To a Snail (1951)
Warlow, Francis W. "Moore's *To a Snail*." *Explicator* 26 (February 1968): Item 51.

MILCAH MARTHA MOORE (fl. 1780s) U.S.
General Works
Coad, Oral S. "An Early American School Book." *Journal of the Rutgers University Library* 33 (June 1970): 46–48.

PAMELA MOORE (1937–1964) U.S.
General Works
Hamblen, Abigail Ann. "Teen-Ager as Novelist: Pamela Moore." *Midwest Quarterly* 7 (Summer 1966): 355–65.

HANNAH MORE (1745–1833) Great Britain
General Works
Newell, A.G. "Early Evangelical Fiction." *Evangelical Quarterly* 38 (1966): 3–21.
Zall, P.M. "The Cool World of Samuel Taylor Coleridge: More for the Millions." *Wordsworth Circle* 4 (Spring 1973): 152–57.

KATHLEEN MOREHOUSE (1904–) U.S.
General Works
"Thank You Kindly, but with Reservations." *North Carolina Folklore* 20 (May 1972): 87–91.
Individual Works
Rain On the Just (1936)
West, John Foster. "Mrs. Morehouse's *Rain On the Just*." *North Carolina Folklore* 19 (March 1971): 47–54.

ELAINE MORGAN (1920–) U.S.
General Works
Bonfante, J. "Naked Ape Is All Wet, Says a Liber-

ated Lady." *Life* (July 21, 1972): 77.

LADY MORGAN, née Sydney Owenson (1783–1859) Great Britain
General Works
Corrigan, Beatrice. "Three Englishwomen in Italy." *Queen's Quarterly* 79 (1972): 147–58.

MARABEL MORGAN (1937–) U.S.
General Works
"Total Fascination." *Time* (March 10, 1975): 77.

MYRA MORRIS (1893?–1966) Australia
General Works
Macartney, Frederick T. "Myra Morris: Memorial Note." *Meanjin Quarterly* 26 (1967): 457–58.

LOIS MOYLES (fl. 1960s) U.S.
General Works
Moss, Howard. "Introducing Lois Moyles." *Works* 1 (Autumn 1967): 4–5.
Individual Works
I Prophesy Summer (1971)
Moore, Rosalie. "The Poet as Catastrophe." *Works* 3 (Summer–Fall 1971): 92–95.

ALICE MUNRO (1931–) Canada
General Works
Dahlie, H. "Unconsummated Relationships: Isolation and Rejection in Alice Munro's Stories." *World Literature Written in English* 11 (1972): 43–48.
Metcalf, John. "A Conversation with Alice Munro." *Journal of Canadian Fiction* 1 (1972): 54–62.

IRIS MURDOCH (1919–) Great Britain
Bibliography
Culley, Ann, with John Feaster. "Criticism of Iris Murdoch: A Selected Checklist." *Modern Fiction Studies* 15 (Autumn 1969): 449–57.
Murray, William M. "A Note on the Iris Murdoch Manuscripts in the University of Iowa Libraries." *Modern Fiction Studies* 15 (Autumn 1969): 445–48.
Widmann, R.L. "An Iris Murdoch Checklist." *Criticism* 10 (1968): 17–29.
General Works
Allen, Diogenes. "Two Experiences of Existence: Jean-Paul Sartre and Iris Murdoch." *International Philosophical Quarterly* 14 (June 1974): 181–87.
Anderson, Thayle K. "Concepts of Love in the

Novels of Iris Murdoch." *Dissertation Abstracts International* 31 (1971): 5385A–86A (Purdue).

Baldanza, Frank. "Iris Murdoch and the Theory of Personality." *Criticism* 7 (1965): 176–89.

Barrows, John. "Iris Murdoch." *John O'London's* (May 4, 1961): 498.

Bryden, Ronald. "Talking to Iris Murdoch." *Listener* (April 4, 1968): 433–34.

Culley, Ann. "Theory and Practice: Characterization in the Novels of Iris Murdoch." *Modern Fiction Studies* 15 (Autumn 1969): 335–46.

Davis, Robert Murray. "On Editing Modern Texts: Who Should Do What, and to Whom?" *Journal of Modern Literature* 3 (1974): 1012–20.

De Mott, Benjamin. "Dirty Words?" *Hudson Review* 18 (Spring 1965): 31–44.

Dick, Bernard F. "The Novels of Iris Murdoch: A Formula for Enchantment." *Bucknell Review* 14 (May 1966): 66–81.

Fast, Laurence E. "Self-Discovery in the Novels of Iris Murdoch." *Dissertation Abstracts International* 31 (1971): 5397A (Oregon).

Felheim, Marvin. "Symbolic Characterization in the Novels of Iris Murdoch." *Texas Studies in Literature and Language* 2 (Summer 1960): 189–97.

German, Howard. "Allusions in the Early Novels of Iris Murdoch." *Modern Fiction Studies* 15 (Autumn 1969): 361–77.

German, Howard. "The Range of Allusions in the Novels of Iris Murdoch." *Journal of Modern Literature* 2 (1971): 57–85.

Gilligan, John T. "The Fiction and Philosophy of Iris Murdoch." *Dissertation Abstracts International* 35 (1974): 1099A–1100A (Wisconsin, Milwaukee).

Gindin, James. "Images of Illusion in the Work of Iris Murdoch." *Texas Studies in Literature and Language* 2 (Summer 1960): 180–88.

Goshgarian, Gary. "Feminist Values in the Novels of Iris Murdoch." *Revue des Langues Vivantes* 40 (1974): 519–27.

Goshgarian, Gary. "From Fable to Flesh: A Study of the Female Characters in the Novels of Iris Murdoch." *Dissertation Abstracts International* 33 (1973): 3583A (Wisconsin).

Halio, Jay L. "A Sense of the Present." *Southern Review* (U.S.) 2 (1966): 952.

Hall, William. " 'The Third Way': The Novels of Iris Murdoch." *Dalhousie Review* 46 (Autumn 1966): 306–18.

Hauerwas, Stanley. "The Significance of Vision: Toward an Aesthetic Ethic." *Studies in Religion* 2 (1972): 36–49.

Hicks, Granville. "Literary Horizons." *Saturday Review* (January 18, 1969): 32.

Hoffman, Frederick J. "Iris Murdoch: The Reality of Persons." *Critique* 7 (1964): 48–57.

Hoffman, Frederick J. "The Miracle of Contingency: The Novels of Iris Murdoch." *Shenandoah* 17 (1965): 49–55.

Hoskins, Robert. "Iris Murdoch's Midsummer Nightmare." *Twentieth Century Literature* 18 (July 1972): 191–98.

Jacobson, Dan. "Farce, Totem and Taboo." *New Statesman* (June 16, 1961): 956–57.

Keates, Lois S. "Varieties of the Quest-Myth in the Early Novels of Iris Murdoch." *Dissertation Abstracts International* 33 (1972): 1730A (Penn.).

Kermode, Frank. "The House of Fiction: Interviews with Seven English Novelists." *Partisan Review* 29 (1963):61–82.

Kuehl, Linda. "Iris Murdoch: The Novelist as Magician/The Magician as Artist." *Modern Fiction Studies* 15 (Autumn 1969): 347–60.

Maes-Jelinek, Hena. "A House for Free Characters: The Novels of Iris Murdoch." *Revue des Langues Vivantes* 29 (1963): 45–69.

Majdiak, Daniel. "Romanticism in the Aesthetics of Iris Murdoch." *Texas Studies in Literature and Language* 14 (Summer 1972): 359–75.

McCabe, Bernard. "The Guises of Love." *Commonweal* (December 3, 1965): 270–73.

Meidner, Olga McDonald. "The Progress of Iris Murdoch." *English Studies in Africa* 4 (March 1961): 17–38.

Morrell, Roy. "Iris Murdoch: The Early Novels." *Critical Quarterly* 9 (Autumn 1967): 272–82.

Nye, Robert. "Ending the World." *John O'London's* (July 5, 1962): 9.

Obumselu, B. "Iris Murdoch and Sartre." *English Literary History* 42 (Summer 1975): 296–317.

O'Connor, William Van. "Iris Murdoch: The Formal and the Contingent." *Critique* 3 (1960): 34–46.

O'Sullivan, Kevin. "Iris Murdoch and the Image of Liberal Man." *Yale Literary Magazine* 131 (1962): 27–36.

Pearson, Gabriel. "Iris Murdoch and the Romantic Novel." *New Left Review* 13–14 (January–April 1962): 137–45.

Pondrom, Cyrena Norman. "Iris Murdoch: An Existentialist?" *Comparative Literature Studies* 5 (1968): 403–19.

Ricks, Christopher. "A Sort of Mystery Novel." *New Statesman* (October 22, 1965): 604–5.

Rockefeller, Larry J. "Comedy and the Early Novels of Iris Murdoch." *Dissertation Abstracts* 29 (1969): 4018A (Bowling Green).

Rose, W.K. "An Interview with Iris Murdoch." *Shenandoah* 19 (1968): 3–22.

Rose, W. K. "Iris Murdoch, Informally: Interview." *Harper's Bazaar* (May 1968): 208.

Schneidermeyer, Wilma F. "The Religious Dimension in the Works of Iris Murdoch." *Dissertation Abstracts International* 35 (1974): 3113A (Southern California).

Souvage, Jacques. "The Novels of Iris Murdoch." *Studia Germanica Gandensia* 4 (1962): 225–52.

Stubbs, Patricia. "Two Contemporary Views on Fiction: Iris Murdoch and Muriel Spark." *English* 23 (Autumn 1974): 102–10.

Taylor, Jane. "Iris Murdoch." *Books and Bookmen* 16 (April 1971): 26–27.

Weatherhead, A. Kingsley. "Backgrounds with Figures in Iris Murdoch." *Texas Studies in Literature and Language* 10 (Winter 1969): 635–48.

Whiteside, George. "The Novels of Iris Murdoch." *Critique* 7 (1964): 27–47.

Wolf, Nancy C. "Philosophical Ambivalence in the Novels of Iris Murdoch." *Dissertation Abstracts International* 33 (1972): 2959A (Connecticut).

Wolfe, Peter. "Philosophical Themes in the Novels of Iris Murdoch." *Dissertation Abstracts* 26 (1965): 3357–58 (Wisconsin).

Individual Works

The Bell (1958)

Ashdown, Ellen Abernethy. "Form and Myth in Three Novels by Iris Murdoch: *The Flight from the Enchanter*, *The Bell*, and *A Severed Head*." *Dissertation Abstracts International* 35 (1975): 5334A–35A (Florida).

Jones, Dorothy. "Love and Morality in Iris Murdoch's *The Bell*." *Meanjin Quarterly* 26 (1967): 85–90.

Kaehele, Sharon, and Howard German. "Discovery of Reality in Iris Murdoch's *The Bell*." *Publications of the Modern Language Association* 82 (1967): 554–63.

McCarthy, Margot. "Dualities in *The Bell*." *Contemporary Review* 213 (1968): 313–17.

McGinnis, Robert M. "Murdoch's *The Bell*." *Expli-*

cator 28 (September 1969): Item 1.

Souvage, Jacques. "Symbol as Narrative Device: An Interpretation of Iris Murdoch's *The Bell*." *English Studies* 43 (1962): 81–96.

Wall, Stephen. "The Bell in *The Bell*." *Essays in Criticism* 13 (July 1963): 265–73.

Bruno's Dream (1968)

Hall, William F. "*Bruno's Dream*: Technique and Meaning in the Novels of Iris Murdoch." *Modern Fiction Studies* 15 (Autumn 1969): 429–43.

Kaye, H. "Delight and Instruction." *New Republic* (February 8, 1969): 19–20.

Thomson, P.W. "Iris Murdoch's Honest Puppetry—The Characters of *Bruno's Dream*." *Critical Quarterly* 11 (Autumn 1969): 277–83.

Tube, Henry. "Women's Rites." *Spectator* (January 17, 1969): 79–80.

A Fairly Honourable Defeat (1970)

Watrin, Jany. "Iris Murdoch's *A Fairly Honourable Defeat*." *Revue des Langues Vivantes* 38 (1972): 46–64.

The Flight from the Enchanter (1956)

Ashdown, Ellen Abernethy. "Form and Myth in Three Novels by Iris Murdoch: *The Flight from the Enchanter*, *The Bell*, and *A Severed Head*." *Dissertation Abstracts International* 35 (1975): 5334A–35A (Florida).

Meidner, Olga McDonald. "Reviewer's Bane: A Study of Murdoch's *The Flight from the Enchanter*." *Essays in Criticism* 11 (October 1961): 435–47.

Sullivan, Zohreh Tawakuli. "Enchantment and the Demonic in Iris Murdoch: *The Flight from the Enchanter*." *Midwest Quarterly* 16 (Spring 1975): 276–97.

Italian Girl (1964)

Kriegel, Leonard. "A Surrender of Symbols." *Nation* (November 9, 1964): 339.

Pagones, Dorrie. "Wanton Waifs and a Roman Woman." *Saturday Review* (September 19, 1964): 48–49.

Tracy, Honor. "Misgivings about Miss Murdoch." *New Republic* (October 10, 1964): 21–22.

Tucker, Martin. "More Iris Murdoch." *Commonweal* (October 30, 1964): 173–74.

The Nice and the Good (1968)

Baldanza, Frank. "*The Nice and the Good*." *Modern Fiction Studies* 15 (Autumn 1969): 417–28.

Byatt, A.S. "Kiss and Make Up." *New Statesman* (January 29, 1968): 113.

Hicks, Granville. "Love Runs Rampant." *Saturday Review* (January 6, 1968): 27–28.

Taubman, Robert. "Not Caring." *Listener* (February 1, 1968): 148.

The Red and the Green (1965)

Berthoff, Warner. "Fortunes of the Novel: Muriel Spark and Iris Murdoch." *Massachusetts Review* 8 (Spring 1967): 301–32.

Bradbury, Malcolm. "The Romantic Miss Murdoch." *Spectator* (September 3, 1965): 293.

Hicks, Granville. "Easter Monday Insights." *Saturday Review* (October 30, 1965): 41–42.

Kemp, Peter. "The Fight against Fantasy: Iris Murdoch's *The Red and the Green*." *Modern Fiction Studies* 15 (Autumn 1969): 403–15.

Rome, Joy. "A Respect for the Contingent: A Study of Iris Murdoch's Novel *The Red and the Green*." *English Studies in Africa* 14 (March 1971): 87–98.

Sullivan, Richard. "Millicent the Magnificent." *Critic* 24 (December 1965–January 1966): 63.

Tucker, Martin. "The Odd Fish in Murdoch's Kettle." *New Republic* (February 5, 1966): 26–28.

A Severed Head (1961)

Ashdown, Ellen Abernethy. "Form and Myth in Three Novels by Iris Murdoch: *The Flight from the Enchanter*, *The Bell*, and *A Severed Head*." *Dissertation Abstracts International* 35 (1975): 5334A–35A (Florida).

Baldanza, Frank. "The Manuscript of Iris Murdoch's *A Severed Head*." *Journal of Modern Literature* 3 (1974): 75–90.

Bryden, Ronald. "Phenomenon." *Spectator* (June 16, 1961): 885.

Cosman, Max. "Priapean Japes." *Commonweal* (June 9, 1961): 286–87.

Jacobson, Dan. "Farce, Totem and Taboo." *New Statesman* (June 16, 1961): 956–57.

Kane, Patricia. "The Furnishings of a Marriage: An Aspect of Characterization in Iris Murdoch's *A Severed Head*." *Notes on Contemporary Literature* 2 (November 1972): 4–5.

Kenney, Alice P. "The Mythic History of *A Severed Head*." *Modern Fiction Studies* 15 (Autumn 1969): 387–401.

Miner, Earl. "Iris Murdoch: The Uses of Love." *Nation* (June 2, 1962): 498–99.

Moody, Philippa. "In the Lavatory of the Athenaeum—Post War English Novels." *Melbourne Critical Review* 6 (1963): 83–92.

O'Connor, William Van. "Iris Murdoch: *A Severed Head*." *Critique* 5 (1962): 74–77.

The Sovereignty of Good (1970)

Griffin, James. "The Fat Ego." *Essays in Criticism* 22 (January 1972): 74–83.

The Time of the Angels (1966)

Eimerl, Sarel. "Choreography of Despair." *Reporter* (November 3, 1966): 45–46.

Hicks, Granville. "Rector of a Dead God." *Saturday Review* (October 29, 1966): 25–26.

Taubman, Robert. "Uncles' War." *New Statesman* (September 16, 1966): 401–2.

Under the Net (1954)

Batchelor, Billie. "Revision in Iris Murdoch's *Under the Net*." *Books at Iowa*, no. 8 (1968): 30–36.

Bradbury, Malcolm. "Iris Murdoch's *Under the Net*." *Critical Quarterly* 4 (Spring 1962): 47–54.

Goldberg, Gerald Jay. "The Search for the Artist in Some Recent British Fiction." *South Atlantic Quarterly* 62 (Summer 1963): 387–401.

Porter, Raymond J. "*Leitmotif* in Iris Murdoch's *Under the Net*." *Modern Fiction Studies* 15 (Autumn 1969): 379–85.

Souvage, Jacques. "The Unresolved Tension: An Interpretation of Iris Murdoch's *Under the Net*." *Revue des Langues Vivantes* 26 (1960): 420–29.

Vickery, John B. "The Dilemmas of Language: Sartre's *La Nausée* and Iris Murdoch's *Under the Net*." *Journal of Narrative Technique* 1 (1971): 69–76.

Widmann, R.L. "Murdoch's *Under the Net*: Theory and Practice of Fiction." *Criticism* 10 (1968): 5–16.

The Unicorn (1963)

Barrett, William. "English Opposites." *Atlantic Monthly* (June 1963): 131–32.

Bradbury, Malcolm. "Under the Symbol." *Spectator* (September 6, 1963): 210–95.

Cook, Eleanor. "Mythical Beasts." *Canadian Forum* 43 (August 1963): 113–14.

Hebblethwaite, Peter. "Out Hunting Unicorns." *Month* (October 1963): 224–28.

Pondrom, Cyrena N. "Review of *The Unicorn*." *Critique* 6 (1963–1964): 177–181.

Whitehorn, Katharine. "Three Women." *Encounter* 21 (December 1963): 78–82.

Tucker, Martin. "Love and Freedom: Golden and Hard Words." *Commonweal* (June 21, 1963): 357–58.

An Unofficial Rose (1962)

Barrett, William. "Rose with Thorns." *Atlantic*

Monthly (June 1962): 108–9.

Hicks, Granville. "The Operations of Love." *Saturday Review* (May 19, 1962): 32.

McDowell, F.P.W. "The Devious Involutions of Human Character and Emotion: Reflections on Some Recent British Novels." *Wisconsin Studies in Contemporary Literature* 4 (Autumn 1963): 353–59.

Miller, Vincent. "Unofficial Roses." *National Review* (September 1, 1962): 194–96.

Miner, Earl. "Iris Murdoch: The Uses of Love." *Nation* (June 2, 1962): 498–99.

Ryan, Marjorie. "Review of *An Unofficial Rose*." *Critique* 5 (1962): 117–21.

A Word Child (1975)

Schwartz, Lynne Sharon. "A Grammarian of Human Relations." *Nation* (October 11, 1975): 343–45.

Mary Noailles Murfree [pseud. Charles Egbert Craddock] (1850–1922) U.S.
Bibliography
Carleton, Reese M. "Mary Noailles Murfree (1850–1922): An Annotated Bibliography." *American Literary Realism* 7 (1974): 293–378.

Cary, Richard. "Mary Noailles Murfree (1850–1922)." *American Literary Realism* 1 (1967): 79–83.

General Works
Lanier, Doris. "Mary Noailles Murfree: An Interview." *Tennessee Historical Quarterly* 31 (Fall 1972): 276–78.

Loyd, Dennis. "Tennessee's Mystery Woman Novelist." *Tennessee Historical Quarterly* 29 (Fall 1970): 272–77.

Reeves, Paschal. "From Halley's Comet to Prohibition." *Mississippi Quarterly* 21 (Fall 1968): 286.

Wood, Ann Douglas. "The Literature of Impoverishment: The Women Local Colorists in America 1865–1914." *Women's Studies* 1 (1972): 3–40.

Individual Works
In the Tennessee Mountains (1884)

Nilles, Mary. "Craddock's Girls: A Look at Some Unliberated Women." *Markham Review* 3 (October 1972): 74–77.

Warfel, Harry R. "Local Color and Literary Artistry: Mary Noailles Murfree's *In the Tennessee Mountains*." *Southern Literary Journal* 3 (Fall 1976): 154–63.

When Old Baldy Spoke (1962)

Dillingham, William B., ed. "*When Old Baldy Spoke*." *Emory University Quarterly* 18 (Summer 1962): 93–106.

Where the Battle Was Fought (1884)

Shuman, R. Baird. "Mary Murfree's Battle." *Tennessee Studies in Literature* 6 (1961): 33–37.

Anna Maria Murray (fl. 1830's) Australia
Individual Works
The Guardian (1838)

Wilson, Gwendoline. "Anna Maria Murray, Authoress of *The Guardian*." *Australian Literary Studies* 3 (1967): 148–49.

Kathleen Mansfield Murry. *See* Katherine Mansfield

N

JULIA NEWBERRY (fl. 1870s) U.S.
General Works
Holmes, J. Welfred. "Three Uncommon Records of the Commonplace." *College Language Association Journal* 9 (March 1966): 215–24.

LORINE NIEDECKER (1903–) U.S.
General Works
Corman, C. "With Lorine." *Chicago Review* 25 (1973): 139–65.

ANAIS NIN (1903–1977) U.S.
Bibliography
Zee, Nancy S. "A Checklist of Nin Materials at Northwestern University Library." *Under the Sign of Pisces* 3 (Spring 1972): 3–11.
General Works
Amoia, Alba. "The Novel of the Future." *Studies in the Twentieth Century*, no. 6 (Fall 1970): 109–17.
Brodsley, Laurel. "Anais Nin and the Novel of the Future." *Delta*, no. 48 (March 1971): 35–39.
Evans, Oliver, "Anais Nin and the Discovery of Inner Space." *Prairie Schooner* 36 (Fall 1962): 217–30.
Freeman, Barbara. "A Dialogue with Anais Nin." *Chicago Review* 24 (1972): 29–35.
Griffith, Paul. "The Jewels of Anais Nin." *Journal of the Otto Rank Association* 5 (1970): 82–91.
Hauser, Marianne. "Anais Nin: Myth and Reality." *Studies in the Twentieth Century*, no. 1 (Fall 1968): 45–50.
Henderson, B. "Do-It-Yourself Publishing." *Publishers Weekly* (August 13, 1973): 31.
Hinz, Evelyn J. "Anais Nin." *Contemporary Literature* 13 (Spring 1972): 225–57.
Killoh, Ellen P. "The Woman Writer and the Element of Destruction." *College English* 34 (October 1972): 31–38.
Kuntz, Paul Grimley. "Art as Public Dream: The Practice and Theory of Anais Nin." *Journal of Aesthetics and Art Criticism* 32 (1974): 525–37.
McBrien, W. "Anais Nin: An Interview." *Twentieth Century Literature* 20 (October 1974): 277–90.
Nin, Anais. "Notes on Feminism." *Massachusetts Review* 13 (Winter–Spring 1972): 25–28.
Nin, Anais. "On Feminism and Creation." *Michigan Quarterly Review* 13 (Winter 1974): 4–13.
Owen, Peter. "Anais Nin." *Times Literary Supplement* (May 19, 1972): 577.
Peck, Ellen M. McK. "Exploring the Feminine: A Study of Janet Lewis, Ellen Glasgow, Anais Nin and Virginia Woolf." *Dissertation Abstracts International* 35 (1974): 3761A (Stanford).
Schneider, Duane. "The Art of Anais Nin." *Southern Review* (U.S.) 6 (1970): 506–14.
Sukenick, Lynn. "Sense and Sensibility in Women's Fiction: Studies in the Novels of George Eliot, Virginia Woolf, Anais Nin and Doris Lessing." *Dissertation Abstracts International* 35 (1975): 4563A (C.U.N.Y.).
Young, Marguerite. "Marguerite Young on Anais Nin." *Voyages* 1 (Fall 1967): 63–65.
Zee, Nancy, "Towards a Definition of the Woman Artist: Notes on the Diaries of Anais Nin." *Oyez Review* (Roosevelt University) 8 (Winter 1973): 49–55.
Zee, Nancy S. "Anais Nin: Beyond the Mask." *Dissertation Abstracts International* 34 (1974): 6671A (Brown).
Zinnes, Harriet. "Anais Nin's Works Reissued." *Books Abroad* 37 (Summer 1963): 283–86.
Individual Works

Cities of the Interior (1959)

Korges, James. "Review of *Collages* and *Cities of the Interior* by Anais Nin and *Henry Miller: Letters to Anais Nin*, and Other Books." *Critique* 7 (1965): 66–81.

Collages (1964)

Korges, James. "Review of *Collages* and *Cities of the Interior* by Anais Nin and *Henry Miller: Letters to Anais Nin*, and Other Books." *Critique* 7 (1965): 66–81.

Diary (1934–)

McEvilly, Wayne. "The Bread of Tradition: Reflections on the Diary of Anais Nin." *Prairie Schooner* 45 (Summer 1971): 161–67.

McEvilly, Wayne. "Portrait of Anais Nin as a Bodhisattva: Reflections on the Diary 1934–1939." *Studies in the Twentieth Century*, no. 1 (Fall 1968): 51–60.

Nin, Anais. "From the Fourth Journal." *Boston University Journal* 19 (1971): 7–10.

Nin, Anais. "Genesis of the Diary." *Voyages* 2 (Fall 1968): 5–13.

Potts, Margaret L. "The Genesis and Evolution of the Creative Personality: A Rankian Analysis of *The Diary of Anais Nin*, Volumes 1–5." *Dissertation Abstracts International* 34 (1974): 4279A–80A (Southern California).

Spencer, Sharon. " 'Femininity' and the Woman Writer: Doris Lessing's *The Golden Notebook* and the *Diary* of Anais Nin." *Women's Studies* 1 (1973): 247–57.

Stern, Daniel. "The Diary of Anais Nin." *Studies in the Twentieth Century*, no. 1 (Fall 1968): 39–43.

Zaller, Robert M. "Anais Nin and the Truth of Feeling." *Arts in Society* 10 (Summer–Fall 1973): 308–12.

Zee, Nancy. "Towards a Definition of the Woman Artist: Notes on the Diaries of Anais Nin." *Oyez Review* (Roosevelt University) 8 (Winter 1973): 49–55.

The Four-Chambered Heart (1950)

Broderick, Catherine V. "A Comparative Thematic Study of François Mauriac's *Genitrix* and Anais Nin's *The Four-Chambered Heart*." *Dissertation Abstracts International* 31 (1971): 4152A (North Carolina).

ADA NISBET (1907–) U.S.
General Works

Nevius, B. "Ada Nisbet." *Nineteenth Century Fiction* 29 (June 1974): 1–2.

CAROLINE ELIZABETH NORTON, née Sheridan (1808–1877) Great Britain
General Works

Hoge, James H. "Caroline Norton, Lord Melbourne, and the Custody of Infants: Fragments of a Correspondence." *Mary Wollstonecraft Newsletter* 1 (July 1972): 1–8.

Olney, Clarke. "Caroline Norton to Lord Melbourne." *Victorian Studies* 8 (March 1965): 255–62.

Rauchbauer, Otto Hans. "Some Unrecorded Letters by Caroline Norton." *Notes and Queries* 17 (September 1970): 335–39.

FLORA NWAPA (1931–) Nigeria
General Works

Conde, M. "Three Female Writers in Modern Africa: Flora Nwapa, Ama Ata Aidoo and Grace Ogot." *Présence Africaine* 82 (1973): 132–43.

James, Adeala. "IDU: Flora Nwapa." *African Literature Today* 5 (1971): 150–52.

O

Joyce Carol Oates (1938–) U.S.
Bibliography
McCormick, Lucienne P. "A Bibliography of Works by and about Joyce Carol Oates." *American Literature* 43 (March 1971): 124–32.
General Works
Andersen, Sally. "The Poetry of Joyce Carol Oates." *Spirit* 39 (1972): 24–29.
Bellamy, J.D. "Dark Lady of American Letters: Interview." *Atlantic Monthly* (February 1972): 63–67.
Bower, W. "Bliss in the First Person." *Saturday Review* (October 26, 1968): 34–35.
Clemons, Walter. "Joyce Carol Oates: Love and Violence." *Newsweek* (December 11, 1972): 72.
Clemons, Walter. "Joyce Carol Oates at Home." *New York Times Book Review* (September 28, 1969): 4.
Dalton, Elizabeth. "Joyce Carol Oates: Violence in the Head." *Commentary* 49 (June 1970): 75–77.
Dike, Donald A. "The Aggressive Victim in the Fiction of Joyce Carol Oates." *Greyfriar* 15 (1974): 13–29.
Fossum, Robert H. "Only Control: The Novels of Joyce Carol Oates." *Studies in the Novel* 7 (Summer 1975): 285–97.
Grant, Mary Kathryn. "The Tragic Vision of Joyce Carol Oates." *Dissertation Abstracts International* 35 (1975): 4520A (Indiana).
Hodge, Marion Cecil, Jr. "What Moment Is Not Terrible? An Introduction to the Work of Joyce Carol Oates." *Dissertation Abstracts International* 35 (1975): 5407A (Tennessee).
"Hunger for Dreams." *Newsweek* (March 23, 1970): 109A.
Kazin, A. "Oates." *Harper's* (August 1971): 78–82.

Kuehl, Linda. "An Interview with Joyce Carol Oates." *Commonweal* (December 5, 1969): 307–10.
Martin, Alice Conkright. "Toward a Higher Consciousness: A Study of the Novels of Joyce Carol Oates." *Dissertation Abstracts International* 35 (1975): 5415A–16A (Northern Illinois).
Oates, Joyce Carol. "Disguised Fiction." *Publications of the Modern Language Association* 89 (1974): 580–81.
Oates, Joyce Carol. "New Heaven and Earth." *Saturday Review* (November 1972): 51–54.
Oates, Joyce Carol. "Writing as a Natural Reaction." *Time* (October 10, 1969): 108.
Pickering, Samuel F., Jr. "The Short Stories of Joyce Carol Oates." *Georgia Review* 28 (Summer 1974): 218–26.
Pinsker, Sanford. "Isaac Bashevis Singer and Joyce Carol Oates: Some Versions of Gothic." *Southern Review* (U.S.) 9 (1973): 895–908.
Stevens, Cynthia C. "The Imprisoned Imagination: The Family in the Fiction of Joyce Carol Oates, 1960–1970." *Dissertation Abstracts International* 35 (1974): 479A (Illinois).
Sullivan, Walter. "The Artificial Demon: Joyce Carol Oates and the Dimensions of the Real." *Hollins Critic* 9 (December 1972): 1–12.
Sullivan, Walter. "Old Age, Death, and Other Modern Landscapes: Good and Indifferent Fables for Our Time." *Sewanee Review* 82 (Winter 1974): 138–47.
"Transformations of Self: An Interview with Joyce Carol Oates." *Ohio Review* 15 (Fall 1973): 51–61.
Wegs, Joyce M. "The Grotesque in Some American Novels of the Nineteen-Sixties: Ken Kesey, Joyce Carol Oates, Sylvia Plath." *Dissertation Abstracts*

International 34 (1974): 7791A–92A (Illinois).

Individual Works

By the North Gate (1963)

Duus, Louise. "Review of *By the North Gate*." *Critique* 7 (1964): 176–77.

Do with Me What You Will (1973)

Burwell, R.M. "Process of Individuation as Narrative Structure: Joyce Carol Oates' *Do with Me What You Will*." *Critique* 17 (1975): 93–106.

A Garden of Earthly Delights (1967)

Burwell, Rose Marie. "Joyce Carol Oates and an Old Master." *Critique* 15 (1973): 48–58.

Marriages and Infidelities (1972)

Abrahams, William. "Stories of a Visionary." *Saturday Review* (October 1972): 76.

Plot (1972)

Walker, Carolyn. "Fear, Love, and Art in Oates' *Plot*." *Critique* 15 (1973): 59–70.

Them (1969)

De Mott, Benjamin. "The Necessity in Art of a Reflective Intelligence." *Saturday Review* (November 22, 1969): 71.

Where Are You Going, Where Have You Been? (1974)

Wegs, Joyce M. " 'Don't You Know Who I Am?': The Grotesque in Oates's *Where Are You Going, Where Have You Been?*" *Journal of Narrative Technique* 5 (1975): 66–72.

Wonderland (1971)

Waller, G.F. "Joyce Carol Oates' *Wonderland*: An Introduction." *Dalhousie Review* 54 (Autumn 1974): 480–90.

Flannery O'Connor (1925–1964) U.S.

Bibliography

Becham, Gerald. "Flannery O'Connor Collection." *Flannery O'Connor Bulletin* 1 (1972): 66–71.

Brittain, Joan T. "Flannery O'Connor: A Bibliography—Part One." *Bulletin of Bibliography* 25 (September–December 1967): 98–100; Part Two, 25 (January–April 1968): 123–24; "Addenda," (May–August 1968): 142.

Cunningham, John. "Recent Works on Flannery O'Connor: A Review-Essay." *Southern Humanities Review* 8 (Summer 1974): 375–88.

Dorsey, J.E. "Carson McCullers and Flannery O'Connor: A Checklist of Graduate Research." *Bulletin of Bibliography* 32 (October–December 1975): 162–67.

Lackey, Allen D. "Flannery O'Connor: A Supplemental Bibliography of Secondary Sources." *Bulletin of Bibliography* 30 (October–December 1973): 170–75.

General Works

Abbot, Louise Hardeman. "Remembering Flannery O'Connor." *Southern Literary Journal* 2 (Spring 1970): 3–25.

Alice, Sister Rose. "Flannery O'Connor: Poet to the Outcast." *Renascence* 16 (Spring 1964): 126–32.

Asals, Frederick J., Jr. "Flannery O'Connor: An Interpretive Study." *Dissertation Abstracts International* 33 (1973): 6897A–98A (Brown).

Asals, Frederick, Jr. "Flannery O'Connor as Novelist: A Defense." *Flannery O'Connor Bulletin* 3 (1974): 23–39.

Barcus, Nancy B. "Psychological Determinism and Freedom in Flannery O'Connor." *Cithara* 12 (1972): 26–33.

Bassan, Maurice. "Flannery O'Connor's Way: Shock with Moral Intent." *Renascence* 15 (Summer 1963): 195–99.

Baumbach, Georgia A. "The Psychology of Flannery O'Connor's Fictive World." *Dissertation Abstracts International* 34 (1973): 304A (Ohio State).

Baumbach, Jonathan. "The Acid of God's Grace: The Fiction of Flannery O'Connor." *Georgia Review* 17 (Fall 1963): 334–46.

Bergup, Sister Bernice. "Themes of Redemptive Grace in the Works of Flannery O'Connor." *American Benedictine Review* 21 (June 1970): 169–91.

Bertrande, Sister. "Four Stories of Flannery O'Connor." *Thought* 37 (1962): 410–26.

Blackwell, Annie Louise. "The Artistry of Flannery O'Connor." *Dissertation Abstracts* 27 (1968): 3862A (Florida State).

Blackwell, Annie Louise. "Flannery O'Connor's Literary Style." *Antigone Review* 10 (1972): 57–66.

Brewster, Rudolph A. "The Literary Devices in the Writings of Flannery O'Connor." *Dissertation Abstracts* 29 (1970): 3572A (Texas State).

Brittain, Joan T. "The Fictional Family of Flannery O'Connor." *Renascence* 19 (Fall 1966): 48–52.

Brittain, Joan T., and Leon V. Driskell. "O'Connor and the Eternal Crossroads." *Renascence* 22 (Autumn 1969): 49–55.

Browning, Preston M., Jr. "Flannery O'Connor and the Demonic." *Modern Fiction Studies* 19 (Spring

1973): 29–41.

Burke, John J., Jr. "Convergence of Flannery O'Connor and Chardin." *Renascence* 19 (Fall 1966): 41.

Burns, Stuart L. "Flannery O'Connor's Literary Apprenticeship." *Renascence* 22 (Autumn 1969): 3–16.

Burns, Stuart L. "Freaks in a Circus Tent: Flannery O'Connor's Christ-Haunted Characters." *Flannery O'Connor Bulletin* 1 (1972): 3–23.

Burns, Stuart L. "O'Connor and the Critics: An Overview." *Mississippi Quarterly* 27 (Fall 1974): 483–95.

Burns, Stuart L. " 'Torn by the Lord's Eye': Flannery O'Connor's Use of Sun Imagery." *Twentieth Century Literature* 13 (October 1967): 154–66.

Carlson, Thomas M. "Flannery O'Connor: The Manichaean Dilemma." *Dissertation Abstracts International* 34 (1973): 2613A (North Carolina).

Carlson, Thomas M. "Flannery O'Connor: The Manichaean Dilemma." *Sewanee Review* 77 (Spring 1969): 254–76.

Cheney, Brainard. "Flannery O'Connor's Campaign for Her Country." *Sewanee Review* 72 (Autumn 1964): 555–58.

Cheney, Brainard. "Miss O'Connor Creates Unusual Humor Out of Ordinary Sin." *Sewanee Review* 71 (Autumn 1963): 644–52.

Cleveland, Carol L. "Psychological Violence: The World of Flannery O'Connor." *Dissertation Abstracts International* 34 (1974): 5959A (St. Louis).

Coleman, Richard. "Flannery O'Connor: A Scrutiny of Two Forms of Her Many-Leveled Art." *Phoenix* 1 (1966): 30–66.

Connolly, Janet Maroney. "The Fiction of Flannery O'Connor." *Dissertation Abstracts* 28 (1967): 670A (Columbia).

Cooper, Arthur. "Picaresque Prophetess." *Newsweek* (July 2, 1973): 66

Cruser, Paul Alexander. "The Fiction of Flannery O'Connor." *Dissertation Abstracts International* 31 (1971): 2910A (Penn.).

Darretta, John L. "The Idea and Image of Retribution in the Fiction of Flannery O'Connor." *Dissertation Abstracts International* 33 (1973): 4406A–7A (Fordham).

Davis, Barnabas. "Flannery O'Connor: Christian Belief in Recent Fiction." *Listening* (Autumn 1965): 5–19.

Davis, Jack and Jane. "Tarwater and Jonah: Two

Reluctant Prophets." *Xavier University Studies* 9 (Spring 1970): 19–27.

Desmond, John Francis. "Christian Historical Analogues in the Fiction of William Faulkner and Flannery O'Connor." *Dissertation Abstracts International* 32 (1972): 3994A (Oklahoma).

Detweiler, Robert. "The Curse of Christ in Flannery O'Connor's Fiction." *Comparative Literature Studies* 3 (1965): 235–45.

"Diverse Readings of Flannery O'Connor." *Sewanee Review* 76 (Spring 1968): 261–356.

Donner, Robert. "She Writes Powerful Fiction." *Sign* 40 (March 1961): 46–48.

Dowell, Bob. "The Moment of Grace in the Fiction of Flannery O'Connor." *College English* 27 (December 1965): 235–39.

Drake, Robert, Jr. " 'The Bleeding Stinking Mad Shadow of Jesus' in the Fiction of Flannery O'Connor." *Comparative Literature Studies* 3 (1965): 183–86.

Drake, Robert, Jr. "Flannery O'Connor and American Literature." *Flannery O'Connor Bulletin* 3 (1974): 1–22.

Drake, Robert, Jr. "Harrowing Evangel of Flannery O'Connor." *Christian Century* (September 30, 1964): 1200–1202.

Drake, Robert Y., Jr. "Miss O'Connor: The Shadow and the Substance." *College English Association Critic* 32 (April 1970): 13.

Drake, Robert Y., Jr. "The Paradigm of Flannery O'Connor's True Country." *Studies in Short Fiction* 6 (Summer 1969): 433–42.

Duffy, Martha. "At Gunpoint." *Time* (November 29, 1971): 87–88.

Duhamel, P. Albert. "Flannery O'Connor's Violent View of Reality." *Catholic World* (February 1960): 280–85.

Dunn, Robert J. "A Mode of Good: Form and Philosophy in the Fiction of Flannery O'Connor." *Dissertation Abstracts International* 32 (1972): 3995A–96A (Michigan).

Dunn, Sister Francis Mary. "Function and Implications of Setting in the Fiction of Flannery O'Connor." *Dissertation Abstracts* 27 (1967): 3043A (Catholic U.).

"Dust for Art's Sake." *Time* (May 30, 1969): 70.

Edelstein, Mark G. "Flannery O'Connor and the Problem of Modern Satire." *Studies in Short Fiction* 12 (Spring 1975): 139–44.

Eggenschwiler, David. "Flannery O'Connor's True

and False Prophets." *Renascence* 21 (Spring 1969): 151.

Farnham, J.F. "The Grotesque in Flannery O'Connor." *America* (May 13, 1961): 277.

Farnham, James F. "Disintegration of Myth in the Writings of Flannery O'Connor." *Connecticut Review* 8 (October 1974): 11–19.

Farnham, James F. "The Essential Flannery O'Connor." *Cross Currents* 15 (Summer 1965): 376–78.

Feeley, Sister M. Kathleen. "Thematic Imagery in the Fiction of Flannery O'Connor." *Southern Humanities Review* 3 (Winter 1968): 14–32.

Finger, Larry L. "Elements of the Grotesque in Selected Works of Welty, Capote, McCullers, and O'Connor." *Dissertation Abstracts International* 33 (1972): 1721A–22A (George Peabody College for Teachers).

Fremantle, Ann. "If a Seed Fall." *Commonweal* (February 16, 1962): 545–46.

Friedman, Melvin J. "By and about Flannery O'Connor." *Journal of Modern Literature* 1 (1970–1971): 288–92.

Friedman, Melvin J. "Flannery O'Connor: Another Legend in Southern Fiction." *English Journal* 51 (April 1962): 233–43.

Friedman, Melvin J. "Flannery O'Connor: The Tonal Dilemma." *Southern Literary Journal* 6 (Spring 1974): 124–29.

Fugin, Katherine, et al. "An Interview with Flannery O'Connor." *Censer* (Fall 1960): 28–30.

Gabel, Sister Mariella. "Ecumenical Core in Flannery O'Connor's Fiction." *American Benedictine Review* 15 (June 1964): 127–43.

Gilman, Richard. "On Flannery O'Connor." *New York Review of Books* (August 21, 1969): 24.

Golden, Robert E. "Violence and Art in Postwar American Literature: A Study of O'Connor, Kosinski, Hawkes, and Pynchon." *Dissertation Abstracts International* 33 (1972): 311A (Rochester).

Gordon, Caroline. "Heresy in Dixie." *Sewanee Review* 77 (Spring 1969): 263–97.

Gordon, Caroline. "Rebels and Revolutionaries: The New American Scene." *Flannery O'Connor Bulletin* 3 (1974): 40–56.

Gordon, Caroline, Robert Drake, Jr., Frederick Asals, Jr., Rosa Lee Walston, and Marion Montgomery. "Panel Discussion." *Flannery O'Connor Bulletin* 3 (1974): 57–78.

Gossett, T.F. "No Vague Believer: Flannery O'Connor and Protestantism." *Southwest Review* 60 (Summer 1975): 256–63.

Gossett, Thomas F. "Flannery O'Connor on Her Fiction." *Southwest Review* 59 (Winter 1974): 34–42.

Gossett, Thomas F. "Flannery O'Connor's Opinions of Other Writers: Some Unpublished Comments." *Southern Literary Journal* 6 (Spring 1974): 70–82.

Gregory, Donald L. "An Internal Analysis of the Fiction of Flannery O'Connor." *Dissertation Abstracts* 28 (1968): 5055A (Ohio State).

Griffith, Albert. "Flannery O'Connor." *America* (November 27, 1965): 674–75.

Hamblen, Abigail A. "Flannery O'Connor's Study of Innocence and Evil." *University Review* (Kansas) 34 (1968): 295–97.

Hand, John T. "Letters to the Laodiceans: The Romantic Quest in Flannery O'Connor." *Dissertation Abstracts International* 32 (1972): 5227A–28A (Kent State).

Hauser, James D. "The Broken Cosmos of Flannery O'Connor: The Design of Her Fiction." *Dissertation Abstracts International* 34 (1973): 1912A (Penn.).

Hawkes, John. "Flannery O'Connor's Devil." *Sewanee Review,* 70 (Summer 1962): 395–407.

Hendin, Josephine. "In Search of Flannery O'Connor." *Columbia Forum* 13 (Spring 1970): 38–41.

Hicks, Granville. "A Cold, Hard Look at Humankind." *Saturday Review* (May 29, 1965): 22–23.

Hicks, Granville. "Literary Horizons." *Saturday Review* (May 10, 1969): 30.

Hicks, Granville. "A Writer at Home with Her Heritage." *Saturday Review* (May 12, 1962): 22–23.

Hoffman, Arnold Ray. "The Sense of Place: Peter de Vries, J. F. Powers and Flannery O'Connor." *Dissertation Abstracts* 31 (1971): 6059A (Michigan).

Hoffman, Eleanor M.R. "A Study of the Major Structures Intrinsic to the Fiction of Flannery O'Connor." *Dissertation Abstracts* 33 (1973): 3649A (Texas).

Howell, Elmo. "The Developing Art of Flannery O'Connor." *Arizona Quarterly* 29 (Autumn 1973): 266–76.

Howell, Elmo. "Flannery O'Connor and the Home

Country." *Renascence* 24 (Summer 1972): 171–76.

Ingram, Forrest L. "O'Connor's Seven-Story Cycle." *Flannery O'Connor Bulletin* 2 (1973): 19–28.

Jacobsen, Josephine. "A Catholic Quartet." *Christian Scholar* 47 (1964): 139–54.

Jeremy, Sister. "Comic Ritual of Flannery O'Connor." *Catholic Library World* 39 (November 1967): 195–200.

Johnson, Rhonda E. "A Translation of Silence: The Fiction of Flannery O'Connor." *Dissertation Abstracts International* 34 (1973): 3403A (S.U.N.Y., Buffalo).

Jones, Bartlett C. "Depth Psychology and Literary Study." *Midcontinent American Studies Journal* 5 (1964): 50–56.

Jordon, Rene. "A Southern Drawl from Beyond the Grave." *British Association for American Studies Bulletin* 12–13 (1966): 99–101.

Katz, Claire. "Flannery O'Connor's Rage of Vision." *American Literature* 46 (March 1974): 54–67.

Katz, Claire Rose. "Flannery O'Connor: A Rage of Vision." *Dissertation Abstracts International* 35 (1975): 6719A (California, Berkeley).

Keller, Jane Carter. "The Comic Spirit in the Works of Flannery O'Connor." *Dissertation Abstracts* 31 (1971): 2922A (Tulane).

Keller, Jane Carter. "The Figures of the Empiricist and the Rationalist in the Fiction of Flannery O'Connor." *Arizona Quarterly* 28 (Autumn 1972): 263–73.

Kellog, Jean D. "Serious Comedy." *Christian Century* (December 21, 1966): 1575–76.

Kellog, Jean D. "We Have Had Our Fall." *Christian Century* (July 9, 1969): 927.

Kirkland, William M. "Flannery O'Connor: The Person and the Writer." *East-West Review* 8 (Summer 1967): 159–63.

Klevar, Harvey. "Image and Imagination: Flannery O'Connor's Front Page Fiction." *Journal of Modern Literature* 4 (1974): 121–32.

Klevar, Harvey Lee. "The Sacredly Profane and Profanely Sacred: Flannery O'Connor and Erskine Caldwell as Interpreters of Southern Cultural and Religious Traditions." *Dissertation Abstracts International* 31 (1971): 5407A–8A (Minnesota).

Lackey, Allen D. "Flannery O'Connor and Her Critics: A Survey and Evaluation of the Critical Response to the Fiction of Flannery O'Connor."

Dissertation Abstracts International 33 (1972): 2383A–84A (Tennessee).

Langford, Roberta B. "The Comic Sense of Flannery O'Connor." *Dissertation Abstracts International* 35 (1974): 2995A–96A (Duke).

Lensing, George. "De Chardin's Ideas in Flannery O'Connor." *Renascence* 18 (Summer 1966): 171–75.

Lipper, Mark. "Blessed Are the Destitute in Flannery O'Connor." *Shippensburg State College Review* (October 1968): 20–23.

Lorch, T. "Flannery O'Connor: Christian Allegorist." *Criticism* 10 (1968): 69–80.

Maloff, Saul. "On Flannery O'Connor." *Commonweal* (August 8, 1969): 490–91.

Martin, Carter. "Flannery O'Connor and Fundamental Poverty." *English Journal* 60 (April 1971): 458–61.

Martin, Carter. "Flannery O'Connor's Early Fiction." *Southern Humanities Review* 7 (Spring 1973): 210–14.

Mary Alice, Sister. "My Mentor, Flannery O'Connor." *Saturday Review* (May 29, 1965): 24–25.

May, John R. "Flannery O'Connor: Critical Consensus and the 'Objective' Interpretation." *Renascence* 27 (Summer 1975): 179–92.

May, John R. "Flannery O'Connor and the New Hermeneutic." *Flannery O'Connor Bulletin* 2 (1973): 29–42.

May, John R. "The Pruning World: Flannery O'Connor's Judgment of Intellectuals." *Southern Humanities Review* 4 (Fall 1970): 325–38.

Mayer, David R. "Blazing Sun and the Relentless Shutter: The Kindred Arts of Flannery O'Connor and Diane Arbus." *Christian Century* (April 30, 1975): 435–40.

Mayer, David R. "The Hermaphrodite and the Host: Incarnation as Vision and Method in the Fiction of Flannery O'Connor." *Dissertation Abstracts International* 34 (1973): 3415A–16A (Maryland).

Mayhew, L.F.S. "Flannery O'Connor: 1925–1964." *Commonweal* (August 21, 1964): 562–63.

McCarthy, J. F. "Human Intelligence versus Divine Truth: The Intellectual in Flannery O'Connor's Works." *English Journal* 55 (December 1966): 1143–48.

McDowell, Frederick P.W. "Toward the Luminous and the Numinous: The Art of Flannery O'Connor." *Southern Review* (U.S.) 9 (1973):

998–1013.

McKenzie, B. "Flannery O'Connor Country: A Photo Essay." *Georgia Review* 29 (Summer 1975): 328–62.

Meaders, Margaret Inman. "Flannery O'Connor: Literary Witch." *Colorado Quarterly* 10 (Spring 1962): 377–86.

Mehl, Duane Paul. "Spiritual Reality in the Works of Flannery O'Connor." *Dissertation Abstracts International* 35 (1975): 3716A (St. Louis).

Mellard, James M. "Violence and Belief in Mauriac and O'Connor." *Renascence* 26 (Spring 1974): 158–68.

"Memento Mori." *Times Literary Supplement* (March 24, 1966): 242.

Merton, Thomas. "The Other Side of Despair." *Critic* 23 (October–November 1965): 13–23.

Montgomery, Marion. "Beyond Symbol and Surface: The Fiction of Flannery O'Connor." *Georgia Review* 22 (Summer 1968): 188–93.

Montgomery, Marion. "Flannery O'Connor: Prophetic Poet." *Flannery O'Connor Bulletin* 3 (1974): 79–94.

Montgomery, Marion. "Flannery O'Connor and the Natural Man." *Mississippi Quarterly* 21 (Fall 1968): 235–42.

Montgomery, Marion. "Flannery O'Connor's Territorial Center." *Criticism* 11 (1969): 5–10.

Montgomery, Marion. "Flannery O'Connor's Transformation of the Sentimental." *Mississippi Quarterly* 25 (Winter 1971–1972): 1–18.

Montgomery, Marion. "In Defense of Flannery O'Connor's Dragon." *Georgia Review* 25 (Fall 1971): 302–16.

Montgomery, Marion. "Miss O'Connor and the Christ-Haunted." *Southern Review* (U.S.) 4 (1968): 665–72.

Montgomery, Marion. "A Note on Flannery O'Connor's Terrible and Violent Prophecy of Mercy." *Forum* 7 (Summer 1969): 4–7.

Montgomery, Marion. "O'Connor and Teilhard de Chardin: The Problem of Evil." *Renascence* 22 (Autumn 1969): 34–42.

Montgomery, Marion. "The Prophet's Eye." *Triumph* 4 (October 1969): 35–36.

Muller, Gilbert Henry. "The City of Woe: Flannery O'Connor's Dantean Vision." *Georgia Review* 23 (Summer 1969): 206–13.

Muller, Gilbert Henry. "Flannery O'Connor and the Catholic Grotesque." *Dissertation Abstracts* 28

(1969): 3193A (Stanford).

Mullins, C. Ross, Jr. "Flannery O'Connor: An Interview." *Jubilee* 11 (June 1963): 34.

Murray, J. "Southland à la Russe." *Critic* 21 (June–July 1963): 26–28.

Mutkeski, Barbara E. "The Teilhard Milieu: Pierre Teilhard de Chardin's Influence on Flannery O'Connor's Fiction." *Dissertation Abstracts International* 34 (1974): 5196A (Fordham).

Nance, William L. "Flannery O'Connor: The Trouble with Being a Prophet." *University Review* (Kansas) 36 (1969): 101–8.

Neligan, Dorris P. "A Room for Flannery." *Columns* 18 (Fall 1972): 3–6.

Nisby, Paul Wayne. "Flannery O'Connor and the Gothic Impulse." *Dissertation Abstracts International* 35 (1975): 892A (Kansas).

"The Novelist and Free Will." *Fresco* 1 (Winter 1961): 100–101.

Oates, Joyce Carol. "The Visionary Art of Flannery O'Connor." *Southern Humanities Review* 7 (Summer 1973): 235–46.

O'Brien, John T. "The Unchristianity of Flannery O'Connor." *Listening* 5 (Winter 1971): 71–81.

Orvell, Miles D. "Flannery O'Connor." *Sewanee Review* 78 (Winter 1970): 184–92.

Padgett, Thomas E., Jr. "The Irony in Flannery O'Connor's Fiction." *Dissertation Abstracts International* 33 (1973): 5192A (Missouri).

Palms, Rosemary H.G. "The Double Motif in Literature: From Origins to an Examination of Three Modern American Novels." *Dissertation Abstracts International* 33 (1972): 321A (Texas).

Pearce, Howard D. "Flannery O'Connor's Ineffable Recognitions." *Genre* 6 (1973): 298–312.

Quinn, J.J. "A Reading of Flannery O'Connor." *Thought* 48 (1973): 520–31.

Rosliep, Raymond. "Flannery O'Connor, 1925–1964." *Georgia Review* 19 (Fall 1965): 368.

Rupp, Richard H. "Flannery O'Connor." *Commonweal* (December 6, 1963): 304–7.

Samuels, Charles Thomas. "Flannery O'Connor: From Theology to Fable." *Book World* (May 4, 1969): 1.

Schott, W. "Flannery O'Connor: Faith's Stepchild." *Nation* (September 13, 1965): 142–44.

Scouten, Kenneth. "The Mythological Dimensions of Five of Flannery O'Connor's Works." *Flannery O'Connor Bulletin* 2 (1973): 59–72.

Shapiro, C. "Heroic Chauvinism." *Novel* 8 (Fall

1974): 78–80.

Shear, Walter. "Flannery O'Connor: Character and Characterization." *Renascence* 20 (Spring 1968): 140–46.

Sherry, Gerard. "An Interview with Flannery O'Connor." *Critic* 21 (June–July 1963): 29–31.

Shinn, Thelma J. "Flannery O'Connor and the Violence of Grace." *Wisconsin Studies in Contemporary Literature* 9 (Winter 1968): 58–73.

Shloss, Carol. "The Limits of Inference: Flannery O'Connor and the Representation of 'Mystery.'" *Dissertation Abstracts International* 35 (1975): 5427A (Brandeis).

Short, Donald Aubrey. "The Concrete in Her Medium: The Fiction of Flannery O'Connor." *Dissertation Abstracts* 30 (1971): 3476A (Pittsburgh).

Smith, J.O. "Ritual and Violence in Flannery O'Connor." *Thought* 41 (1966): 545–60.

Sonnenfeld, Albert. "Flannery O'Connor: The Catholic Writer as Baptist." *Contemporary Literature* 13 (Autumn 1972): 445–57.

Spiegel, Alan. "A Theory of the Grotesque in Southern Fiction." *Georgia Review* 26 (Winter 1972): 426–37.

Spivey, Ted R. "Flannery O'Connor's View of God and Man." *Studies in Short Fiction* 1 (Spring 1964): 200–206.

Stelzmann, Rainulf. "Shock and Orthodoxy: An Interpretation of Flannery O'Connor's Novels and Short Stories." *Xavier University Studies* 2 (March 1963): 4–21.

Stephens, Martha. "Flannery O'Connor and the Sanctified-Sinner Tradition." *Arizona Quarterly* 24 (Autumn 1968): 223–39.

Stephens, Martha. "An Introduction to the Work of Flannery O'Connor." *Dissertation Abstracts* 29 (1969): 3157A (Indiana).

Stern, Richard. "Flannery O'Connor: A Remembrance and Some Letters." *Shenandoah* 16 (1965): 5–10.

Strassberg, Mildred P. "Religious Commitment in Recent American Fiction: Flannery O'Connor, Bernard Malamud, John Updike." *Dissertation Abstracts International* 32 (1972): 6457A (S.U.N.Y., Stony Brook).

Sullivan, Walter. "The Achievement of Flannery O'Connor." *Southern Humanities Review* 2 (Summer 1968): 303–9.

Sweeney, Francis. "One Gets the Blood of the Narrator on One's Hands." *New York Times Book Review* (February 13, 1972): 30.

Taylor, Henry. "The Halt Shall Be Gathered Together: Physical Deformity in the Fiction of Flannery O'Connor." *Western Humanities Review* 22 (Autumn 1968): 325–38.

TeSelle, S.M. "Experience of Coming to Belief." *Theology Today* 32 (July 1975): 159–65.

True, Michael D. "Flannery O'Connor: Backwoods Prophet in the Secular City." *Papers on Language and Literature* 5 (1969): 209–23.

Vande Kieft, Ruth M. "Judgment in the Fiction of Flannery O'Connor." *Sewanee Review* 76 (Spring 1968): 337–56.

Walker, Alice. "Beyond the Peacock: The Reconstruction of Flannery O'Connor." *Ms.* (December 1975): 77.

Walsh, Thomas F. "The Devils of Hawthorne and Flannery O'Connor." *Xavier University Studies* 5 (January 1966): 117–22.

Walston, Rosa Lee. "Flannery: An Affectionate Recollection." *Flannery O'Connor Bulletin* 1 (1972): 55–60.

Walston, Rosa Lee. "Flannery O'Connor—A Good Writer Is Hard to Find." *Columns* 7 (Fall 1965): 8–13.

Walston, Rosa Lee. "Flannery O'Connor as Seen by a Friend." *Carrell* 14 (1974): 16–24.

Wilson, James D. "Luis Buñel, Flannery O'Connor and the Failure of Charity." *Minnesota Review*, NRP 4 (Spring 1973): 158–62.

Wylder, Jean. "Flannery O'Connor: A Reminiscence and Some Letters." *North American Review* 225 (Spring 1970): 58–65.

Wynne, J.F. "Sacramental Irony of Flannery O'Connor." *Southern Literary Journal* 7 (Spring 1975): 33–49.

Individual Works

The Artificial Nigger (1964)

Byrd, Turner F. "Ironic Dimension in Flannery O'Connor's *The Artificial Nigger*." *Mississippi Quarterly* 21 (Fall 1968): 243–51.

Goss, James. "The Double Action of Mercy in *The Artificial Nigger*." *Christianity and Literature* 23 (Spring 1974): 36–45.

Hays, Peter L. "Dante, Tobit, and *The Artificial Nigger*." *Studies in Short Fiction* 5 (Spring 1968): 263–68.

The Church and the Fiction Writer (1957)

Hegarty, Charles M. "A Note on Flannery O'Connor." *Studies in Short Fiction* 9 (Fall 1972): 409–10.

The Comforts of Home (1960)

Millichap, Joseph R. "The Pauline 'Old Man' in Flannery O'Connor's *The Comforts of Home*." *Studies in Short Fiction* 11 (Winter 1974): 96–99.

The Displaced Person (1954)

Fitzgerald, Robert. "The Countryside and the True Country." *Sewanee Review* 70 (Summer 1962): 380–84.

Joselyn, Sister M. "Thematic Centers in *The Displaced Person*." *Studies in Short Fiction* 1 (Winter 1964): 85–92. .

Male, Roy R. "The Two Versions of *The Displaced Person*." *Studies in Short Fiction* 7 (Summer 1970): 450–57.

Everything That Rises Must Converge (1965)

Coffey, Warren. "Flannery O'Connor." *Commentary* 40 (November 1965): 93–99.

Desmond, John F. "The Lessons of History: Flannery O'Connor's *Everything That Rises Must Converge*." *Flannery O'Connor Bulletin* 1 (1972): 39–45.

Esch, Robert M. "O'Connor's *Everything That Rises Must Converge*." *Explicator* 27 (April 1969): Item 58.

Kane, Patricia. "Flannery O'Connor's *Everything That Rises Must Converge*." *Critique* 8 (1965): 89–91.

Kann, Jean Marie. "*Everything That Rises Must Converge*." *Catholic World* (December 1966): 154–59.

Maida, Patricia Dinneen. " 'Convergence' in Flannery O'Connor's *Everything That Rises Must Converge*." *Studies in Short Fiction* 7 (Fall 1970): 549–55.

Montgomery, Marion. "On Flannery O'Connor's *Everything That Rises Must Converge*." *Critique* 13 (1971): 15–29.

Snow, Ollye Tine. "The Functional Gothic in Flannery O'Connor." *Southwest Review* 50 (Summer 1965): 286–99.

Sullivan, Walter. "Flannery O'Connor, Sin, and Grace: *Everything That Rises Must Converge*." *Hollins Critic* 2 (September 1965): 1.

Good Country People (1955)

Jones, Bartlett C. "Depth Psychology and Literary Study." *Midcontinent American Studies Journal* 5

(1964): 50–56.

Smith, Anneliese. "O'Connor's *Good Country People*." *Explicator* 33 (December 1974): Item 30.

A Good Man Is Hard to Find (1955)

Brittain, J.T. "O'Connor's *A Good Man Is Hard to Find*." *Explicator* 26 (September 1967): Item 1.

Brown, Ashley. "Grotesque Occasions." *Spectator* (September 6, 1968): 330–32.

Doxey, William S. "A Dissenting Opinion of Flannery O'Connor's *A Good Man Is Hard to Find*." *Studies in Short Fiction* 10 (Spring 1973): 199–204.

Kropf, C.R. "Theme and Setting in *A Good Man Is Hard to Find*." *Renascence* 24 (Summer 1972): 177–80.

Marks, W.S., III. "Advertisements for Grace: Flannery O'Connor's *A Good Man Is Hard to Find*." *Studies in Short Fiction* 4 (Fall 1966): 19–27.

Martin, Sister M. "O'Connor's *A Good Man Is Hard to Find*." *Explicator* 24 (October 1965): Item 19.

Matchie, Thomas Frederick. "Mythical Flannery O'Connor: A Psycho-Mythic Study of *A Good Man Is Hard To Find*." *Dissertation Abstracts International* 36 (1975): 277A (Wisconsin).

Montgomery, Marion. "Miss Flannery's *A Good Man Is Hard To Find*." *Denver Quarterly* 3 (Spring 1968): 1–19.

Greenleaf (1956)

Asals, Frederick, Jr. "The Mythic Dimensions of Flannery O'Connor's 'Greenleaf.' " *Studies in Short Fiction* 5 (Summer 1968): 317–30.

The Lame Shall Enter First (1962)

Asals, Frederick J., Jr. "Hawthorne, Mary Ann, and *The Lame Shall Enter First*." *Flannery O'Connor Bulletin* 2 (1973): 3–18.

Asals, Frederick, Jr. "Flannery O'Connor's *The Lame Shall Enter First*." *Mississippi Quarterly* 23 (Spring 1970): 103–20.

Kane, Patricia. "Flannery O'Connor's *The Lame Shall Enter First*." *Critique* 8 (1965): 85–88.

Spivey, Ted. "Flannery O'Connor's View of God and Man." *Studies in Short Fiction* 1 (Spring 1964): 200–206.

Spivey, Ted R. "Flannery's South: Don Quixote Rides Again." *Flannery O'Connor Bulletin* 1 (1972): 46–53.

Leaden Tract Against Complacency and Contraception (1955)

Montgomery, Marion. "Flannery O'Connor's

Leaden Tract Against Complacency and Contraception." *Arizona Quarterly* 24 (Summer 1968): 133–46.

The Life You Save May Be Your Own (1953)

Desmond, John. "The Shifting of Mr. Shiftlet: Flannery O'Connor's *The Life You Save May Be Your Own.*" *Mississippi Quarterly* 28 (Winter 1974–1975): 55–59.

Griffith, A.J. "Flannery O'Connor's Salvation Road." *Studies in Short Fiction* 3 (Spring 1966): 329–33.

Hegarty, Charles M. "A Man Thought Not Yet a Whole One: Mr. Shiftlet's Genesis." *Flannery O'Connor Bulletin* 1 (1972): 24–38.

Parker's Back (1965)

Browning, Preston M., Jr. " 'Parker's Back': Flannery O'Connor's Iconography of Salvation by Profanity." *Studies in Short Fiction* 6 (Fall 1969): 525–35.

Driskell, Leon. " 'Parker's Back' vs. 'The Partridge Festival': Flannery O'Connor's Critical Choice." *Georgia Review* 21 (Winter 1967): 476–90.

Fahey, William A. "Flannery O'Connor's 'Parker's Back.' " *Renascence* 20 (Spring 1968): 162.

The Partridge Festival (1961)

Driskell, Leon. " 'Parker's Back' vs. 'The Partridge Festival': Flannery O'Connor's Critical Choice." *Georgia Review* 21 (Winter 1967): 476–90.

A Temple of the Holy Ghost (1954)

Mayer, David R. "Apologia for the Imagination: Flannery O'Connor's *A Temple of the Holy Ghost.*" *Studies in Short Fiction* 11 (Spring 1974): 147–52.

The Train (1948)

Harrison, Margaret. "Hazel Motes in Transit: A Comparison of Two Versions of Flannery O'Connor's *The Train* with Chapter One of *Wise Blood.*" *Studies in Short Fiction* 8 (Spring 1971): 287–93.

A View of the Woods (1957)

Kane, Patricia. "Flannery O'Connor's *A View of the Woods.*" *Critique* 8 (1965): 85–91.

The Violent Bear It Away (1960)

Ballif, Algene, "A Southern Allegory—*The Violent Bear It Away.*" *Commentary* 30 (October 1960): 358–62.

Bower, Robert O. "Hope vs. Despair in the New Gothic Novel." *Renascence* 13 (Spring 1961): 147–52.

Burns, Stuart L. "Flannery O'Connor's *The Violent*

Bear It Away: Apotheosis in Failure." *Sewanee Review* 76 (Spring 1968): 319–36.

Desmond, John F. "The Mystery of the Word and the Act: *The Violent Bear It Away.*" *American Benedictine Review* 24 (September 1973): 342–47.

Duhamel, P. Albert. "Flannery O'Connor's Violent View of Reality." *Catholic World* (February 1960): 280–85.

Fahey, William A. "Out of the Eater: Flannery O'Connor's Appetite for Truth." *Renascence* 20 (Autumn 1967): 22–29.

Ferris, Sumner J. "The Outside and the Inside: Flannery O'Connor's *The Violent Bear It Away.*" *Critique* 3 (1960): 11–19.

Jeremy, Sister. "*The Violent Bear It Away*: A Linguistic Education." *Renascence* 17 (Fall 1964): 11–16.

May, John R. "*The Violent Bear It Away*: The Meaning of the Title." *Flannery O'Connor Bulletin* 2 (1973): 83–86.

Mayer, David R. "*The Violent Bear It Away*: Flannery O'Connor's Shaman." *Southern Literary Journal* 4 (Spring 1972): 41–54.

McCown, Robert M. "The Education of a Prophet: A Study of Flannery O'Connor's *The Violent Bear It Away.*" *Kansas Magazine* (1962): 73–78.

Muller, Gilbert H. "*The Violent Bear It Away*: Moral and Dramatic Sense." *Renascence* 22 (Autumn 1969): 17–25.

Nolde, M. Simon. "*The Violent Bear It Away*: A Study in Imagery." *Xavier University Studies* 1 (Spring 1961–1962): 180–94.

Smith, Francis J. "O'Connor's Religious Viewpoint in *The Violent Bear It Away.*" *Renascence* 22 (Winter 1970): 108–12.

Trowbridge, Clinton W. "The Symbolic Vision of Flannery O'Connor: Patterns of Imagery in *The Violent Bear It Away.*" *Sewanee Review* 76 (Spring 1968): 298–318.

Wise Blood (1952)

Asals, Frederick, Jr. "The Road to *Wise Blood.*" *Renascence* 21 (Summer 1969): 181–94.

Burns, Stuart L. "The Evolution of *Wise Blood.*" *Modern Fiction Studies* 16 (Summer 1970): 147–62.

Burns, Stuart L. "Structural Patterns in *Wise Blood.*" *Xavier University Studies* 8 (July 1969): 32–43.

Burrows, Miles. "Little Monsters." *New Statesman* (February 2, 1968): 146.

Dula, Martha A. "Evidence of the Prelapsarian in

Flannery O'Connor's *Wise Blood.*" *Xavier University Studies* 11 (Winter 1972): 1–12.

Green, James L. "Enoch Emery and His Biblical Namesakes in *Wise Blood.* "*Studies in Shot Fiction* 10 (Fall 1973): 417–19.

Harrison, Margaret. "Hazel Motes in Transit: A Comparison of Two Versions of Flannery O'Connor's *The Train* with Chapter One of *Wise Blood.*" *Studies in Short Fiction* 8 (Spring 1971): 287–93.

Lawson, Lewis A. "Flannery O'Connor and the Grotesque: *Wise Blood.*" *Renascence* 17 (Spring 1965): 137–47.

Littlefield, Daniel F., Jr. "Flannery O'Connor's *Wise Blood*: 'Unparalleled Prosperity' and Spiritual Chaos." *Mississippi Quarterly* 23 (Spring 1970): 121–33.

McCullagh, James C. "Symbolism and the Religious Aesthetic: Flannery O'Connor's *Wise Blood.*" *Flannery O'Connor Bulletin* 2 (1973): 43–58.

Rechnitz, Robert M. "Passionate Pilgrim: Flannery O'Connor's *Wise Blood.*" *Georgia Review* 19 (Fall 1965): 310–16.

Tate, James Oliver, Jr. "Flannery O'Connor and *Wise Blood*: The Significance of the Early Draft." *Dissertation Abstracts International* 35 (1975): 2828A (Columbia).

GRACE OGOT (fl. 1960s–1970s) Kenya
General Works

Conde, M. "Three Female Writers in Modern Africa: Flora Nwapa, Ama Ata Aidoo and Grace Ogot." *Présence Africaine* 82 (1973): 132–43.

MARGARET OLIPHANT, née Wilson (1828–1897) Scotland

General Works

Colby, Vineta. "William Wilson, Novelist." *Notes and Queries* 13 (February 1966): 60–66.

Leavis, Q.D. "Mrs. Oliphant." *Listener* (December 18, 1969): 891–92.

Lochhead, Marion. "Margaret Oliphant: A Half-Forgotten Victorian." *Quarterly Review* 299 (July 1961): 300–310.

Mosier, William E. "Mrs. Oliphant's Literary Criti-

cism." *Dissertation Abstracts* 28 (1968): 3644A–45A (Northwestern).

Watson, Kathleen. "George Eliot and Mrs. Oliphant: A Comparison in Social Attitudes." *Essays in Criticism* 19 (October 1969): 410–19.

Individual Works
A Beleaguered City (1880)

Colby, Robert and Vineta. "*A Beleaguered City*: A Fable for the Victorian Age." *Nineteenth Century Fiction* 16 (March 1962): 283–301.

TILLIE OLSEN (1913–) U.S.
General Works

O'Connor, William Van. "The Short Stories of Tillie Olsen." *Studies in Short Fiction* 1 (Fall 1963): 21–25.

ORINDA. *See* Katherine Philips

MARTHA OSTENSO (1900–1963) U.S.
Individual Works
Wild Geese (1925)

Mullins, S.G. "Some Remarks on a Theme in Martha Ostenso's *Wild Geese.*" *Culture* 23 (December 1962): 359–62.

OUIDA [pseud. of Marie Louise de la Ramée] (1839–1908) Great Britain
General Works

"Is the Ghost of Ouida There?" *Listener* (July 22, 1965): 126.

"Homage to the Longhorn." *Listener* (April 23, 1970): 543.

ROCHELLE OWENS (1936–) U.S.
General Works

Goulianos, J. "Women and the Avant-Garde Theater: Interview." *Massachusetts Review* 13 (Winter–Spring 1972): 257–61.

CYNTHIA OZICK (1928–) U.S.
Individual Works
Trust (1966)

Goodheart, Eugene. "Review of *Trust.*" *Critique* 9 (1966): 99–102.

P

P.K. PAGE (1916–) Canada
General Works
Smith, A.J.M. "The Poetry of P.K. Page." *Canadian Literature*, no. 50 (Autumn 1971): 17–34.

VIOLET PAGET [pseud. Vernon Lee] (1856–1935) Great Britain
General Works
Cary, Richard. "Vernon Lee's Vignettes of Literary Acquaintances." *Colby Library Quarterly* 9 (September 1970): 179–99.
Cary, Richard. "Violet Paget to Sarah Orne Jewett." *Colby Library Quarterly* 9 (December 1970): 235–43.
Gettman, Royal A. "Vernon Lee: Exponent of Aestheticism." *Prairie Schooner* 42 (Spring 1968): 47–55.
Ormond, Richard. "John Singer Sargent and Vernon Lee." *Colby Library Quarterly* 9 (September 1970): 154–78.
Pantazzi, Sybille. "Carlo Placci and Vernon Lee: Their Letters and Their Friends." *English Miscellany* 12 (1961): 97–122.
Individual Works
Miss Brown (1884)
Ormond, Leonee. "Vernon Lee as a Critic of Aestheticism in *Miss Brown*." *Colby Library Quarterly* 9 (September 1970): 131–54.

GRACE PALEY (1922–) U.S.
General Works
Gold, Ivan. "On Having Grace Paley Once More Among Us." *Commonweal* (October 25, 1968): 111–12.
Malin, Irving. "The Verve of Grace Paley." *Genesis West* 1 (Fall 1963): 73–78.

Midwood, B. "Short Visits with Five Writers and One Friend." *Esquire* (November 1970): 151–52.

LADY SOPHIA MATILDA PALMER (1852–1915) Great Britain
General Works
Chapman, J.K., ed. "A Political Correspondence of the Gladstone Era." *American Philosophical Society Transactions* 61 (March 1971): 5–52.

NETTIE PALMER [pseud. of Janet Gertrude Higgins] (1885–) Australia
General Works
Barocchi, Guido. "Nettie Palmer." *Overland*, no. 32 (1965): 37–38.
Levy, Esther. "Yours as Ever . . . N. P." *Meanjin Quarterly* 24 (1965): 329–33.
McLeod, Jessie. "Nettie Palmer: Some Personal Memories." *Overland*, no. 31 (1965): 20–21.

EMMELINE PANKHURST, née Goulden (1858–1928) Great Britain
General Works
Zacharis, John C. "Emmeline Pankhurst: An English Suffragette Influences America." *Speech Monographs* 38 (August 1971): 198–206.

GAIL PARENT (fl. 1970s) U.S.
General Works
Smith, Andrew. "Focus on Gail Parent: Interview." *Harper's Bazaar* (January 1974): 50.

DOROTHY PARKER (1893–1967) U.S.
General Works
Amory, C. "Celebrity Register." *McCall's* (July 1963): 144.
Brown, J.M. "High Spirits in the Twenties." *Hori-*

zon (New York) 4 (July 1962): 33–41.

Cooper, Wyatt. "Whatever You Think Dorothy Parker Was Like, She Wasn't." *Esquire* (July 1968): 57.

Gingrich, A. "Entrée to the World of Dorothy Parker." *Esquire* (January 1962): 4.

"Guinevere of the Round Table." *Time* (June 16, 1967): 94.

James, Clive. "Nickel and Ivory." *New Statesman* (April 27, 1973): 623–24.

"Low Spirits." *Times Literary Supplement* (April 6, 1973): 395.

"Queen of the Round Table." *Newsweek* (June 19, 1967): 43.

Sokolov, R.A. "Wittiest Woman." *Newsweek* (October 12, 1970): 124.

LINDA PASTAN (1932–) U.S.
General Works
Jellema, Roderick. "The Poetry of Linda Pastan." *Voyages* 2 (Spring 1969): 73–74.

MARGARET PASTON (fl. 1441–1478) Great Britain
General Works
Davis, Norman. "Margaret Paston's Uses of 'Do.' " *Neuphilologische Mitteilungen* 73 (1972): 55–62.

MARY PATTERSON (1928–1973) U.S.
General Works
Nichols, L. "Couple." *New York Times Book Review* (February 6, 1966): 8.

PAX [pseud.]. *See* Mary Cholmondeley

ELIZABETH PEABODY (1804–1894) U.S.
General Works
Stern, Madeleine B. "Elizabeth Peabody's Foreign Library (1840)." *American Transcendental Quarterly* 20, Supplement (1973): 5–12.

Turner, A. "Elizabeth Peabody Visits Lincoln, February 1865." *New England Quarterly* 48 (March 1975): 116–24.

Wilson, J.B. "Grimm's Law and the Brahmins." *New England Quarterly* 38 (June 1965): 234–39.

MARY HERBERT, COUNTESS OF PEMBROKE (1561–1621) Great Britain
Individual Works
Psalms (1694–1695)
"Text and Manuscript Variants of the Countess of

Pembroke's *Psalms*." *Review of English Studies* 26 (February 1975): 1–18.

Waller, G. F. "This Matching of Contraries: Calvinism and Courtly Philosophy in the Sidney *Psalms*." *English Studies* 55 (1974): 22–31.

FLORENCE PERCY [pseud.]. *See* Elizabeth Akers Allen

ELEANOR PERRY (fl. 1960s) U.S.
General Works
"Behind the Lens." *Time* (March 20, 1972): 93.

Meade, Marion. "Prime of Ms. Perry." *McCall's* (June 1972): 52.

"People Are Talking About. . . ." *Vogue* (September 1970): 375.

GRACE PERRY (fl. 1940s) Australia
General Works
New, William H. "Grace Perry's House of Poetry." *Poetry Australia* 8 (1972): 45–55.

JULIA PETERKIN (1880–1961) U.S.
General Works
Cheney, Brainard. "Can Julia Peterkin's 'Genius' Be Revived for Today's Black Myth-Making?" *Sewanee Review* 80 (Winter 1972): 173–79.

Henry, Louis Lee. "Julia Peterkin: A Biographical and Critical Study." *Dissertation Abstracts* 26 (1966): 4659 (Florida State).

Landess, Thomas H. "Julia Peterkin: A Critical Study." *Dissertation Abstracts International* 34 (1973): 323A (South Carolina).
Individual Works
The Collected Short Stories of Julia Peterkin (1970)
Coker, Elizabeth Boatwright. "An Appreciation of Julia Peterkin and *The Collected Short Stories of Julia Peterkin*." *South Carolina Review* 3 (June 1971): 3–7.

ANN PETRY, née Lane (1911–) U.S.
General Works
Shinn, Thelma. "Women in the Novels of Ann Petry." *Critique* 16 (1974): 110–20.
Individual Works
In Darkness and Confusion (1947)
Adams, George R. "Riot as Ritual: Ann Petry's *In Darkness and Confusion*." *Negro American Literature Forum* 6 (1972): 54.
Tituba of Salem Village (1964)
Morsberger, Robert E. "The Further Transforma-

tion of Tituba." *New England Quarterly* 47 (September 1974): 456–58.

ELIZABETH STUART PHELPS (1815–1852) U.S.
General Works
Starrsell, Christine. "Elizabeth Stuart Phelps: A Study in Female Rebellion." *Massachusetts Review* 13 (Winter–Spring 1972): 239–56.

KATHERINE PHILIPS [known as "the Matchless Orinda"] (1631–1664) Great Britain
General Works
Roberts, William. "The Dating of Orinda's French Translations." *Philological Quarterly* 49 (January 1970): 56–67.
Roberts, William. "Saint-Amant, Orinda and Dryden's *Miscellany.*" *English Language Notes* 1 (March 1964): 191–96.

PHILOMELA [pseud.]. *See* Elizabeth Rowe

MARGE PIERCY (fl. 1970s) U.S.
General Works
Schreiber, Ron. "Symposium: What's New in American and Canadian Poetry." *New* 15 (April–May 1971): 92–97.
"Young Hopefuls." *Saturday Review/World* (December 14, 1974): 102.
Zee, Nancy S. "Marge Piercy: A Collage." *Oyez Review* (Roosevelt University) 9 (Spring 1975): 87–94.

HELEN PINKERTON (fl. 1950s) Great Britain
Individual Works
Error Pursued (1959)
Bowers, Edgar. "The Poems of Helen Pinkerton." *Spectrum* 5 (Summer 1961): 97–105.

JEAN PLAIDY [pseud.]. *See* Eleanor Alice Burford Hibbert

SYLVIA PLATH [pseud. Victoria Lucas] (1932–1963) U.S.
Bibliography
Alvarez, A. "Sylvia Plath: The Cambridge Collection." *Cambridge Review* (February 7, 1969): 246–47.
General Works
Aird, Eileen M. "Variants in a Tape Recording of Fifteen Poems by Sylvia Plath." *Notes and Queries*

19 (February 1972): 59–61.
Alvarez, A. "Sylvia Plath." *Review* 9 (October 1963): 20–26.
Alvarez, A. "Sylvia Plath." *Tri-Quarterly* 7 (Fall 1966): 65–107.
Ashford, Deborah. "Sylvia Plath's Poetry: A Complex of Irreconcilable Antagonisms." *Concerning Poetry* 7 (1974): 62–69.
Baker, A.T. "Poetry Today: Low Profile, Flatted Voice." *Time* (July 13, 1971): 61.
Barnard, Caroline K. "God's Lioness: The Poetry of Sylvia Plath." *Dissertation Abstracts International* 34 (1974):5935A (Brown).
"Blood Jet Is Poetry." *Time* (June 10, 1966): 118.
Boyers, Robert. "Sylvia Plath: The Trepanned Veteran." *Centennial Review* 13 (1969): 138–53.
Capek, Mary Ellen S. " 'Perfection Is Terrible': A Study of Sylvia Plath's Poetry." *Dissertation Abstracts International* 34 (1974): 6629A (Wisconsin).
Clair, William F. "That Rare, Random Descent: The Poetry and Paths of Sylvia Plath." *Antioch Review* 26 (Winter 1966–1967): 552–60.
Cooley, Peter. "Autism, Autoeroticism, Auto-da-fé: The Tragic Poetry of Sylvia Plath." *Hollins Critic* 10 (February 1973): 1–15.
Cox, C.B., and A.R. Jones. "After the Tranquilized Fifties: Notes on Sylvia Plath and James Baldwin." *Critical Quarterly* 6 (Summer 1964): 107–22.
Davison, P. "Inhabited by a Cry: Last Poetry of Sylvia Plath." *Atlantic Monthly* (August 1966): 76–77.
Donovan, Josephine. "Sexual Politics in Sylvia Plath's Short Stories." *Minnesota Review,* NRP 4 (Spring 1973): 150–57.
Duffy, M. "Two Lives." *Time* (November 24, 1975): 101–2.
Duffy, Martha. "The Triumph of a Tormented Poet." *Life* (November 12, 1971): 38A–38B.
"Early Poems by Sylvia Plath." *Cambridge Review* (February 7, 1969): 244–49.
Eriksson, Pamela D. "Some Thoughts on Sylvia Plath." *Unisa English Studies* 10 (June 1972): 45–52.
Fraser, G.S. "A Hard Nut to Crack from Sylvia Plath." *Contemporary Poetry* 1 (Spring 1973): 1–12.
Gordon, Lydia Caroline. " 'From Stone to Cloud': A Critical Study of Sylvia Plath." *Dissertation Abstracts International* 35 (1975): 2820A (Penn.).

Hobsbaum, Philip. "The Temptation of Giant Despair." *Hudson Review* 25 (Winter 1972–1973): 596–612.

Holbrook, David. "Sylvia Plath and the Problem of Violence in Art." *Cambridge Review* (February 7, 1969): 249–50.

Homberger, Eric. "I Am I." *Cambridge Review* (February 7, 1969): 251–52.

Homberger, Eric. "The Uncollected Plath." *New Statesman* (September 22, 1972): 404–5.

Howard, Maureen. "Letters Home." *New York Times Book Review* (December 14, 1975): 1–2.

Hoyle, James F. "Sylvia Plath: A Poetry of Suicidal Mania." *Literature and Psychology* 18 (1968): 187–203.

Jefferson, M. "Who Was Sylvia?" *Newsweek* (December 22, 1975): 83.

Jones. A.R. "Necessity and Freedom: The Poetry of Robert Lowell, Sylvia Plath and Anne Sexton." *Critical Quarterly* 7 (Spring 1965): 11–30.

Kissick, Gary. "Plath: A Terrible Perfection." *Nation* (September 16, 1968): 245–47.

Levine, Ellen Sue. "From Water to Land: The Poetry of Sylvia Plath, James Wright and W. S. Merwin." *Dissertation Abstracts International* 35 (1975): 4532A (Washington).

Libby, Anthony. "God's Lioness and the Priest of Sycorax: Plath and Hughes." *Contemporary Literature* 15 (Summer 1974): 386–405.

Lindberg–Seyersted, Brita. "Notes on Three Poems by Sylvia Plath." *Edda* 74 (1974): 47–54.

Lindberg–Seyersted, Brita. "On Sylvia Plath's Poetry." *Edda* 72 (1972): 54–59.

Martin, Wendy. " 'God's Lioness'—Sylvia Plath, Her Prose and Poetry." *Women's Studies* 1 (1973): 191–98.

McKay, D.F. "Aspects of Energy in the Poetry of Dylan Thomas and Sylvia Plath." *Critical Quarterly* 16 (Spring 1974): 53–68.

Megna, Jerome F. "The Two-World Division in the Poetry of Sylvia Plath." *Dissertation Abstracts International* 33 (1972): 760A (Ball State).

Meissner, William. "The Rise of the Angel: Life through Death in the Poetry of Sylvia Plath." *Massachusetts Studies in English* 3 (1971): 34–39.

Newlin, Margaret. "The Suicide Bandwagon." *Critical Quarterly* 14 (Winter 1972): 367–78.

Newman, Charles. "Candor Is the Only Wile." *Tri-Quarterly* 7 (Fall 1966): 39–64.

Oates, Joyce Carol. "The Death Throes of Romanticism: The Poems of Sylvia Plath." *Southern Review* (U.S.) 9 (1973): 501–22.

Oberg, Arthur K. "Sylvia Plath and the New Decadence." *Chicago Review* 20 (1968): 66–73.

Oettle, Pamela. "Sylvia Plath's Last Poems." *Balcony* 3 (1965): 47–50.

Ostriker, Alicia. " 'Fact' as Style: The Americanization of Sylvia." *Language and Style* 1 (1968): 201–12.

Perloff, Marjorie. "Angst and Animism in the Poetry of Sylvia Plath." *Journal of Modern Literature* 1 (1970): 57–74.

Perloff, Marjorie. "Extremist Poetry: Some Versions of the Sylvia Plath Myth." *Journal of Modern Literature* 2 (1972): 581–88.

Phillips, Robert. "The Dark Funnel: A Reading of Sylvia Plath." *Modern Poetry Studies* 3 (Spring 1972): 49–74.

Plath, A. S. "Sylvia Plath on Her Love and Marriage." *Mademoiselle* (July 1975): 82–87.

Procopiow, Norma. "Sylvia Plath and the New England Mind." *Thoth* 13 (1974): 3–15.

Romano, J. "Sylvia Plath Reconsidered." *Commentary* 57 (April 1974): 47–52.

Rosenstein, Harriet. "Reconsidering Sylvia Plath." *Month* (September 1972): 44.

Rosenstein, Harriet. "To the Most Wonderful Mummy . . . a Girl Ever Had." *Ms.* (December 1975): 45–49.

"Russian Roulette." *Newsweek* (June 20, 1966): 109A–109B.

Smith, Pamela A. "Unitive Urge in the Poetry of Sylvia Plath." *New England Quarterly* 45 (September 1972): 323–39.

Spendal, R.J. "Sylvia Plath's Cut." *Modern Poetry Studies* 6 (Autumn 1975): 128–34.

Spender, Stephen. "Warnings from the Grave." *New Republic* (June 18, 1966: 23–26.

Stainton, Rita T. "Vision and Voice in Three Poems by Sylvia Plath." *Windless Orchard*, no. 17 (Spring 1974): 31–36.

Stainton, Rita Tomasallo. "The Magician's Girl: Power and Vulnerability in the Poetry of Sylvia Plath." *Dissertation Abstracts International* 35 (1975): 2828A (Rutgers).

Steiner, George. "In Extremis." *Cambridge Review* (February 7, 1969): 247–49.

Stolanoff, E.A. "Sylvia Plath." *Mademoiselle* (September 1971): 160–61.

Sumner, Nan McCowan. "Sylvia Plath." *Research*

Studies 38 (1970): 112–21.

Taylor, Andrew. "Sylvia Plath's Mirror and Beehive." *Meanjin Quarterly* 33 (1974): 256–65.

Taylor, Eleanor Ross. "Sylvia Plath's Last Poems." *Poetry* 109 (January 1967): 260–62.

Uroff, Margaret D. "Sylvia Plath on Motherhood." *Midwest Quarterly* 15 (Autumn 1973): 70–90.

Uroff, Margaret D. "Sylvia Plath's Women." *Concerning Poetry* 7 (1974): 45–56.

Wegs, Joyce M. "The Grotesque in Some American Novels of the Nineteen-Sixties: Ken Kesey, Joyce Carol Oates, Sylvia Plath." *Dissertation Abstracts International* 34 (1974): 7791A–92A (Illinois).

Individual Works

Ariel (1966)

Bierman, Larry. "The Vivid Tulips Eat My Oxygen: An Essay On Sylvia Plath's *Ariel*." *Windless Orchard*, no. 4 (Spring 1971): 44–46.

Davis, Robin R. "The Honey Machine: Imagery Patterns in *Ariel*." *New Laurel Review* 1 (1972): 23–31.

Davis, William V. "Sylvia Plath's *Ariel*." *Modern Poetry Studies* 3 (Autumn 1972): 176–84.

Perloff, Marjorie. "On the Road to *Ariel*: The 'Transitional' Poetry of Sylvia Plath." *Iowa Review* 4 (Spring 1973): 94–110.

The Bell Jar (1963)

Himelick, Raymond. "Notes on the Care and Feeding of Nightmares: Burton, Erasmus, and Sylvia Plath." *Western Humanities Review* 28 (Fall 1974): 313–26.

Levy, Laurie. "Outside *The Bell Jar*." *Ohio Review* 15 (Spring 1973): 67–73.

Milliner, Gladys W. "The Tragic Imperative: *The Awakening* and *The Bell Jar*." *Mary Wollstonecraft Newsletter* 2 (December 1973): 21–27.

Perloff, Marjorie. "A Ritual for Being Born Twice: Sylvia Plath's *The Bell Jar*." *Contemporary Literature* 13 (Autumn 1972): 507–22.

Smith, S. "Attitudes Counterfeiting Life: The Irony of Artifice in Sylvia Plath's *The Bell Jar*." *Critical Quarterly* 17 (Autumn 1975): 247–60.

The Colossus (1962)

Smith, Pamela. "Architectonics: Sylvia Plath's *Colossus*." *Ariel* 4 (1973): 4–21.

Crossing the Water (1960)

Boyers, Robert. "On Sylvia Plath." *Salmagundi* 21 (1973): 96–104.

Dyroff, Jan M. "Sylvia Plath: Perceptions in *Crossing the Water*." *Art and Literature* 1 (1972): 49–50.

Hughes, Ted. "Sylvia Plath's *Crossing the Water*: Some Reflections." *Critical Quarterly* 13 (Summer 1971): 165–72.

Richmond, Lee J. "Books Covered and Uncovered: *Crow* by Ted Hughes; *Crossing the Water . . .* by Sylvia Plath." *Erasmus Review* 1 (1971): 157–62.

The Disquieting Muses (1957)

Melander, Ingrid. "*The Disquieting Muses*: A Note on a Poem by Sylvia Plath." *Research Studies* 39 (1971): 53–54.

Elm (1962)

Hakeem, A. "Sylvia Plath's *Elm* and Munch's *The Scream*." *English Studies* 55 (1974): 531–37.

The Hanging Man (1955)

Balitas, Vincent D. "A Note on Sylvia Plath's *The Hanging Man*." *Notes and Queries* 22 (May 1975): 208.

Lady Lazarus (1971)

Burnham, Richard E. "Sylvia Plath's *Lady Lazarus*." *Contemporary Poetry* 1 (Winter 1973): 42–46.

The Manor Garden (1960)

Megna, Jerome F. "Plath's *The Manor Garden*." *Explicator* 30 (March 1972): Item 58.

Tulips (1961)

Meissner, William. "The Opening of the Flower: The Revelation of Suffering in Sylvia Plath's *Tulips*." *Contemporary Poetry* 1 (Spring 1973): 13–17.

Watercolor of Grantchester Meadows (1959)

Melander, Ingrid. "*Watercolor of Grantchester Meadows*: An Early Poem by Sylvia Plath." *Moderna Sprak* 65 (1971): 1–5.

Jane Porter (1776–1850) Great Britain
General Works

Helms, Randel. "Another Source for Poe's *Arthur Gordon Pym*." *American Literature* 41 (January 1970): 572–75.

Katherine Anne Porter (1890–) U.S.
Bibliography

Waldrip, Louise D. "A Bibliography of the Works of Katherine Anne Porter." *Dissertation Abstracts* 27 (1967): 4269A (Texas).

General Works

Allen, Charles A. "The Nouvelles of Katherine Anne Porter." *University Review* (Kansas) 29 (1962): 87–93.

Amory, C. "Celebrity Register." *McCall's* (April 1963): 184.

Baker, Howard, "The Upward Path: Notes on the Work of Katherine Anne Porter." *Southern Review* (U.S.) 4 (1968): 1–19.

Baldeshwiler, Eileen. "Structural Patterns in Katherine Anne Porter's Fiction." *South Dakota Review* 11 (Summer 1973): 45–53.

Bedford, Sybille. "Voyage to Everywhere." *Spectator* (November 16, 1962): 703–4.

"Best Years." *Newsweek* (July 31, 1961): 78.

Core, George. "The Best Residuum of Truth." *Georgia Review* 20 (Fall 1966): 278–91.

Cruttwell, Patrick. "Swift, Miss Porter, and the 'Dialect of the Tribe.' " *Shenandoah* 17 (1966): 27–38.

Domadio, Stephen. "The Collected Miss Porter." *Partisan Review* 33 (1966): 278–84.

Ephron, Nora. "A Strange Kind of Simplicity." *New York Times Book Review* (May 5, 1968): 8.

Farrinton, Thomas A. "The Control of Imagery in Katherine Anne Porter's Fiction." *Dissertation Abstracts International* 34 (1973): 767A (Illinois).

Featherstone, Joseph. "Katherine Anne Porter's Harvest." *New Republic* (September 4, 1965): 23–26.

Flood, Ethelbert. "Christian Language in Modern Literature." *Culture* 22 (March 1961): 28–42.

Frankel, H. "Author." *Saturday Review* (September 25, 1965): 36.

Gaunt, Marcia E. "Imagination and Reality in the Fiction of Katherine Anne Porter and John Cheever: Implications for Curriculum." *Dissertation Abstracts International* 33 (1972): 2933A (Purdue).

Givner, Joan. "Katherine Anne Porter, Eudora Welty, and 'Ethan Brand.' " *Italia Francescana* 1 (1974): 32–37.

Givner, Joan. "Porter's Subsidiary Art." *Southwest Review* 59 (Summer 1974): 265–76.

Gordon, Caroline. "Katherine Anne Porter and the ICM." *Harper's* (November 1964): 146–48.

Greene, George. "Brimstone and Roses: Notes on Katherine Anne Porter." *Thought* 36 (1961): 421–40.

Hagopian, John V. "Katherine Anne Porter: Feeling, Form, and Truth." *Four Quarters* 12 (November 1962): 1–10.

Hartley, Lodwick. "Katherine Anne Porter." *Southern Literary Journal* 6 (Spring 1974): 139–50.

Hertz, Robert Neil. "Rising Waters: A Study of Katherine Anne Porter." *Dissertation Abstracts* 25 (1964): 3571–72 (Cornell).

Howell, Elmo. "Katherine Porter as a Southern Writer." *South Carolina Review* 4 (December 1971): 5–15.

Johnson, James William. "Another Look at Katherine Anne Porter." *Virginia Quarterly Review* 36 (Autumn 1960): 598–613.

Johnson, Shirley E. "Love Attitudes in the Fiction of Katherine Anne Porter." *West Virginia University Bulletin: Philological Papers* 13 (December 1961): 82–93.

"Katherine Anne Porter." *Publishers Weekly* (February 12, 1973): 36.

"Katherine Anne Porter: A Birthday Tribute." *Yale Review* 55 (Winter 1966): 265–90.

Keily, Robert. "The Craft of Despondency." *Daedalus* 92 (Spring 1963): 220–37.

Krishnamurthi, Matighatta G. "Katherine Anne Porter: A Study in Themes." *Dissertation Abstracts* 28 (1967): 682A–83A (Wisconsin).

Ledbetter, Nan W. "The Thumbprint: A Study of People in Katherine Anne Porter's Fiction." *Dissertation Abstracts* 28 (1967): 252A–53A (Texas).

Lopez, Hank, and Katherine Anne Porter. "A Country and Some People I Love." *Harper's* (September 1965): 58–68.

Marsden, Malcolm M. "Love as Threat in Katherine Anne Porter's Fiction." *Twentieth Century Literature* 13 (April 1967): 29–38.

Miles, Lee R. "Unused Possibilities: A Study of Katherine Anne Porter." *Dissertation Abstracts International* 34 (1973): 784A–85A (California, Los Angeles).

Moss, Howard. "No Safe Harbor." *New Yorker* (April 28, 1962): 165–73.

Nance, William L. "Katherine Anne Porter and Mexico." *Southwest Review* 55 (Spring 1970): 143–53.

Nance, William L. "The Principle of Rejection: A Study of the Thematic Unity in the Fiction of Katherine Anne Porter." *Dissertation Abstracts* 24 (1963): 1172–73 (Notre Dame).

Nance, William L. "Variations on a Dream: Katherine Anne Porter and Truman Capote." *Southern Humanities Review* 3 (Fall 1969): 338–45.

Nichols, L. "Miss Porter." *New York Times Book Review* (April 22, 1962): 8.

"Notes of a Survivor." *Time* (May 4, 1970): 99–100.

Ohsugi, Hiroaki. "Tragic Vision of Katherine Anne Porter." *Studies in English Literature*, English

Number (1962): 77–90.

Partridge, Colin. "'My Familiar Country': An Image of Mexico in the Work of Katherine Anne Porter." *Studies in Short Fiction* 7 (Fall 1970): 597–614.

Pinkerton, Jane. "Katherine Anne Porter's Portrayal of Black Resentment." *University Review* (Kansas) 36 (1970): 315–17.

Plante, Patricia R. "Katherine Anne Porter: Misanthrope Acquitted." *Xavier University Studies* 2 (December 1963): 87–91.

Porter, Katherine Anne. "From the Notebooks of Katherine Anne Porter." *Southern Review* (U.S.) 1 (1965): 570–73.

Porter, Katherine Anne. "On First Meeting T. S. Eliot." *Shenandoah* 12 (1961): 25–26.

Pritchett, V.S. "Stories and Stories." *New Statesman* (January 10, 1964): 47–48.

Redden, Dorothy Sue. "The Legend of Katherine Anne Porter." *Dissertation Abstracts* 26 (1966): 6722–23 (Stanford).

Rockwell, Jeanne. "The Magic Cloak." *Michigan Quarterly Review* 5 (Fall 1966): 283–84.

Rosliep, R. "Kodachrome: Katherine Anne Porter." *Catholic World* (March 1963): 342.

Rubin, Louis D., Jr. "We Get Along Together Just Fine." *Four Quarters* 12 (March 1963): 30–31.

Ruoff, James E. "Katherine Anne Porter Comes to Kansas." *Midwest Quarterly* 4 (Summer 1963): 305–14.

Ryan, Marjorie. "*Dubliners* and the Stories of Katherine Anne Porter." *American Literature* 31 (January 1960): 464–73.

Schwartz, Edward G. "The Fictions of Memory." *Southwest Review* 45 (Summer 1960): 204–15.

Shapiro, K. "Emily Dickinson and Katherine Anne Porter." *Poetry* 98 (April 1961): 2–3.

Sullivan, Walter. "Katherine Anne Porter: The Glories and Errors of Her Ways." *Southern Literary Journal* 3 (Fall 1970): 111–21.

Sutherland, Donald. "Ole Woman River: A Correspondence with Katherine Anne Porter." *Sewanee Review* 74 (Summer 1966): 554–67.

Taubman, Robert. "A First-Class Passenger." *New Statesman* (November 2, 1962): 619–20.

Thompson, Barbara. "The Art of Fiction 29—Katherine Anne Porter: An Interview." *Paris Review* 4 (Winter–Spring 1963): 87–114.

Van Zyl, John. "Surface Elegance, Grotesque Content—A Note on the Short Stories of Katherine Anne Porter." *English Studies in Africa* 9 (September 1966): 168–75.

Vliet, Vida A. "The Shape of Meaning: A Study of the Development of Katherine Anne Porter's Fictional Form." *Dissertation Abstracts* 29 (1968): 1550A (Penn. State).

Warren, Robert Penn. "Uncorrupted Consciousness: The Stories of Katherine Anne Porter." *Yale Review* 55 (Winter 1966): 280–90.

Welty, Eudora. "The Eye of the Story." *Yale Review* 55 (Winter 1966): 265–74.

Wiesenfarth, Joseph. "Negatives of Hope: A Reading of Katherine Anne Porter." *Renascence* 25 (Winter 1973): 85–94.

Yosha, Lee William. "The World of Katherine Anne Porter." *Dissertation Abstracts* 21 (1961): 3795–96 (Michigan).

Individual Works

The Cracked Looking-Glass (1940)

Wiesenfarth, Joseph. "Illusion and Allusion: Reflections in *The Cracked Looking-Glass*." *Four Quarters* 12 (November 1962): 30–37.

The Downward Path to Wisdom (1944)

Hartley, Lodwick. "Stephen's Lost World: The Background of Katherine Anne Porter's *The Downward Path to Wisdom*." *Studies in Short Fiction* 6 (Fall 1969): 574–79.

Flowering Judas (1930)

Bluefarb, Sam. "Loss of Innocence in *Flowering Judas*." *College Language Association Journal* 7 (March 1964): 256–62.

Bride, Sister Mary. "Laura and the Unlit Lamp." *Studies in Short Fiction* 1 (Fall 1963): 61–63.

Gottfried, Leon. "Death's Other Kingdom: Dantesque and Theological Symbolism in *Flowering Judas*." *Publications of the Modern Language Association* 84 (1969): 112–24.

Gross, Beverly. "The Poetic Narrative: A Reading of *Flowering Judas*." *Style* 11 (Spring 1968): 129–39.

Madden, David. "The Charged Image in Katherine Anne Porter's *Flowering Judas*." *Studies in Short Fiction* 7 (Spring 1970): 277–89.

Redden, Dorothy S. "*Flowering Judas*: Two Voices." *Studies in Short Fiction* 6 (Winter 1969): 194–204.

The Grave (1944)

Bell, Vereen M. "*The Grave* Revisited." *Studies in Short Fiction* 2 (Fall 1965): 39–45.

Brooks, Cleanth. "On *The Grave*." *Yale Review* 55

(Winter 1966): 275–79.

Curley, Daniel. "Treasure in *The Grave*." *Modern Fiction Studies* 9 (Winter 1963–1964): 377–84.

Joselyn, Sister Mary. "*The Grave* as Lyrical Short Story." *Studies in Short Fiction* 1 (Spring 1964): 216–21.

Kramer, Dale. "Notes on Lyricism and Symbols in *The Grave*." *Studies in Short Fiction* 2 (Summer 1965): 331–36.

Prater, William. "*The Grave*: Form and Symbol." *Studies in Short Fiction* 6 (Spring 1969): 336–38.

Hacienda (1934)

Hendrick, George. "Katherine Anne Porter's *Hacienda*." *Four Quarters* 12 (November 1962): 24–29.

Perry, Robert L. "Porter's *Hacienda* and the Theme of Change." *Midwest Quarterly* 6 (Summer 1965): 403–15.

He (1940)

Deasy, Brother Paul Francis. "Reality and Escape." *Four Quarters* 12 (January 1963): 28–31.

The Jilting of Granny Weatherall (1940)

Barnes, Daniel R. and Madeline T. "The Secret Sin of Granny Weatherall." *Renascence* 21 (Spring 1969): 162–65.

Becker, Laurence A. "*The Jilting of Granny Weatherall*: The Discovery of Pattern." *English Journal* 55 (December 1966): 1164–69.

Cowser, Robert G. "Porter's *The Jilting of Granny Weatherall*." *Explicator* 21 (December 1962): Item 34.

Wiesenfarth, Joseph. "Internal Opposition in Porter's 'Granny Weatherall.'" *Criticism* 11 (1969): 47–55.

Wolfe, Peter. "The Problems of Granny Weatherall." *College Language Association Journal* 11 (December 1967): 142–48.

Maria Concepcion (1940)

Hafley, James. "*Maria Concepcion*: Life Among the Ruins." *Four Quarters* 12 (November 1962): 11–17.

Noon Wine (1937)

Howell, Elmo. "Katherine Anne Porter and the Southern Myth: A Note on *Noon Wine*." *Louisiana Studies* 11 (Fall 1972): 252–59.

Pierce, Marvin. "Point of View: Katherine Anne Porter's *Noon Wine*." *Ohio University Review* 3 (1961): 95–113.

Smith, J. Oates. "Porter's *Noon Wine*: A Stifled Tragedy." *Renascence* 17 (Spring 1965): 157–62.

Thomas, M. Wynn. "Strangers in a Strange Land: A Reading of *Noon Wine*." *American Literature* 47 (May 1975): 230–46.

Walsh, Thomas F. "The *Noon Wine* Devils." *Georgia Review* 22 (Spring 1968): 90–96.

Pale Horse, Pale Rider (1939)

Yannella, Philip R. "The Problems of Dislocation in *Pale Horse, Pale Rider*." *Studies in Short Fiction* 6 (Fall 1969): 637–42.

Youngblood, Sarah. "Structure and Imagery in Katherine Anne Porter's *Pale Horse, Pale Rider*." *Modern Fiction Studies* 5 (Winter 1959–1960): 344–52.

Ship of Fools (1962)

Adams, Robert Hickman. "The Significance of Point of View in Katherine Anne Porter's *Ship of Fools*." *Dissertation Abstracts* 26 (1965): 2201 (Southern California).

Alexander, Jean. "Katherine Anne Porter's Ship in the Jungle." *Twentieth Century Literature* 11 (January 1966): 179–88.

Baumgartner, Paul R. "From Medieval Fool to Renaissance Rogue: *Cocke Lorell's Bote* and the Literary Tradition." *Annuale Mediaevale* 1 (1960): 57–91.

Curley, Daniel. "Katherine Anne Porter: The Larger Plan." *Kenyon Review* 25 (1963): 671–95.

Finkelstein, Sidney. "*Ship of Fools*." *Mainstream* 15 (September 1962): 42–48.

Hartley, Lodwick. "Dark Voyagers: A Study of Katherine Anne Porter's *Ship of Fools*." *University Review* (Kansas) 30 (1963): 83–94.

Heilman, Robert B. "*Ship of Fools*: Notes on Style." *Four Quarters* 12 (November 1962): 46–55.

Hendrick, George. "Hart Crane Aboard the *Ship of Fools*: Some Speculations." *Twentieth Century Literature* 9 (April 1963): 3–9.

Hertz, Robert N. "Sebastian Brant and Porter's *Ship of Fools*." *Midwest Quarterly* 6 (Summer 1965): 389–401.

Janeway, E. "For Katherine Anne Porter *Ship of Fools* Was a Lively Twenty-Two-Year Voyage." *New York Times Book Review* (April 1, 1962): 4–5.

Joselyn, Sister Mary. "On the Making of *Ship of Fools*." *South Dakota Review* 1 (May 1964): 46–52.

Kirkpatrick, Smith. "*The Ship of Fools*." *Sewanee Review* 71 (Winter 1963): 94–98.

Liberman, M. M. "The Responsibility of the Novelist: The Critical Reception of *Ship of Fools.*" *Criticism* 8 (1966): 377–88.

Liberman, M.M. "The Short Story as Chapter in *Ship of Fools.*" *Criticism* 10 (1968): 65–71.

Liberman, M.M. "Some Observations on the Genesis of *Ship of Fools*: A Letter from Katherine Anne Porter." *Publications of the Modern Language Association* 84 (1969): 136–37.

McIntyre, John P. "*Ship of Fools* and Its Publicity." *Thought* 38 (1963): 211–20.

Miller, Paul W. "Katherine Porter's *Ship of Fools*: A Masterpiece Manqué." *University Review* (Kansas) 32 (1965): 151–57.

Osta, Winifred H. "The Journey Pattern in Four Contemporary American Novels." *Dissertation Abstracts International* 31 (1970): 2933A (Arizona).

Ruoff, James, and Del Smith. "Katherine Anne Porter on *Ship of Fools.*" *College English* 24 (February 1963): 396–97.

Ryan, Marjorie. "Katherine Anne Porter: *Ship of Fools* and the Short Stories." *Bucknell Review* 12 (March 1964): 51–63.

Ryan, Marjorie. "Review of *Ship of Fools.*" *Critique* 5 (1962): 94–99.

Solotaroff, Theodore. "*Ship of Fools* and the Critics." *Commentary* 34 (October 1962): 277–86.

Spence, Jon. "Looking-Glass Reflections: Satirical Elements in *Ship of Fools.*" *Sewanee Review* 82 (Spring 1974): 316–30.

Walton, Gerald. "Katherine Anne Porter's Use of Quakerism in *Ship of Fools.*" *University of Mississippi Studies in English* 7 (1966): 15–23.

Wescott, Glenway. "Katherine Anne Porter: The Making of a Novel." *Atlantic Monthly* (April 1962): 43–49.

Theft (1940)

Givner, Joan. "A Re-reading of Katherine Anne Porter's *Theft.*" *Studies in Short Fiction* 6 (Summer 1969): 463–65.

Praeger, Leonard. "Getting and Spending: Porter's *Theft.*" *Personalist* 41 (Spring 1961): 230–34.

Stein, William B. "*Theft*: Porter's Politics of Modern Love." *Personalist* 41 (Winter 1960): 223–28.

Wiesenfarth, Joseph. "The Structure of Katherine Anne Porter's *Theft.*" *Cithara* 10 (1971): 64–71.

Beatrix Potter (1866–1943) Great Britain
Bibliography
"Collamore Collection of Beatrix Potter Goes to the Free Library of Philadelphia." *American Book Collector* 18 (April 1968): 8.

Deval, Laurie. "Bibliography of Beatrix Potter." *Book Collector* 15 (Winter 1966): 454–59.

General Works
Gilpatrick, N. "Secret Life of Beatrix Potter." *Natural History* 81 (October 1972): 38–41.

Kanfer, S. "Rabbit Run." *Time* (July 5, 1971): 67.

"Letter from the Creator of Peter Rabbit." *American Book Collector* 16 (April 1966): 10.

Linder, L. "Beatrix Potter's Code Writing." *Horn Book Magazine* 39 (1963): 141–55.

Messer, P.B. "Beatrix Potter: Classic Novelist of the Nursery." *Elementary English* 45 (March 1968): 325–33.

"Peter Rabbit's Mother." *Time* (August 26, 1966): 82.

Individual Works
The Journal of Beatrix Potter (1881–1897)
Hamer, Douglas, "*The Journal of Beatrix Potter*: Some Corrections." *Notes and Queries* 16 (June 1969): 221.

Sendak, Maurice. "*Journal of Beatrix Potter.*" *Publishers Weekly* (July 11, 1966): 130–33.

Dawn Powell (1897–1965) U.S.
General Works
Josephson, Matthew. "Dawn Powell: A Woman of Esprit." *Southern Review* (U.S.) 9 (1973): 18–52.

Katharine Susannah Prichard (1884–) Australia
General Works
Hewett, Dorothy. " 'Excess of Love': The Irreconcilable in Katharine Susannah Prichard." *Overland*, no. 43 (1969): 27–31.

Lindsay, Jack. "The Novels of Katharine Susannah Prichard." *Meanjin Quarterly* 20 (1961): 366–87.

Malos, Ellen. "Jack Lindsay's Essay on Katharine Susannah Prichard's Novels." *Meanjin Quarterly* 22 (1963): 413–16.

Malos, Ellen. "Some Major Themes in the Novels of Katharine Susannah Prichard." *Australian Literary Studies* 1 (1963): 32–41.

Sadlier, Richard. "The Writings of Katharine Susannah Prichard: A Critical Evaluation." *Westerly*, no. 3 (1961): 31–35.

Williams, Justina. "Rage That Engenders: The Last Decade of Katharine Susannah Prichard." *Southerly* 32 (1972): 17–29.

Individual Works

Brumly Innes (1972)

D.D. and M.M.M. "A Note on *Brumly Innes*." *Komos* 2 (1972): 139–40.

Williams, Margaret. "Natural Sexuality: Katharine Prichard's *Brumly Innes*." *Meanjin Quarterly* 32 (1973): 91–93.

ROBERTA STONE PRYOR [pseud.]. *See* Cecelia Holland

R

ANN RADCLIFFE (1764–1823) Great Britain
General Works

Coolidge, Archibald C., Jr. "Charles Dickens and Mrs. Radcliffe: A Farewell to Wilkie Collins." *Dickensian* 58 (May 1962): 112–16.

Durant, David S., Jr. "Ann Radcliffe's Novels: Experiments in Setting." *Dissertation Abstracts International* 32 (1972): 5225A–26A (North Carolina).

Epstein, Lynne. "Ann Radcliffe's Gothic Landscape of Fiction and the Various Influences upon It." *Dissertation Abstracts International* 32 (1972): 5735A (N.Y.U.).

Epstein, Lynne. "Mrs. Radcliffe's Landscapes: The Influence of Three Landscape Painters on Her Nature Descriptions." *Hartford Studies in Literature* 1 (1969): 107–20.

Gregor, Arthur. "Visionary Landscapes." *Poetry* 98 (June 1961): 186–89.

Pound, Edward Fox. "The Influence of Burke and the Psychological Critics on the Novels of Ann Radcliffe." *Dissertation Abstracts* 25 (1964): 1198 (Washington).

Ronald, Margaret A. "Functions of Setting in the Novel: From Mrs. Radcliffe to Charles Dickens." *Dissertation Abstracts International* 31 (1971): 5373A (Northwestern).

Rothstein, Eric. "The Lessons of *Northanger Abbey*." *University of Toronto Quarterly* 44 (Fall 1974): 14–30.

Smith, Nelson Charles. "The Art of Gothic: Ann Radcliffe's Major Novels." *Dissertation Abstracts* 29 (1968): 240A–41A (Washington).

Smith, Nelson Charles. "Sense, Sensibility and Ann Radcliffe." *Studies in English Literature, 1500–1900* 13 (Autumn 1973): 577–90.

Stoler, John A. "Ann Radcliffe: The Novel of Suspense and Terror." *Dissertation Abstracts International* 32 (1972): 5203A (Arizona).

Swigart, Ford H., Jr. "A Study of the Imagery in the Gothic Romances of Ann Radcliffe." *Dissertation Abstracts* 27 (1967): 2509A–10A (Pittsburgh).

Thomas, Donald. "The First Poetess of Romantic Fiction: Ann Radcliffe, 1764–1823." *English* 15 (Autumn 1964): 91–95.

Ware, Marcolm. "Mrs. Radcliffe's 'Picturesque Embellishment.'" *Tennessee Studies in Literature* 5 (1960): 67–71.

Individual Works

The Mysteries of Udolpho (1794)

Allen, M. L. "The Black Veil: Three Versions of a Symbol." *English Studies* 47 (1966): 286–89.

Beaty, Frederick L. "Mrs. Radcliffe's Fading Gleam." *Philological Quarterly* 42 (January 1963): 126–29.

Christensen, Merton A. "Udolpho, Horrid Mysteries and Coleridge's Machinery of the Imagination." *Wordsworth Circle* 2 (Autumn 1971): 153–59.

MARY ANN RADCLIFFE (fl. 1800's) Great Britain
General Works

Adams, Donald K. "The Second Mrs. Radcliffe." *Mystery and Detection Annual* 1 (1972): 48–64.

C.E. RAIMOND [pseud.]. *See* Elizabeth Robins

KATHLEEN RAINE (1908–) Great Britain
General Works

Bevington, H. "Land Unknown." *New York Times Book Review* (October 12, 1975): 5–6.

Foltinek, H. "The Primitive Element in the Poetry of Kathleen Raine." *English Studies* 42 (1961): 15–20.

Mills, Ralph J., Jr. "The Visionary Poetry of Kathleen Raine." *Renascence* 14 (Spring 1962): 139.

Pritchett, V. S. "Love Among the Villas." *New Statesman* (November 23, 1973): 778–80.

Aɴ Rᴀɴᴅ (1905–) U.S. (Born in Russia)
General Works

"The Chairman's Favorite Author." *Time* (September 30, 1974): 87–88.

Cook, Bruce. "Ayn Rand: A Voice in the Wilderness." *Catholic World* (May 1965): 119–25.

"Disturber of the Peace." *Mademoiselle* (May 1962): 172–73.

Ephron, Nora. "A Strange Kind of Simplicity." *New York Times Book Review* (May 5, 1968): 8.

Houtz, Judy. "The End of the Intellectual." *Sequoia* 6 (Spring 1961): 20–23.

Kobler, John. "Curious Cult of Ayn Rand." *Saturday Evening Post* (November 11, 1961): 98–101.

Letwin, William. "A Credo for the Ultras." *Reporter* (October 11, 1962): 56–62.

Lugenbehl, D. "Argument for an Objective Standard of Value (with Reply by W. Dwyer)." *Personalist* 55 (Spring 1974): 155–64.

Michelson, Peter. "Fictive Babble." *New Republic* (February 21, 1970): 21–24.

Nozick, Robert. "On the Randian Argument." *Personalist* 52 (Spring 1971): 282–99.

Root, E. Merrill. "What About Ayn Rand?" *National Review* (January 16, 1960): 76–77.

"Russian-American Author Born Eccentric." *Newsweek* (March 27, 1961): 104–5.

Schroder, Charles Frederick. "Ayn Rand: Far Right Prophetess." *Christian Century* (December 13, 1961): 1493–95.

"Who Is an Objectivist?" *Western World Review* 2 (Fall 1967): 11–14.

Wills, Garry. "But Is Ayn Rand Conservative?" *National Review* (February 27, 1960): 139.

Jᴜᴅɪᴛʜ Rᴀsᴄᴏᴇ (1942–) U.S.
General Works

Schorer, Mark. "Judith Rascoe." *Esquire* (October 1972): 134.

Bᴇᴀᴛʀɪᴄᴇ Rᴀᴠᴇɴᴇʟ (1870–1956) U.S.
Individual Works
The Arrow of Lightning (1925)

Rubin, Louis D., Jr. "The Poetry of Beatrice Ravenel." *South Carolina Review* 1 (November 1968): 55–75.

Mᴀʀᴊᴏʀɪᴇ Kɪɴɴᴀɴ Rᴀᴡʟɪɴɢs (1896–1953) U.S.
General Works

Bellman, Samuel Irving. "Marjorie Kinnan Rawlings: A Solitary Sojourner in the Florida Backwoods." *Kansas Quarterly* 2 (Spring 1970): 78–87.

Bigelow, Gordon E. "Marjorie Kinnan Rawlings' Wilderness." *Sewanee Review* 73 (Spring 1965): 299–310.
Individual Works
Lord Bill of the Suwanee River (1963)

Bigelow, Gordon E. "Marjorie Kinnan Rawlings: *Lord Bill of the Suwanee River.*" *Southern Folklore Quarterly* 27 (1963): 113–31.

Secret River (1955)

Bellman, Samuel I. "Writing Literature for Young People: Marjorie Kinnan Rawlings' *Secret River* of the Imagination." *Costerus* 9 (1973): 19–27.

The Yearling (1938)

Bellman, Samuel I. "Marjorie Kinnan Rawlings' Existentialist Nightmare *The Yearling.*" *Costerus* 9 (1973): 9–18.

Lɪᴢᴇᴛᴛᴇ Wᴏᴏᴅᴡᴏʀᴛʜ Rᴇᴇsᴇ (1856–1935) U.S.
General Works

Dietrich, Mae. "Lizette Woodworth Reese." *Emily Dickinson Bulletin* 15 (1970): 114–22.

Malin, Vincent D. "Lizette Reese Stimulates Effective Writing." *Baltimore Bulletin of Education* 43 (1965–1966): 36–44.

Turnbull, G. H. "Miss Reese and Her Loyal Critic." *Menckeniana* 17 (1966): 9–11.
Individual Works
Tears (1909)

Burch, F.F. "Tennyson and Milton: Sources of Reese's *Tears.*" *American Notes and Queries* 1 (April 1963): 115–17.

Mᴀx Rᴇɪɴᴇʀ [pseud.]. *See* Janet Taylor Caldwell

Jᴇᴀɴɴᴇ Rᴇᴊᴀᴜɴɪᴇʀ (1934–) U.S.
General Works

"What It Takes to Be a Lady Author Anymore." *Life* (November 7, 1969): 91–92.

Mᴀʀʏ Rᴇɴᴀᴜʟᴛ [pseud. of Mary Challans] (1905–) Great Britain

General Works

Burns, Landon C., Jr. "Men Are Only Men: The Novels of Mary Renault." *Critique* 6 (1963–1964): 102–21.

"Imagining the Past." *Times Literary Supplement* (August 23, 1974): 893–94.

Individual Works

The Persian Boy (1972)

Dick, Bernard F. "The Herodotean Novelist." *Sewanee Review* 81 (Autumn 1973): 864–69.

AGNES REPPLIER (1858–1950) U.S.

General Works

Horchler, Dora. "The Essays of Agnes Repplier: An Invitation to Reading." *Modern Age* 5 (Summer 1961): 311–16.

MURIEL RESNIK (1921?–) U.S.

General Works

Poirer, N. "Miracle on Broadway." *Saturday Evening Post* (April 25, 1964): 83–86.

JEAN RHYS (1894–) West Indies

General Works

Braybrooke, Neville. "The Return of Jean Rhys." *Caribbean Quarterly* 16 (December 1970): 43–46.

Cantwell, M. "I'm a Person at a Masked Ball without a Mask: Interview." *Mademoiselle* (October 1974): 170–71.

Mellown, Elgin W. "Characters and Themes in the Novels of Jean Rhys." *Contemporary Literature* 13 (Autumn 1972): 458–75.

Wyndham, Francis. "Introduction to Jean Rhys." *London Magazine*, o.s. 7* (January 1960): 15–18.

ADRIENNE RICH (1931–) U.S.

General Works

Boyers, Robert. "On Adrienne Rich: Intelligence and Will." *Salmagundi* 22–23 (1973): 132–48.

Carruth, Hayden. "To Solve Experience." *Poetry* 109 (January 1967): 267–68.

Flynn, Gale. "The Radicalization of Adrienne Rich." *Hollins Critic* 11 (October 1974): 1–15.

Kalstone, David. "Talking with Adrienne Rich." *Saturday Review* (April 22, 1972): 56–59.

"Looking for Life." *Newsweek* (December 24, 1973): 84–85.

Plumly, Stanley, Wayne Dodd, and Walter Trevis. "Talking with Adrienne Rich." *Ohio Review* 13 (Spring 1971): 28.

Spiegelman, W. "Voice of the Survivor: The Poetry of Adrienne Rich." *Southwest Review* 60 (Autumn 1975): 370–88.

LAURA ELIZABETH RICHARDS (1850–1943) U.S.

Bibliography

Calhoun, Philo, and Howell J. Heaney. "A Checklist of Separately Published Works of Laura E. Richards." *Colby Library Quarterly* 5 (December 1961): 337–43.

Cary, Richard. "Some Richards Manuscripts and Correspondence." *Colby Library Quarterly* 5 (December 1961): 344–56.

General Works

Calhoun, Philo. "More Steps Westward: A Personal Recollection of Laura E. Richards." *Colby Library Quarterly* 5 (December 1961): 326–36.

DOROTHY MILLER RICHARDSON (1872–1957) Great Britain

Bibliography

Glikin, Gloria. "Checklist of Writings by Dorothy M. Richardson." *English Literature in Transition* 8 (1965): 1–11.

General Works

Allentuck, Marcia. "Dorothy Richardson on William Blake and the Broadside: An Unrecorded Appraisal." *Blake Studies* 3 (Spring 1971): 195–96.

Bell, Millicent. "The Single Self." *New Republic* (October 20, 1973): 23–27.

Craig, Patricia. "Dorothy Richardson—'The Damned Egotistical Self.'" *Books and Bookmen* 18 (September 1973): 43–45.

Gilbert, Sandra M. "A Painful Case." *Nation* (September 20, 1975): 246–47.

Glikin, Gloria. "Through the Novelist's Looking Glass." *Kenyon Review* 31 (1969): 297–319.

Glikin, Gloria. "Variations on a Method." *James Joyce Quarterly* 2 (Fall 1964): 42–49.

Haule, James Mark. "The Theme of Isolation in the Fiction of Dorothy M. Richardson, Virginia Woolf, and James Joyce." *Dissertation Abstracts International* 35 (1975): 7905A–6A (Wayne State).

Kaplan, Sydney. " 'Featureless Freedom' or Ironic Submission: Dorothy Richardson and May Sinclair." *College English* 32 (May 1971): 914–17.

Kaplan, Sydney Janet. "The Feminine Consciousness in the Novels of Five Twentieth Century British Women." *Dissertation Abstracts Interna-*

tional 32 (1971): 4615A (California, Los Angeles).

Manning, Olivia. "The Future of the Novel." *John O'London's* (December 20, 1962): 556–60.

Odle, R. I. "Dorothy Richardson." *New York Times Book Review* (October 22, 1967): 48.

Pritchett, V.S. "Moral Gymnasium." *New Statesman* (May 5, 1967): 619.

Rose, Shirley. "Dorothy Richardson: The First Hundred Years, a Retrospective View." *Dalhousie Review* 53 (Spring 1973): 92–96.

Rose, Shirley. "Dorothy Richardson Recalls Yeats." *Ireland* 7 (Spring 1972): 96–102.

Rose, Shirley. "Dorothy Richardson's Focus on Time." *English Literature in Transition* 17 (1974): 163–72.

Tudor, Kathleen R. "The Androgynous Mind in W.B. Yeats, D.H. Lawrence, Virginia Woolf and Dorothy Richardson." *Dissertation Abstracts International* 35 (1974): 1126A–27A (Toronto).

Individual Works

Pilgrimage (1915–1938)

Glikin, Gloria. "Dorothy M. Richardson: The Personal 'Pilgrimage.' " *Publications of the Modern Language Association* 78 (1963): 586–600.

Glikin, Gloria H. "Dorothy Richardson's *Pilgrimage*: A Critical Study." *Dissertation Abstracts* 25 (1964): 1209 (N.Y.U.).

Kaplan, Sydney. " 'Featureless Freedom' or Ironic Submission: Dorothy Richardson and May Sinclair." *College English* 32 (May 1971): 914–17.

Rose, Shirley. "Dorothy Richardson's Theory of Literature: The Writer as Pilgrim." *Criticism* 12 (1970): 20–37.

Rose, Shirley. "The Unmoving Center: Consciousness in Dorothy Richardson's *Pilgrimage*." *Contemporary Literature* 10 (Summer 1969): 366–82.

HENRY HANDEL RICHARDSON [pseud. of Ethel Florence Richardson Robertson] (1870–1946) Australia

Bibliography

Wittrock, Verna D. "Henry Handel Richardson: An Annotated Bibliography of Writings About Her." *English Literature in Transition* 7 (1964): 146–87.

General Works

Barnes, John. "Henry Handel Richardson." *Biblionews and Australian Notes and Queries* 3 (1969): 23–25.

Clark, Dymphna. "The Aurora Borealis: Henry Handel Richardson as a Translator." *Quadrant* 18 (1973): 21–30.

Clutton-Brock, M.H. "Mrs. Lins: Sister to Henry Handel Richardson." *Southerly* 27 (1967): 46–59.

Elliott, William D. "H.H. Richardson: The Education of an Australian Realist." *Studies in the Novel* 4 (Summer 1972): 141–53.

Elliott, William D. "Scandinavian Influences in the Novels of H. H. Richardson." *Discourse* 12 (Spring 1969): 249–54.

Green, Dorothy. "Henry Handel Richardson: Mimes and Kelly." *Meanjin Quarterly* 31 (1972): 162–66.

Green, Dorothy. " 'I Will Say Music, Too . . .': A Note on Henry Handel Richardson's Songs." *Meanjin Quarterly* 32 (1973): 466–67.

Green, Dorothy. "A Poet in Prose Who Saw 'With Energy.' " *Hemisphere* 13 (1969): 22–27.

Heseltine, H.P. "Criticism and the Individual Talent." *Meanjin Quarterly* 31 (1972): 10–24.

Jeffares, A. Norman. "Richard Mahony Exile." *Journal of Commonwealth Literature* 6 (January 1969): 106–19.

Kaplan, Sydney Janet. "The Feminine Consciousness in the Novels of Five Twentieth Century British Women." *Dissertation Abstracts International* 32 (1971): 4615A (California, Los Angeles).

Phillips, A.A. "A Harmony of Minds: Dorothy Green's Study of Henry Handel Richardson." *Meanjin Quarterly* 33 (1974): 80–85.

Wilkes, G.A. "Henry Handel Richardson: Some Uncollected Writings." *Southerly* 22 (1963): 6.

Individual Works

The Fortunes of Richard Mahony (1930)

Elliott, William D. "*The Fortunes of Richard Mahony*: A Critical Appraisal." *Dissertation Abstracts* 28 (1967): 2243A (Michigan).

Elliott, William D. "French Influences in *The Fortunes of Richard Mahony*." *Discourse* 11 (Winter 1968): 108–15.

Foster, I.M. "Richard Mahony's Tragedy." *Australian Literary Studies* 4 (1970): 279–80.

Green, Dorothy. "The Pilgrim Soul: The Philosophical Structure of *The Fortunes of Richard Mahony*." *Meanjin Quarterly* 28 (1969): 328–37.

Kiernan, Brian. "*The Fortunes of Richard Mahony*." *Southerly* 29 (1969): 199–209.

Loder, Elizabeth. *The Fortunes of Richard Mahony*:

Dream and Nightmare." *Southerly* 25 (1965): 251–63.

Stewart, Ken. "Dr. Richardson and Dr. Mahony." *Southerly* 33 (1973): 74–79.

Stewart, Kenneth. "History and Fiction in *The Fortunes of Richard Mahony.*" *Teaching History* 4 (1970): 24–39.

Stewart, Kenneth. "The Prototype of Richard Mahony." *Australian Literary Studies* 4 (1970): 227–40.

The Getting of Wisdom (1910)

Elliott, William D. "Richardson's Realism and *The Getting of Wisdom.*" *Discourse* 12 (Spring 1969): 112–16.

Maurice Guest (1908)

Kiernan, Brian. "Romantic Conventions and *Maurice Guest.*" *Southerly* 28 (1968): 286–94.

Loder, Elizabeth. "*Maurice Guest*: An Innocent Abroad." *Balcony* 4 (1966): 34–37.

Loder, Elizabeth. "*Maurice Guest*: Some Nineteenth-Century Progenitors." *Southerly* 26 (1966): 94–105.

Palmer, Anthony J. "A Link with Late Nineteenth-Century Decadence in *Maurice Guest.*" *Australian Literary Studies* 5 (1972): 366–73.

Stewart, Ken. "*Maurice Guest* and the Siren Voices." *Australian Literary Studies* 5 (1972): 352–65.

The Young Cosima (1939)

Green, Dorothy. "*The Young Cosima.*" *Australian Literary Studies* 4 (1970): 215–26.

Triebel, L.A. "*The Young Cosima.*" *Australian Literary Studies* 1 (1963): 53–57.

Laura Riding, Mrs. Jackson (1901–) U.S.
General Works

"An Ambition Beyond Poetry." *Times Literary Supplement* (February 9, 1973): 151–52; (March 9, 1973): 268.

Jackson, Laura Riding. "Correspondence: The Cult of 'Connections.'" *Private Library* 6 (Autumn 1973): 133–41.

Jackson, Laura Riding. "A Postscript." *Private Library* 5 (Autumn 1972): 139–47.

Raiziss, Sonia. "An Appreciation." *Chelsea* 12 (September 1962): 28–31.

Anne Ridler, née Bradby (1912–) Great Britain
General Works

Kliewer, Warren. "Theological Form in Anne Ridler's Plays." *Approach*, no. 52 (Summer 1964): 22–32.

Morgan, Kathleen E. "The Holiness of the Heart's Affections: Aspects of the Poetry of Anne Ridler." *English* 16 (Spring 1966): 2–5.

Jessie Belle Rittenhouse (1869–1948) U.S.
General Works

Cohen, Edward H. "The Letters of Sara Teasdale to Jessie B. Rittenhouse." *Resources for American Literary Studies* 4 (1974): 225–27.

Amélie Rives, Princess Troubetzkoy (1863–1945) U.S.
General Works

Gallup, Donald. "More Letters of American Writers." *Yale University Library Gazette* 37 (1962): 30–35.

Taylor, Welford D. "Amélie Rives: A Virginia Princess." *Virginia Cavalcade* 12 (Spring 1963): 11–17.

Individual Works

Shadows of Flames (1915)

Taylor, Welford D. "A 'Soul' Remembers Oscar Wilde." *English Literature in Transition* 14 (1971): 43–48.

Judith Rives (fl. 1830s) U.S.
General Works

Moore, John H. "Judith Rives of Castle Hill." *Virginia Cavalcade* 13 (Spring 1964): 30–35.

Elizabeth Madox Roberts (1886–1941) U.S.
General Works

Hawley, Isabel L. "Elizabeth Madox Roberts: Her Development as Self-Conscious Narrative Artist." *Dissertation Abstracts International* 31 (1971): 4163A (North Carolina).

Murphy, John J. "Elizabeth Madox Roberts and the Civilizing Consciousness." *Kentucky Historical Society Register* 64 (April 1966): 110–20.

Nilles, Mary. "Social Development in the Poetry of Elizabeth Madox Roberts." *Markham Review* 2 (September 1969): 18–22.

Nilles, Mary E. "The Rise and Decline of a Literary Reputation: Vagaries in the Career of Elizabeth Madox Roberts." *Dissertation Abstracts International* 33 (1972): 2945A–46A (N.Y.U.).

Spears, Woodridge. "Elizabeth Madox Roberts: A Biographical and Critical Study." *Dissertation Ab-*

stracts 20 (1960): 3753–54 (Kentucky).

Warren, Robert Penn. "Elizabeth Madox Roberts: Life Is from Within." *Saturday Review* (March 2, 1963): 20.

Individual Works

On the Mountainside (1932)

Foster, Ruel E. "An Undiscovered Source for Elizabeth Madox Roberts' *On the Mountainside.*" *West Virginia University Bulletin: Philological Papers* 15 (June 1966): 57–61.

ETHEL FLORENCE RICHARDSON ROBERTSON. *See* Henry Handel Richardson

ELIZABETH ROBINS [pseud. C. E. Raimond] (1865–1952) U.S.

General Works

Marcus, Jane C. "Elizabeth Robins." *Dissertation Abstracts* 34 (1973): 3414A (Northwestern).

HARRIET H. ROBINSON (1825–1911) U.S.

General Works

Schneir, Miriam. "Harriet H. Robinson: An American Mill Girl." *Ms.* (August 1972): 12.

JILL ROBINSON, née Schary (fl. 1970s) U.S.

Individual Works

Bed Time Story (1974)

Gottlieb, A. "Bed Time Story." *New York Times Book Review* (October 27, 1974): 42–43.

ELLEN ROSS, née McGregor (1816?–1892) Canada

General Works

Wallock, Jeffrey L. "Ellen Ross (1816?–1892): 'Violet Keith and All That Sort of Thing.'" *Journal of Canadian Fiction* 3 (1974): 80–88.

MARTIN ROSS [pseud.] *See* Violet Florence Martin

CHRISTINA GEORGINA ROSSETTI (1830–1894) Great Britain

Bibliography

Fraser, R.S. "The Rossetti Collection of Janet Camp Troxell: A Survey with Some Sidelights." *Princeton University Library Chronicle* 33 (Spring 1972): 146–75.

Weideman, Rebecca S. "A Critical Bibliography of Christina Rossetti." *Dissertation Abstracts International* 31 (1970): 6075A–76A (Texas).

General Works

Adlard, John. "Christina Rossetti: Strategies of Loneliness." *Critical Review* 15 (1972): 146–50

Baumbach, Frances E. "Relativity and Polarity in Christina Rossetti." *Dissertation Abstracts* 29 (1968): 1889A (Wisconsin).

Cook, Wister J. "The Sonnets of Christina Rossetti: A Comparative Prosodic Analysis." *Dissertation Abstracts International* 32 (1972): 6419A–20A (Auburn).

Crump, R.W. "Eighteen Moments' Monuments: Christina Rossetti's 'Bouts Rimes' Sonnets in the Troxell Collection." *Princeton University Library Chronicle* 33 (Spring 1972): 210–29.

Curran, Stuart. "The Lyric Voice of Christina Rossetti." *Victorian Poetry* 9 (Autumn 1971): 287–99.

Herendeen, Warren. "The Midsummer Eves of Shakespeare and Christina Rossetti." *Victorian Newsletter* 41 (Spring 1972): 24–26.

Honnighausen, Gisela. "Emblematic Tendencies in the Works of Christina Rossetti." *Victorian Poetry* 10 (Spring 1972): 1–15.

Kmetz, Gail. "With Stillness That Is Almost Paradise: Romanticism and Mysticism in the Poetry of Christina Rossetti." *Dissertation Abstracts International* 34 (1973): 3405A–6A (Columbia).

Kohl, James. "A Medical Comment on Christina Rossetti." *Notes and Queries* 15 (November 1968): 423–24.

Kohl, James A. "Sparks of Fire: Christina Rossetti's Artistic Life." *Dissertation Abstracts* 30 (1970): 2972A (Delaware).

Owen, Marion. "Christina Rossetti: 'Affairs of the Heart.'" *Humanities Association Bulletin* 21 (Summer 1970): 16–25.

Packer, Lona Mosk. "Christina Rossetti." *Times Literary Supplement* (December 24, 1964): 1163.

Packer, Lona Mosk. "Controversy: Christina Rossetti." *Victorian Studies* 8 (March 1965): 278–80.

Packer, Lona Mosk. "F. S. Ellis and the Rossettis: A Publishing Venture and Misadventure, 1870." *Western Humanities Review* 16 (Summer 1962): 243–53.

Packer, Lona Mosk. "Swinburne and Christina Rossetti: Atheist and Anglican." *University of Toronto Quarterly* 33 (October 1963): 30–42.

Putt, S. Gorley. "Christina Rossetti, Alms-giver." *English* 13 (Autumn 1961): 222–23.

Ricks, Christopher. " 'O Where Are You Going?':
W. H. Auden and Christina Rossetti." *Notes and
Queries* 7 (December 1960): 472.

Standley, Fred L. "Christina Georgina to Dante
Gabriel: An Unpublished Letter." *English Language Notes* 5 (June 1968): 283–85.

Individual Works

Acme (1906)

Janowitz, K.E. "The Antipodes of Self: Three
Poems of Christina Rossetti." *Victorian Poetry* 11
(Autumn 1973): 195–205.

Amor Mundi (1865)

Brzenk, Eugene J. "*Up-Hill* and Down by Christina
Rossetti." *Victorian Poetry* 10 (Winter 1972):
367–71.

A Birthday (1857)

Festa, Conrad. "Symbol and Meaning in *A Birthday*." *English Language Notes* 11 (September
1973): 50–56.

Lynde, Richard D. "A Note on the Imagery in
Christina Rossetti's *A Birthday*." *Victorian Poetry* 3
(Autumn 1965): 261–63.

Goblin Market and Other Poems (1862)

Festa, Conrad. "Studies in Christina Rossetti's
Goblin Market and Other Poems." *Dissertation Abstracts* 30 (1970): 5407A (South Carolina).

Weathers, Winston. "Christina Rossetti: The Sisterhood of Self." *Victorian Poetry* 3 (Spring 1965):
81–89.

Il Rossegiar Dell' Oriente (1868)

Kohl, James A. "Christina Rossetti's *Il Rossegiar
Dell' Oriente*." *Antigonish Review* 2 (Summer
1971): 47–61.

Monna Innominata (1862)

Wenger, Helen H. "The Influence of the Bible in
Christina Rossetti's *Monna Innominata*." *Christian
Scholar's Review* 3 (1973): 15–24.

A Nightmare (1896)

De Groot, H.B. "Christina Rossetti's *A Nightmare*:
A Fragment Completed." *Review of English Studies* 24 (February 1973): 48–52.

A Pageant and Other Poems (1881)

Uffelman, Larry K. "Christina Rossetti's *A Pageant
and Other Poems*: An Annotated Critical Edition."
Dissertation Abstracts 30 (1970): 5422A (Kansas
State).

Waller, John O. "Christ's Second Coming:
Christina Rossetti and the Premillennialist,
William Dodsworth." *Bulletin of the New York
Public Library* 73 (September 1969): 465–82.

Restive (1906)

Janowitz, K.E. "The Antipodes of Self: Three
Poems of Christina Rossetti." *Victorian Poetry* 11
(Autumn 1973): 195–205.

Songs in a Cornfield (1863)

Packer, Lona Mosk. "Christina Rossetti's *Songs in a
Cornfield*: A Misprint Uncorrected." *Notes and
Queries* 9 (March 1962): 97–100.

Spring Quiet (1847)

Janowitz, K.E. "The Antipodes of Self: Three
Poems of Christina Rossetti." *Victorian Poetry* 11
(Autumn 1973): 195–205.

Up-Hill (1861)

Brzenk, Eugene J. "*Up-Hill* and Down by Christina
Rossetti." *Victorian Poetry* 10 (Winter 1972):
367–71.

MARIA FRANCESCA ROSSETTI (1827–1876) Great
Britain

General Works

Packer, L.M. "Maria Francesca to Dante Gabriel
Rossetti: Some Unpublished Letters." *Publications
of the Modern Language Association* 79 (1964):
613–19.

ELIZABETH ROWE [pseud. Philomela] (1674–1737)
Great Britain

General Works

Chapman, C.H. "Benjamin Colman and Philomela."
New England Quarterly 42 (June 1969): 214–31.

Richetti, John J. "Mrs. Elizabeth Rowe: The Novel
as Polemic." *Publications of the Modern Language
Association* 82 (1967): 522–29.

MARY ROWLANDSON, née White (c. 1635–c.–1678)
U.S.

Individual Works

*The Sovereignty & Goodness of God, Together with the
Faithfulness of His Promises Displayed; Being a
Narrative of the Captivity and Restauration of Mrs.
Mary Rowlandson* (1682)

Diebold, Robert K. "A Critical Edition of Mrs. Mary
Rowlandson's Captivity Narrative." *Dissertation
Abstracts International* 33 (1972): 2368A (Yale).

Leach, Douglas Edward. "The When's of Mary
Rowlandson's Captivity." *New England Quarterly*
34 (September 1961): 352–63.

SUSANNA HASWELL ROWSON (1762–1824) U.S.
(Born in Great Britain)

General Works

Brandt, Ellen B. "Susanna Haswell Rowson: A Critical Biography." *Dissertation Abstracts International* 35 (1974): 2214A (Penn.).

Giffen, J.C. "Susanna Rowson and Her Academy." *Antiques* 98 (September 1970): 436–40.

Martin, Wendy. "Profile: Susanna Rowson, Early American Novelist." *Women's Studies* 2 (1974): 1–8.

Weil, Dorothy L. "Susanna Rowson, the Young Lady's Friend." *Dissertation Abstracts International* 35 (1974): 3705A–6A (Cincinnati).

GABRIELLE ROY (1909–) Canada
General Works

Grosskurth, Phyllis. "Gabrielle Roy." *Canadian Literature*, no. 42 (Autumn 1969): 6–13.

ANNE NEWPORT ROYALL (1769–1854) U.S.
General Works

Griffith, Lucille. "Anne Royall in Alabama." *Alabama Review* 21 (January 1968): 53–63.

MURIEL RUKEYSER (1913–) U.S.
General Works

Carruth, Hayden. "The Closest Permissible Approximation." *Poetry* 101 (February 1963): 358–60.

Individual Works
Waterlily Fire (1962)

Adkins, Joan F. "The Esthetics of Science: Muriel Rukeyser's *Waterlily Fire*." *Contemporary Poetry* 1 (Winter 1973): 23–27.

LAVINIA RUSS, née Faxon (1904–) U.S.
Individual Works
A High Old Time, or, How to Enjoy Being a Woman Over Sixty (1972)

Bannon, B.A. "Story behind the Book: *A High Old Time, or, How to Enjoy Being a Woman Over Sixty*." *Publishers Weekly* (April 3, 1972): 46–47.

S

VICTORIA MARY SACKVILLE-WEST (1892–1962)
Great Britain
General Works
Annan, Noel. "Love and Friendship." *New States-man* (October 26, 1973): 601–2.

Auchincloss, K. "Duality of Love." *Newsweek* (November 5, 1973): 99A.

Gordan, John D. "Letters to an Editor: Georgia Poetry 1912–1922: An Exhibition from the Berg Collection." *Bulletin of the New York Public Library* 71 (May 1967): 300.

Haight, Gordon S. "The Permissive Edwardians." *Yale Review* 63 (Spring 1974): 416–21.

MacKnight, Nancy Margaret. "Vita: A Portrait of V. Sackville-West." *Dissertation Abstracts International* 35 (1975): 7914A (Columbia).

Nicolson, B. "Robin and Lady Sackville." *Burlington Magazine* 112 (January 1970): 37–43.

Parmacek, S.L. "Pèche Melba." *Time* (November 12, 1973): 128.

"Poet's Rose Garden." *Vogue* (October 1961): 129–31.

Rosenthal, M. "One for the Vita Market." *New York Times Book Review* (July 28, 1974): 6.

"Sackville-West: A Tower for Her." *Newsweek* (April 24, 1961): 100–101.

Sayre, N. "Portrait of a Marriage." *New York Times Book Review* (October 28, 1973): 2–3.

SONIA SANCHEZ (1934–) U.S.
General Works
Clarke, Sebastian. "Black Magic Woman: Sonia Sanchez and Her Work." *Présence Africaine* 78 (1971): 253–61.

Clarke, Sebastian. "Sonia Sanchez and Her Work." *Black World* 20 (June 1971): 44.

Palmer, R. Roderick. "The Poetry of Three Revolutionists: Don L. Lee, Sonia Sanchez and Nikki Giovanni." *College Language Association Journal* 15 (September 1971): 25–36.

MARI SANDOZ (1901–1966) U.S.
General Works
Lowe, David. "A Meeting with Mari Sandoz." *Prairie Schooner* 42 (Spring 1968): 21–26.

"Mari Sandoz: 1935." *Prairie Schooner* 41 (Summer 1967): 172–77.

Nicoll, Bruce H. "Mari Sandoz: Nebraska Loner." *American West* 2 (Spring 1965): 32–36.

Rice, Minnie C. "Mari Sandoz: Biography of the Old West." *Midwest Review* (Spring 1960): 44–49.

Stauffer, Helen Arlene Winter. "Mari Sandoz: A Study of the Artist as a Biographer." *Dissertation Abstracts International* 35 (1975): 5429A (Nebraska).

Switzer, Dorothy Nott. "Mari Sandoz's Lincoln Years: A Personal Recollection." *Prairie Schooner* 45 (Summer 1971): 107–15.

Walton, Kathleen. "Mari Sandoz: An Initial Critical Appraisal." *Dissertation Abstracts International* 32 (1971): 461A (Delaware).

MAY SARTON (1912–) U.S.
General Works
Bannon, B.A. "May Sarton." *Publisher Weekly* (June 24, 1974): 16–17.

Putney, Paula G. "Sister of the Mirage and Echo: An Interview with May Sarton." *Contempora* 2 (1972): 1–6.

Taylor, Henry. "Home to a Place Beyond Exile: The Collected Poems of May Sarton." *Hollins Critic* 11 (June 1974): 1–16.

DOROTHY LEIGH SAYERS (1893–1957) Great Britain
Bibliography
Christopher, J.R. "A Sayers Bibliography: Part 4." *Unicorn* 2 (1973): 28–30.
General Works
Bernikow, L. "Such a Strange Lady." *New York Times Book Review* (November 9, 1975): 51.
Burleson, James Bernard, Jr. "A Study of the Novels of Dorothy L. Sayers." *Dissertation Abstracts* 26 (1965): 2204 (Texas).
Fairman, Marion Baker. "The Neo-Medieval Plays of Dorothy L. Sayers." *Dissertation Abstracts* 23 (1962): 1016–17 (Pittsburgh).
Green, Martin. "The Detection of a Snob." *Listener* (March 14, 1963): 461–64.
Heilbrun, Carolyn. "Sayers, Lord Peter and God." *American Scholar* 37 (Spring 1968): 324–34.
Peters, Margot, and Agate N. Krouse. "Women and Crime: Sexism in Allingham, Sayers, and Christie." *Southwest Review* 59 (Spring 1974): 144–52.
Rickman, H.P. "From Detection to Theology: The Work of Dorothy Sayers." *Hibbert Journal* 60 (1962): 290–96.
Smith, Sheldon Moody. "Three British Christians." *National Review* (May 18, 1971): 545–48.
Soloway, Sara L. "Dorothy Sayers: Novelist." *Dissertation Abstracts International* 32 (1971): 2105A (Kentucky).
Individual Works
Gaudy Night (1935)
Ray, Laura K. "The Mysteries of *Gaudy Night*: Feminism, Faith and the Depths of Character." *Mystery and Detection Annual* 3 (1974): 272–85.

DOROTHY SCARBOROUGH (1878–1935) U.S.
General Works
Neatherlin, James W. "Dorothy Scarborough: Form and Milieu in the Work of a Texas Writer." *Dissertation Abstracts International* 34 (1973): 3421A–22A (Iowa).

GLADYS SCHMITT (1909–1972) U.S.
General Works
Fuller, Edmund. "Gladys Schmitt." *American Scholar* 30 (Summer 1961): 411–17.

OLIVE SCHREINER [pseud. Ralph Iron] (1865–1920) South Africa

Bibliography
Rive, Richard M. "Olive Schreiner: A Critical Study and a Checklist." *Studies in the Novel* 4 (Summer 1972): 231–51.
General Works
Beeton, Ridley. "Two Notes on Olive Schreiner's Letters." *Research in African Literature* 3 (Fall 1972): 180–89.
Jacobson, Dan. "Olive Schreiner: A South African Writer." *London Magazine* 10 (February 1971): 5–21.
Laredo, Ursula. "Olive Schreiner." *Journal of Commonwealth Literature* 6 (December 1969): 107–24.

VIDA DUTTON SCUDDER (1861–1954) U.S.
General Works
Frederick, Peter J. "Vida Dutton Scudder: The Professor as Social Activist." *New England Quarterly* 43 (September 1970): 407–31.

CATHARINE MARIA SEDGWICK (1789–1867) U.S.
General Works
Gallup, Donald. "More Letters of American Writers." *Yale University Library Gazette* 37 (1962): 30–35.
Individual Works
Hope Leslie, or Early Times in the Massachusetts (1827)
Bell, Michael D. "History and Romance Convention in Catharine Sedgwick's *Hope Leslie*." *American Quarterly* 22 (Summer 1970): 213–21.

ANYA SETON (1916–) U.S.
Individual Works
Devil Water (1962)
"Best-Seller." *New Yorker* (May 12, 1962): 34.

ANNA SEWARD (1747–1809) Great Britain
General Works
Mackerness, E.D. "Some Anna Seward Marginalia." *Notes and Queries* 9 (May 1962): 176.
Rousseau, G.S. "Anna Seward to William Hayley: A Letter from the Swan of Lichfield." *Harvard Library Bulletin* 15 (1967): 273–80.
Woolley, James D. "Johnson as Despot: Anna Seward's Rejected Contribution to Boswell's *Life*." *Modern Philology* 70 (November 1972): 140–45.

FANNY SEWARD (fl. 1860s) U.S.
General Works
Johnson, Patricia C., ed. "Stumping for Lincoln in 1860: Excerpts from the Diary of Fanny Seward." *University of Rochester Library Bulletin* 16 (Autumn 1960): 1–15.

ELIZABETH MISSING SEWELL (1815–1906) Great Britain
General Works
Frerichs, Sarah Cutts. "Elizabeth Missing Sewell: A Minor Novelist's Search for the *Via Media* in the Education of Women in the Victorian Era." *Dissertation Abstracts International* 35 (1975): 7303A (Brown).

ANNE SEXTON, née Harvey (1928–1974) U.S.
General Works
Axelrod, Rise B. "The Transforming Art of Anne Sexton." *Concerning Poetry* 7 (1974): 6–13.
Fein, Richard J. "The Demon of Anne Sexton." *English Record* 18 (October 1967): 16–21.
Jones, A. R. "Necessity and Freedom: The Poetry of Robert Lowell, Sylvia Plath and Anne Sexton." *Critical Quarterly* 7 (Spring 1965): 11–30.
Kevles, Barbara. "The Art of Poetry 15: Anne Sexton." *Paris Review* 13 (Summer 1971): 158–91.
Levertov, Denise. "Anne Sexton: Light Up the Cave." *Ramparts* (December 1974): 61–63.
Marx, Patricia. "Interview with Anne Sexton." *Hudson Review* 18 (Winter 1965–1966): 560–70.
McClatchy, J.D. "Anne Sexton: Somehow to Endure." *Centennial Review* 19 (1975): 1–36.
McDonnell, Thomas P. "Light in a Dark Journey." *America* (May 13, 1967): 729–31.
Mizejewski, Linda. "Sappho to Sexton: Woman Uncontained." *College English* 35 (December 1973): 340–45.
Mood, John J. "*A Bird Full of Bones*: Anne Sexton— A Visit and a Reading." *Chicago Review* 23 (1972): 107–23.
Newlin, Margaret. "The Suicide Bandwagon." *Critical Quarterly* 14 (Winter 1972): 367–78.
O'Brien, John. "R.I.P. . . . Anne Sexton." *Oyez Review* (Roosevelt University) 9 (Spring 1975): 45–49.
Smith, Hal. "Anne Sexton." *Epoch* 12 (Fall 1962): 124–26.
Zollman, Sol. "Criticism, Self-Criticism, No Trans-

formation: The Poetry of Robert Lowell and Anne Sexton." *Literature and Ideology* 9 (1971): 29–36.
Individual Works
For My Lover . . . (1968)
Shoz, Ira. "Anne Sexton's *For My Lover . . .*: Feminism in the Classroom." *College English* 34 (May 1973): 1082–93.
Live or Die (1966)
Boyers, Robert. "*Live or Die:* The Achievement of Anne Sexton." *Salmagundi* 2 (1967): 61–71.
Legler, Philip. "O Yellow Eye." *Plamuk* 110 (May 1967): 125–27.
Transformations (1971)
Armstrong, Roberta R. "Sexton's *Transformations*: Beyond Confessionalism." *Iowa English Bulletin: Yearbook* 24 (1974): 57–66.

MARGERY SHARP (1905–) Great Britain
Individual Works
The Nutmeg Tree (1941)
Bullough, Geoffrey. "Literary Relations of Shaw's Mrs. Warren." *Philological Quarterly* 41 (January 1962): 339–58.

MARY WOLLSTONECRAFT SHELLEY, née Godwin (1797–1851) Great Britain
Bibliography
Juel-Jensen, Bent. "Contemporary Collectors, 43." *Book Collector* 15 (Summer 1966): 152–74.
General Works
Brown, T.J. "Some Shelley Forgeries by 'Major Byron.'" *Keats-Shelley Memorial Bulletin* 14 (1963): 47–54.
Huntley, Reid De Berry. "Thomas Wolfe's Idea of the Imagination: Similarities to the Views of the Nineteenth Century." *Dissertation Abstracts International* 31 (1970): 390A (North Carolina).
Lovell, Ernest J. "Byron, Mary Shelley, and Madame de Staël." *Keats-Shelley Journal* 14 (1965): 13.
Luke, Hugh J., Jr. "Sir William Laurence: Physician to Shelley and Mary." *Papers on Language and Literature* 1 (1965): 141–52.
Lund, Mary G. "Mary Shelley's Father." *Discourse* 12 (Winter 1969): 130–35.
Massey, Irvin. "Mary Shelley, Walter Scott, and 'Maga.'" *Notes and Queries* 9 (November 1962): 420–21.
Newmann, Bonnie R. "Mary Shelley." *Dissertation Abstracts International* 33 (1973): 5689A (New Mexico).

Nitchie, Elizabeth. "Mary Shelley, Traveler." *Keats-Shelley Journal* 10 (1961): 29–42.

Nitchie, Elizabeth. "Shelley at Eton: Mary Shelley vs Jefferson Hogg." *Keats-Shelley Memorial Bulletin* 11 (1960): 48–54.

Palacio, Jean de. "Mary Shelley's Latin Studies: Her Unpublished Translation of Apuleius." *Revue de Littérature Comparée* 38 (1964): 564–71.

Powers, Katherine R. "The Influence of William Godwin on the Novels of Mary Shelley." *Dissertation Abstracts International* 33 (1973): 4359A (Tennessee).

Raymond, William O. "Browning and the Harriet Westbrook Shelley Letters." *University of Toronto Quarterly* 32 (January 1963): 184–92.

Rieger, James. "Shelley's Paterin Beatrice." *Studies in Romanticism* 4 (Spring 1965): 169–84.

Rose, Catherine Papadopoulou. "Shelley's View of Women." *Dissertation Abstracts* 21 (1960): 1186 (Claremont).

Wade, Philip T. "Influence and Intent in the Prose Fiction of Percy and Mary Shelley." *Dissertation Abstracts* 27 (1967): 3021A (North Carolina).

Warman, Christopher. "A Woman Who Made Room at the Top." *London Times* (August 7, 1972): 5.

Individual Works

Falkner (1837)

Ozolins, Aija. "The Novels of Mary Shelley: From *Frankenstein* to *Falkner*." *Dissertation Abstracts International* 33 (1972): 2389A (Maryland).

The Fortunes of Perkin Warbeck (1830)

Dunleavy, Gareth W. "Two New Mary Shelley Letters and the 'Irish' Chapters of *Perkin Warbeck*." *Keats-Shelley Journal* 13 (1964): 6–9.

Frankenstein, or the Modern Prometheus (1818)

Arnold, Donna. "Frankenstein's Monster: Paragon or Paranoiac?" *Trace* 54 (Autumn 1964): 285–87.

Bloom, Harold. "Frankenstein, or The New Prometheus." *Partisan Review* 32 (1965): 611–18.

Callahan, Patrick J. "Frankenstein, Bacon, and the 'Two Truths.'" *Extrapolation* 14 (1972): 39–48.

Coleman, William E. "On the Discrimination of Gothicisms." *Dissertation Abstracts International* 31 (1970): 2871A (C.U.N.Y.).

Crafts, Stephen. "*Frankenstein*: Camp Curiosity or Premonition?" *Catalyst* 3 (Summer 1967): 96–103.

Cude, Wilfred. "Mary Shelley's Modern Prometheus: A Study in the Ethics of Scientific Creativity." *Dalhousie Review* 52 (Summer 1972): 212–25.

Dunn, R.J. "Narrative Distance in *Frankenstein*." *Studies in the Novel* 6 (Winter 1974): 408–17.

Fleck, P.D. "Mary Shelley's Notes to Shelley's Poems and *Frankenstein*." *Studies in Romanticism* 6 (Summer 1967): 226–54.

Gaylin, Willard. "The Frankenstein Myth Becomes a Reality—We Have the Awful Knowledge to Make Exact Copies of Human Beings." *New York Times Magazine* (March 5, 1972): 12–13.

Greene, D. Randolf. "The Romantic Prometheus: Varieties of the Heroic Quest." *Dissertation Abstracts International* 35 (1974): 403A (Wisconsin).

Hume, Robert D. "Gothic versus Romantic: A Revaluation of the Gothic Novel." *Publications of the Modern Language Association* 84 (1969): 282–90.

Kmetz, G. "Mary Shelley: In the Shadow of *Frankenstein*." *Ms.* (February 1975): 12–16.

Levine, George. "*Frankenstein* and the Tradition of Realism." *Novel* 7 (Fall 1973): 14–30.

Lund, Mary Graham. "The Faustian Theme in Mary Shelley's *Frankenstein*." *Western World Review* 2 (Fall 1967): 6–10.

Lund, Mary Graham. "Mary Godwin Shelley and the Monster." *University of Kansas City Review* 28 (1962): 253–58.

Lund, Mary Graham. "Shelley as Frankenstein." *Forum* 4 (Fall 1963): 28–31.

Lyles, William H. "Mary Shelley and *Frankenstein*." *Times Literary Supplement* (August 2, 1974): 834–35.

Mays, Milton A. "*Frankenstein*—Mary Shelley's Black Theodicy." *Southern Humanities Review* 3 (Spring 1969): 146–53.

McKenney, John L. "Nietzsche and the Frankenstein Creature." *Dalhousie Review* 41 (Spring 1961): 40–48.

Nelson, Lowry, Jr. "Night Thoughts on the Gothic Novel." *Yale Review* 52 (Winter 1963): 236–57.

Ozolins, Aija. "The Novels of Mary Shelley: From *Frankenstein* to *Falkner*." *Dissertation Abstracts International* 33 (1972): 2389A (Maryland).

Palmer, D.J., and R.E. Dowse. "*Frankenstein*: A Moral Fable." *Listener* (August 23, 1962): 281–84.

Pollin, Burton R. "Philosophical and Literary Sources of *Frankenstein*." *Comparative Literature* 17 (1965): 97–108.

Pollin, Burton R. " 'Rappaccini's Daughter'—Sources and Names." *Names* 14 (1966): 30–35.

Rao, E. Nageswara. "The Significance of *Frankenstein*." *Triveni* 37 (1968): 20–26.

Rieger, James. "Dr. Polidori and the Genesis of *Frankenstein*." *Studies in English Literature, 1500–1900* 3 (Autumn 1963): 461–72.

Robinson, Charles E. "Mary Shelley and the Roger Dodsworth Hoax." *Keats-Shelley Journal* 24 (1975): 20–28.

Rosenberg, Samuel. "The Horrible Truth about *Frankenstein*." *Life* (March 15, 1968): 74B–84.

Swingle, L. J. "Frankenstein's Monster and Its Romantic Relatives: Problems of Knowledge in English Romanticism." *Texas Studies in Literature and Language* 15 (Spring 1973): 51–65.

Tropp, Martina. "Mary Shelley's Monster: A Study of *Frankenstein*." *Dissertation Abstracts International* 34 (1973): 1871A (Boston).

Wade, Phil. "On the Occasion of the 150th Birthday of Frankenstein's Monster: Some Thoughts on His Parentage." *South Atlantic Bulletin* 34 (1969):10.

Journals (1814–1844)

Feldman, Paula Renee. "The Journals of Mary Wollstonecraft Shelley: An Annotated Edition." *Dissertation Abstracts International* 35 (1975): 6663A (Northwestern).

The Last Man (1826)

Hildebrand, William H. "On Three Prometheuses: Shelley's Two and Mary's One." *Serif* 11 (Summer 1974): 3–11.

Luke, Hugh J., Jr. "*The Last Man*: Mary Shelley's Myth of the Solitary." *Prairie Schooner* 39 (Winter 1965–1966): 316–27.

Miller, Arthur. "*The Last Man*: A Study of the Eschatological Theme in English Poetry and Fiction from 1806 through 1839." *Dissertation Abstracts* 28 (1967): 687A (Duke).

The Parvenue (1836)

Pollin, Burton R. "Mary Shelley as *The Parvenue*." *Review of English Literature* 8 (July 1967): 9–21.

FRANCES SHERIDAN (1724–1766) Great Britain
General Works

Sheldon, Esther K. "Frances Sheridan's Comedies: Three Stages in the Development of Her Comic Art." *Theater Annual* 26 (1970): 1–23.

DORA SIGERSON SHORTER (1866–1918) Great Britain
General Works

Hanley, E.A. "Dora Sigerson Shorter: Late Victorian Romantic." *Victorian Poetry* 3 (Autumn 1965): 223–34.

PENELOPE SHUTTLE (1947–) Great Britain
General Works

"To Be a Prodigy." *Times Educational Supplement* (June 12, 1970): 9–10.

LYDIA HUNTLEY SIGOURNEY (1791–1865) U.S.
General Works

Green, David Bonnell. "William Wordsworth and Lydia Huntley Sigourney." *New England Quarterly* 37 (December 1964): 527–31.

Wood, Ann Douglas. "Mrs. Sigourney and the Sensibility of Inner Space." *New England Quarterly* 45 (June 1972): 163–81.

LOUISA SIMPSON [pseud.]. *See* Harriette Arnow

MAY SINCLAIR (1865–1946) Great Britain
Bibliography

Boll, T.E.M. "May Sinclair: A Check List." *Bulletin of the New York Public Library* 74 (September 1970): 454–67.

Boll, T.E.M. "On the May Sinclair Collection." *Library Chronicle* (Penn.) 27 (1961): 1–15.

Robb, Kenneth A. "May Sinclair: An Annotated Bibliography of Writings about Her." *English Literature in Transition* 16 (1973): 177–231.

General Works

Boll, T.E.M. "May Sinclair and the Medico-Psychological Clinic of London." *Proceedings of the American Philosophical Society* (August 22, 1962): 310–26.

Boll, T.E.M. "The Mystery of Charlotte Mew and May Sinclair: An Inquiry." *Bulletin of the New York Public Library* 74 (September 1970): 445–53.

Davidow, Mary C. "The Charlotte Mew–May Sinclair Relationship: A Reply." *Bulletin of the New York Public Library* 75 (April 1971): 295–300.

Kaplan, Sydney Janet. "The Feminine Consciousness in the Novels of Five Twentieth Century British Women." *Dissertation Abstracts International* 32 (1971): 4615A (California, Los Angeles).

Kinnamon, Rebeccah Ann. "May Sinclair's Fiction of the Supernatural." *Dissertation Abstracts International* 35 (1975): 6143A (Duke).

Zegger, Hrisey Dimitrakis. "May Sinclair's Psychological Novels." *Dissertation Abstracts International* 32 (1971): 1537A (N.Y.U.).

Individual Works
Mary Olivier: A Life (1919)

Kaplan, Sydney. " 'Featureless Freedom' or Ironic Submission: Dorothy Richardson and May Sinclair." *College English* 32 (May 1971): 914–17.

DAME EDITH SITWELL (1887–1964) Great Britain
Bibliography
Ehrstine, John W., and Douglas D. Rich. "Edith Sitwell: A Critical Bibliography, 1951–1973." *Bulletin of Bibliography* 31 (July–September 1974): 111–16.

General Works
Bell, A.S. "Rache." *Times Literary Supplement* (November 6, 1970): 1301; (December 4, 1970): 1422.

Bennett, Gordon Willard. "The Form and Sensibility of Edith Sitwell's Devotional Poems: A Study of Baroque Tradition." *Dissertation Abstracts International* 30 (1969): 2520A (Kansas).

Brophy, James. "Edith Sitwell: Modern Metaphysical." *Renascence* 15 (Spring 1963): 152–56.

Brophy, James. "Empire of Shade: A Reading of Edith Sitwell's Poetry." *Dissertation Abstracts* 27 (1966): 197A (Columbia).

Burnett, Hugh, and Feliks Topolski. "Six English Self-Portraits." *Harper's* (April 1965): 56–58.

Driberg, Tom, "Edith Sitwell at Home: A Partial Recall." *Encounter* 26 (May 1966): 51–55.

Falk, Carol Joyce Thompson. "The Poetic Vision of Edith Sitwell." *Dissertation Abstracts International* 31 (1971): 4767A (North Dakota).

Green, Timothy. "I Am an Electric Eel in a Pool of Catfish." *Life* (January 4, 1963): 60–62.

Griffith, Philip M. "Carolinian Conversations: Recollections of a Visit with Dame Edith Sitwell, March 1957." *Nimrod* 13 (Winter 1969): 10–18.

Harrington, David V. "The 'Metamorphosis' of Edith Sitwell." *Criticism* 9 (1967): 80–91.

Hoffman, Daniel. "Two Ladies of Legend." *Reporter* (December 28, 1967): 41–43.

Hollowood, Bernard. "For the British It's Odd Man In." *New York Times Magazine* (January 24, 1965): 48.

Holroyd, Michael. "A Delightful but Deleterious Trio." *Book World* (September 23, 1968): 5.

Husain, F.N. "Edith Sitwell in the Symbolist Tradition." *Dissertation Abstracts* 26 (1966): 5437 (Minnesota).

Jennings, Elizabeth. "Dame Edith." *Spectator* (December 18, 1964): 837.

Kitchen, Laurence. "Edith Sitwell: 1887–1964." *Listener* (December 17, 1964): 980.

Launx, Eyre de. "Montegufoni." *New Yorker* (September 10, 1966): 198.

Levi, Peter. "The Death of Poets." *Month* (February 1965): 114–19.

Lewis, Jenny. "Edith Sitwell Letters." *British Museum Quarterly* 30 (Autumn 1965): 17–22.

McKenna, John Paul. "The Early Poetry of Edith Sitwell." *Dissertation Abstracts* 24 (1964): 3752 (Columbia).

Mills, Ralph J., Jr. "The Development of Apocalyptic Vision in Five Modern Poets." *Dissertation Abstracts* 24 (1963): 3753 (Northwestern).

Mills, Ralph J., Jr. "Edith Sitwell: Prophetess to an Age." *Christian Century* (May 19, 1965): 652–55.

Mills, Ralph J., Jr. "The Poetic Roles of Edith Sitwell." *Chicago Review* 14 (1961): 33–64.

Misko, Ellen. "A Study of Dame Edith Sitwell's 'Later Poems: 1940–1945.' " *Dissertation Abstracts* 33 (1972): 1735A (Loyola, Chicago).

Nandakumar, Prema. "Edith Sitwell, 1887–1964." *Aryan Path* 36 (November 1965): 501–8.

Osborne, Charles. "Sitwell and Walton." *London Magazine* 2 (December 1962): 60–62.

Ower, John. "Edith Sitwell: Metaphysical Medium and Metaphysical Message." *Twentieth Century Literature* 16 (October 1970): 253–67.

Ower, John. "A Golden Labyrinth: Edith Sitwell and the Theme of Time." *Renascence* 26 (Summer 1974): 207–17.

Ower, John B. "Cosmic Aristocracy and Cosmic Democracy in Edith Sitwell." *Contemporary Literature* 12 (Autumn 1971): 527–53.

Parker, Derek. "Edith Sitwell." *Poetry Review* 56 (Spring 1965): 18–23.

"Peacock Poetry." *Newsweek* (December 21, 1964): 57.

"People Are Talking About. . . ." *Vogue* (July 1960): 62.

Pryce-Jones, Alan. "Edith Sitwell: Holding Court Among Straw Men." *Commonweal* (May 14, 1965): 241–43.

Robb, Margaret. "The Growth of a Poet." *Colorado Quarterly* 13 (Autumn 1964): 151–64.

Spender, Stephen. "Dame Edith Sitwell's Show."

New Republic (December 2, 1967): 21–22.

Spender, Stephen. "Edith Sitwell, Poet." *Observer Weekend Review* (December 13, 1964): 28.

Spender, Stephen. "Exotic Specimens." *New York Times Book Review* (September 22, 1968): 5.

Stanford, Derek. "Dame Edith Sitwell and the Transatlantic Muse." *Month* (July 1960): 13–20.

Symons, Julian. "Miss Edith Sitwell Have and Had and Heard." *London Magazine* 4 (November 1964): 50–63.

Turnell, Martin. "Edith, Ian and All That." *Ramparts* (April 1965): 55–59.

Vickery, John B. "*Golden Bough*: Impact and Archetype." *Virginia Quarterly Review* 39 (Winter 1963): 37–57.

Weeks, Edward. "The Peripatetic Reviewer." *Atlantic Monthly* (February 1965): 135–36.

Weintraub, Stanley. "Making the Best of It." *New York Times Book Review* (October 22, 1967): 4.

Welvaert, Marie-Laurentina. "The Gold-Dust Imagery of Edith Sitwell." *St. Louis Quarterly* 3 (1965): 399–418.

White, Eric W. "With All Guns Firing." *Times Literary Supplement* (April 29, 1965): 336.

Individual Works
Gold Coast Customs (1929)

Ower, John B. "Black Oracle: Theme and Motif in Edith Sitwell's *Gold Coast Customs*." *Cithara* 12 (1972): 3–25.

Still Falls the Rain (1940)

Brophy, James D. "Sitwell's *Still Falls the Rain*." *Explicator* 29 (December 1970): Item 36.

Jacobs, Willis D. "Sitwell's *Still Falls the Rain*." *Explicator* 31 (September 1972): Item 5.

Three Poems of the Atomic Age (1945)

Cuffel, K.D. "The Shadow of Cain: Themes in Dame Edith Sitwell's Later Poetry." *Personalist* 46 (Autumn 1965): 517–26.

Mollie Skinner (1876–1955) Australia
General Works
Porter, Peter. "Collaborations." *New Statesman* (November 16, 1973): 741–42.

Jonathan Slick [pseud.]. *See* Ann Sophia Stephens

Agnes Smedley (1890–1950) U.S.
General Works
Piercy, Marge. "Reconsideration: Agnes Smedley: Dirt-Poor Daughter of Earth." *New Republic* (December 14, 1974): 19–20.

Charlotte Turner Smith (1749–1806) Great Britain
General Works
Ehrenpreis, Anne Henry. "*Northanger Abbey*: Jane Austen and Charlotte Smith." *Nineteenth Century Fiction* 25 (December 1970): 343–48.

Fry, Carrol L. "Charlotte Smith, Popular Novelist." *Dissertation Abstracts International* 31 (1971): 5360A (Nebraska).

Hunt, Bishop C., Jr. "Wordsworth and Charlotte Smith." *Wordsworth Circle* 1 (Summer 1970): 85–103.

Magee, William H. "The Happy Marriage: The Influence of Charlotte Smith on Jane Austen." *Studies in the Novel* 7 (Spring 1975): 120–32.

Pollin, Burton R. "Keats, Charlotte Smith, and the Nightingale." *Notes and Queries* 13 (May 1966): 180–81.

Turner, Rufus Paul. "Charlotte Smith (1749–1806): New Light on Her Life and Literary Career." *Dissertation Abstracts* 27 (1966): 189A (Southern California).

Whiting, George W. "Charlotte Smith, Keats, and the Nightingale." *Keats-Shelley Journal* 12 (1963): 4–8.

Individual Works
The Romance of Real Life (1799)

Howard, Edward G. "An Unrecorded Baltimore Imprint from Philadelphia." *Papers of the Bibliographical Society of America* 61 (1967): 121–23.

Elizabeth Oakes Smith [pseud. Ernest Helfenstein] (1806–1893) U.S.
General Works
Harding, Walter. "Elizabeth Oakes Smith on Thoreau." *Thoreau Society Bulletin* 110 (Winter 1970): 2–3.

Florence Margaret Smith. *See* Stevie Smith

Lillian Smith (1897–1966) U.S.
General Works
Besal, Dorothy. "Lillian Smith, Prophet for Our Time." *Community* 24 (June 1965): 3.

Blackwell, Louise, and Frances Clay. "Lillian Smith, Novelist." *College Language Association Journal* 15 (June 1972): 452–58.

Brockway, George P. "You Do It Because You Love Somebody." *Saturday Review* (October 22, 1966): 53–54.

Hall, Giles G., Jr. "The Social Criticism of Lillian Smith." *Dissertation Abstracts International* 33 (1973): 3647A (Georgia).

"Herald of the Dream." *Time* (October 7, 1966): 36–37.

Long, Margaret. "The Sense of Her Presence: A Memorial for Lillian Smith." *New South* 21 (Fall 1966): 71–77.

"Memory of a Large Christmas." *Life* (December 15, 1961): 90–94.

Sugg, Redding S., Jr. "Lillian Smith and the Condition of Women." *South Atlantic Quarterly* 71 (Spring 1972): 155–64.

Sullivan, Margaret. "Lillian Smith: Public Image and Personal Vision." *Mad River Review* 2 (Summer–Fall 1967): 3–21.

Individual Works

Strange Fruit (1944)

Hamblen, Abigail Ann. "*Strange Fruit*: Harvest." *Forum* 5 (Summer 1967): 31–33.

Marcus, Fred H. "*Cry, the Beloved Country* and *Strange Fruit*: Exploring Man's Inhumanity to Man." *English Journal* 51 (December 1962): 609–16.

Thorburn, Neil. "*Strange Fruit* and Southern Tradition." *Midwest Quarterly* 12 (Winter 1971): 157–71.

PAULINE URMSON SMITH (1883–1959) Great Britain (Born in South Africa)

General Works

Beeton, D.R. "Pauline Smith and South African Literature in English." *Unisa English Studies* 11 (March 1973): 35–50.

Eglington, Charles. " 'Quaintness' in Pauline Smith: Observations on Her Style and Dialogue." *English Studies in Africa* 3 (March 1960): 48–56.

Haresnape, Geoffrey. "A Note on Pauline Smith's Presentation of Country Life." *English Studies in Africa* 9 (March 1966): 83–86.

Haresnape, Geoffrey. "Pauline Smith and Arnold Bennett." *English Studies in Africa* 6 (September 1963): 144–48.

Haresnape, Geoffrey. "Pauline Smith and the Place of Her Inspiration." *English Studies in Africa* 6 (March 1963): 70–76.

Ravenscroft, Arthur. "Pauline Smith." *Review of*

English Literature 4 (April 1963): 55–67.

Individual Works

Why and How I Became an Author (1913)

Haresnape, Geoffrey. "A Note about Pauline Smith's Unpublished Essay: *Why and How I Became an Author*." *English Studies in Africa* 6 (September 1963): 149–50.

STEVIE SMITH [pseud. of Florence Margaret Smith] (1902–1971) Great Britain

General Works

Peel, Muriel. "Half in Love with Easeful Death." *Books and Bookmen* 16 (June 1971): 6–7.

VIVIAN SMITH (1933–) Australia

Individual Works

The Other Meaning (1956)

Irvin, Margaret. " 'That Subtle Country of My Heart': The Poetry of *The Other Meaning*." *Poetry Magazine* 1 (1969): 33–36.

EDITH ANNA OENONE SOMERVILLE (1861–1949) Ireland

General Works

Flanagan, Thomas. "The Big House of Ross-Drishane." *Kenyon Review* 28 (1966): 54–78.

Individual Works

The Charlotte (1894)

Pritchett, V.S. "Anglo-Irish Attitudes." *New Statesman* (March 9, 1973): 343.

SUSAN SONTAG (1933–) U.S.

General Works

Boyers, Robert. "On Susan Sontag and the New Sensibility." *Salmagundi* 1 (1966): 27–38.

Ellmann, Mary. "The Sensational Susan Sontag." *Atlantic Monthly* (September 1966): 59–63.

Heilbrun, Carolyn G. "Speaking of Susan Sontag." *New York Times Book Review* (August 27, 1967): 2.

Kent, L. "Susan Sontag Speaks Up: Interview." *Vogue* (August 1971): 88.

Kock, Stephen. "On Susan Sontag." *Tri-Quarterly* 7 (Fall 1966): 153–60.

Marx, Leo. "Susan Sontag's 'New Left' Pastoral: Notes on Revolutionary Pastoralism in America." *Tri-Quarterly* 23–24 (Spring 1972): 552–75.

McCormack, Robert. "Interpretations." *Tamarack Review* 40 (Summer 1966): 67–73.

McCourt, J. "Promised Lands." *Film Comment* 11

(July 1975): 36.

Nairn, Tom. "New Sensibility." *New Statesman* (March 24, 1967): 408–9.

"People Are Talking About. . . ." *Vogue* (June 1966): 96–97.

Phillips, William. "Radical Styles." *Partisan Review* 36 (1969): 388–400.

"Promised Lands." *Film Library Quarterly* 8 (1975): 36–37.

Rubin, L.D., Jr. "Susan Sontag and the Camp Followers." *Sewanee Review* 82 (Summer 1974): 503–10.

Solotaroff, Theodore. "Death in Life." *Commentary* 44 (November 1967): 87–89.

Tobach, James. "Whatever You'd Like Susan Sontag to Think, She Doesn't." *Esquire* (July 1968): 59–60.

Wain, John. "Song of Myself, 1963." *New Republic* (September 21, 1963): 26.

Individual Works
Styles of Radical Will (1969)

Houston, Gary. "Susan Sontag." *Michigan Quarterly Review* 9 (Fall 1970): 272–75.

VIRGINIA SORENSEN (1912–) U.S.
General Works

Bradford, Mary L. "Virginia Sorensen: A Saving Remnant." *Dialog* 4 (Autumn 1969): 56–64.

MURIEL SPARK (1918–) Great Britain
General Works

Baldanza, Frank. "Muriel Spark and the Occult." *Wisconsin Studies in Contemporary Literature* 6 (Summer 1965): 190–203.

Berthoff, Warner. "Fortunes of the Novel: Muriel Spark and Iris Murdoch." *Massachusetts Review* 8 (Spring 1967): 301–32.

Bradbury, Malcolm. "Muriel Spark's Fingernails." *Critical Quarterly* 14 (Autumn 1972): 241–50.

Byatt, A.S. "Whittled and Spikey Art." *New Statesman* (December 15, 1967): 848.

Dobie, Ann B. "Muriel Spark's Definition of Reality." *Critique* 12 (1970): 20–27.

Dobie, Ann B., and Carl Wooton. "Spark and Waugh: Similarities by Coincidence." *Midwest Quarterly* 13 (Summer 1972): 423–34.

Grosskurth, Phyllis. "The World of Muriel Spark: Spirits or Spooks?" *Tamarack Review* 39 (Spring 1966): 62–67.

Hynes, Joseph. "After Marabar: Reading Forster, Robbe-Grillet, Spark." *Iowa Review* 5 (Winter 1974): 120–26.

Hynes, Samuel. "Prime of Muriel Spark." *Commonweal* (February 23, 1962): 562–68.

Jacobsen, Josephine. "A Catholic Quartet." *Christian Scholar* 47 (1964): 139–54.

Jones, Jacqueline Ann. "The Absurd in the Fiction of Muriel Spark." *Dissertation Abstracts International* 36 (1975): 317A–18A (Penn.).

Kermode, Frank. "The House of Fiction: Interviews with Seven English Novelists." *Partisan Review* 29 (1963): 61–82.

Keyser, Barbara E.Y. "The Dual Vision of Murial Spark." *Dissertation Abstracts International* 32 (1972): 4005A (Tulane).

Laffin, Gerry S. "Muriel Spark's Portrait of the Artist as a Young Girl." *Renascence* 24 (Summer 1972): 213–23.

Laffin, Gerry S. "Unresolved Dualities in the Novels of Muriel Spark." *Dissertation Abstracts International* 34 (1974): 4268A (Wisconsin).

Legris, Maurice R. "Muriel Spark's Use of the Non-Material: Prolegomena to a Theological Critique." *Dissertation Abstracts International* 34 (1974): 7763A–64A (Oregon).

Mansfield, Joseph G. "Another World Than This: The Gothic and the Catholic in the Novels of Muriel Spark." *Dissertation Abstracts International* 34 (1974): 5980A (Iowa).

Mayne, Richard. "Fiery Particle: On Muriel Spark." *Encounter* 25 (December 1965): 61–68.

McLeod, Patrick G. "Vision and the Moral Encounter: A Reading of Muriel Spark's Novels." *Dissertation Abstracts International* 34 (1973): 1286A–87A (Rice).

Mobley, Jonnie P. "Toward Logres: The Operation of Efficacious Grace in Novels by C. S. Lewis, Charles Williams, Muriel Spark, and Gabriel Fielding." *Dissertation Abstracts International* 34 (1974): 4274A (Southern California).

Murphy, Carol. "A Spark of the Supernatural." *Approach*, no. 60 (Summer 1966): 26–30.

Potter, Nancy A.J. "Muriel Spark: Transformer of the Commonplace." *Renascence* 17 (Spring 1965): 115–20.

Raven, Simon. "Heavens Below." *Spectator* (September 20, 1963): 354.

Reed, Douglas. "Taking Cocktails with Life." *Books and Bookmen* 16 (August 1971): 10–14.

Schneider, Harold W. "A Writer in Her Prime:

The Fiction of Muriel Spark." *Critique* 5 (1962): 28–45.

Spark, Muriel. "My Conversion." *Twentieth Century* 170 (Autumn 1961): 58–63.

Spark, Muriel. "The Poet's House." *Encounter* 30 (May 1968): 48–50.

Stanford, Derek. "The Early Days of Miss Muriel Spark." *Critic* 20 (April–May 1962): 49–53.

Stanford, Derek. "The Work of Muriel Spark: An Essay on Her Fictional Method." *Month* (August 1962): 92–99.

Stubbs, Patricia. "Two Contemporary Views on Fiction: Iris Murdoch and Muriel Spark." *English* 23 (Autumn 1974): 102–10.

Sullivan, Walter. "Updike, Spark and Others." *Sewanee Review* 74 (Summer 1966): 709–16.

Individual Works

The Bachelors (1960)

Updike, John. "Creatures of the Air." *New Yorker* (September 30, 1961): 161–67.

The Comforters (1957)

Kermode, Frank. "The Prime of Miss Muriel Spark." *New Statesman* (September 27, 1963): 397–99.

Doctors of Philosophy (1963)

Mutalik-Desai, A.A. "*Doctors of Philosophy*, a Play by Muriel Spark: A Review." *Parashuramia* (March 1964): 56–60.

The Driver's Seat (1970)

Richmond, V.B. "The Darkening Vision of Muriel Spark." *Critique* 15 (1973): 71–85.

The Girls of Slender Means (1963)

Casson, Allan. "Review of *The Girls of Slender Means*." *Critique* 7 (1964): 94–96.

Soule, George. "Must a Novelist Be an Artist?" *Carleton Miscellany* 5 (Spring 1964): 92–98.

Not to Disturb (1971)

Richmond, V.B. "The Darkening Vision of Muriel Spark." *Critique* 15 (1973): 71–85.

The Prime of Miss Jean Brodie (1962)

Dobie, Ann B. "*The Prime of Miss Jean Brodie*: Muriel Spark Bridges the Credibility Gap." *Arizona Quarterly* 25 (Autumn 1969): 217–28.

Lodge, David. "The Uses and Abuses of Omniscience: Method and Meaning in Muriel Spark's *The Prime of Miss Jean Brodie*." *Critical Quarterly* 12 (Autumn 1970): 235–57.

The Public Image (1968)

Richmond, V.B. "The Darkening Vision of Muriel Spark." *Critique* 15 (1973): 71–85.

Robinson (1958)

Ohmann, C.B. "Muriel Spark's *Robinson*." *Critique* 8 (1965): 70–84.

CATHERINE HELEN SPENCE (1825–1910) Australia
General Works

Walker, R.B. "Catherine Helen Spence: Unitarian Utopian." *Australian Literary Studies* 5 (1971): 31–41.

Walker, R.B. "Catherine Helen Spence and South Australian Politics." *Australian Journal of Politics and History* 15 (1969): 35–46.

Wightman, Jennifer. "A Practical Dreamer: Catherine Helen Spence." *Meanjin Quarterly* 33 (1974): 89–92.

ANNE BETHEL SPENCER, née Scales (1882–) U.S.
General Works

Greene, Johnny Lee. "Anne Spencer: A Study of Her Life and Poetry." *Dissertation Abstracts International* 36 (1975): 312A (North Carolina).

ELIZABETH SPENCER (1921–) U.S.
General Works

Bunting, Charles T. " 'In That Time and at That Place': The Literary World of Elizabeth Spencer." *Mississippi Quarterly* 28 (Fall 1975): 435–60.

Burger, Nash K. "Elizabeth Spencer's Three Mississippi Novels." *South Atlantic Quarterly* 63 (Summer 1964): 351–62.

Cole, Hunter M. "Windsor in Spencer and Welty: A Real and an Imaginary Landscape." *Notes on Mississippi Writers* 7 (Spring 1974): 2–11.

Cole, Hunter McKelva. "Elizabeth Spencer at Sycamore Fair." *Notes on Mississippi Writers* 6 (Winter 1974): 81–86.

Haley, Josephine. "An Interview with Elizabeth Spencer." *Notes on Mississippi Writers* 1 (Fall 1968): 42–53.

Kauffman, Stanley. "Sense and Sensibility." *New Republic* (June 26, 1965): 27–28.

Spencer, Elizabeth. "On Writing Fiction." *Notes on Mississippi Writers* 3 (Fall 1970): 71–72.

JEAN STAFFORD (1915–) U.S.
General Works

Jenson, Sid. "The Noble Wicked West of Jean Stafford." *Western American Literature* 7 (Winter 1973): 261–70.

Vickery, Olga W. "Jean Stafford and the Ironic Vision." *South Atlantic Quarterly* 61 (Autumn 1962): 484–91.

Vickery, Olga W. "The Novels of Jean Stafford." *Critique* 5 (1962): 14–26.

Individual Works

The Catherine Wheel (1952)

Mann, J.W. "Toward New Archetypal Forms: Jean Stafford's *The Catherine Wheel.*" *Critique* 17 (1975): 77–92.

The Mountain Lion (1947)

Burns, Stuart L. "Counterpoint in Jean Stafford's *The Mountain Lion.*" *Critique* 9 (1967): 20–32.

Gelfant, Blanche H. "*The Mountain Lion* by Jean Stafford." *New Republic* (May 10, 1975): 22–25.

CHRISTINA STEAD (1902–) Australia
General Works

Clemons, W. "Penny Pinchers." *Newsweek* (June 2, 1975): 72.

Geering, R.G. "The Achievement of Christina Stead." *Southerly* 22 (1962): 193–212.

Geering, R.G. "Christina Stead in the 1960's." *Southerly* 28 (1968): 26–36.

Jamison, Greeba. "Christina Stead—'Can't Help Being Original.'" *Walkabout* 36 (1969): 36–37.

Pybus, Rodney. "The Light and the Dark: The Fiction of Christina Stead." *Stand* 10 (1968): 30–37.

Thomas, Tony. "Christina Stead." *Westerly*, no. 4 (1970): 46–53.

Wilding, Michael. "Christina Stead's Australian Novels." *Southerly* 27 (1967): 20–33.

Individual Works

The Man Who Loved Children (1965)

Burns, Graham. "The Moral Design of *The Man Who Loved Children.*" *Critical Review* 14 (1971): 38–61.

Katz, Alfred H. "Some Psychological Themes in a Novel by Christina Stead." *Literature and Psychology* 15 (1965): 210–15.

The Salzburg Tales (1934)

Thomas, Tony. "Christina Stead: *The Salzburg Tales, Seven Poor Men of Sydney.*" *Westerly*, no. 4 (1969): 46–53.

Seven Poor Men of Sydney (1935)

Green, Dorothy. "Chaos or a Dancing Star? Christina Stead's *Seven Poor Men of Sydney.*" *Meanjin Quarterly* 27 (1967): 150–61.

Miller, Anthony. "*Seven Poor Men of Sydney.*" *Westerly*, no. 2 (1967): 61–66.

Thomas, Tony. "Christina Stead: *The Salzburg Tales, Seven Poor Men of Sydney.*" *Westerly*, no. 4 (1969): 46–53.

GERTRUDE STEIN (1874–1946) U.S.
Bibliography

Gallup, Donald. "Du Côté de Chez Stein." *Book Collector* 19 (Summer 1970): 169–84.

General Works

Baker, William D. "Lighting Birthday Candles for Gertrude Stein." *Widening Circle* 1 (1973): 1–2.

Beer, Patricia. "At the Court of Queen Gertrude." *Times Literary Supplement* (November 8, 1974): 1252.

Bloom, E.F. "Three Steins." *Texas Quarterly* 13 (Summer 1970): 15–22.

Bloome, Gayle C.B. "Gertrude Stein's Concepts of the Self and Her Literary Characters." *Dissertation Abstracts International* 34 (1973): 1892A (Michigan).

Brinnin, John. "Gertrude Stein in America." *Atlantic Monthly* (October 1960): 98–106.

Chase, Mary Ellen. "Five Literary Portraits." *Massachusetts Review* 3 (Spring 1962): 511–16.

Cooper, Douglas. "Gertrude Stein and Juan Gris." *Apollo* 93 (January 1971): 28–35.

Copeland, Carolyn F. "Narrative Technique in the Works of Gertrude Stein." *Dissertation Abstracts International* 34 (1974): 5960A–61A (Iowa).

Davis, D. "Americans in Paris." *Newsweek* (December 14, 1970): 80–81B.

Duffy, M. "Steinways." *Time* (March 4, 1974): 82.

Dupee, F. W. "Gertrude Stein." *Commentary* 33 (June 1962): 519–23.

Fendelman, E. "Happy Birthday, Gertrude Stein." *American Quarterly* 27 (March 1975): 99–107.

Fitz, L.T. "Gertrude Stein and Picasso: The Language of Surfaces." *American Literature* 45 (May 1973): 228–37.

Flanner, J. "Memory Is All." *New Yorker* (December 15, 1975): 141–42.

Gallup, Donald. "Introducing Gertrude Stein." *Widening Circle* 1 (1973): 6–10.

Gervasi, Frank. "The Liberation of Gertrude Stein." *Saturday Review* (August 21, 1971): 13–14.

Glassco, John. "Memoirs of Montparnasse." *Tamarack Review* 50–51 (1969): 5–19.

Haas, Robert B. "A Bolt of Energy, or Why I Still

Read Gertrude Stein." *Widening Circle* 1 (1973): 14–15.

Haas, Robert B. "Gertrude Stein Talking—A Transatlantic Interview." *UCLAN* 8 (Summer 1962): 3–11.

Harrison, Gilbert. "A Remembrance." *Widening Circle* 1 (1973): 18–19.

Hoffman, Michael J. "The Development of Abstractionism in the Writing of Gertrude Stein to 1913." *Dissertation Abstracts* 25 (1964): 475–76 (Penn.).

Hoffman, Michael J. "Gertrude Stein and William James." *Personalist* 47 (Spring 1966): 226–33.

Hoffman, Michael J. "Gertrude Stein in the Psychology Laboratory." *American Quarterly* 17 (Spring 1965): 127–32.

Hughes, R. "Patrons and Roped Climbers." *Time* (December 14, 1970): 76.

Jefferson, M. "Passionate Friend." *Newsweek* (January 7, 1974): 67–68.

Kazin, Alfred. "The Mystery of Gertrude Stein." *Reporter* (February 18, 1960): 48–52.

Kostelanetz, Richard. "Gertrude Stein: The New Literature." *Hollins Critic* 12 (June 1975): 1–16.

Leibowitz, H. "Charmed Circle." *New York Times Book Review* (February 3, 1974): 1–2.

Lord, James. "Where the Pictures Were: A Memoir." *Prose* 7 (1973): 133–87.

McCaffrey, John. " 'Any of Mine Without Music to Help Them': The Operas and Plays of Gertrude Stein." *Yale/Theater* 4 (Summer 1973): 27–39.

McMillan, Samuel Hubert, Jr. "Gertrude Stein, the Cubists, and the Futurists." *Dissertation Abstracts* 25 (1964): 2985 (Texas).

Mellow, James R. "Gertrude Stein Rediscovers America." *Columbia Forum*, n.s. 3 (Winter 1974): 20–29.

Mellow, J. R. "Stein Salon Was the First Museum of Modern Art." *New York Times Magazine* (December 1, 1968): 48–51.

Meyerowitz, Patricia. "Say Yes to Everything." *Widening Circle* 1 (1973): 20–22.

Moers, Ellen. "The Angry Young Women." *Harper's* (December 1963): 88–95.

More de Morinni, Clara. "Miss Stein and the Ladies." *New Republic* (November 11, 1967): 17–19.

Nazzaro, Linda, " 'A Piece of Coffee': A Stylistic Description of the Work of Gertrude Stein." *English Review* 13 (1973): 50–54.

Nichol, Bishop. "Some Beginning Writings on Gertrude Stein's Theories of Personality." *Open Letter*, 2d ser. 2 (1972): 41–47.

Prescott, P.S. "Up in Gertie's Room." *Newsweek* (February 11, 1974): 92.

Purdy, Strother B. "Gertrude Stein at Marienbad." *Publications of the Modern Language Association* 85 (1970): 1096–1105.

Roe, Nancy E. "Gertrude Stein: Rhetoric and the 'Modern Composition.' " *Dissertation Abstracts International* 32 (1972): 6450A (Michigan).

Rogers, W.G. "I Remember Gertrude." *Widening Circle* 1 (1973): 23.

Rose, F. "G. Stein." *Vogue* (January 1971): 89.

Rose, Sir Francis. "A Gift of Roses." *Widening Circle* 1 (1973): 25–27.

"Salute to Gertrude Stein." *Time* (March 22, 1963): 97–98.

Shaw, Barnett. "Encounter with Gertrude Stein, Paris, 1944." *Texas Quarterly* 9 (Autumn 1966): 21–23.

Shaw, Sharon. "Gertrude Stein and Henry James: The Difference between Accidence and Coincidence." *Pembroke Magazine* 5 (1974): 95–101.

Shults, Donald. "Gertrude Stein and the Problems of Time." *Kyushu American Literature* 11 (1968): 59–71.

Sprigge, Elizabeth. "To Begin with Beginning." *Widening Circle* 1 (1973): 28–30.

Steele, O.L., Jr. "Gertrude Stein and Ellen Glasgow: Memoir of a Meeting." *American Literature* 33 (March 1961): 76–77.

Steiner, Wendy Lois. "Gertrude Stein's Portrait Form." *Dissertation Abstracts International* 36 (1975): 331A–32A (Yale).

"Steiniana." *New Yorker* (March 11, 1974): 27–29.

Steloff, Frances. "The Making of an American Visit: Gertrude Stein." *Confrontation* 8 (Spring 1974): 9–17.

Stewart, Allegra. "Flat Land as Explanation." *Widening Circle* 1 (1973): 31–33.

Stewart, Laurence D. "Gertrude Stein and the Vital Dead." *Mystery and Detection Annual* 1 (1972): 102–23.

Sutherland, Donald. "Alice and Gertrude and Others." *Prairie Schooner* 45 (Winter 1971–1972): 284–99.

Sutherland, Donald. "Ole Woman River: A Correspondence with Katherine Anne Porter." *Sewanee Review* 74 (Summer 1966): 554–67.

Sutherland, Donald. "A Passion for the World."

Widening Circle 1 (1973): 34–35.

Sutton, William A. "All Life Is Important." *Widening Circle* 1 (1973): 36–37.

Thomson, Virgil. "No Diminution of Power." *Widening Circle* 1 (1973): 38.

Thurman, J.A. "A Rose Is a Rose Is a Rose." *Ms.* (February 1974): 54–57.

Van Vechten, Carl. "More Laurels for Our Gertrude." *Confrontation* 8 (Spring 1974): 18–19.

Wasserstrom, W. "Sursymamericubealism of Gertrude Stein." *Twentieth Century Literature* 21 (February 1975): 90–106.

Wright, George T. "Gertrude Stein and Her Ethic of Self-Containment." *Tennessee Studies in Literature* 8 (1963): 17–23.

Yates, Peter. "A Portrait of Gertrude Stein." *Forum* 3 (Summer 1960): 62–66.

Individual Works

The Autobiography of Alice B. Toklas (1933)

Alkon, Paul K. "Visual Rhetoric in *The Autobiography of Alice B. Toklas.*" *Critical Inquiry* 1 (June 1975): 849–81.

Barry, Joseph. "Miss Toklas on Her Own." *New Republic* (March 30, 1963): 21–23.

Friedrich, O. "Grave of Alice B. Toklas." *Esquire* (January 1968): 98–103.

Harrison, Gilbert A. "Alice B. Toklas." *New Republic* (March 18, 1967): 24.

Lord, James. "Where the Pictures Were: A Memoir." *Prose* 7 (1973): 133–87.

Mellers, Wilfred. "Toklas." *New Statesman* (November 29, 1963): 792–93.

Sutherland, Donald. "The Conversion of Alice B. Toklas." *Colorado Quarterly* 17 (Autumn 1968): 129–41.

"Together Again." *Time* (March 17, 1967): 34.

A Box (1913?)

George, Jonathan C. "Stein's *A Box.*" *Explicator* 31 (February 1973): Item 42.

Four Saints in Three Acts (1934)

Prideaux, T. "Four Patron Saints in One Great Act." *Life* (April 23, 1971): 56–60.

Shapiro, Harriet. "*Four Saints in Three Acts*: An Interview." *Intellectual Digest* 3 (October 1973): 22–26.

Melanchtha (1909)

Bridgman, Richard. " 'Melanchtha.' " *American Literature* 33 (November 1961): 350–59.

Paris France (1940)

Barry, Joseph. "*Paris France* Reviewed." *Widening Circle* 1 (1973): 3–5.

Malone, Kemp. "Observations on *Paris France.*" *Papers on Language and Literature* 3 (1967): 159–78.

Portraits and Prayers (1934)

Hoffman, Michael J. "Gertrude Stein's *Portraits.*" *Twentieth Century Literature* 11 (October 1965): 115–22.

Tender Buttons (1914)

Anderson, Peter S. "Gertrude Stein's *Tender Buttons*: Two Rosaries." *Poet and Critic* 1 (Winter 1965): 32–42.

Cooper, David D. "Gertrude Stein's 'Magnificent Asparagus': Horizontal Vision and Unmeaning in *Tender Buttons.*" *Modern Fiction Studies* 20 (Autumn 1974): 337–49.

Garvin, Harry R. "The Human Mind and *Tender Buttons.*" *Widening Circle* 1 (1973): 11–13.

Schmitz, Neil. "Gertrude Stein as Post-Modernist: The Rhetoric of *Tender Buttons.*" *Journal of Modern Literature* 3 (1974): 1203–18.

Three Lives (1908)

Maynard, Reid. "Abstractionism in Gertrude Stein's *Three Lives.*" *Ball State University Forum* 13 (Winter 1972–1973): 68–71.

IDA FRANCES STELOFF (1887–) U.S.

General Works

"In Touch with Genius." *Journal of Modern Literature* 4 (1975): 749–887.

Morgan, Kathleen E. "Frances Steloff and the Gotham Book Mart." *Journal of Modern Literature* 4 (1975): 737–48.

ANN SOPHIA STEPHENS [pseud. Jonathan Slick] (1813–1886) U.S.

General Works

Stern, Madeleine B. "Ann S. Stephens: Author of the First Beadle Dime Novel, 1860." *Bulletin of the New York Public Library* 64 (June 1960): 303–22.

Stern, Madeleine B. "The First Beadle Dime Novel and Its Author." *American Book Collector* 14 (October 1963): 27.

SUSAN STERN (fl. 1970s) U.S.

Individual Works

With the Weathermen (1975)

Prescott, Peter S. "Stormy Weather." *Newsweek* (June 30, 1975): 64.

MARY STEWART (1916–) Great Britain
General Works

Duffy, M. "On the Road to Manderley." *Time* (April 12, 1971): 96.

Hemming, F. W. J. "Mary Queen of Hearts." *New Statesman* (November 5, 1965): 698–99.

ANNIS STOCKTON (fl. 1760s) U.S.
General Works

Burt, Nathaniel. "Outpost of Sensibility: Or the Literary Tradition of the Town of Princeton from Annis Stockton to John O'Hara." *Princeton University Library Chronicle* 28 (Spring 1967): 156–70.

SARAH STODART (fl. 1790s) Great Britain
General Works

Barke, John R. "Some Early Correspondence of Sarah Stodart and the Lambs." *Huntington Library Quarterly* 24 (November 1960): 59–69.

ELIZABETH DREW STODDARD (1832–1902) U.S.
General Works

Kraft, James. "An Unpublished Review by Henry James." *Studies in Bibliography* 20 (1967): 267–73.

CAROLYN STOLOFF (fl. 1970s) U.S.
Individual Works

Dying to Survive (1973)

Sylvester, Janet. "Embracing the Fugitive." *Works* 4 (Summer 1973): 109–12.

KATE STONE (fl. 1860s) U.S.
General Works

Williams, Ora G. "Muskets and Magnolias: Four Civil War Diaries by Louisiana Girls." *Louisiana Studies* 4 (Fall 1965): 187–99.

RUTH STONE (1915–) U.S.
General Works

Gross, Harvey. "On the Poetry of Ruth Stone: Selections and Commentary." *Iowa Review* 3 (Spring 1972): 94–106.

CHARLOTTE CARMICHAEL STOPES (1841–1929) Great Britain
General Works

McAleer, John J. "Charlotte Stopes—Spindle-Side Shakespearean." *Shakespeare Newsletter* 12 (November 1962): 38.

HARRIET BEECHER STOWE (1811–1896) U.S.
Bibliography

Adams, John R. "Harriet Beecher Stowe (1811–1896)." *American Literary Realism* 2 (1969): 160–64.

General Works

Allen, Peter R. "Lord Macaulay's Gift to Harriet Beecher Stowe: The Solution to a Riddle in Trevelyan's Life." *Notes and Queries* 17 (January 1970): 23–24.

Baxter, Annette K. "Women's Studies and American Studies: The Uses of the Interdisciplinary." *American Quarterly* 26 (October 1974): 433–39.

Cooke, George Willis. "Harriet Beecher Stowe." *Emerson Society Quarterly* 63 (1971): 2–10.

Cooper, Alice Adair. "Harriet Beecher Stowe: A Critical Study." *Dissertation Abstracts International* 26 (1965): 121 (Harvard).

Emig, Janet A. "The Flower in the Cleft: The Writings of Harriet Beecher Stowe." *Bulletin of History and Philosophy of Ohio* 21 (October 1963): 223–38.

"God Was Her Co-Author." *Newsweek* (April 8, 1963): 96.

Goldman, Maureen. "American Women and the Puritan Heritage: Anne Hutchinson to Harriet Beecher Stowe." *Dissertation Abstracts International* 35 (1975): 1503A–4A (Boston).

Graham, Thomas. "Harriet Beecher Stowe and the Question of Race." *New England Quarterly* 46 (December 1973): 614–22.

"Harriet Beecher Stowe Issue." *Emerson Society Quarterly* 49 (1967): 1–80.

Hovet, Theodore R. "Christian Revolution: Harriet Beecher Stowe's Response to Slavery and the Civil War." *New England Quarterly* 47 (December 1974): 535–49.

Hovet, Theodore R. "Harriet Beecher Stowe's Holiness Crusade Against Slavery." *Dissertation Abstracts International* 31 (1970): 2919A (Kansas).

Jacobson, Dan. "Down the River." *New Statesman* (October 12, 1962): 490–91.

Jones, Michael O. " 'Ye Must Contrive Allers to Keep Jest the Happy Medium Between Truth and Falsehood': Folklore and the Folk in Mrs. Stowe's Fiction." *New York Folklore Quarterly* 27 (December 1971): 357–69.

Lebedun, J. "Harriet Beecher Stowe's Interest in Sojourner Truth, Black Feminist." *American Literature* 46 (November 1974): 359–63.

Lentricchia, Frank, Jr. "Harriet Beecher Stowe and Byron Whirlwind." *Bulletin of the New York Public Library* 70 (April 1966): 218–28.

Lombard, Charles M. "Harriet Beecher Stowe's Attitude Towards French Romanticism." *College Language Association Journal* 11 (March 1968): 236–40.

Lynn, Kenneth S. "Mrs. Stowe and the American Imagination." *New Republic* (June 29, 1963): 20–21.

Manierre, William R. "A Southern Response to Mrs. Stowe: Two Letters of John R. Thompson." *Virginia Magazine of History and Biography* 69 (January 1961): 83–92.

Marotta, Kenny R. "The Literary Relationship of George Eliot and Harriet Beecher Stowe." *Dissertation Abstracts International* 35 (1974): 3751A (Johns Hopkins).

McCullough, David. "The Unexpected Mrs. Stowe." *American Heritage* 24 (August 1973): 4.

Miller, Eleanor A. "The Christian Philosophy in the New England Novels of Harriet Beecher Stowe." *Dissertation Abstracts International* 32 (1971): 445A (Nevada).

Moers, Ellen. "The Angry Young Women." *Harper's* (December 1963): 88–95.

"Mrs. Stowe—Painter." *American Heritage* 24 (August 1973): 6–7.

Murray, Alex L. "Harriet Beecher Stowe on Racial Segregation in the Schools." *American Quarterly* 12 (Winter 1960): 518–19.

Rotundo, Barbara. "Harriet Beecher Stowe and the Mythmakers." *American Notes and Queries* 12 (May–June 1974): 131–33.

"Stowe and Day Houses to Be Open Next Year." *Emerson Society Quarterly* 51 (1968): 74–75.

Trautmann, Frederick. "Harriet Beecher Stowe's Public Readings in New England." *New England Quarterly* 47 (June 1974): 279–89.

Van Why, Joseph F. "Bulletin for September, 1961." *Stowe, Beecher, Hooker, Seymour, Day Foundation Bulletin* 1 (September 1961): 2–14.

Van Why, Joseph F. "History in Houses: Harriet Beecher Stowe House in Nook Farm." *Antiques* 94 (September 1968): 376–81.

Van Why, Joseph F. "Letters of Harriet Beecher Stowe." *Stowe, Beecher, Hooker, Seymour, Day Foundation Bulletin* 1 (September 1960): 4–15.

Van Why, Joseph F. "Nook Farm." *Stowe, Beecher, Hooker, Seymour, Day Foundation Bulletin* 1 (September 1962): 1–34.

Individual Works

Ida May: The Story of Things Actual and Possible (1854)

Liedel, Donald E. "The Puffing of *Ida May*: Publishers Exploit the Antislavery Novel." *Journal of Popular Culture* 3 (Fall 1969): 287–306.

Pearl of Orr's Island (1862)

Jobes, Katharine T. "From Stowe's Eagle Island to Jewett's 'A White Heron.' " *Colby Library Quarterly* 10 (December 1974): 515–21.

Poems (1967)

Moran, John M., Jr., ed. "Collected Poems of Harriet Beecher Stowe." *Emerson Society Quarterly* 49 (1967): 1–100.

Sam Lawson's Fireside Stories (1871)

Flory, Claude R. "Huck, Sam and the Small-Pox." *Mark Twain Journal* 12 (Winter 1964–1965): 1–2.

Uncle Tom's Cabin (1852)

Allen, Walter. "*Uncle Tom's Cabin* Revisited." *Listener* (August 11, 1966): 197–200.

Boatwright, James. "Reconsideration: Totin' de Weery Load." *New Republic* (September 1, 1973): 29–32.

Brandstadter, Evan. "Uncle Tom and Archy Moore: The Antislavery Novel as Ideological Symbol." *American Quarterly* 26 (May 1974): 160–75.

Brown, Dorothy S. "Thesis and Theme in *Uncle Tom's Cabin*." *English Journal* 58 (December 1969): 1330–34.

Burgess, Anthony. "Making de White Boss Frown." *Encounter* 27 (July 1966): 54–58.

Cassara, Ernest. "The Rehabilitation of Uncle Tom: Significant Themes in Mrs. Stowe's Antislavery Novel." *College Language Association Journal* 17 (December 1973): 230–40.

Cox, J.F. "*Uncle Tom's Cabin*: A Pre-Raphaelite's Reaction." *Notes and Queries* 22 (March 1975): 111–12.

Davuall, Severn. "*Uncle Tom's Cabin*: The Sinister Side of the Patriarchy." *New England Quarterly* 35

(March 1963): 3–22.

Grimsted, David. "*Uncle Tom* from Page to Stage: Limitations of Nineteenth-Century Drama." *Quarterly Journal of Speech* 56 (October 1970): 235–44.

Haley, Alex. "In *Uncle Tom* Are Our Guilt and Hope." *New York Times Magazine* (March 1, 1964): 23.

Hamblen, Abigail Ann. "Uncle Tom and 'Nigger Jim': A Study in Contrasts and Similarities." *Mark Twain Journal* 11 (Fall 1961): 13–16.

Hill, Herbert. "*Uncle Tom,* an Enduring American Myth." *Crisis* 72 (May 1965): 289–95.

Hudson, Benjamin F. "Another View of *Uncle Tom.*" *Phylon* 24 (1963): 79–87.

Kaspin, Albert. "*Uncle Tom's Cabin* and 'Uncle' Akim's Inn: More on Harriet Beecher Stowe and Turgenev." *Slavic and East European Journal* 9 (Spring 1965): 47–55.

Kirkham, E. Bruce. "The First Editions of *Uncle Tom's Cabin*: A Bibliographic Study." *Papers of the Bibliographical Society of America* 65 (1971): 365–82.

Kirkham, E. Bruce. "Harriet Beecher Stowe and the Genesis, Composition and Revision of *Uncle Tom's Cabin.*" *Dissertation Abstracts* 29 (1968): 4492A–93A (North Carolina).

Lee, Joseph. "Uncle Tom's Little Red Cabin." *University College Quarterly* 11 (November 1965): 15–24.

Levin, David. "American Fiction as Historical Evidence: Reflections on *Uncle Tom's Cabin.*" *Negro American Literature Forum* 5 (1971): 132–36.

Lippman, Monroe. "Uncle Tom and His Poor Relations: American Slavery Plays." *Southern Speech Journal* 28 (Spring 1963): 183–97.

McDowell, John H. "Original Scenery and Documents for Productions of *Uncle Tom's Cabin.*" *Revue D'Histoire du Théâtre* 15 (January–March 1963): 71–79.

Merideth, Robert. "The Revival of *Uncle Tom's Cabin.*" *Phylon* 24 (1963): 300–302.

Meserve, W. J., and R. I. Meserve. "*Uncle Tom's Cabin* and Modern Chinese Drama." *Modern Drama* 17 (March 1974): 57–66.

Miller, Randall M. "Mrs. Stowe's Negro: George Harris' Negritude in *Uncle Tom's Cabin.*" *Colby Library Quarterly* 10 (December 1974): 521–26.

Oliver, Egbert S. "The Little Cabin of Uncle Tom." *College English* 26 (February 1965): 355–61.

Opperman, Harry. "Two Ghost Editions of *Uncle Tom's Cabin.*" *Papers of the Bibliographical Society of America* 65 (1971): 295–96.

Pickens, Donald K. "Uncle Tom Becomes Nat Turner: A Commentary on Two American Heroes." *Negro American Literature Forum* 3 (1969): 45–48.

Reed, Kenneth T. "*Uncle Tom's Cabin* and the Heavenly City." *College Language Association Journal* 12 (December 1968): 150–54.

Rexroth, Kenneth. "*Uncle Tom's Cabin.*" *Saturday Review* (January 11, 1969): 71.

Smylie, James H. "*Uncle Tom's Cabin* Revisited: The Bible, the Romantic Imagination, and the Sympathies of Christ." *Interpretation* 27 (1973): 67–85.

Steele, Thomas J. "Tom and Eva: Mrs. Stowe's Two Dying Christs." *Negro American Literature Forum* 6 (1972): 85–90.

Strout, Cushing. "*Uncle Tom's Cabin* and the Portent of Millennium." *Yale Review* 57 (Spring 1968): 375–85.

"Uncle Tom: That Enduring Old Image." *American Heritage* 23 (December 1971): 50–57.

"Uncle Tom's Message: The Book of War and Freedom." *Times Literary Supplement* (October 4, 1963): 777–78.

Van Hoy, Milton S. "Two Allusions to Hungary in *Uncle Tom's Cabin.*" *Phylon* 34 (1973): 433–35.

Van Why, Joseph F., and E. Bruce Kirkham. "A Note on Two Pages of the Manuscript of *Uncle Tom's Cabin.*" *Papers of the Bibliographical Society of America* 66 (1972): 433–34.

Ward, John William. "I've Been Reading *Uncle Tom's Cabin,* as a Matter of Historical Fact." *Columbia University Forum* 9 (Winter 1966): 42–47.

IDAH MEACHAM STROBRIDGE (1855–1932) U.S.

General Works

Amaral, Anthony. "Idah Meacham Strobridge: First Woman of Nevada Letters." *Nevada Historical Society Quarterly* 10 (Fall 1967): 5–12.

JANE STUART (1942–) U.S.

Bibliography

Woodbridge, Hensley C. "Jesse and Jane Stuart: A Bibliography-Supplement." *Jack London Newsletter* 2 (September–December 1969): 118–20; 3 (January–April 1970): 37–41; 5 (May–August 1972): 139–41; 5 (September–December 1972):

184–85; 6 (January–April 1973): 55–56; 6 (May–August 1973): 89–90.

RUTH SUCKOW (1892–1960) U.S.
General Works

Hamblen, Abigail Ann. "Protestanism in Three American Novels." *Forum* 3 (Fall–Winter 1960): 40–43.

Hamblen, Abigail Ann. "Ruth Suckow and Thomas Wolfe: A Study in Similarity." *Forum* 3 (Winter 1961): 27–31.

Kissane, Leedice McAnelly. "Ruth Suckow: Interpreter of the Mind of Mid-America (1900–1933)." *Dissertation Abstracts* 28 (1968): 3674A (Minnesota).

McAlpin, Sister Sara. "Enlightening the Commonplace: The Art of Sarah Jewett, Willa Cather and Ruth Suckow." *Dissertation Abstracts International* 32 (1971): 2061A (Penn.).

Muehl, Lois B. "Ruth Suckow's Art of Fiction." *Books at Iowa*, no. 13 (1970): 3–12.

Paluka, Frank. "Ruth Suckow: A Calendar of Letters." *Books at Iowa*, no. 1 (1964): 34–40; no. 2 (1964): 31–42.

Stewart, Margaret O'Brien. "A Critical Study of Ruth Suckow's Fiction." *Dissertation Abstracts* 21 (1960): 1195–96 (Illinois).
Individual Works
The Folks (1934)

Hamblen, Abigail Ann. "Ruth Suckow's *The Folks*: Universality in Iowa." *Cresset* 27 (March 1964): 8–11.

MARTHA SUMMERHAYS (fl. 1870s) U.S.
Individual Works
Vanished Arizona (c. 1870)

Powell, Laurence C. "Martha Summerhays' *Vanished Arizona*." *Westways* 63 (July 1971): 16–19.

JACQUELINE SUSANN (1921–1974) U.S.
General Works

Bannon, B.A. "Jacqueline Susann." *Publishers Weekly* (April 2, 1973): 12–14.

"Blockbusters." *Newsweek* (June 6, 1966): 101A–3.

Davidson, Sara. "Jacqueline Susann: The Writing Machine." *Harper's* (October 1969): 65–71.

"Doris Day Remembers: My Friend Jackie." *Ladies' Home Journal* (January 1975): 58.

Ebert, A. "Fears of the Famous." *Good Housekeeping* (May 1973): 107.

"How Green Is Her Valley." *Newsweek* (February 5, 1968): 70–71.

Howard, J. "Happiness Is Being Number 1." *Life* (August 19, 1966): 69–70.

"Jackie's Machine." *Time* (June 20, 1969): 88.

"Jacqueline Susann's Bedtime Stories: Interview." *Today's Health* (September 1971): 30–33.

Kasindorf, M. "Jackie Susann Picks Up the Marbles." *New York Times Magazine* (August 12, 1973): 11.

"More Guys and Dolls." *Newsweek* (June 2, 1969): 98.

Purdy, Ken W. "Valley of the Dollars." *Saturday Evening Post* (February 24, 1968): 76–78.

Reed, Rex. "Remembering Jacqueline Susann." *Ladies' Home Journal* (January 1975): 52.
Individual Works
Valley of the Dolls (1966)

Seiden, Lewis S. "*Valley of the Dolls* by Jacqueline Susann." *Psychology Today* (July 1967): 13–14.

ROSEMARY SUTCLIFF (1920–) Great Britain
Bibliography

"Rosemary Sutcliff." *Horn Book Magazine* 36 (1960): 248.

General Works

Colwell, E.H. "Rosemary Sutcliff—Lantern Bearer." *Horn Book Magazine* 36 (1960): 200–205.

MAY SWENSON (1919–) U.S.
General Works

Howard, Richard. "May Swenson." *Tri-Quarterly* 7 (Fall 1966): 119–31.

Knudson, R. "Two Poets." *American Library Association Bulletin* 2 (November 1971): 1046–47.

Stanford, Ann. "May Swenson: The Art of Perceiving." *Southern Review* (U.S.) 5 (1969): 58–75.

T

IDA MINERVA TARBELL (1857–1944) U.S.
General Works
Hamilton, V. V. "Gentlewoman and the Robber Baron." *American Heritage* 21 (April 1970): 78–86.

ELIZABETH TAYLOR (1912–) Great Britain
General Works
Bailey, Paul. "Artist in Miniature." *New Statesman* (August 10, 1973): 192–93.
Liddell, Robert. "The Novels of Elizabeth Taylor." *Review of English Literature* 1 (February 1960): 54–61.

SARA TEASDALE (1884–1933) U.S.
Bibliography
Buchan, Vivian. "Sara Teasdale (1884–1933)." *Bulletin of Bibliography* 25 (September–December 1967): 94–97; 26 (January–April 1968): 120–23.
General Works
Cohen, Edward H. "The Letters of Sara Teasdale to Jessie B. Rittenhouse." *Resources for American Literary Studies* 4 (1974): 225–27.

EMILY LADY TENNYSON, née Sellwood (1813–1896) Great Britain
General Works
Hoge, James O. "The Letters of Emily Lady Tennyson." *Dissertation Abstracts International* 31 (1971): 4718A (Virginia).

ELLEN TERNAN (fl. 1870s) Great Britain
General Works
Staples, Leslie C. "Ellen Ternan—Some Letters." *Dickensian* 61 (January 1965): 30–35.

OCTAVE THANET [pseud.]. *See* Alice French

CELIA LAIGHTON THAXTER (1835–1894) U.S.
General Works
Cary, Richard. "The Multicolored Spirit of Celia Thaxter." *Colby Library Quarterly* 6 (December 1964): 512–36.
Vaughan, Dorothy M. "Celia Thaxter's Library." *Colby Library Quarterly* 6 (December 1964): 536–49.
Westbrook, P.D. "Celia Thaxter: Seeker of the Unattainable." *Colby Library Quarterly* 6 (December 1964): 500–12.

DOROTHY THOMPSON (1894–1961) U.S.
General Works
Heilbrun, Carolyn. "Dorothy Thompson: A Legend in Her Own Time." *Ms.* (August 1972): 36.

FLORA THOMPSON (1877?–1947) Great Britain
General Works
Fowles, John. "A Lost World." *New Statesman* (August 3, 1973): 154–55.
Lipson, E. R. "Laura/Flora of Lark Rise." *New York Times Book Review* (July 21, 1974): 23.

KAY THOMPSON (1911–) U.S.
General Works
Reed, Rex. "Rex Reed on Kay Thompson: You've Never Seen Anything Like Her." *Harper's Bazaar* (November 1972): 114–15.

MARIANNE THORNTON (1797–1887) Great Britain
General Works
Hair, P.E.H. "Marianne Thornton, 1886." *Notes and Queries* 18 (November 1971): 419–20.

HESTER LYNCH THRALE, Mrs. Piozzi (1741–1821) Great Britain

General Works

Bell, A.S. "A Late View of Mrs. Piozzi." *Notes and Queries* 18 (September 1971): 337–38.

Burnim, Kalman A. "The Letters of Sarah and William Siddons to Hester Lynch Piozzi in the John Rylands Library." *Bulletin of the John Rylands Library* 52 (Autumn 1969): 46–95.

Corrigan, Beatrice. "Three Englishwomen in Italy." *Queen's Quarterly* 79 (1972): 147–58.

Hyde, Mary. "The Impossible Friendship." *Harvard Library Bulletin* 20 (1972): 5–37.

Lustig, Irma S. "Boswell at Work: The 'Animadversions' on Mrs. Piozzi." *Modern Language Review* 67 (January 1972): 11–30.

Menagh, Diana. "An Edition of the Letters of Marianne Frances (1790–1832) to Hester Lynch Piozzi (1741–1821), 1808–1810." *Dissertation Abstracts International* 35 (1975): 2223A (C.U.N.Y.).

Myers, Sylvia H. "The Ironies of Education." *Aphra* 4 (Spring 1973): 61–72.

Riely, John C. "Bozzy and Piozzi: The History of Literary Friendship and Rivalry." *Dissertation Abstracts International* 32 (1972): 4577A–78A (Penn.).

Riely, John C. "Johnson's Last Years with Mrs. Thrale: Facts and Problems." *Bulletin of the John Rylands Library* 57 (Autumn 1974): 196–212.

Riely, John C. "Lady Knight's Role in the Boswell–Piozzi Rivalry." *Philological Quarterly* 51 (October 1972): 961–65.

Riely, J.C., and Alvaro Ribeiro. "Mrs. Thrale in the *Tour*." *Papers of the Bibliographical Society of America* 69 (1975): 151–63.

Spacks, Patricia Meyer. "Scrapbook of a Self: Mrs. Piozzi's Late Journals." *Harvard Library Bulletin* 18 (1970): 221–47.

Weinbrot, H.D. "Samuel Johnson's 'Short Song of Congratulation' and the Accompanying Letter to Mrs. Thrale: The Huntington Library Manuscripts." *Huntington Library Quarterly* 34 (November 1970): 79–80.

Yung, K.K. "The Association Books of Johnson, Boswell, and Mrs. Piozzi in the Johnson Birthplace Museum." *New Rambler*, no. 112 (1972): 23–44.

CHARLOTTE ELIZABETH TONNA, née Browne (1790–1846) Great Britain
General Works

Kovacevic, Ivanka, and Barbara S. Kanna. "Blue Book into Novel: The Forgotten Industrial Fiction of Charlotte Elizabeth Tonna." *Nineteenth Century Fiction* 25 (September 1970): 152–73.

CATHERINE TRAILL (1802–1899) Canada
General Works

Collard, E. "Botanist in the Backwoods: The Career of Catherine Traill." *Country Life* 147 (1970): 182–83.

Gairdner, William D. "Traill and Moodie: Two Realities." *Journal of Canadian Fiction* 1 (1972): 35–42.

Thomas, Clara. "Journeys to Freedom." *Canadian Literature*, no. 51 (Winter 1972): 11–19.

PAMELA LYNDON TRAVERS (1906–) Australia
General Works

Roddy, J. "Visit with the Real Mary Poppins." *Look* (December 13, 1966): 84.
Individual Works

Mary Poppins (1934)

Lingeman, R.R. "Visit with Mary Poppins and P.L. Travers." *New York Times Magazine* (December 25, 1966): 12–13.

"Mary Poppins." *New Yorker* (October 20, 1962): 44–45.

DIANA TRILLING, née Rubin (1905–) U.S.
General Works

Fraser, G.S. "Impolite Essays." *Partisan Review* 32 (1965): 127–33.

SARAH KIRBY TRIMMER (1741–1810) Great Britain
General Works

"Sarah Trimmer, 1741–1810: Revolutionary in a Lace Cap." *Times Educational Supplement* (December 16, 1961): 830.

FRANCES TROLLOPE (1780–1863) Great Britain
General Works

Chaloner, W. H. "Mrs. Trollope and the Early Factory System." *Victorian Studies* 4 (September 1960): 159–66.

U

Fligar, Martha Weber. "Mrs. Trollope's Valentine to Cincinnati." *Bulletin of History and Philosophy of Ohio* 18 (January 1960): 13–18.

DOROTHY UHNAK (1930?–) U.S.
General Works
"Seven Who Do the Whodunits." *Newsweek* (March 22, 1971): 103.

EVELYN UNDERHILL (1875–1941) Great Britain
General Works
Kirby, Sister Mary Xavier. "The Writings of Evelyn Underhill: A Critical Analysis." *Dissertation Abstracts* 26 (1966): 6043–44 (Penn.).

V

FRANCES FULLER VICTOR (1826–1902) U.S.
General Works
Mills, Hazel Emery. "The Emergence of Frances Fuller Victor—Historian." *Oregon Historical Quarterly* 62 (1961): 309–34.

ETHEL LILIAN VOYNICH, née Boole (1864–1960) Great Britain
Individual Works
The Gadfly (1897)
Fremantle, Anne. "Return of the Gadfly." *Commonweal* (May 12, 1961): 167–71.

W

DIANE WAKOWSKI (1937–) U.S.
General Works
Gerber, Philip L., and Robert J. Gemmett, eds. "A Terrible War: A Conversation with Diane Wakowski." *Far Point* 4 (Spring–Summer 1970): 44–54.

ANNE WALDMAN (1945?–) U.S.
General Works
Braudy, S. "Queen Anne." *Newsweek* (November 22, 1971): 128.

ALICE WALKER (1944–) U.S.
General Works
Callahan, John. "Reconsideration: The Higher Ground of Alice Walker." *New Republic* (September 14, 1974): 21–22.
Coles, Robert. "To Try Men's Souls." *New Yorker* (February 27, 1971): 104–6.
Fowler, Carolyn. "Solid at the Core." *Freedomways* 14 (1974): 59–62.
Hairston, Loyle. "Work of Rare Beauty and Power." *Freedomways* 11 (1971): 170–77.
Smith, Barbara. "The Souls of Black Women." *Ms.* (February 1974): 42.
Washington, Mary Helen. "Black Women Myth and Image Makers." *Black World* 23 (August 1974): 10–18.
Individual Works
In Love and Trouble (1973)
Washington, Mary Helen. "Review of *In Love and Trouble*." *Black World* 23 (October 1974): 51–52.
Revolutionary Petunias (1973)
Ward, Jerry. "Review of *Revolutionary Petunias*." *College Language Association Journal* 17 (September 1973): 127–29.
Washington, Mary Helen. "Review of *Revolutionary Petunias*." *Black World* 22 (September 1973): 51.
The Third Life of Orange Copeland (1970)
Schorer, Mark. "Novels and Nothingness." *American Scholar* 40 (Winter 1970–1971): 168–74.

KATH WALKER [pseud. of Kathleen Dalziel] (fl. 1940s) Australia
General Works
Baysting, Arthur. "Kath Walker: Poet and Propagandist." *New Zealand Listener* (September 25, 1972): 17.
Doobov, Ruth. "The New Dreamtime: Kath Walker in Australian Literature." *Australian Literary Studies* 6 (1973): 46–55.

MARGARET WALKER (1915–) U.S.
General Works
Giddings, Paula. " 'A Shoulder Hunched Against a Sharp Concern': Some Themes in the Poetry of Margaret Walker." *Black World* 21 (December 1971): 20–25.

ELIZABETH HELY WALSHE (1835?–1869) Canada(?)
Individual Works
Cedar Creek (1863)
Brodie, Alexander H. "*Cedar Creek*: Bibliography of Canadiana." *Humanities Association Bulletin* 22 (Spring 1971): 56–62.

EDA LOU WALTON (1894–1961) U.S.
General Works
Belitt, Ben. "ELW: A Homage." *New Mexico Quarterly* 33 (Autumn 1963): 266–71.
Greenhood, David. "Eda Lou Walton's Use of Her Native Scene." *New Mexico Quarterly* 33 (Autumn 1963): 253–65.

MAISIE WARD (1889–1975) Great Britain
General Works
Sheed, W. "Frank Sheed and Maisie Ward: Writers, Publishers and Parents." *New York Times Book Review* (April 2, 1972): 2.

MRS. HUMPHRY WARD, née Mary Augusta Arnold (1851–1920) Great Britain
General Works
Musil, Caryn M. "Art and Ideology: The Novels and Times of Mrs. Humphry Ward." *Dissertation Abstracts International* 35 (1974): 3694A (Northwestern).
Norton-Smith, J. "An Introduction to Mrs. Humphry Ward, Novelist." *Essays in Criticism* 18 (October 1968): 420–28.
Peterson, William S. "J. H. Shorthouse and Mrs. Humphry Ward: Two New Letters." *Notes and Queries* 18 (July 1971): 259–61.
Peterson, William S. "Robert Browning and Mrs. Humphry Ward." *Browning Newsletter* 7 (Fall 1971): 13–14.
Tomalin, Claire. "Mary Augusta." *New Statesman* (October 19, 1973): 569.
Webster, Norman W. "Mrs. Humphry Ward: A Retrospect." *Cornhill Magazine*, no. 1059 (Spring 1969): 223–33.
Williams, Kenneth E. "Faith, Intention, and Fulfillment: The Religious Novels of Mrs. Humphry Ward." *Dissertation Abstracts* 30 (1970): 2553A–54A (Temple).
Individual Works
Lady Connie (1916)
Knoepflmacher, U. C. "The Rival Ladies: Mrs. Ward's *Lady Connie* and Lawrence's *Lady Chatterley's Lover*." *Victorian Studies* 4 (December 1960): 141–58.
Robert Elsmere (1888)
Laski, Marghanita. "Words from *Robert Elsmere*." *Notes and Queries* 8 (June 1961): 229–30.
Peterson, William S. "Gladstone's Review of *Robert Elsmere*: Some Unpublished Correspondence." *Review of English Studies* 21 (November 1970): 442–61.
Peterson, William S. "Mrs. Humphry Ward on *Robert Elsmere*: Six New Letters." *Bulletin of the New York Public Library* 74 (November 1970): 587–97.

SHEILA WATSON (1919–) Canada
Individual Works
The Double Hook (1959)
Corbett, Nancy J. "Closed Circle." *Canadian Literature*, no. 61 (Summer 1974): 46–53.
Lennox, John Watt. "The Past: Themes and Symbols of Confrontation in *The Double Hook* and *Le Torrent*." Journal of Canadian Fiction 2 (1973): 70–72.
Mitchell, Beverley. "Association and Allusion in *The Double Hook*." *Journal of Canadian Fiction* 2 (1973): 63–69.
Morriss, Margaret. "The Elements Transcended." *Canadian Literature*, no. 42 (Autumn 1969): 56–71.

HARRIET WEAVER (1908–) U.S.
General Works
Firth, John. "Harriet Weaver's Letters to James Joyce, 1915–1920." *Studies in Bibliography* 20 (1967): 151–88.
Pritchett, V.S. "Passion of the Virgin." *New Statesman* (November 27, 1970): 715–16.

MARY WEBB (1881–1927) Great Britain
Bibliography
Sanders, Charles. "Mary Webb: An Annotated Bibliography of Writings About Her." *English Literature in Transition* 9 (1966): 119–36.
General Works
Davis, W. Eugene. "The Poetry of Mary Webb: An Invitation." *English Literature in Transition* 11 (1968): 95–101.
Sanders, Charles. "Mary Webb: An Introduction." *English Literature in Transition* 9 (1966): 115–18.
Individual Works
The Golden Arrow (1916)
Sanders, Charles. "*The Golden Arrow*: Mary Webb's 'Apocalypse of Love.' " *English Literature in Transition* 10 (1967): 1–8.
Precious Bane (1924)
Sanders, Charles. "Webb's *Precious Bane*, Book 3, Chapter 2." *Explicator* 25 (October 1966): Item 10.

PHYLLIS WEBB (1927–) Canada
General Works
Hulcoop, John. "Phyllis Webb and the Priestess of Motion." *Canadian Literature*, no. 32 (Spring

1967): 29–39.

Sonthoff, Helen W. "Structure of Loss: The Poetry of Phyllis Webb." *Canadian Literature*, no. 9 (Summer 1961): 15–22.

EUDORA WELTY (1909–) U.S.

Bibliography

Cole, Hunter McKelva. "Book Reviews by Eudora Welty: A Checklist." *Bulletin of Bibliography* 23 (January–April 1963): 240.

Gross, Seymour L. "Eudora Welty: A Bibliography of Criticism and Comment." *Secretary's News Sheet*, no. 45 (1960): 1–32.

Jordan, Leona. "Eudora Welty: Selected Criticism." *Bulletin of Bibliography* 20 (January–April 1960): 14–15.

Keller, Dean H. "A Footnote to Eudora Welty: A Checklist." *Bulletin of Bibliography* 24 (January–April 1965): 138.

McDonald, W.U., Jr. "Eudora Welty Manuscripts: An Annotated Finding List." *Bulletin of Bibliography* 24 (September–December 1965): 44–46.

McDonald, W.U., Jr. "Eudora Welty Manuscripts: A Supplementary Annotated Finding List." *Bulletin of Bibliography* 31 (July–September 1974): 95.

Polk, Noel. "A Eudora Welty Checklist." *Mississippi Quarterly* 26 (Fall 1973): 662–93.

Williams, G.W. "An Addition to *Secretary's News Sheet*, no. 45, p. 11." *Secretary's News Sheet*, no. 48 (1962): 6.

General Works

Aldridge, John W. "Eudora Welty: Metamorphosis of a Southern Lady Writer." *Saturday Review* (April 18, 1970): 21.

Allen, J.A. "Eudora Welty: The Three Moments." *Virginia Quarterly Review* 51 (Autumn 1975): 605–27.

Appel, Alfred, Jr. "The Short Stories of Eudora Welty." *Dissertation Abstracts* 27 (1967): 4241A (Columbia).

Armes, Nancy Ruth. "The Feeder: A Study of the Fiction of Eudora Welty and Carson McCullers." *Dissertation Abstracts International* 35 (1975): 2817A (Illinois).

Blackwell, Louise. "Eudora Welty and the Rubber Fence Family." *Kansas Magazine* (1965): 73–76.

Brown, Ashley. "Eudora Welty and the Myths of Summer." *Shenandoah* 20 (1969): 20–35.

Buckley, William F., Jr. "The Southern Imagination: An Interview w8ith Eudora Welty and Walker Percy." *Mississippi Quarterly* 26 (Fall 1973): 493–516.

Bunting, Charles T. "'The Interior World': An Interview with Eudora Welty." *Southern Review* (U.S.) 8 (1972): 711–35.

Burger, Nash K. "Eudora Welty's Jackson." *Shenandoah* 20 (1969): 3–15.

Buswell, Mary Catherine. "The Love Relationships of Women in the Fiction of Eudora Welty." *West Virginia University Bulletin: Philological Papers* 13 (December 1961): 94–106.

Buswell, Mary Catherine. "The Mountain Figure in the Fiction of Eudora Welty." *West Virginia University Bulletin: Philological Papers* 19 (July 1972): 50–63.

Clemons, W. "Meeting Miss Welty." *New York Times Book Review* (April 12, 1970): 2.

Cole, Hunter M. "Windsor in Spencer and Welty: A Real and an Imaginary Landscape." *Notes on Mississippi Writers* 7 (Spring 1974): 2–11.

Cooley, John R. "Blacks as Primitives in Eudora Welty's Fiction." *Ball State University Forum* 14 (Summer 1973): 20–28.

Curley, Daniel. "Eudora Welty and the Quondam Obstruction." *Studies in Short Fiction* 5 (Spring 1968): 209–24.

Daniel, Robert W. "Eudora Welty: The Sense of Place." *South* 26 (1962): 276–86.

East, Charles. "The Search for Eudora Welty." *Mississippi Quarterly* 26 (Fall 1973): 477–82.

"Eudora Welty." *Publishers Weekly* (May 15, 1972): 30–31.

"Eudora Welty's World in the 30's." *Mademoiselle* (September 1971): 162–65.

Finger, Larry L. "Elements of the Grotesque in Selected Works of Welty, Capote, McCullers, and O'Connor." *Dissertation Abstracts International* 33 (1972): 1721A–22A (George Peabody College for Teachers).

"Five Tributes." *Shenandoah* 20 (1969): 36–39.

Fleischauer, John F. "The Focus of Mystery: Eudora Welty's Prose Style." *Southern Literary Journal* 5 (Spring 1973): 64–79.

Folsom, Gordon R. "Form and Substance in Eudora Welty." *Dissertation Abstracts* 21 (1960): 621 (Wisconsin).

Gill, B. "Inconstant Past." *New Yorker* (December

25, 1971): 66–68.

Givner, Joan. "Katherine Anne Porter, Eudora Welty, and 'Ethan Brand.'" *Italia Francescana* 1 (1974): 32–37.

Hardy, John Howard. "The Achievement of Eudora Welty." *Southern Humanities Review* 2 (Summer 1968): 269–78.

Hembree, Charles William. "Narrative Technique in the Fiction of Eudora Welty." *Dissertation Abstracts International* 35 (1975): 6139A–40A (Oklahoma).

Hinton, Jane Lee. " 'Out of All Times of Trouble': The Family in the Fiction of Eudora Welty." *Dissertation Abstracts International* 35 (1975): 7906A (Vanderbilt).

Howell, Elmo. "Eudora Welty and the Use of Place in Southern Fiction." *Arizona Quarterly* 28 (Autumn 1972): 248–56.

Howell, Elmo. "Eudora Welty's Comedy of Errors." *South Atlantic Quarterly* 69 (Autumn 1970): 469–79.

Inge, M. Thomas. "Eudora Welty as Poet." *Southern Humanities Review* 2 (Summer 1968): 310–12.

Isaacs, Neil D. "Four Notes on Eudora Welty." *Notes on Mississippi Writers* 2 (Fall 1969): 42–54.

Jones, Alun R. "A Frail Traveling Coincidence: Three Later Stories by Eudora Welty." *Shenandoah* 20 (1969): 40–53.

King, William P. "A Thematic Study of the Fiction of Eudora Welty." *Dissertation Abstracts International* 33 (1973): 3652A–53A (George Peabody College for Teachers).

Kuehl, L. "Eudora Welty: Interview." *Paris Review* 14 (Fall 1972): 73–97.

Landess, Thomas H. "The Function of Taste in the Fiction of Eudora Welty." *Mississippi Quarterly* 26 (Fall 1973): 543–58.

Lief, Ruth Ann. "A Progression of Answers." *Studies in Short Fiction* 2 (Summer 1965): 343–50.

Masserand, Anne M. "Eudora Welty's Travellers: The Journey Theme in Her Short Stories." *Southern Literary Journal* 3 (Spring 1971): 39–48.

McFarland, Ronald E. "Vision and Perception in the Works of Eudora Welty." *Markham Review* 2 (February 1971): 94–99.

Oates, Joyce Carol. "The Art of Eudora Welty." *Shenandoah* 20 (1969): 54–57.

Opitz, Kurt. "Eudora Welty: The Order of a Captive Soul." *Critique* 7 (1964–1965): 79–91.

Pickett, Nell Ann. "Colloquialism as a Style in the First-Person-Narrator Fiction of Eudora Welty." *Mississippi Quarterly* 26 (Fall 1973): 559–76.

Rouse, Sarah Allman. "Place and People in Eudora Welty's Fiction: A Portrait of the Deep South." *Dissertation Abstracts* 23 (1962): 3901 (Florida State).

Smith, Carol P. "The Journey Motif in the Collected Works of Eudora Welty." *Dissertation Abstracts International* 32 (1972): 5807A–8A (Maryland).

Stanford, Donald E. "Eudora Welty and the Pulitzer Prize." *Southern Review* (U.S.) 9 (1973): 20–23.

Tapley, Philip Allen. "The Portrayal of Women in Selected Short Stories by Eudora Welty (Volumes I and II)." *Dissertation Abstracts International* 35 (1975): 5429A–30A (Louisiana State).

Tarbox, Raymond. "Eudora Welty's Fiction: The Salvation Theme." *American Imago* 29 (Spring 1972): 70–91.

Thompson, Victor H. " 'Life's Impact Is Oblique': A Study of Obscurantism in the Writings of Eudora Welty." *Dissertation Abstracts International* 33 (1972): 1745A (Rutgers).

Vande Kieft, Ruth M. "The Mysteries of Eudora Welty." *Georgia Review* 15 (Fall 1961): 343–57.

Vande Kieft, Ruth M. "The Vision of Eudora Welty." *Mississippi Quarterly* 26 (Fall 1973): 517–42.

Vickery, Olga W. "Review of *Eudora Welty* by Ruth M. Vande Kieft." *Critique* 6 (1963): 136–38.

Welty, Eudora. "Must the Novelist Crusade?" *Atlantic Monthly* (October 1965): 104–8.

Welty, Eudora. "Some Notes on Time in Fiction." *Mississippi Quarterly* 26 (Fall 1973): 483–92.

Wild, Rebecca Smith. "Studies in the Shorter Fiction of Elizabeth Bowen and Eudora Welty." *Dissertation Abstracts* 27 (1966): 490A (Michigan).

Yardley, Jonathan. "The Last Good One?" *New Republic* (May 9, 1970): 33–36.

Individual Works

The Burning (1955)

Howell, Elmo. "Eudora Welty's Civil War Story." *Notes on Mississippi Writers* 2 (Spring 1969): 3–12.

Wild, Rebecca. "The Prophetic Strain in Eudora Welty's *The Burning*." *Essays and Studies* 20 (1973): 23–38.

The Bride of the Innisfallen (1955)

Harrell, Don. "Death in Eudora Welty's *The Bride of the Innisfallen*." *Notes on Contemporary Literature* 3 (September 1973): 2–7.

Clytie (1941)

Griffith, Albert J. "The Numinous Vision: Eudora Welty's *Clytie*." *Studies in Short Fiction* 4 (Fall 1966): 80–82.

Death of a Traveling Salesman (1936)

Griffith, Albert J. "Welty's *Death of a Traveling Salesman*." *Explicator* 20 (January 1962): Item 38.

Jones, William M. "Eudora Welty's Use of Myth in *Death of a Traveling Salesman*." *Journal of American Folklore* 73 (January–March 1960): 18–23.

Vickery, John B. "William Blake and Eudora Welty's *Death of a Traveling Salesman*." *Modern Language Notes* 76 (November 1961): 625–32.

Delta Wedding (1946)

Prenshaw, Peggy. "Cultural Patterns in Eudora Welty's *Delta Wedding* and the Demonstrators." *Notes on Mississippi Writers* 3 (Fall 1970): 51–70.

The Golden Apples (1949)

Blackwell, Louise. "Eudora Welty: Proverbs and Proverbial Phrases in *The Golden Apples*." *Southern Folklore Quarterly* 30 (1966): 332–41.

Bryant, J.A., Jr. "See Double in *The Golden Apples*." *Sewanee Review* 82 (Spring 1974): 300–315.

Carson, Franklin D. " 'The Song of Wandering Aengus': Allusions in Eudora Welty's *The Golden Apples*." *Notes on Mississippi Writers* 6 (Spring 1973): 14–18.

Harris, Wendell V. "The Thematic Unity of Welty's *The Golden Apples*." *Texas Studies in Literature and Language* 6 (Spring 1964): 92–95.

Jones, W. M. "The Plot as Search." *Studies in Short Fiction* 5 (Fall 1967): 37–43.

McHaney, Thomas L. "Eudora Welty and the Multitudinous Golden Apples." *Mississippi Quarterly* 26 (Fall 1973): 589–624.

Keela, the Outcast Indian Maiden (1941)

May, Charles E. "*Le Roi Mehaigne* in Welty's *Keela, the Outcast Indian Maiden*." *Modern Fiction Studies* 18 (Winter 1972–1973): 559–66.

McDonald, W. U., Jr. "Welty's *Keela*: Irony, Ambiguity, and the Ancient Mariner." *Studies in Short Fiction* 1 (Fall 1963): 59–61.

Ladies in Spring (1955)

Bolsterli, Margaret. "Mythic Elements in *Ladies in Spring*." *Notes on Mississippi Writers* 6 (Winter 1974): 69–72.

Lilly Daw and the Three Ladies (1941)

Drake, Robert Y., Jr. "Comments on Two Eudora Welty Stories." *Mississippi Quarterly* 13 (Summer 1960): 123–31.

Livvie (1943)

Henley, Elton F. "Confinement-Escape Symbolism in Eudora Welty's *Livvie*." *Iowa English Yearbook* 10 (Fall 1965): 60–63.

Smith, Julian. "*Livvie*: Eudora Welty's Song of Solomon." *Studies in Short Fiction* 5 (Fall 1967): 73–74.

Losing Battles (1970)

Boatwright, James. "Speech and Silence in *Losing Battles*." *Shenandoah* 25 (1974): 3–14.

Bradford, M. E. "Looking Down from a High Place: The Serenity of Miss Welty's *Losing Battles*." *Recherches Anglaises et Américaines* 4 (1971): 92–97.

Gossett, Louise Y. "Eudora Welty's New Novel: The Comedy of Loss." *Southern Literary Journal* 3 (Fall 1970): 122–37.

Kreyling, Michael. "Myth and History: The Foes of *Losing Battles*." *Mississippi Quarterly* 26 (Fall 1973): 639–50.

McMillen, William E. "Conflict and Resolution in Welty's *Losing Battles*." *Critique* 15 (1973): 110–24.

Moore, Carol A. "The Insulation of Illusion and *Losing Battles*." *Mississippi Quarterly* 26 (Fall 1973): 651–58.

Rubin, Louis D., Jr. "Everything Brought Out in the Open: Eudora Welty's *Losing Battles*." *Hollins Critic* 7 (June 1970): 1–12.

A Memory (1954)

Lief, Ruth Ann. "A Progression of Answers." *Studies in Short Fiction* 2 (Summer 1965): 343–50.

Old Mr. Marblehall (1936)

Davis, Charles E. "Welty's *Old Mr. Marblehall*." *Explicator* 30 (February 1972): Item 40.

Detweiler, Robert. "Eudora Welty's Blazing Butterfly: The Dynamics of Response." *Language and Style* 6 (1973): 58–71.

Travis, Mildred K. "A Note on *Wakefield* and *Old Mr. Marblehall*." *Notes on Contemporary Literature* 4 (May 1974): 9–10.

One Time, One Place: Mississippi in the Depression/Snapshot Album (1971)

Bradford, M.E. "Miss Eudora's Picture Book." *Mississippi Quarterly* 26 (Fall 1973): 659–62.

Curley, Daniel. "A Time Exposure." *Notes on Mississippi Writers* 5 (Spring 1972): 11–14.

The Optimist's Daughter (1969)

Brooks, Cleanth. "The Past Reexamined in *The*

Optimist's Daughter." *Mississippi Quarterly* 26 (Fall 1973): 577–88.

Davenport, Guy. "Primal Visions." *National Review* (June 23, 1972): 697.

Price, Reynolds. "The Onlooker Smiling: An Early Reading of *The Optimist's Daughter.*" *Shenandoah* 20 (1969): 59–73.

Stuckey, W.J. "Use of Marriage in Welty's *The Optimist's Daughter.*" *Critique* 17 (1975): 36–46.

Petrified Man (1954)

Cochran, Robert W. "Welty's *Petrified Man.*" *Explicator* 27 (December 1968): Item 25.

Helterman, Jeffrey. "Gorgons in Mississippi: Eudora Welty's *Petrified Man.*" *Notes on Mississippi Writers* 7 (Spring 1974): 12–20.

Kraus, W. Keith. "Welty's *Petrified Man.*" *Explicator* 29 (April 1971): Item 63.

Richmond, Lee J. "Symbol and Theme in Eudora Welty's *Petrified Man.*" *English Journal* 60 (December 1971): 1201–3.

Ringe, Donald A. "Welty's *Petrified Man.*" *Explicator* 18 (February 1960): Item 32.

A Piece of News (1937)

Hollenbaugh, Carol. "Ruby Fisher and Her Demon Lover." *Notes on Mississippi Writers* 7 (Fall 1974): 63–68.

McDonald, William U., Jr. "Eudora Welty's Revisions of *A Piece of News.*" *Studies in Short Fiction* 7 (Spring 1970): 232–47.

The Ponder Heart (1954)

Dosenbury, Winifred. "*Baby Doll* and *The Ponder Heart.*" *Modern Drama* 3 (February 1961): 393–95.

Sir Rabbit (1949)

Carson, Franklin D. "The Passage of Time in Eudora Welty's *Sir Rabbit.*" *Studies in Short Fiction* 12 (Summer 1975): 284–86.

A Still Moment (1943)

Thompson, Victor H. "The Natchez Trace in Eudora Welty's *A Still Moment.*" *Southern Literary Journal* 6 (Fall 1973): 59–69.

A Visit of Charity (1936)

Bradham, Jo Allen. "*A Visit of Charity*: Menippean Satire." *Studies in Short Fiction* 1 (Summer 1964): 258–63.

May, Charles E. "The Difficulty of Loving in *A Visit of Charity.*" *Studies in Short Fiction* 6 (Spring 1969): 338–41.

Palmer, Melvin Delmar. "Welty's *A Visit of Charity.*" *Explicator* 22 (May 1964): Item 69.

Toole, William B. "The Texture of *A Visit of Charity.*" *Mississippi Quarterly* 20 (Winter 1966–1967): 43–46.

The Whistler (1938)

McDonald, William U., Jr. "Welty's 'Social Consciousness': Revisions of *The Whistler.*" *Modern Fiction Studies* 16 (Summer 1970): 193–98.

Why I Live at the P.O. (1941)

Blackwell, Louise. "Eudora Welty and the Rubber Fence Family." *Kansas Magazine* (1965): 73–76.

Drake, Robert Y., Jr. "Comments on Two Eudora Welty Stories." *Mississippi Quarterly* 13 (Summer 1960): 123–31.

A Worn Path (1941)

Daly, Saralyn. "*A Worn Path* Retrod." *Studies in Short Fiction* 1 (Winter 1964): 133–39.

Donlan, D. "*A Worn Path*: Immortality of Stereotype." *English Journal* 62 (April 1973): 549–50.

Howell, Elmo. "Eudora Welty's Negroes: A Note on *A Worn Path.*" *Xavier University Studies* 9 (Spring 1970): 28–32.

Isaacs, Neil D. "Life for Phoenix." *Sewanee Review* 71 (Winter 1963): 75–81.

Moss, Grant, Jr. "*A Worn Path* Retold." *College Language Association Journal* 15 (December 1971): 144–52.

Russell, Diarmuid. "First Work." *Shenandoah* 20 (1969): 16–19.

Seidl, Frances. "Eudora Welty's Phoenix." *Notes on Mississippi Writers* 6 (Fall 1973): 53–55.

Trefan, Sara. "Welty's *A Worn Path.*" *Explicator* 24 (February 1966): Item 56.

Welty, Eudora. "Artists on Criticism of Their Art: 'Is Phoenix Jackson's Grandson Really Dead?' " *Critical Inquiry* 1 (September 1974): 219–21.

Welty, Eudora. "*A Worn Path.*" *Critical Inquiry* 1 (September 1974): 222–28.

DAME REBECCA WEST [pseud. of Cecily Isabel Fairfield] (1892–) Great Britain

General Works

"And They All Lived Unhappily Ever After." *Times Literary Supplement* (July 26, 1974): 779.

Clemons, W. "Happy Egotists." *Newsweek* (October 7, 1974): 103.

Curtis, Anthony. "Social Improvements and Literary Disasters." *Listener* (February 15, 1973): 211–13.

Hellman, Lillian. "H. G. Wells and Rebecca West." *New York Times Book Review* (October 13, 1974): 4–5.

Hicks, Jim. "Specialist in Traitors, Spies, and Weeds." *Life* (September 30, 1966): 55–56.

"In Communion with Reality." *Times Literary Supplement* (December 21, 1973): 1553–55.

Kobler, Turner S. "The Eclecticism of Rebecca West." *Critique* 13 (1971): 30–49.

Orlich, Sister Mary. "The Novels of Rebecca West: A Complex Unity." *Dissertation Abstracts* 27 (1967): 2540A (Notre Dame).

Rainer, Dachine. "Rebecca West: Disturber of the Peace." *Commonweal* (May 10, 1968): 227–30.

"Redbook Dialogue: Peter O'Toole and Rebecca West." *Redbook* (March 1964): 56–74.

Redd, Tony N. "Rebecca West: Master of Reality." *Dissertation Abstracts International* 33 (1973): 4431A (South Carolina).

Trilling, Diana. "The Jaguar and the Panther." *Times Literary Supplement* (November 22, 1974): 1301–2.

Weintraub, Stanley. "Literary Liaison." *New Republic* (October 5, 1974): 19–20.

West, Rebecca. "Testimony of Four Peers." *Esquire* (December 1971): 157.

Redd, Tony N. "Rebecca West: Master of Reality." *Dissertation Abstracts International* 33 (1973): 4431A (South Carolina).

Trilling, Diana. "The Jaguar and the Panther." *Times Literary Supplement* (November 22, 1974): 1301–2.

Weintraub, Stanley. "Literary Liaison." *New Republic* (October 5, 1974): 19–20.

West, Rebecca. "Testimony of Four Peers." *Esquire* (December 1971): 157.

JANE WEST (1758–1852) Great Britain
Individual Works
A Gossip's Story (1796)
Moler, Kenneth L. "*Sense and Sensibility* and Its Sources." *Review of English Studies* 17 (November 1966): 413–19.

JESSAMYN WEST (1907–) U.S.
Bibliography
Shivers, Alfred S. "Jessamyn West." *Bulletin of Bibliography* 28 (January–March 1971): 1–3.
General Works
Flanagan, John T. "The Fiction of Jessamyn West." *Indiana Magazine of History* 67 (1971): 299–316.
Graham, Lee. "An Interview with Jessamyn West." *Writer's Digest* 47 (May 1967): 24–27.

"Richard Nixon, Jessamyn West Help to Honor Paul S. Smith." *Quaker Life* (April 1966): 117.
Individual Works
Love, Death, and the Ladies' Drill Team (1955)
Katope, Christopher G. "West's *Love, Death, and the Ladies' Drill Team.*" *Explicator* 23 (December 1964): Item 27.

EDITH WHARTON, NÉE JONES (1862–1937) U.S.
Bibliography
Plante, Patricia R. "The Critical Reception of Edith Wharton's Fiction in America and England with an Annotated Enumerative Bibliography of Wharton Criticism from 1900 to 1961." *Dissertation Abstracts* 23 (1962): 1706 (Boston).
Tuttleton, James W. "Edith Wharton: An Essay in Bibliography." *Resources for American Literary Studies* 3 (1973): 163–202.
General Works
"Age of Edith." *Newsweek* (January 29, 1962): 82.
Ammons, Elizabeth Miller. "Edith Wharton's Heroines: Studies in Aspiration and Compliance." *Dissertation Abstracts International* 35 (1975): 7292A (Illinois).
Anderson, Hilton. "Edith Wharton and the Vulgar American." *Southern Quarterly* 7 (October 1968): 17–22.
Anderson, Hilton. "Edith Wharton as Fictional Heroine." *South Atlantic Quarterly* 69 (Winter 1970): 118–23.
Anderson, Hilton. "A Whartonian Woman in *Dodsworth*." *Sinclair Lewis Newsletter* 1 (Spring 1969): 5–6.
Anderson, Quentin. "Edith Wharton." *New York Times Book Review* (August 31, 1975): 1–2.
Baril, James Ronald. "Vision as Metaphorical Perception in the Fiction of Edith Wharton." *Dissertation Abstracts* 31 (1970): 1258A (Colorado).
Baxter, Annette K. "Caste and Class: Howells' Boston and Wharton's New York." *Midwest Quarterly* 4 (Summer 1963): 353–61.
Bell, Millicent. "The Eagle and the Worm." *London Magazine* 6 (July 1966): 5–46.
Bretschneider, Margaret Ann. "Edith Wharton: Patterns of Rejection and Denial." *Dissertation Abstracts* 30 (1970): 3935A (Case Western Reserve).
Buchan, Alexander M. "Edith Wharton and 'The Elusive Bright-Winged Thing.'" *New England Quarterly* 37 (September 1964): 343–62.
Buitenhuis, Peter. "Edith Wharton and the First

World War." *American Quarterly* 18 (Fall 1966): 493–505.

Cargas, Harry J. "Seeing, But Not Living: Two Characters from James and Wharton." *New Laurel Review* 1 (1972): 5–7.

Clarke, Gerald. "Popping the Stays." *Time* (September 1, 1975): 59–61.

Clough, David. "Edith Wharton's War Novels: A Reappraisal." *Twentieth Century Literature* 19 (January 1973): 1–14.

Coard, Robert L. "Names in the Fiction of Edith Wharton." *Names* 13 (1965): 1–10.

Cohn, Jan. "The Houses of Fiction: Domestic Architecture in Howells and Edith Wharton." *Texas Studies in Literature and Language* 15 (Fall 1973): 537–49.

Crane, Joan St. C. "Rare or Seldom-Seen Dust Jackets of American First Editions, 8." *Serif* 9 (Summer 1972): 36–37; 9 (Fall 1972): 45–47.

Duggan, Margaret M., ed. "Edith Wharton's *Gatsby* Letter." *Fitzgerald-Hemingway Annual* (1972): 85–87.

Featherstone, Joseph L. "Mrs. Wharton and Mr. James." *New Republic* (May 29, 1965): 21–24.

Gleason, James J. "After Innocence: The Later Novels of Edith Wharton." *Dissertation Abstracts* 30 (1969): 1564A–65A (Ohio State).

Greenwood, Florence Joan Voss. "A Critical Study of Edith Wharton's Short Stories and *Nouvelles*." *Dissertation Abstracts* 23 (1962): 234–35 (Stanford).

Grumbach, Doris. "Reconsideration: Edith Wharton." *New Republic* (April 21, 1973): 29–30.

Hamblen, Abigail Ann. "Edith Wharton in New England." *New England Quarterly* 38 (June 1965): 239–44.

Hemmer, Sister Jean Marie. "A Study of Setting in the Major Novels of Edith Wharton." *Dissertation Abstracts* 25 (1964): 3571 (Fordham).

Hewitt, Rosalie. "Aristocracy and the Modern American Novel of Manners: Edith Wharton, F. Scott Fitzgerald, Ellen Glasgow, and James Gould Cozzens." *Dissertation Abstracts* 31 (1970): 4163A (Purdue).

Hierth, Harrison E. "The Class Novel." *College English Association Critic* 27 (December 1964): 1–4.

Howe, Irving. "The Achievement of Edith Wharton." *Encounter* 19 (July 1962): 45–52.

Jacoby, Victoria A.D. "A Study of Class Values and the Family in the Fiction of Edith Wharton." *Dissertation Abstracts International* 33 (1972): 2379A (Stanford).

Jones, Ann Maret. "Three American Responses to World War One: Wharton, Empey, and Bourne." *Dissertation Abstracts* 31 (1970): 1802A (Wisconsin).

Karl, Frederick R. "Three Conrad Letters in the Edith Wharton Papers." *Yale University Library Gazette* 44 (1970): 148–51.

Kraft, Stephanie B. "Women and Society in the Novels of George Eliot and Edith Wharton." *Dissertation Abstracts International* 34 (1973): 2632A (Rochester).

Kronenberger, Louis. "Edith Wharton's New York: Two Period Pieces." *Michigan Quarterly Review* 4 (Winter 1965): 3–13.

Kronenberger, Louis. "Mrs. Wharton's Literary Museum." *Atlantic Monthly* (September 1968): 98–102.

Krupnick, Mark L. "Stephen Crane and Edith Wharton: Two Essays in the Literature of Disinheritance." *Dissertation Abstracts* 30 (1969): 1567A (Brandeis).

"Last Survivor." *Time* (June 5, 1964): 101–2.

Lavison, Richard H. "Hermann Sudermann and Edith Wharton." *Revue de Littérature Comparée* 41 (1967): 125–31.

Lawson, Richard H. "The Influence of Gottfried Keller on Edith Wharton." *Revue de Littérature Comparée* 42 (1968): 366–79.

L'Enfant, Julia Chandler. "Edith Wharton and Virginia Woolf: Tradition and Experiment in the Modern Novel." *Dissertation Abstracts International* 35 (1975): 4531A (Louisiana State).

Lewis, Katherine Ann. "Satire and Irony in the Later Novels of Edith Wharton." *Dissertation Abstracts* 29 (1968): 608A (Stanford).

Lewis, R.W.B. "Edith Wharton: The Beckoning Quarry." *American Heritage* 26 (October 1975): 53–56.

Lindberg, Gary H. "Edith Wharton and the Rhetoric of Manners." *Dissertation Abstracts* 28 (1967): 4637A (Stanford).

Maynard, Moira. "The Medusa's Face: A Study of Character and Behavior in the Fiction of Edith Wharton." *Dissertation Abstracts* 32 (1971): 2096A (N.Y.U.).

McDowell, Margaret B. "Edith Wharton's Ghost Stories." *Criticism* 12 (1970): 133–52.

McDowell, Margaret B. "Viewing the Custom of Her Country: Edith Wharton's Feminism." *Contemporary Literature* 15 (Autumn 1974): 521–38.

McManis, Jo Agnew. "Edith Wharton's Hymn to Respectability." *Southern Review* (U.S.) 7 (1971): 986–93.

McManis, Jo Agnew. "Edith Wharton's Treatment of Love: A Study of Conventionality and Unconventionality in Her Fiction." *Dissertation Abstracts* 28 (1967): 2689A (Louisiana State).

Mizener, Arthur. "Scott Fitzgerald and Edith Wharton." *Times Literary Supplement* (July 7, 1966): 595.

Molley, Chester N. "The Artemis–Athene and Venus Polarity in the Works of Edith Wharton: A Mythological Dimension with Psychological Implications." *Dissertation Abstracts International* 32 (1971): 6442A (Penn. State).

Moss, R.F. "Edith Wharton: A Biography." *Saturday Review* (August 9, 1975): 36–37.

Parker, Jeraldine. " 'Uneasy Survivors': Five Women Writers, 1896–1923." *Dissertation Abstracts International* 34 (1973): 1927A (Utah).

Phelps, Donald. "Edith Wharton and the Invisible." *Prose* 7 (1973): 227–45.

Pitlick, Mary Louise. "Edith Wharton's Narrative Technique: The Major Phase." *Dissertation Abstracts* 26 (1965): 3347–48 (Wisconsin).

Plante, Patricia R. "Edith Wharton: A Prophet Without Due Honor." *Midwest Review*, Summer (1962): 16–22.

Plante, Patricia R. "Edith Wharton and the Invading Goths." *Midcontinent American Studies Journal* 5 (1964): 18–23.

Plante, Patricia R. "Edith Wharton as Short Story Writer." *Midwest Quarterly* 4 (Summer 1963): 363–69.

Prescott, P.S. "Portrait of a Lady." *Newsweek* (September 22, 1975): 75–76.

Pritchett, V.S. "A Friend for Destiny." *New Statesman* (December 22, 1972): 946–47.

Puknat, E.M., and S.B. Puknat. "Edith Wharton and Gottfried Keller." *Comparative Literature* 21 (1969): 245–54.

Rothwell, K.S. "From Society to Babbitry: Lewis' Debt to Edith Wharton." *Journal of the Central Mississippi Valley American Study Association* (Spring 1960): 32–37.

Sasaki, Miyoko. "The Sense of Horror in Edith Wharton." *Dissertation Abstracts International* 34 (1974): 7244A (Yale).

Semel, Sister Ann. "A Study of the Thematic Design in the Four Major Novels of Edith Wharton." *Dissertation Abstracts* 32 (1972): 2707A (Notre Dame).

Shelton, Frank W. "The Family in the Novels of Wharton, Faulkner, Cather, Lewis and Dreiser." *Dissertation Abstracts International* 32 (1972): 5244A (North Carolina).

Thomas, J.D. "Three American Tragedies: Notes on the Responsibilities of Fiction." *South Central Bulletin* 20 (1960): 11–15.

Tintner, A.R. "James' Mock Epic: *The Velvet Glove*, Edith Wharton and Other Late Tales." *Modern Fiction Studies* 17 (Winter 1971–1972): 483–99.

Todd, R. "Edith Wharton." *Atlantic Monthly* (November 1975): 114–16.

Tuttleton, James Wesley. "Edith Wharton: Form and the Epistemology of Artistic Creation." *Criticism* 10 (1968): 334–51.

Tuttleton, James Wesley. "Edith Wharton: High Priestess of Reason." *Personalist* 47 (Summer 1966): 382–98.

Tuttleton, James Wesley. "Edith Wharton: The Archeological Motive." *Yale Review* 61 (Summer 1972): 562–74.

Tuttleton, James Wesley. "Edith Wharton and the Novel of Manners." *Dissertation Abstracts* 24 (1963): 3345–46 (North Carolina).

Tuttleton, James Wesley. "Henry James and Edith Wharton: Fiction as the House of Fame." *Midcontinent American Studies Journal* 7 (1966): 25–36.

Tuttleton, James Wesley. "Leisure, Wealth and Luxury: Edith Wharton's Old New York." *Midwest Quarterly* 7 (Summer 1966): 337–52.

Tuttleton, James Wesley. "The President and the Lady: Edith Wharton and Theodore Roosevelt." *Bulletin of the New York Public Library* 69 (January 1965): 49–57.

Wegelin, Christof. "Edith Wharton and the Twilight of the International Novel." *Southern Review* (U.S.) 5 (1969): 398–418.

Wegelin, Christof. "The Rise of the International Novel." *Publications of the Modern Language Association* 77 (1962): 305–10.

White, Charles J. "The Intelligent Acceptance of Given Conditions: Moral and Social Attitudes, and Their Relationship to Social Change in the Novels of Edith Wharton, John P. Marquand and James Gould Cozzens." *Dissertation Abstracts Interna-*

tional 34 (1973): 1943A (Penn.).

Winner, Viola Hopkins. "Convention and Prediction in Edith Wharton's *Fast and Loose*." *American Literature* 42 (March 1970): 50–69.

Wolfe, Robert F. "The Restless Women of Edith Wharton." *Dissertation Abstracts International* 35 (1974): 1130A (Columbia).

Individual Works

After Holbein (1911)

McDowell, Margaret B. "Edith Wharton's *After Holbein* 'A Paradigm of the Human Condition.'" *Journal of Narrative Technique* 1 (1971): 49–58.

The Age of Innocence (1920)

Cartwright, Faith Carman Watton. "*The Age of Innocence* by Edith Wharton: A Critical and Annotated Edition." *Dissertation Abstracts* 32 (1970): 1466A (Nebraska).

Doyle, Charles Clay. "Emblems of Innocence: Imagery Patterns in Wharton's *The Age of Innocence*." *Xavier University Studies* 10 (Fall 1971): 19–26.

Evans, Elizabeth. "Musical Allusions in *The Age of Innocence*." *Notes on Contemporary Literature* 4 (May 1974): 4–7.

Gargano, James W. "*The Age of Innocence*: Art or Artifice." *Research Studies* 38 (1970): 22–28.

Ishimoto, Kimi. "On *The Age of Innocence*." *Essays in Literature and Thought* 25 (March 1963): 14–16.

Jacobson, Irving. "Perception, Communication, and Growth as Correlative Theme in Edith Wharton's *The Age of Innocence*." *Agora* 2 (1973): 68–82.

Lamar, Lillie B. "Edith Wharton and the Book of Common Prayer." *American Notes and Queries* 7 (November 1968): 38–39.

Lamar, Lillie B. "Edith Wharton's Foreknowledge in *The Age of Innocence*." *Texas Studies in Literature and Language* 8 (Fall 1966): 385–89.

Murphy, John J. "The Satiric Structure of Wharton's *The Age of Innocence*." *Markham Review* 2 (May 1970): 1–4.

Niall, Brenda. "Prufrock in Brownstone: Edith Wharton's *The Age of Innocence*." *Southern Review* (Australia) 4 (1971): 203–14.

The Children (1928)

Bruccoli, Matthew J. "Hidden Printings in Edith Wharton's *The Children*." *Studies in Bibliography* 15 (1962): 269–73.

Hamblen, Abigail A. "The Jamesian Note in Edith Wharton's *The Children*." *University of Kansas City Review* 31 (1965): 209–11.

The Custom of the Country (1913)

Ammons, Elizabeth. "The Business of Marriage in Edith Wharton's *The Custom of the Country*." *Criticism* 16 (1974): 326–38.

McHaney, Thomas L. "Fouqué's *Undine* and Edith Wharton's *Custom of the Country*." *Revue de Littérature Comparée* 45 (1971): 180–86.

Ethan Frome (1911)

Bernard, Kenneth. "Imagery and Symbolism in *Ethan Frome*." *College English* 23 (December 1961): 178–84.

Brennan, Joseph X. "*Ethan Frome*: Structure and Metaphor." *Modern Fiction Studies* 7 (Winter 1961–1962): 347–56.

Iyengar, K.R. Srinivasa. "A Note on *Ethan Frome*." *Literary Criterion* 5 (1962): 168–78.

Shuman, R. Baird. "The Continued Popularity of *Ethan Frome*." *Revue des Langues Vivantes* 37 (1971): 257–63.

The Hermit and the Wild Woman (1908)

Tintner, Adeline R. "*The Hermit and the Wild Woman*: Edith Wharton's Fictioning of Henry James." *Journal of Modern Literature* 4 (1974): 32–42.

The House of Mirth (1905)

Bristol, Marie. "Life Among the Ungentle Genteel: Edith Wharton's *The House of Mirth* Revisited." *Western Humanities Review* 16 (Autumn 1962): 371–74.

Friman, Anne. "Determinism and Point of View in *The House of Mirth*." *Papers on Language and Literature* 2 (1966): 175–78.

Gargano, James W. "*The House of Mirth*: Social Futility and Faith." *American Literature* 44 (March 1972): 137–43.

Hierth, Harrison E. "The Class Novel." *College English Association Critic* 27 (December 1964): 1–4.

Loney, G.M. "Edith Wharton and *The House of Mirth*: The Novelist Writes for the Theater." *Modern Drama* 4 (September 1961): 152–63.

McIlvaine, Robert. "Edith Wharton's American Beauty Rose." *Journal of American Studies* 7 (August 1973): 183–85.

Trilling, Diana. "*The House of Mirth*: Revisited." *American Scholar* 32 (Winter 1962–1963): 113–28.

Vella, Michael Wayne. "Technique and Theme in *The House of Mirth*." *Markham Review* 2 (May 1970): 17–20.

Wolff, Cynthia G. "Lily Bart and the Beautiful

Death." *American Literature* 46 (March 1974): 16–40.

The Valley of Decision (1902)

Murphy, John J. "Edith Wharton's Italian Triptych: *The Valley of Decision.*" *Xavier University Studies* 4 (May 1965): 85–94.

PHILLIS WHEATLEY (1753?–1784) U.S.
General Works

Bridenbaugh, Carol. "The Earliest Published Poem of Phillis Wheatley." *New England Quarterly* 42 (December 1969): 583–84.

Burroughs, Margaret G. "Do Birds of a Feather Flock Together?" *Jackson State Review* 6 (1974): 61–73.

Collins, Terence. "Phillis Wheatley: The Dark Side of the Poetry." *Phylon* 36 (1975): 78–88.

"E Pluribus Unum."*Crisis* 82 (August 1975): 254.

Giddings, Paula. "Critical Evaluation of Phillis Wheatley." *Jackson State Review* 6 (1974): 74–81.

Holder, Kenneth R. "Some Linguistic Aspects of the Heroic Couplet in the Poetry of Phillis Wheatley." *Dissertation Abstracts International* 34 (1974): 5144A (North Texas State).

Huddleston, Eugene L. "Matilda's 'On Reading the Poems of Phillis Wheatley, the African Poetess.'" *Early American Literature* 5 (Winter 1970–1971): 57–67.

Kuncio, Robert C. "Some Unpublished Poems of Phillis Wheatley." *New England Quarterly* 43 (June 1970): 287–97.

Matson, R. Lynn. "Phillis Wheatley—Soul Sister?" *Phylon* 33 (1972): 222–30.

Nwoga, Donatus I. "Humanitarianism and the Criticism of African Literature, 1770–1810." *Research in African Literature* 3 (Fall 1972): 171–79.

Parks, Carole A. "Phillis Wheatley Comes Home." *Black World* 23 (February 1974): 92–97.

Porter, Dorothy B. "Historical and Bibliographical Data of Phillis Wheatley's Publications." *Jackson State Review* 6 (1974): 54–60.

Robinson, William H. "Phillis Wheatley: Colonial Quandary." *College Language Association Journal* 9 (September 1965): 25–38.

Silverman, Kenneth. "Four New Letters by Phillis Wheatley." *Early American Literature* 8 (Winter 1973–1974): 257–71.

"Special Issue: The Phillis Wheatley Poetry Festival, November 4–7, 1973." *Jackson State Review* 6 (1974): 1–107.

Weight, Glenn S. "Anniversary of Phillis Wheatley Remains an Inspiration to All." *Negro History Bulletin* 25 (January 1962): 91–92.

PHYLLIS AYAME WHITNEY (1903–) U.S.
General Works

Duffy, M. "On the Road to Manderley." *Time* (April 12, 1971): 96.

KATE DOUGLAS WIGGIN (1856–1923) U.S.
General Works

Forman, H.J. "Kate Douglas Wiggin: A Woman of Letters." *Southern California Quarterly* 44 (December 1962): 273–85.

FRANCES LUCY WIGHTMAN, Mrs. Arnold (d. 1901) Great Britain
General Works

McCarthy, Patrick J. "Mrs. Matthew Arnold." *Texas Studies in Literature and Language* 12 (Winter 1971): 647–62.

McCarthy, Patrick J. "Mrs. Matthew Arnold: Some Considerations and Some Letters." *Harvard Library Bulletin* 17 (1969): 385–403.

ELLA WHEELER WILCOX (1850–1919) U.S.
General Works

Gallup, Donald. "More Letters of American Writers." *Yale University Library Gazette* 37 (1962): 30–35.

Haeffner, Paul. "Auden and Ella Wheeler Wilcox." *Notes and Queries* 9 (March 1962): 110–11.

Lewis, Naomi. "Wilcox Revisited." *New Statesman* (December 24, 1971): 901.

Pittock, Malcolm. "In Defense of Ella Wheeler Wilcox." *Durham University Journal* 65 (December 1972): 86–89.

LAURA INGALLS WILDER (d. 1957) U.S.
General Works

Anderson, D.N. "Little More About Laura: Her Relatives in Wisconsin." *Elementary English* 41 (March 1964): 297–99.

Jacobs, W.J. "Frontier Faith Revisited: The Little House Books of Laura Ingalls Wilder." *Horn Book Magazine* 41 (1965): 465–73.

Kies, C. "Laura and Mary and the 3 R's." *Peabody Journal of Education* 44 (September 1966): 110–13.

Mortensen, L.H. "Little Houses and Magnificent

Mansions." *Elementary English* 45 (May 1968): 672–73.

Thurman, Evelyn. "On the Trail of Laura Ingalls Wilder." *Instructor* 84 (February 1975): 78–79.

Ward, N. "Laura Ingalls Wilder: An Appreciation." *Elementary English* 50 (October 1973): 1025–27.

Individual Works

The First Four Years (1971)

Elliott, C. "Little Houses." *Time* (March 15, 1971): 91–92.

ANNE WILKINSON, née Gibbons (1910–1961) Canada

General Works

Smith, A.J.M. "A Reading of Anne Wilkinson." *Canadian Literature*, no. 10 (Autumn 1961): 33–39.

IRIS WILKINSON. *See* Robin Hyde

SYLVIA WILKINSON (1940–) U.S.

General Works

Chappell, Fred. "Unpeaceable Kingdoms: The Novels of Sylvia Wilkinson." *Hollins Critic* 8 (April 1971): 1–10.

VINNIE WILLIAMS (fl. 1950s–1960s) U.S.

Individual Works

Walk Egypt (1960)

Hall, Wade. "Humor and Folklore in Vinnie Williams' *Walk Egypt*." *Southern Folklore Quarterly* 26 (1962): 225–331.

SARA PAYSON WILLIS (pseud. Fanny Fern) (1811–1872) U.S.

General Works

Adams, J. Donald. "Speaking of Books." *New York Times Book Review* (April 17, 1960): 2.

McGinnis, Patricia I. "Fanny Fern, American Novelist." *Biblion* 2 (Spring 1969): 2–37.

White, William. "Fanny Fern to Walt Whitman: An Unpublished Letter." *American Book Collector* 11 (May 1961): 9.

ETHEL WILSON (1890–) Canada

General Works

Hinchcliffe, Peter M. " 'To Keep the Memory of So Worthy a Friend': Ethel Wilson as an Elegist." *Journal of Canadian Fiction* 2 (1973): 62–67.

Sonthoff, Helen W. "The Novels of Ethel Wilson."

Canadian Literature, no. 26 (Autumn 1965): 33–42.

Urbas, Jeanette. "Equations and Flutes." *Journal of Canadian Fiction* 1 (1972): 69–73.

Urbas, Jeanette. "Perquisites of Love." *Canadian Literature*, no. 59 (Winter 1974): 6–15.

Individual Works

Hetty Dorval (1947)

MacDonald, R.D. "Serious Whimsy." *Canadian Literature*, no. 63 (Winter 1975): 40–51.

Pacey, Desmond. "Ethel Wilson's First Novel." *Canadian Literature*, no. 29 (Summer 1966): 43–55.

The Innocent Traveller (1949)

New, W.H. "The Irony of Order: Ethel Wilson's *The Innocent Traveller*." *Criticism* 10 (1968–1969): 22–30.

Mrs. Golightly and Other Stories (1961)

McLaw, Catherine M. "The Initiation of Mrs. Golightly." *Journal of Canadian Fiction* 1 (1972): 52–55.

GLADYS MARY WILSON, née Baldwin (1915?–) Great Britain

General Works

"New Literary Light." *Newsweek* (October 5, 1970): 44.

ANNE GOODWIN WINSLOW (d. 1959) U.S.

General Works

White, Helen, and Redding S. Sugg, Jr. "Lady into Artist: The Literary Achievement of Anne Goodwin Winslow." *Mississippi Quarterly* 22 (Fall 1969): 289–302.

KATHLEEN WINSOR (1919–) U.S.

General Works

"11,623 Hours." *Newsweek* (May 24, 1965): 114.

ELIZABETH WINSTANLEY (b. 1818?) Great Britain

Individual Works

Shifting Scenes in Theatrical Life (1859)

Irvin, Eric. "The Mrs. Siddons of Sydney, Part I." *Theatre Notebook* 25 (Spring 1971): 97–103.

SARAH WISTER (1761–1804) U.S.

Individual Works

Journal of Life in Philadelphia (1777–1778)

Holmes, J. Welfred. "Three Uncommon Records of the Commonplace." *College Language Association Journal* 9 (March 1966): 215–24.

MARY WOLLSTONECRAFT, Mrs. Godwin (1759–1797) Great Britain
Bibliography
Todd, Janet M., and Florence Boos. "Checklist for Mary Wollstonecraft." *Mary Wollstonecraft Newsletter* 1 (April 1973): 1–5.
General Works
Allentuck, Marcia. "Mary Wollstonecraft." *Times Literary Supplement* (December 9, 1960): 797.
Boos, Florence S. "The Biographies of Mary Wollstonecraft." *Mary Wollstonecraft Newsletter* 1 (April 1973): 6–10.
Brown, Lloyd W. "Jane Austen and the Feminist Tradition." *Nineteenth Century Fiction* 28 (December 1973): 321–38.
Cobb, Richard. "Radicalism and Wreckage." *Times Literary Supplement* (September 6, 1974): 941–44.
Hare, Robert Rigby. "Charles Brockden Brown's *Ormond*: The Influence of Rousseau, Godwin, and Mary Wollstonecraft." *Dissertation Abstracts* 28 (1968): 4599A (Maryland).
Harper, George Mills. "Mary Wollstonecraft's Residence with Thomas Taylor the Platonist." *Notes and Queries* 9 (December 1962): 461–64.
Hickey, Damon D. "Mary Wollstonecraft and *The Female Reader*." *English Language Notes* 13 (December 1975): 128–29.
McGavran, Margaret R. "Mary and Margaret: The Triumph of Woman." *Dissertation Abstracts International* 34 (1973): 1248A (Cornell).
Nixon, Edna. "Mary Wollstonecraft, English Feminist." *History Today* 20 (September 1970): 655–62.
Peter, Mary. "A Portrait of Mary Wollstonecraft Godwin by John Opie in the Tate Gallery." *Keats-Shelley Memorial Bulletin* 14 (1963): 1–3.
Sage, Lorna. "Rights and Wrongs: On Mary Wollstonecraft." *Encounter* 43 (December 1974): 67–72.
Sambrook, James. "Some Heirs of Goldsmith: Poets of the Poor in the Late Eighteenth Century." *Studies in Burke and His Time* 11 (Fall 1969): 1348–61.
Sanders, Marion K. "A Slight Case of Library Fever or, How Not to Write a Book." *Harper's* (April 1962): 68–71.
Sunstein, E.W. "Mary Wollstonecraft: Another Brother and Corrected Dating." *Notes and Queries* 22 (January 1975): 25–26.
Tims, Margaret. "The Rights of Men and Women." *Aryan Path* 43 (February 1972): 63–68.

Tomalin, Claire. "A Fallen Woman." *New Statesman* (May 21, 1971): 712.
Tomkievicz, Shirley. "The First Feminist." *Horizon* (New York) 14 (Spring 1972): 114–19.
Individual Works
A Vindication of the Rights of Woman, with Strictures on Political and Moral Subjects (1792)
Hardt, Ulrich Hermann. "A Critical Edition of Mary Wollstonecraft's *A Vindication of the Rights of Woman, with Strictures on Political and Moral Subjects*." *Dissertation Abstracts International* 35 (1975): 5404A–5A (Oregon).
Hayden, Lucy K. "A Rhetorical Analysis of Mary Wollstonecraft's *A Vindication of the Rights of Woman*." *Dissertation Abstracts International* 32 (1972): 5185A (Michigan).
Poston, Carol H. "Mary Wollstonecraft's *A Vindication of the Rights of Woman*: A Critical and Annotated Edition." *Dissertation Abstracts International* 34 (1973): 2575A (Nebraska).
Poston, Carol H., and Janet M. Todd. "Some Textual Variations in the First Two Editions of *A Vindication of the Rights of Woman*." *Mary Wollstonecraft Journal* 2 (1974): 27–29.
Todd, Janet M. "The Language of Sex in *A Vindication of the Rights of Woman*." *Mary Wollstonecraft Newsletter* 1 (April 1973): 10–17.
Tomalin, Claire. "Mary Wollstonecraft and the Rights of Women." *Listener* (January 20, 1972): 77–79.

MRS. HENRY WOOD, née Ellen Price (1814–1887) Great Britain
General Works
Ross, Alan S.C. "Some Words from Mrs. Henry Wood." *Notes and Queries* 21 (January 1974): 25–26.
Ross, Alan S.C. "To Go A-Blackberrying." *Notes and Queries* 20 (August 1973): 284–85.
Individual Works
East Lynne (1861)
Maison, Margaret M. "Adultresses in Agony." *Listener* (January 19, 1961): 133–34.

SARAH WOOD (1759–1855) U.S.
General Works
Fife, Hilda M. "Madam Wood's 'Recollections.'" *Colby Library Quarterly* 7 (September 1965): 89–115.

VIRGINIA WOOLF (1882–1941) Great Britain
Bibliography

Haight, Gordon S. "Virginia Woolf." *Yale Review* 62 (Spring 1973): 426–31.

Hale, Nancy. "Half-Glimpses of Genius." *Virginia Quarterly Review* 49 (Spring 1973): 309–12.

Kirkpatrick, B.J. "Additions to the Bibliography of Virginia Woolf." *Book Collector* 13 (Spring 1964): 70.

Laing, D.A. "An Addendum to the Virginia Woolf Bibliography." *Notes and Queries* 19 (September 1972): 338.

Novak, Jane. "Recent Criticism of Virginia Woolf: January 1970–June 1972: Abstracts of Published Criticism and Unpublished Dissertations." *Virginia Woolf Quarterly* 1 (Fall 1972): 141–55.

Weiser, Barbara. "Criticism of Virginia Woolf from 1956 to the Present: A Selected Checklist with an Index to Studies of Separate Works." *Modern Fiction Studies* 18 (Autumn 1972): 477–86.

General Works

Abrahams, William. "The Indispensable Virginia Woolf." *Atlantic Monthly* (February 1973): 93–95.

Alexander, Sally Jeanette. "Outsiders and Educated Men's Daughters: The Feminist as Heroine in Six Novels of Virginia Woolf." *Dissertation Abstracts International* 35 (1975): 3723A (Florida State).

Anderson, Patrick. "Essays after Tea." *Spectator* (November 11, 1966): 620.

Annan, Noel. "Virginia Woolf." *Listener* (June 15, 1972): 794–95.

Ariail, Jacqueline A. "An Elegy for Androgyny." *Iowa English Bulletin: Yearbook* 24 (1974): 13–20.

Bagnold, Enid. "Virginia." *Adam*, no. 364–66 (1972): 15.

Barnett, Alan Wayne. "Who Is Jacob? The Quest for Identity in the Writing of Virginia Woolf." *Dissertation Abstracts* 26 (1965): 2742 (Columbia).

Batchelor, J.B. "Feminism in Virginia Woolf." *English* 17 (Spring 1968): 1–7.

Bazin, Nancy Topping. "Virginia Woolf's Quest for Equilibrium." *Modern Language Quarterly* 32 (September 1971): 305–19.

Beja, Morris. "Matches Struck in the Dark: Virginia Woolf's Moments of Vision." *Critical Quarterly* 6 (Summer 1964): 137–52.

Beker, Miroslav. "Virginia Woolf's Appraisal of Joseph Conrad." *Studia Romanica et Anglica* 12 (December 1961): 17–22.

Bell, Barbara Currie, and Carol Ohmann. "Virginia Woolf's Criticism: A Polemical Preface." *Critical Inquiry* 1 (December 1974): 361–71.

Bell, Carolyn W. "A Study of Virginia Woolf's 'Moment of Vision.'" *Dissertation Abstracts International* 34 (1973): 761A (Texas).

Bell, Millicent. "Virginia Woolf Now." *Massachusetts Review* 14 (Autumn 1973): 655–87.

Bell, Quentin. "The Biographer, the Critic, and the Lighthouse." *Ariel* 2 (1971): 94–101.

Bloom, L.D. "They All Cried Woolf." *Novel* 7 (Spring 1974): 255–66.

Bree, Germaine. "Two Vintage Years: France, 1913; England, 1922." *Virginia Woolf Quarterly* 1 (Summer 1973): 19–30.

Brophy, Brigid. "Modern Classic." *New Statesman* (March 29, 1963): 463–64.

Chalfant, Thomas H. "The Marriage of Granite and Rainbow: Virginia Woolf as Biographer." *Dissertation Abstracts International* 32 (1971): 3298A (Wisconsin).

Chapman, Marjorie D. "Virginia Woolf's Recurrent Imagery: An Approach to the World of Her Imagination." *Dissertation Abstracts International* 31 (1971): 5391A–92A (New Brunswick).

Chapman, Robert T. "The 'Enemy' vs Bloomsbury." *Adam*, no. 364–366 (1972): 81–84.

Collet, Georges-Paul. "Jacques-Émile Blanche and Virginia Woolf." *Comparative Literature* 17 (1965): 73–81.

Conklin, Anna M. "Historical and Sociocultural Elements in the Novels of Virginia Woolf." *Dissertation Abstracts International* 35 (1974): 3730A (North Carolina).

Cumings, Melinda F. "Visionary Ritual in the Novels of Virginia Woolf." *Dissertation Abstracts International* 33 (1973): 3638A (Wisconsin).

Cwiakala-Piatkowska, Jadwiga. "The Feminist Pamphlets of Virginia Woolf." *Kwartalnik Neofilologiczny* 19 (1972): 271–79.

Daziel, Bradford Dudley. "'The Sentence in Itself Beautiful': A Study of Virginia Woolf's Mannerist Fiction." *Dissertation Abstracts International* 36 (1975): 1520A–21A (Boston).

Deiman, Werner J. "History, Pattern, and Continuity in Virginia Woolf." *Contemporary Literature* 15 (Winter 1974): 49–66.

Delord, J. "Virginia Woolf's Critical Essays." *Revue des Langues Vivantes* 29 (1963): 126–31.

De Mott, Benjamin. "Radiant Deviations." *Saturday*

Review (January 1973): 67–68.

Di Battista, Maria A. "The Romance of the Self: The Early Novels of Virginia Woolf." *Dissertation Abstracts International* 34 (1974): 7227A (Yale).

DiBona, Helene R. "The Fiction of Virginia Woolf: A Quest for Reality." *Dissertation Abstracts International* 31 (1971): 6599A (California, Berkeley).

Digartani, John L. "Wagnerian Patterns in the Fiction of Joseph Conrad, D.H. Lawrence, Virginia Woolf, and James Joyce." *Dissertation Abstracts International* 34 (1974): 7745A (Wisconsin).

Edmiston, S. "Bookmaking of Virginia and Leonard Woolf." *Craft Horizon* 34 (August 1974): 24–25.

Eiland, Howard Avery. "Double Vision in Conrad, Woolf, and Mann." *Dissertation Abstracts International* 35 (1975): 7300A (Yale).

Farwell, M.R. "Virginia Woolf and Androgyny." *Contemporary Literature* 16 (Autumn 1975): 433–51.

Featherstone, Joseph. "Mrs. Woolf as Essayist." *New Republic* (February 10, 1968): 6.

Fleishman, Avrom. "The Latest Woolf Offering." *Studies in the Novel* 5 (Winter 1973): 559–66.

Fleishman, Avrom. "Woolf and McTaggart." *English Literary History* 36 (December 1969): 719–38.

Fox, Stephen D. "The Novels of Virginia Woolf and Nathalie Sarraute." *Dissertation Abstracts International* 31 (1971): 5399A (Emory).

Francis, Herbert E., Jr. "Virginia Woolf and 'the Moment.'" *Emory University Quarterly* 16 ((Fall 1960): 139–51.

Franks, Gabriel. "Virginia Woolf and the Philosophy of G. E. Moore." *Personalist* 50 (Spring 1969): 222–40.

Freeman, Alma Susan. "The Androgynous Ideal: A Study of Selected Novels by D.H. Lawrence, James Joyce and Virginia Woolf." *Dissertation Abstracts International* 35 (1975): 877A–78A (Rutgers).

Frye, Joanne M.S. "Toward a Form for Paradox: Image and Idea in the Novels of Virginia Woolf." *Dissertation Abstracts International* 35 (1975): 4518A (Indiana).

Gairdner, William D. "Consciousness in the Novels of Virginia Woolf." *Dissertation Abstracts International* 31 (1971): 6055A (Stanford).

Garnett, David. "Virginia Woolf." *American Scholar* 34 (Summer 1965): 371–86.

"Genius and Madness." *Newsweek* (September 7, 1964): 85B–86.

Goldman, Mark. "Virginia Woolf and E.M. For-Reader." *Publications of the Modern Language Association* 80 (1965): 275–84.

Goldman, Mark. "Virginia Woolf and E.M. Forster: A Critical Dialogue." *Texas Studies in Literature and Language* 7 (Winter 1966): 387–400.

Goldman, Morris Irving. "Virginia Woolf and the Art of Criticism." *Dissertation Abstracts* 20 (1960): 4111 (Minnesota).

Gross, John. "Life Itself." *New Statesman* (December 31, 1965): 1030–31.

Haller, Evelyn H. "The Search for 'Life Itself': Characterization and Its Relation to Form in the Novels of Virginia Woolf." *Dissertation Abstracts* 29 (1969): 3140A (Emory).

Hartman, Geoffrey H. "Virginia's Web." *Chicago Review* 14 (1961): 20–32.

Haule, James Mark. "The Theme of Isolation in the Fiction of Dorothy M. Richardson, Virginia Woolf, and James Joyce." *Dissertation Abstracts International* 35 (1975): 7905A–6A (Wayne State).

Henig, Suzanne. "D.H. Lawrence and Virginia Woolf." *D. H. Lawrence Review* 2 (1969): 265–71.

Henig, Suzanne. "Virginia Woolf and Lady Murasaki." *Literature East and West* 11 (December 1967): 421–27.

Higdon, David L. "Three Studies of Virginia Woolf." *Studies in the Novel* 3 (Spring 1971): 108–16.

Hilsinger, Serena Sue. "Insubstantial Pageant: A Reading of Virginia Woolf's Novels." *Dissertation Abstracts* 25 (1965): 4700 (Connecticut).

Hoffman, Charles G. "'From Lunch to Dinner': Virginia Woolf's Apprenticeship." *Texas Studies in Literature and Language* 10 (Winter 1969): 609–27.

Holroyd, M. "Virginia Woolf and Her World." *Horizon* (New York) 17 (Summer 1975): 49–56.

Hulcoop, John F. "Virginia Woolf's Diaries: Some Reflections After Reading Them and a Censure of Mr. Holroyd." *Bulletin of the New York Public Library* 75 (September 1971): 301–10.

Hungerford, Edward Arthur. "The Narrow Bridge of Art: Virginia Woolf's Early Criticism." *Dissertation Abstracts* 21 (1961): 2295–96 (N.Y.U.).

Hunting, Constance. "Three More Hazards Towards Virginia Woolf." *Journal of Modern Literature* 4 (1974): 155–59.

Irons, Evelyn. "An Evening with Virginia Woolf." *New Yorker* (March 30, 1963): 115–21.

Julien, Hershey. "Virginia Woolf: Post-Impressionist Novelist." *Dissertation Abstracts* 29 (1969): 4490A (New Mexico).

Kaplan, Sydney Janet. "The Feminine Consciousness in the Novels of Five Twentieth Century British Women." *Dissertation Abstracts International* 32 (1971): 4615A (California, Los Angeles).

Kelley, Alice Van Buren. "Fact and Vision: A Study of the Novels of Virginia Woolf." *Dissertation Abstracts International* 32 (1972): 4615A–16A (C.U.N.Y.).

Kenney, Susan M. "Fin in the Water: A Study of Virginia Woolf." *Dissertation Abstracts* 29 (1969): 4004A–5A (Cornell).

King, Merton Pruett. "The Price of Awareness: Virginia Woolf as a Practitioner-Critic." *Dissertation Abstracts* 23 (1962): 1704 (Texas).

Kumar, Shiv K. "Memory in Virginia Woolf and Bergson." *University of Kansas City Review* 26 (1960): 235–39.

Kumar, Shiv K. "Virginia Woolf and Bergson's 'Memoire par Excellence.'" *English Studies* 41 (1960): 313–18.

Lakshmi, Vjay. "The Solid and the Intangible: Virginia Woolf's Theory of the Androgynous Mind." *Literary Criterion* 10 (1971): 28–34.

Lakshmi, Vjay. "The Unviewed Room: An Interpretation of the Room Analogy in Virginia Woolf's Critical Writings." *Rajasthan University Studies in English* 6 (1972): 64–69.

L'Enfant, Julia Chandler. "Edith Wharton and Virginia Woolf: Tradition and Experiment in the Modern Novel." *Dissertation Abstracts International* 35 (1975): 4531A (Louisiana State).

Lund, Mary Graham. "The Androgynous Moment: Woolf and Eliot." *Renascence* 12 (Winter 1960): 74–78.

Madison, Elizabeth C. "Reality and Imagery in the Novels of Virginia Woolf and Nathalie Sarraute." *Dissertation Abstracts International* 34 (1974): 7765A–66A (Indiana).

Majundar, R. "Virginia Woolf and Thoreau." *Thoreau Society Bulletin* 109 (Fall 1969): 4–5.

Mansfield, Katherine. "Fifteen letters from K.M. to

Virginia Woolf." *Adam*, no. 370–375 (1973): 19–24.

Manuel, M. "Virginia Woolf as the Common Reader." *Literary Criterion* 7 (1966): 28–32.

Matro, Thomas Gaetano. "Life as Creative Activity in the Early Novels of Virginia Woolf." *Dissertation Abstracts International* 35 (1975): 905A–6A (Rutgers).

Maxwell, W. "Virginia Stephen/Virginia Woolf." *New Yorker* (February 3, 1973): 88–90.

McIntyre, Clara F. "Is Virginia Woolf a Feminist?" *Personalist* 41 (Spring 1960): 176–84.

Mendez, Charlotte W. "I Need a Little Language." *Virginia Woolf Quarterly* 1 (Fall 1972): 87–105.

Mendez, Charlotte W. "Language, Mystery and Selfhood in the Novels of Virginia Woolf." *Dissertation Abstracts International* 34 (1973): 1287A (Syracuse).

Moers, E. "Letters of Virginia Woolf." *New York Times Book Review* (November 23, 1975): 2.

Morgenstern, Barry S. "Like a Work of Art: The Narrative Voices in the Novels of Virginia Woolf." *Dissertation Abstracts International* 32 (1972): 6443A–44A (Penn. State).

Naremore, James. "A World without a Self: The Novels of Virginia Woolf." *Novel* 5 (Winter 1972): 122–34.

Naremore, James Otis. "The World without a Self: Style in the Novels of Virginia Woolf." *Dissertation Abstracts International* 31 (1971): 1283A (Wisconsin).

Nicolson, Nigel, and Joanne Trautmann. "Virginia Woolf's Unpublished Letters on the Occasion of Her Marriage." *Ms.* (November 1975): 94.

Novak, Jane. "Virginia Woolf—'A Fickle Jacobean.'" *Virginia Woolf Newsletter* 3 (April 1972): 1–8.

Oates, Joyce Carol. "Disguised Fiction." *Publications of the Modern Language Association* 89 (1974): 580–81.

Oberbeck, S.K. "Fragile Genius." *Newsweek* (November 20, 1972): 126.

Olson, Stanley. "North from Richmond, South from Bloomsbury." *Adam*, no. 364–366 (1972): 70–74.

Ozick, Cynthia. "Mrs. Virginia Woolf." *Commentary* 56 (August 1973): 33–44.

Pachmuss, Temira. "Dostoevsky, Werfel, and Virginia Woolf: Influences and Confluences." *Comparative Literature Studies* 9 (1972): 416–28.

Painter, George. "Proust and Virginia Woolf." *Adam*, no. 364–366 (1972): 17–23.

Parasuram, Laxmi S. "Virginia Woolf: The Treatment of Natural Phenomena in Six Novels." *Dissertation Abstracts International* 33 (1973): 5741A–42A (Kentucky).

Parsons, Trekkie. "Virginia Woolf's Last Letters." *Times Literary Supplement* (July 13, 1973): 808.

Peck, Ellen M. McK. "Exploring the Feminine: A Study of Janet Lewis, Ellen Glasgow, Anais Nin and Virginia Woolf." *Dissertation Abstracts International* 35 (1974): 3761A (Stanford).

Phillips, Ann H. "The Anonymous Self: A Study of Virginia Woolf's Novels." *Dissertation Abstracts International* 32 (1972): 5801A (Stanford).

Pritchett, V.S. "Pale Precocious Genius." *New Statesman* (June 16, 1972): 827–28.

Pritchett, V.S. "Who's Afraid of Virginia Woolf." *New Statesman* (November 25, 1966): 790.

Rahman, Shaista. "Virginia Woolf and Reality: The Artist, the Intellectual and the Mystic in the Novels." *Dissertation Abstracts International* 34 (1973): 3428A (C.U.N.Y.).

Ramsay, Warren. "The Claims of Language: Virginia Woolf as Symbolist." *English Literature in Transition* 4 (1961): 12–17.

Richardson, Betty. "Beleaguered Bloomsbury: Virginia Woolf, Her Friends, and Their Critics." *Papers on Language and Literature* 10 (1974): 207–21.

Robinson, Deborah S. " 'Frigidity' and the Aesthetic Vision: A Study of Karen Horney and Virginia Woolf." *Dissertation Abstracts International* 35 (1974): 2294A–95A (Rochester).

Rogat, Ellen H. "The Virgin in the Bell Biography." *Twentieth Century Literature* 20 (April 1974): 96–113.

Rogat, Ellen H. "Visiting the Berg Collection." *Virginia Woolf Miscellany* 1 (1973): 1–2.

Rubenstein, Roberta. "The Evolution of an Image: Virginia Woolf and the 'Glove of Life.' " *Antigonish Review* 15 (Autumn 1973): 43–50.

Rubenstein, Roberta. "Virginia Woolf and *Anna Karenina*." *Descant* 16 (1972): 37–41.

Rubenstein, Roberta. "Virginia Woolf and the Russian Point of View." *Comparative Literature Studies* 9 (1972): 196–206.

Rubenstein, Roberta. "Virginia Woolf, Chekhov, and *The Rape of the Lock*." *Dalhousie Review* 54

(Autumn 1974): 429–35.

Sakamoto, Tadanobu. " 'Modern Novels' and 'Modern Fiction': A Study of Some Discrepancies." *Studies in English Literature,* English Number (1967): 215–28.

Samuelson, Ralph. "More Than One Room of Her Own: Virginia Woolf's Critical Dilemmas." *Western Humanities Review* 19 (Summer 1965): 249–56.

Schaefer, Josephine Alice O'Brien. "The Three-Fold Nature of Reality in the Novels of Virginia Woolf." *Dissertation Abstracts* 23 (1962): 238–39 (Stanford).

Schlack, Beverly A. "Literary Allusions in Selected Novels of Virginia Woolf: A Study in Criticism." *Dissertation Abstracts International* 35 (1974): 3008A (N.Y.U.).

Seltzer, Alvin Jay. "Chaos in the Novel in Chaos." *Dissertation Abstracts International* 32 (1971): 984A (Penn. State).

Shanahan, Mary Steussy. "Order and Chaos in the Novels of Virginia Woolf." *Dissertation Abstracts International* 31 (1971): 1292A (Wisconsin).

Shields, Ellen F. "Characterization in the Novels of Virginia Woolf." *Dissertation Abstracts* 27 (1967): 3880A (Illinois).

Shoukri, Doris Enright-Clark. "The Nature of Being in Woolf and Duras." *Contemporary Literature* 12 (Summer 1971): 317–28.

Simon, Irene. "Some Aspects of Virginia Woolf's Imagery." *English Studies* 41 (1960): 180–96.

Smith, J. Oates. "Henry James and Virginia Woolf: The Art of Relationships." *Twentieth Century Literature* 10 (October 1964): 119–29.

Smith, Michael A. "The Personality of the Essayist: Virginia Woolf and Thomas Mann." *Dissertation Abstracts International* 35 (1974): 3772A (Oregon).

Spater, George A. "The Monks House Library." *American Book Collector* 21 (May 1971): 18–20.

Spater, George A. "The Monks House Library." *Virginia Woolf Quarterly* 1 (Spring 1973): 60–65.

Spater, George A. "Monks House, 1970." *Virginia Woolf Quarterly* 1 (Fall 1972): 106–9.

Spater, George A. "The Paradise Road Publications of the Hogarth Press." *American Book Collector* 21 (January 1971): 18.

Sukenick, Lynn. "Sense and Sensibility in Women's Fiction: Studies in the Novels of George Eliot,

Virginia Woolf, Anais Nin and Doris Lessing." *Dissertation Abstracts International* 35 (1975): 4563A (C.U.N.Y.).

Talamantes, Florence. "Virginia Woolf and Alfonsina Storni: Kindred Spirits." *Virginia Woolf Quarterly* 1 (Spring 1973): 4–21.

Trautmann, Joanne. "A Talk with Nigel Nicolson." *Virginia Woolf Quarterly* 1 (Fall 1972): 38–44.

Tudor, Kathleen R. "The Androgynous Mind in W.B. Yeats, D.H. Lawrence, Virginia Woolf and Dorothy Richardson." *Dissertation Abstracts International* 35 (1974): 1126A–27A (Toronto).

Vogelsang, John D. "The Wave of Self in Time to Break: D.H. Lawrence and Virginia Woolf." *Dissertation Abstracts International* 35 (1974): 1677A (S.U.N.Y., Buffalo).

Watts, Janet. "Dear Quentin: Janet Watts Interviews Mr. Bell of Bloomsbury." *Virginia Woolf Quarterly* 1 (Fall 1972): 111–16.

Webb, Igor Michael. "Sense and Sensibility: A Study of the Influence of English Aesthetics from Ruskin to Roger Fry on Ford Madox Ford and Virginia Woolf." *Dissertation Abstracts International* 32 (1972): 4638A (Stanford).

Weems, Benjamin Francis. "Virginia Woolf's Use of Imagery in Her Search for Values." *Dissertation Abstracts* 26 (1965): 2764 (Columbia).

Woolf, Virginia. "Three Characters." *Adam*, no. 364–366 (1972): 24–30.

Zak, Michele W. "Feminism and the New Novel." *Dissertation Abstracts International* 34 (1974): 5215A (Ohio State).

Zwerdling, A. "Virginia Woolf In and Out of Bloomsbury." *Sewanee Review* 83 (Summer 1975): 510–23.

Individual Works

Between the Acts (1941)

Basham, C. "*Between the Acts*." *Durham University Journal* 52 (March 1960): 87–94.

Deiman, Werner J. "Virginia Woolf's *Between the Acts*: The Culmination of a Career and the Resolution of a Vision." *Dissertation Abstracts* 27 (1967): 4245A–46A (Yale).

Fox, Stephen D. "The Fish Pond as Symbolic Center in *Between the Acts*." *Modern Fiction Studies* 18 (Autumn 1972): 467–73.

Gibson, Susan M. "Our Part Is to Be the Audience: Virginia Woolf's *Between the Acts*." *Gypsy Scholar* 2 (1974): 5–12.

Kenney, Susan M. "Two Endings: Virginia Woolf's

Suicide and *Between the Acts*." *University of Toronto Quarterly* 44 (Summer 1975): 265–89.

Naremore, James. "The 'Orts and Fragments' in *Between the Acts*." *Ball State University Forum* 14 (Winter 1973): 59–69.

Quick, Jonathan R. "The Shattered Moment: Form and Crisis in *Mrs. Dalloway* and *Between the Acts*." *Mosaic* 7 (1974): 127–36.

Shanahan, Mary Steussy. "*Between the Acts*: Virginia Woolf's Final Endeavor in Art." *Texas Studies in Literature and Language* 14 (Spring 1972): 123–38.

Summerhayes, Don. "Society, Morality, Analogy: Virginia Woolf's World *Between the Acts*." *Modern Fiction Studies* 9 (Winter 1963–1964): 329–37.

Watkins, Renee. "Survival in Discontinuity: Virginia Woolf's *Between the Acts*." *Massachusetts Review* 10 (Spring 1969): 356–76.

Wilkinson, Ann Yanko. "A Principle of Unity in *Between the Acts*." *Criticism* 8 (1966): 53–63.

Flush: A Biography (1933)

Bishop, Morchard. "Towards a Biography of Flush." *Times Literary Supplement* (December 15, 1966): 1180.

Szladits, Lola. "The Life, Character and Opinion of Flush the Spaniel." *Bulletin of the New York Public Library* 74 (April 1970) 211–18.

A Haunted House (1944)

De Araujo, Victor. "*A Haunted House*—The Shattered Glass." *Studies in Short Fiction* 3 (Winter 1966): 157–64.

Jacob's Room (1922)

Morgenstern, Barry. "The Self-Conscious Narrator in *Jacob's Room*." *Modern Fiction Studies* 18 (Autumn 1972): 351–61.

The Lady in the Looking-Glass (1929)

Chapman, R.T. "*The Lady in the Looking-Glass*: Modes of Perception in a Short Story by Virginia Woolf." *Modern Fiction Studies* 18 (Autumn 1972): 331–37.

The Mark on the Wall (1919)

Delbaere-Garant, Jeanne. "*The Mark on the Wall*: Virginia Woolf's World in a Snailshell." *Revue des Langues Vivantes* 40 (1974): 457–65.

Miss Ormerod (1924)

Robb, Kenneth. "Virginia Woolf's *Miss Ormerod*." *American Notes and Queries* 7 (January 1969): 71.

Mr. Bennett and Mrs. Brown (1924)

Goestsch, Paul. "A Source of Virginia Woolf's *Mr.*

Bennett and Mrs. Brown." *English Literature in Transition* 7 (1964): 188–89.

Kreutz, Irving. "Mr. Bennett and Mrs. Woolf." *Modern Fiction Studies* 8 (Summer 1962): 103–15.

Mrs. Dalloway (1925)

Ames, Kenneth J. "Elements of Mock-Heroic in Virginia Woolf's *Mrs. Dalloway.*" *Modern Fiction Studies* 18 (Autumn 1972): 363–74.

Beker, Miroslav. "London as a Principle of Structure in *Mrs. Dalloway.*" *Modern Fiction Studies* 18 (Autumn 1972): 375–85.

Benjamin, A.S. "Towards an Understanding of the Meaning of Virginia Woolf's *Mrs. Dalloway.*" *Wisconsin Studies in Contemporary Literature* 6 (Summer 1965): 214–27.

Blanchard, Margaret. "Socialization in *Mrs. Dalloway.*" *College English* 34 (November 1972): 287–307.

Conn, Peter J. "Woolf's *Mrs. Dalloway.*" *Explicator* 30 (February 1971): Item 2.

Fortin, Rene E. "Sacramental Imagery in *Mrs. Dalloway.*" *Renascence* 18 (Fall 1965): 23–31.

Gelfant, Blanche H. "Love and Conversion in *Mrs. Dalloway.*" *Criticism* 8 (1966): 229–45.

Ghiselin, Brewster. "Virginia Woolf's Party." (Sewanee Review 80 (Winter 1972): 47–50.

Gillen, Francis. " 'I Am This, I Am That': Shifting Distance and Movement in *Mrs. Dalloway.*" *Studies in the Novel* 4 (Fall 1972): 484–93.

Graves, Nora C. "The Case of Mrs. Dalloway." *Virginia Woolf Quarterly* 1 (Spring 1973): 51–59.

Higdon, D.L., and Jean Wyatt. "*Mrs. Dalloway* Revisited." *Publications of the Modern Language Association* 89 (1974): 178–80.

Hildick, Wallace. "Author's Alterations." *New Statesman* (October 8, 1965): 522; (October 15, 1965); 560; (October 29, 1965): 645.

Hildick, Wallace. "In that Solitary Room." *Kenyon Review* 27 (1965): 302–17.

Hoffman, C.G. "From Short Story to Novel: The Manuscript Revisions of Virginia Woolf's *Mrs. Dalloway.*" *Modern Fiction Studies* 14 (Summer 1968): 171–86.

Latham, Jacqueline E.M. "Archetypal Figures in *Mrs. Dalloway.*" *Neuphilologische Mitteilungen* 71 (1970): 480–88.

Latham, Jacqueline E.M. "The Manuscript Revisions of Virginia Woolf's *Mrs. Dalloway*: A Postscript." *Modern Fiction Studies* 18 (Autumn 1972): 475–76.

Latham, Jacqueline E.M. "The Model of Clarissa Dalloway—Kitty Maxse." *Notes and Queries* 16 (July 1969): 262–63.

Latham, Jacqueline E.M. "The Origin of *Mrs. Dalloway.*" *Notes and Queries* 13 (March 1966): 98–99.

Latham, Jacqueline E.M. "Thessaly and the 'Colossal Figure' in *Mrs. Dalloway.*" *Notes and Queries* 16 (July 1969): 263–65.

Lewis, A. J. "From *The Hours* to Mrs. Dalloway." *British Museum Quarterly* 28 (Summer 1964): 15–18.

Miller, David N. "Authorial Point of View in Virginia Woolf's *Mrs. Dalloway.*" *Journal of Narrative Technique* 2 (1972): 125–32.

Mollach, Francis L. "Thematic and Structural Unity of *Mrs. Dalloway.*" *Thoth* 5 (1964): 62–73.

Moody, A.D. "The Unmasking of Clarissa Dalloway." *Review of English Literature* 3 (January 1962): 67–79.

Page, Alex. "A Dangerous Day: Mrs. Dalloway Discovers Her Double." *Modern Fiction Studies* 7 (Summer 1961): 115–24.

Pennr, Catherine S. "The Sacred Will in *Mrs. Dalloway.*" *Thoth* 12 (1972): 3–20.

Philipson, Morris. "Mrs. Dalloway, 'What's the Sense of Your Parties?' " *Critical Inquiry* 1 (September 1974): 123–48.

Pritchard, W.H. "Understanding Virginia." *Hudson Review* 26 (Summer 1973): 367–74.

Quick, Jonathan R. "The Shattered Moment: Form and Crisis in *Mrs. Dalloway* and *Between the Acts.*" *Mosaic* 7 (1974): 127–36.

Rachman, Shalom. "Clarissa's Attic: Virginia Woolf's *Mrs. Dalloway* Reconsidered." *Twentieth Century Literature* 18 (January 1972): 3–18.

Raina, M.L. "A Reading of *Mrs. Dalloway.*" *Indian Journal of English Studies* 8 (1967): 59–71.

Roll-Hansen, Diderik. "Peter Walsh's Seven League Boots: A Note on *Mrs. Dalloway.*" *English Studies* 50 (1969): 301–4.

Rosenberg, Stuart. "Match in the Crocus: Obtrusive Art in Virginia Woolf's *Mrs. Dalloway.*" *Modern Fiction Studies* 13 (Summer 1967): 211–20.

Saagpakk, Paul F. "Psychological Elements in British Novels from 1890–1930." *Dissertation Abstracts* 27 (1966): 782A (Columbia).

Sakamoto, Tadanobu. "Virginia Woolf: 'Mrs. Dalloway in Bond Street' and *Mrs. Dalloway.*" *Studies in English Literature*, English Number (1974): 75–

88.

Samuels, Marilyn S. "The Symbolic Functions of the Sun in *Mrs. Dalloway.*" *Modern Fiction Studies* 18 (Autumn 1972): 387–99.

Schlack, Beverly Ann. "A Freudian Look at *Mrs. Dalloway.*" *Literature and Psychology* 23 (1973): 49–58.

Schoff, Francis G. "Mrs. Dalloway and Mrs. Ramsay." *Iowa English Yearbook* 9 (Fall 1964): 54–60.

Sharma, O.P. "Feminism as Aesthetic Vision: A Study of Virginia Woolf's *Mrs. Dalloway.*" *Panjab University Research Bulletin* 2 (1971): 1–10.

Shields, E.F. "The American Edition of *Mrs. Dalloway.*" *Studies in Bibliography* 27 (1974) 157–75.

Shields, E.F. "Death and Individual Values in *Mrs. Dalloway.*" *Queen's Quarterly* 80 (1973): 79–89.

Snow, Lotus. "The Heat of the Sun: The Double in *Mrs. Dalloway.*" *Research Studies* 41 (1973): 75–83.

Strong, Paul. "The Light in the Garden: Imagery in *Mrs. Dalloway, To the Lighthouse,* and *The Waves.*" *Dissertation Abstracts International* 34 (1974): 4288A–89A (Wisconsin).

Wyatt, J.M. "*Mrs. Dalloway*: Literary Allusion as Structural Metaphor." *Publications of the Modern Language Association* 88 (1973): 440–51; Discussion, 89 (1974): 178–80, 580–81.

Night and Day (1919)

Cumings, Melinda F. "*Night and Day*: Virginia Woolf's Visionary Synthesis of Reality." *Modern Fiction Studies* 18 (Autumn 1972): 339–49.

Sharma, O.P. "Virginia Woolf's *Night and Day.*" *Indian Journal of English Studies* 12 (1971): 55–66.

Zuckerman, Joanne P. "Anne Thackeray Ritchie as the Model for Mrs. Hilbery in Virginia Woolf's *Night and Day.*" *Virginia Woolf Quarterly* 1 (Spring 1973): 32–46.

Orlando (1928)

German, Howard, and Sharon Kaehele. "The Dialectic of Time in *Orlando.* "*College English* 24 (October 1962): 35–41.

Graham, John. "The 'Caricature Value' of Parody and Fantasy in *Orlando.*" *University of Toronto Quarterly* 30 (July 1961): 346–66.

Hoffman, Charles G. "Fact and Fantasy in *Orlando*: Virginia Woolf's Manuscript Revisions." *Texas Studies in Literature and Language* 10 (Fall 1968): 435–44.

Miller, Walter James, and Dorothy Dinnerstein. "Woolf's *Orlando.*" *Explicator* 19 (March 1961):

Item 37.

Rubenstein, Roberta."*Orlando*: Virginia Woolf's Improvisations on a Russian Theme." *Forum for Modern Language Studies* 9 (April 1973): 166–69.

Sakamoto, Tadanobu. "*Orlando*: What Happened in It." *Hiroshima Studies in English Language and Literature* 19 (1972): 22–33.

Samuelson, Ralph. "Virginia Woolf: *Orlando* and the Feminist Spirit." *Western Humanities Review* 15 (Winter 1961): 51–58.

Steele, Philip L. "Virginia Woolf's Spiritual Autobiography." *Topic* 9 (Fall 1969): 64–74.

Stewart, Jack F. "Historical Impressionism in *Orlando.*" *Studies in the Novel* 5 (Spring 1973): 71–85.

To the Lighthouse (1927)

Boyd, Elizabeth F. " 'Luriana Lurilee.' " *Notes and Queries* 10 (October 1963): 380–81.

Cohn, Ruby. "Art in *To the Lighthouse.*" *Modern Fiction Studies* 8 (Summer 1962): 127–36.

Corsa, Helen S. "*To the Lighthouse*: Death, Mourning, and Transfiguration." *Literature and Psychology* 21 (1971): 115–31.

Fromm, Harold. "*To the Lighthouse*: Music and Sympathy." *English Miscellany* 19 (1968): 181–95.

Hashmi, Shahnaz. "Indirect Style in *To the Lighthouse.*" *Indian Journal of English Studies* 2 (1961): 112–20.

Higdon, David Leon. "Mrs. Ramsay's First Name." *Virginia Woolf Quarterly* 1 (Winter 1973): 46–47.

Hoffman, A.C. "Subject and Object and the Nature of Reality: The Dialectic of *To the Lighthouse.*" *Texas Studies in Literature and Language* 13 (Winter 1972): 691–703.

Joyner, Nancy. "The Underside of the Butterfly: Lessing's Debt to Woolf." *Journal of Narrative Technique* 4 (1974): 204–11.

Kaehele, Sharon, and Howard German. "*To the Lighthouse*: Symbol and Vision." *Bucknell Review* 10 (May 1962): 328–46.

Lavin, J.A. "The First Editions of Virginia Woolf's *To the Lighthouse.*" *Proof* 2 (1972): 185–211.

Liberto, Sarah. "The 'Perpetual Pageant' of Art and Life in *To the Lighthouse.*" *Descant* 9 (1965): 35–43.

Lilienfeld, C. Jane. "The Necessary Journey: Virginia Woolf's Voyage to the Lighthouse." *Dissertation Abstracts International* 36 (1975): 321A–22A (Brandeis).

May, Keith M. "The Symbol of 'Painting' in Virginia Woolf's *To the Lighthouse*." *Review of English Literature* 8 (April 1967): 91–98.

Osgerby, J.R. "Virginia Woolf's *To the Lighthouse*." *Use of English* 15 (Winter 1963): 115–24.

Patterson, Frank M. "The Brackets in *To the Lighthouse*." *English Record* 16 (February 1966): 28–29.

Pratt, Annis. "Sexual Imagery in *To the Lighthouse*: A New Feminist Approach." *Modern Fiction Studies* 18 (Autumn 1972): 417–31.

Proudfit, Sharon Wood. "Lily Briscoe's Painting: A Key to Personal Relationships in *To the Lighthouse*." *Criticism* 13 (1971): 26–38.

Rose, Phyllis. "Mrs. Ramsay and Mrs. Woolf." *Women's Studies* 1 (1973): 199–216.

Schoff, Francis G. "Mrs. Dalloway and Mrs. Ramsay." *Iowa English Yearbook* 9 (Fall 1964): 54–60.

Sharma, O.P. "Feminism as Aesthetic Vision and Transcendence: A Study of Virginia Woolf's *To the Lighthouse*." *Panjab University Research Bulletin* 3 (1972): 1–8.

Strong, Paul. "The Light in the Garden: Imagery in *Mrs. Dalloway*, *To the Lighthouse*, and *The Waves*." *Dissertation Abstracts International* 34 (1974): 4288A–89A (Wisconsin).

Warner, John M. "Symbolic Patterns of Retreat and Reconciliation in *To the Lighthouse*." *Discourse* 12 (Summer 1969): 376–92.

Whitehead, Lee M. "The Shawl and the Skull: Virginia Woolf's 'Magic Mountain.'" *Modern Fiction Studies* 18 (Autumn 1972): 401–15.

The Voyage Out (1915)

Leaska, Mitchell A. "Virginia Woolf's *The Voyage Out*: Character Deduction and the Function of Ambiguity." *Virginia Woolf Quarterly* 1 (Winter 1973): 18–41.

The Waves (1931)

Gorsky, Susan. "'The Central Shadow': Characterization in *The Waves*." *Modern Fiction Studies* 18 (Autumn 1972): 449–66.

Graham, J.W. "Point of View in *The Waves*: Some Services of Style." *University of Toronto Quarterly* 39 (April 1970): 193–211.

Heine, Elizabeth. "The Evolution of the Interludes in *The Waves*." *Virginia Woolf Quarterly* 1 (Fall 1972): 60–80.

Katz, Judith N. "Rooms of Their Own: Forms and Images of Liberation in Five Novels." *Dissertation Abstracts International* 34 (1973): 1283A (Penn.

State).

King, Merton P. "The Androgynous Mind and *The Waves*." *University Review* (Kansas) 30 (1964): 221–24.

King, Merton P. "*The Waves* and the Androgynous Mind." *University Review* (Kansas) 30 (1963): 128–34.

McConnell, Frank D. "'Death Among the Apple Trees': *The Waves* and the World of Things." *Bucknell Review* 16 (December 1968): 23–39.

Payne, Michael. "The Eclipse of Order: The Ironic Structure of *The Waves*." *Modern Fiction Studies* 15 (Summer 1969): 209–18.

Rantavaara, Irma. "'Ing'-forms in the Service of Rhythm and Style in Virginia Woolf's *The Waves*." *Neuphilologische Mitteilungen* 61 (1960): 79–97.

Richardson, Robert O. "Point of View in Virginia Woolf's *The Waves*." *Texas Studies in Literature and Language* 14 (Winter 1973): 691–709.

Shanahan, Mary Steussy. "The Artist and the Resolution of *The Waves*." *Modern Language Quarterly* 36 (March 1975): 54–74.

Stewart, Jack F. "Existence and Symbol in *The Waves*." *Modern Fiction Studies* 18 (Autumn 1972): 433–47.

Strong, Paul. "The Light in the Garden: Imagery in *Mrs. Dalloway*, *To the Lighthouse*, and *The Waves*." *Dissertation Abstracts International* 34 (1974): 4288A–89A (Wisconsin).

Tobin, Gloria J. "Virginia Woolf's *The Waves* and *The Years* as Novel of Vision and Novel of Fact." *Dissertation Abstracts International* 35 (1974): 483A (Wisconsin).

Webb, Igor M. "'Things in Themselves': Virginia Woolf's *The Waves*." *Modern Fiction Studies* 17 (Winter 1971–1972): 570–73.

The Years (1937)

Hoffman, Charles G. "Virginia Woolf's Manuscript Revisions of *The Years*." *Publications of the Modern Language Association* 84 (1969): 79–89.

Marder, Herbert. "Beyond the Lighthouse: *The Years*." *Bucknell Review* 15 (March 1967): 61–70.

Proudfit, Sharon W. "Virginia Woolf: Reluctant Feminist in *The Years*." *Criticism* 17 (1975): 59–73.

Radin, Grace. "'I Am Not a Hero': Virginia Woolf and the First Version of *The Years*." *Massachusetts Review* 16 (Winter 1975): 195–208.

Tobin, Gloria J. "Virginia Woolf's *The Waves* and

The Years as Novel of Vision and Novel of Fact." *Dissertation Abstracts International* 35 (1974): 483A (Wisconsin).

CONSTANCE FENIMORE WOOLSON (1840–1894) U.S.
Bibliography

Moore, Rayburn S. "Constance Fenimore Woolson 1840–1894." *American Literary Realism*, no. 3 (Summer 1968): 36–38.
General Works

Milledge, Luetta U. "Theme and Characterization in the Fiction of Constance Fenimore Woolson." *Dissertation Abstracts International* 32 (1972): 5745A–46A (Georgia).

Monteiro, George. "William Dean Howells: Two Mistaken Attributions." *Papers of the Bibliographical Society of America* 56 (1962): 254–57.

DOROTHY WORDSWORTH (1771–1855) Great Britain
General Works

Crawford, Walter B. "A Three-Decker Novel in Wordsworth's Library, 1802." *Notes and Queries* 11 (January 1964): 16–17.

Hardwick, Elizabeth. "Amateurs: Dorothy Wordsworth." *New York Review of Books* (November 30, 1972): 3–4.

Moorman, Mary. "Dorothy Wordsworth, 1771–1855." *Contemporary Review* 219 (1971): 313–21.

Moorman, Mary. "William and Dorothy Wordsworth." *Essays by Divers Hands* 37 (1973): 75–94.

Nabholtz, John R. "Dorothy Wordsworth and the Picturesque." *Studies in Romanticism* 3 (Winter 1964): 118–28.
Individual Works

Journals (1896)

Brownstein, Rachel Mayer. "The Private Life: Dorothy Wordsworth's *Journals*." *Modern Language Quarterly* 34 (March 1973): 48–63.

Laski, Marghanita. "Dorothy Wordsworth's *Journals*." *Notes and Queries* 9 (June 1962): 223–26; 9 (July 1962): 271–72; 9 (August 1962): 296–97.

Rogers, John E., Jr. " 'Dearest Friend': A Study of Dorothy Wordsworth's *Journals*." *Dissertation Abstracts International* 35 (1974): 1632A–33A (Penn. State).

Siemens, Reynold. "The Writings of Dorothy Wordsworth: The MSS Journals, Dove Cottage Facsimiles, University of Alberta." *Wordsworth Circle* 2 (Summer 1971): 104–6.

MARY WORDSWORTH (1770–1859) Great Britain
Individual Works

Journal (1820)

Abrams, Kenneth Theodore. "Mary Wordsworth's Journal of a Tour of Belgium and Holland, 1823." *Dissertation Abstracts* 26 (1965): 3322 (Cornell).

Partridge, A.C. "Unpublished Wordsworthiana: The Continental Tour of 1820, Described in Mary Wordsworth's *Journal*." *English Studies in Africa* 6 (March 1963): 1–6.

JANE WORKMAN (fl. 1800–1810) U.S.
Individual Works

Liberty in Louisiana (1804)

Watson, Charles S. "A Denunciation on the Stage of Spanish Rule: Jane Workman's *Liberty in Louisiana* (1804)." *Louisiana History* 11 (Summer 1970): 245–58.

FRANCES WRIGHT (1795–1852) U.S. (Born in Scotland)

General Works

Lane, Margaret. "Frances Wright (1795–1852): The Great Experiment." *Contemporary Review* 218 (1971): 7–14.

JUDITH WRIGHT (1915–) Australia
Bibliography

Anderson, Hugh. "A Bibliography of Judith Wright." *Australian Literary Studies* 3 (1968): 312–13.

General Works

Brennan, G.A. "The Aborigine in the Works of Judith Wright." *Westerly*, no. 4 (1972): 46–50.

Brissender, R.F. "Five Senses." *Australian Quarterly* 36 (March 1964): 85–91.

Ewers, John K. "The Genius of Judith Wright." *Westerly*, no. 3 (1968): 42–51.

Hay, R.G. "Judith Wright's Achievement." *Australian Literary Studies* 3 (1967): 30–33.

Irvin, Margaret. "Judith Wright's 'Dark Gift.' " *Twentieth Century Literature* 13 (October 1967): 131–34.

Jurgensen, Manfred. "The Poetry of Judith Wright." *Makar* 7 (1971): 18–35.

Kellaway, Frank. "The Collected Poems of Judith Wright." *Overland*, no. 50–51 (1972): 90–92.

Kohli, Devindra. "The Crystal Glance of Love:

Judith Wright as Love Poet." *Journal of Commonwealth Literature* 6 (June 1971): 42–52.

Mares, F.H. "The Poetry of Judith Wright." *Australian Literary Studies* 3 (1967): 24–29.

McAuley, James. "Some Poems of Judith Wright." *Australian Literary Studies* 3 (1968): 201–13.

Phillips, A.A. "Provincialism and Australian Culture." *Meanjin Quarterly* 25 (1966): 265–74.

Ryan, J.S. "Judith Wright and the Bushranger: A Haunting." *Westerly*, no. 4 (1972): 51–54.

Wilkes, G.A. "The Later Poetry of Judith Wright." *Southerly* 25 (1965): 163–71.

Wilson, Richard. "The Short Stories of Judith Wright." *Australian Literary Studies* 1 (1963): 58–61.

ELINOR WYLIE, née Hoyt (1885–1928) U.S.
General Works

Angoff, Charles. "Recollections—Elinor Wylie, Thomas Mann, Joseph Hergesheimer, James Stephens, Logan Clendening." *Literary Review* 10 (Winter 1966–1967): 169–79.

Collura, Ida Mary. "Elinor Wylie's Prose: A Study in Conflict." *Dissertation Abstracts* 23 (1962): 2133 (Pittsburgh).

Farr, Judith Banzer. " 'Language from Spirit': The Art of Elinor Wylie." *Dissertation Abstracts* 27 (1966): 202A (Yale).

Gordon, John D. "A Legend Revisited: Elinor Wylie." *American Scholar* 38 (Summer 1969): 459–68.

Gray, Thomas A. "Elinor Wylie: The Puritan Marrow and the Silver Filigree." *Arizona Quarterly* 19 (Winter 1963): 343–57.

Homsley, Bonnie S. "The Life of Elinor Wylie." *Dissertation Abstracts International* 33 (1973): 5725A–26A (Wisconsin).

Kelly, Edward H. " 'The Eagle and the Mole': The Affective Fallacy Revisited." *English Record* 21 (December 1970): 57–59.

Linneman, M. Rose Ann. "Donne as Catalyst in the Poetry of Elinor Wylie, Wallace Stevens, Herbert Read, and William Empson." *Xavier University Studies* 1 (Summer–Fall 1962): 264–72.

Saul, George Brandon. " 'Icy Song': The Verse of Elinor Wylie." *Bulletin of the New York Public Library* 69 (November 1965): 618–22.

Wright, Celeste Turner. "Elinor Wylie: The Glass Chimaera and the Minotaur." *Twentieth Century Literature* 12 (April 1966): 15–26.
Individual Works
Velvet Shoes (1921)

Wertenbaker, Thomas J., Jr. "Into the Poet's Shoes." *English Journal* 53 (May 1964): 370–72.

Y

CHARLOTTE MARY YONGE (1823–1901) Great Britain

General Works

Dennis, Barbara. "The Two Voices of Charlotte Yonge." *Durham University Journal* 65 (March 1973): 181–88.

Foster, Shirley. "Unpublished Letters of C.M. Yonge." *Notes and Queries* 17 (September 1970): 339–41.

Green, David Bonnell. "Two Popular Novelists of the Fifties and Their Publisher: Letters." *Notes and Queries* 10 (December 1963): 450–54.

Green, Roger Lancelyn. "Words from C.M. Yonge." *Notes and Queries* 8 (September 1961): 355.

Hayter, Alethea. "The Sanitary Idea and a Victorian Novelist." *History Today* 19 (December 1969): 840–47.

Laski, Marghanita. "Words from Some Domestic Novels of C. M. Yonge." *Notes and Queries* 7 (December 1960): 459–65.

Stark, Myra C. "The Clever Woman of the Family—And What Happened to Her." *Mary Wollstonecraft Journal* 2 (1974): 13–20.

Troubridge, St. Vincent. "Words from C.M. Yonge." *Notes and Queries* 8 (June 1961): 232.

Webb, William. "A Charlotte Yonge Reference." *Notes and Queries* 12 (February 1965): 60.

Webb, William. "Charlotte Yonge Story Identified." *Notes and Queries* 21 (June 1974): 216.

Individual Works

The Heir of Redclyffe (1853)

Maxwell, J. C. "An Aeschylus Quotation in *The Heir of Redclyffe*." *Notes and Queries* 14 (February 1967): 63.

MARGUERITE YOUNG (1909–) U.S.

General Works

McEvilly, Wayne. "The Philosopher without Answers: A Look at Metaphysics and Marguerite Young." *Studies in the Twentieth Century,* no. 3 (Spring 1969): 73–81.

Individual Works

Miss MacIntosh, My Darling (1965)

Byatt, A.S. "The Obsession with Amorphous Mankind: Marguerite Young's Strange Best-Seller." *Encounter* 27 (September 1966): 63–69.

Goyen, William. "A Fable of Illusion and Reality." *New York Times Book Review* (September 12, 1965): 5.

Walters, Raymond, Jr. "In and Out of Books." *New York Times Book Review* (September 12, 1965): 8.

Z

CHARLOTTE ZOLOTOW (pseud. Charlotte Bookman)
(1915–) U.S.
General Works
Mercier, J. "Charlotte Zolotow." *Publishers Weekly*
(June 10, 1974): 8–9.

Index